NORTH CAROLINA

S O U T H

C A R O L I N A

FT. PRINCE GEORGE

KEOWEE R.

1775

ECA

TUGALOO R.

1775

FT. CHARLOTTE

1775

BROAD R.

1773

FT. JAMES

LITTLE R.

BUFFALO LICK

RIGHTSBOROUGH

AUGUSTA

1775

SILVER BLUFF

BLUE SPRINGS

SAVANNAH R.

OGEECHEE R.

1775

R

G

OCMULGEE R.

OCONEE R.

1775

1776

EBENEZER

1776

1773

CHARLESTON

1775

SAVANNAH

ALTAMAHA R.

1773

FT. BARRINGTON

1776

SUNBURY

DARIEN

1774

ST. MARY'S R.

FT. WILLIAM

A

SEMINOLES

SPALDINGS LOWER STORE

ST. AUGUSTINE

SOCHTE

CUSCOWILLA

SUWANNEE R.

1774

SPALDINGS UPPER STORE

BLUE SPRINGS

BILL BLACKARD

William Bartram and
the American Revolution
on the Southern Frontier

Portrait of William Bartram by Charles William Peale (1808)
Courtesy of Independence National Historical Park, Philadelphia

William Bartram and the American Revolution on the Southern Frontier

Edward J. Cashin

University of South Carolina Press

Published in Columbia, South Carolina, by the
University of South Carolina Press

Manufactured in the United States of America

04 03 02 01 00   5 4 3 2 1

Library of Congress Cataloging-in-Publication Data

Cashin, Edward J., 1927–
    William Bartram and the American Revolution on the Southern frontier :
the context for Bartram's Travels / Edwin J. Cashin.
    p. cm.
Includes bibliographical references and index.
    ISBN 1-57003-325-0 (alk. paper)
    1. Southern States—History—Revolution, 1775–1783. 2. Bartram,
William, 1739–1823—Journeys—Southern States. 3. Southern
States—Description and travel. 4. Bartram, William, 1739–1823. Travels
through North & South Carolina, Georgia, east & west Florida, the
Cherokee country, the extensive territories of the Muscogulges, or Creek
Confederacy, and the country of the Chactaws. 5. Indians of North
America—Southern States—History—18th century. 6. Travelers—Southern
States—Biography. 7. Naturalists—United States—Biography. I. Title.

E230.5.S7 C38 2000
917.504'3—dc21   99-050699

Endpaper: Map of Bartram's travels across the southern frontier.
Drawn by Bill Blackard

*For my sisters, Margie, Kay, and Eleanor
and my brothers, Dan and Bob*

Contents

Illustrations and Maps

Illustrations

Maps

Preface

William Bartram would be surprised at the number of his admirers two hundred years after the publication of his book, and he would be pleased that trails named for him lure latter-day adventurers into the wildernesses he loved. In the overlong title of his book, he listed all those places he visited, as if laying claim to them: *Travels through North & South Carolina, Georgia, East and West Florida, the Cherokee Country, the Extensive Territories of the Muscogulges, or Creek Confederacy, and the Country of the Chactaws.* Scores of historic markers commemorate his passing and link him in memory to those who came after. From the Nantahala Mountains in North Carolina to Pensacola on the Gulf Coast, plaques tell the traveler that William Bartram crossed the southern frontier at the time of the American Revolution.

My own reaction, upon first reading *Travels,* was one of admiration for a man so courageous that he could ride alone through a wild and dangerous country, and paddle a canoe through thrashing alligators, a man who was so sensitive to beauty, so curious about living things, so attuned to the spiritual. A later, slowly dawning realization was that Bartram had left out the context of his travels. He did not explain what was going on in the places he visited. Incredibly, he neglected to mention the American Revolution, the crucial event of our history. What else, I wondered, had he omitted? And why? The search for answers revealed that Bartram became closely acquainted with the movers and shapers of events in the course of his travels. More interesting than that, this Quaker actually participated in a military adventure!

In company with all those who write about John and William Bartram, father and son, I am indebted to Francis Harper, the indefatigible Bartram sleuth who went where William Bartram went and sorted out his tangled chronology. Several persons have been most helpful in my own efforts to follow Bartram. Frederick Holder of Seneca, South Carolina, took my brother and me on a tour through Oconee County, South Carolina, following Bartram's route and locating the sites of Indian villages. Later, Fred read the manuscript and made valuable suggestions. My wife and I walked along Warwoman Creek and found the waterfall that enraptured the explorer. We liked the beautiful Cowee Valley so well that we invested in a weekend cottage alongside the traces of the old federal pike through the Cherokee country, which must have been the trail Bartram traveled earlier. Nearby historic markers tell of "Cherokee Victory" and "Cherokee Defeat" in 1760 and 1761; Bartram paused in his journey to ponder what happened in those bloody battles.

My son and I followed Bartram's route across Georgia and Alabama to Mobile and Pensacola. Ned Jenkins, director of Fort Toulouse–Jackson Park, took us to some of the village sites along the Tallapoosa River. Davida Hastie, local historian of Stockton, Alabama, showed us the area Bartram explored along the Tensaw River. Dot Jones of the Historic Wrightsboro Foundation put my sister and me on the right road as we traced Bartram's route in the survey of Georgia's land cession of 1773. Carolyn Hodges of Darien took my wife and me on a boat tour of the Altamaha River marshlands, and we saw Broughton Island, more primitive now than when William Bartram visited Henry Laurens's rice plantation. The silence was broken only by the sound of our motor, and we apologized to the ospreys for disturbing their nesting.

The professionals who staff the libraries and archives listed in the bibliography were unfailingly helpful and considerate. I acknowledge the kindness shown my daughter (this research involved the whole family) and me by Brenda Burgess who showed us the earl of Derby's collection of Bartram's early drawings and gave us a private tour of the earl's Georgian mansion. It is always a pleasure to revisit the Clements Library and to renew acquaintances with John Dann, John Harriman, and Rob Cox. Bryan McKown of the South Carolina Department of Archives and History kindly corrected my inaccuracies about Fort Prince George and Keowee. For graciously volunteering information, I thank Patrick M. Demere, Dr. Henry McKinnon, John Britton Wells III, and Elliott Edwards. I appreciate the advice of Tom Fleming and Kathryn Braund. I am indebted to Peter Wood for his careful reading and valuable suggestions. I thank my successive student assistants who have worked on this project: Ann Cowan, John Meadows, Eddie Cashin, Eric Leiden, and Sera Silverman.

Two stories took shape in the course of this research. One, of course, is that of the adventures of William Bartram; the other is about the onset of the American Revolution on the southern frontier. Readers who are interested only in Bartram might be annoyed by the intrusion of politics and violence into this story. I ask them to consider that Bartram must have been far more annoyed. The two great Indian Nations of the southern frontier, the Creek and the Cherokee, are central to both elements of this history, Bartram's botanizing and the eruption of war. By following Bartram about, we realize that the southern frontier was a coherent entity, united by the uneasy coexistence of Indians and British colonials. A recent televised documentary on the American Revolution devoted only one episode out of six to the Revolution in the South and completely omitted events west of the Savannah River. While representative of Americans' collective memory of the Revolution, the interpretation is disappointing. William Bartram deliberately reminds us of the natural wonders of the southern frontier, and inadvertently he makes us realize how the Revolution reached from Charlestown to the Mississippi.

Abbreviations

APS	American Philosophical Society, Philadelphia
CRG	*Colonial Records of Georgia*
FHQ	*Florida Historical Quarterly*
GHS	Georgia Historical Society
HSP	Historical Society of Pennsylvania, Philadelphia
LC	Library of Congress
NYHS	New York Historical Society, New York, N.Y.
PRO, AO	British Public Records Office, Audit Office, Kew, England
PRO, CO	British Public Records Office, Colonial Office, Kew, England
RRG	*Revolutionary Records of Georgia*
SHC	Southern Historical Collection, University of North Carolina
WLCL	William L. Clements Library, University of Michigan
W&MQ	*William and Mary Quarterly*

Prologue

*John Bartram has a son who I hope will perpetuate both
his father's and his own name, for the advancement of
natural philosophy as well as science in general.*
Lionel Chalmers to John Bartram, April 7, 1773

Try as he might, John Bartram could never persuade his fifth son, Billy, to enter a useful occupation. He bought books on medicine and surgery, but Billy refused to read a page. He apprenticed him to a merchant in Philadelphia, but Billy disliked clerking. Benjamin Franklin offered him a job as a printer's engraver, but Billy did not care for the confines of a print shop. All during Billy's teenage years and into his twenties, his father and his father's friends tried to get him to work so as to earn a living, to no avail.[1]

It was partly John Bartram's example that deterred Billy from indoor work. John loved nature in all its forms, and his greatest delight was in botanizing through places where few others had gone. Only a romantic could say, as John did, "My head runs all upon the works of God in Nature, it is through that telescope I see God in all his glory."[2] When Billy was only four, John Bartram toured western Pennsylvania and New York, noting observations about the manners and customs of the Indians of the interior.[3] What John Bartram did and what he was acted as a greater influence upon Billy Bartram than all the urgings and admonitions about finding a job.

Billy Bartram and his twin sister, Elizabeth, were born on April 20, 1739, at home at Kingsessing on the Schuylkill River, outside Philadelphia. John Bartram's first wife, Mary Maris, whom he married in 1723 when he was 27, died in 1727, leaving him with two surviving sons, Isaac and Richard. In 1728 John purchased the stone house at Kingsessing and brought to it his second wife, Ann Mendenhall. John enlarged his house as his family grew, sons James,

1

Moses, John, and Benjamin, daughters Mary and Ann, in addition to the twins.[4] The stone house could scarce contain them all.

In 1733 John Bartram began selling plants to Peter Collinson, a wealthy and politically well-located Quaker merchant who kept a garden outside London. Until Collinson died in 1768, he acted as John Bartram's agent and Billy's mentor. The mature William Bartram appreciated the role played by Collinson: "It was principally through the interest of Collinson that he [John Bartram] became acquainted, and entered into a correspondence with, many of the most celebrated literary characters in Europe, and was elected a member of the Royal Society of London, of Stockholm, etc."[5] Among the correspondents, all plant fanciers, were Sir Hans Sloane, founder of the British Museum, Carl Linnaeus of Sweden, who devised the modern method of cataloging plants, and Dr. John Fothergill, a Quaker whose garden was second only to the royal gardens at Kew in its variety.[6] John Bartram did more to populate British gardens with native American plants than any other professional gardener.

Billy Bartram developed a talent for drawing and at age 14 accompanied his father on a tour of the Catskill Mountain region.[7] John sent Collinson some of Billy's sketches of birds and plants with the comment, "Botany and drawing is his darling delight, am afraid he can't settle to any business else."[8] Collinson expressed astonishment and delight at the quality of Billy's work and showed them to his London friends.[9]

In 1761 Billy's restlessness, as well as his dislike for the latest effort to involve him in business, caused him to leave Kingsessing for an extended visit to his uncle William Bartram's home, Ashwood, in the Cape Fear region of North Carolina.[10] The long war with France ended in 1763 with the Treaty of Paris, by which Britain obtained French Canada, Louisiana east of the Mississippi, and Spanish Florida. John Bartram suggested that Peter Collinson use his connections at court to get him a commission to explore the new acquisitions. Collinson gained the attention of young King George's friend and tutor, the earl of Bute, and secured an appointment for his American friend. In muted triumph, he wrote to John that the "King has named thee his Botanist . . . now thy wishes are in some degree accomplished to range over Georgia and the Floridas."[11]

John Bartram, at age 65, still retained his enthusiasm for new discoveries and lost little time in getting started on his last expedition. He collected Billy at Ashwood and organized for the journey at Charlestown. There Billy met friends who proved to be invaluable help to him later. John Bartram's cryptic account of their travels through Georgia and Florida, published by a Florida promoter named William Stork, only hints at the fascination Florida held for Billy.[12] The young man, twenty-six at the time, decided to remain in Florida as an indigo planter on the St. Johns River, much to the chagrin of his father, who confided to Collinson, "Nothing will do with him now, but he will be a planter . . . this frolic of his . . . hath drove me to great straits."[13] John extended credit, and his Charlestown friends, Laurens and Lamboll, helped outfit the prospective planter. The experiment proved a disastrous failure. A year later Henry Laurens rescued Billy, near death from malnutrition and fevers. "Though a worthy, ingenious man," Laurens wrote John, Billy lacked the "resolution" necessary for the management of a plantation. Laurens called him "poor Billy Bartram."[14] More bad news followed; Billy had turned down a surveyor's job offered him by the royal engineer William G. DeBrahm and had been shipwrecked off the coast of Florida.[15]

Billy survived the wreck and returned to his father's house. He refused to surrender his dreams. Through Collinson's good offices, he secured modest commissions to draw marine shells for the duchess of Portland and mollusks and turtles for Dr. Fothergill.[16] Billy must have cherished one of Collinson's last letters to him: "When art is arrived to such perfection to copy close after nature, who can describe the pleasure but them that feel it, to see the moving pencil display a sort of paper creation, which may endure for ages, [to] transfer a name with applause to posterity."[17] Even though Billy had to leave Philadelphia again, pestered by creditors, to find refuge at Ashwood, he cherished his dream. In 1772 he took the initiative in proposing an expedition to Dr. Fothergill. Would the good doctor sponsor him in the collection and drawing of plants in Florida and the Indian country? Fothergill liked the idea, and Billy hurried back to Kingsessing to prepare for his great adventure.[18]

During his years on the southern frontier, Billy took copious notes, originally intended only for Dr. Fothergill. As he explored from one end of the British American frontier to the other, the American Revolution changed the course of history. Billy Bartram's quest for personal independence, the maturation of Billy into William, coincided with the national assertion of independence. William Bartram transcribed notes into his epic *Travels* after the successful completion of the Revolution and during the drafting of the Constitution that defined the new nation. Convinced that Providence directed events for the betterment of mankind, he believed that those great contemporaries who gathered in Philadelphia were engaged in building a political edifice that would be a model for the world. "I forsee the Magnificent structure and would be instrumental in its advancement," he wrote as he prepared his text.[19] His America, purged of wars and other human foibles, he saw as a garden filled with marvelous plants whose beauty matched their curative powers. If Americans lived in communion with nature; if they would heed the moral law implanted in themselves; if they treated the people of the interior with the respect that fellow humans deserve, then the country would be blessed with greatness and its people with happiness. His book was his best tool in building the magnificent structure.

William Bartram traveled a great distance from Charlestown to the Mississippi, but the difference in maturity between the failed indigo planter of 1766 and the author of *Travels* was more vast.

1

The Georgia Coast

I

[March] 30th: At night arived in Sight of the Lighthouse which stands on an island just within the Barr. In the morning we saild up to Charlestown.

Harper, *Travels*

As the brigantine *Charlestown Packet* crossed the bar into Charlestown harbor on a pleasant spring morning in 1773, a tide of emotions surged in the breast of one of the voyagers. William Bartram viewed the world differently from most other passengers and, indeed, from most other people. On the voyage when it seemed that the ship would be wrecked in a violent storm and people cowered in fear, Bartram marveled at the power and mystery of the Creator. When the wind dashed a bird onto the deck, Bartram drew its portrait.[1] After the storm he mused that "nothing can be more sublime than the view of the encircling horizon after the turbulent winds have taken their flight. . . ."[2] Now the first sight of the landscape made him think of the "first appearance of the earth to man at the creation."[3] William Bartram had the sensitive soul of a poet. He saw the world as Adam might have before the world lost its harmony. His universe still resounded with music and meaning; every living thing gave glory to the Creator. His great delight lay in the exploration of nature with the hope of benefiting mankind through his discoveries. His ability to draw living things gained him recognition from the naturalists of his day. Without seeking membership, he had been elected to the Philadelphia Society, which merged with the American Philosophical Society in 1769. He appreciated the honor but had never attended a meeting.[4]

5

One of Bartram's fellow passengers might have told him a great deal about the southern frontier. Sgt. White Outerbridge had come to Georgia with Oglethorpe's regiment in 1737. When the regiment disbanded in 1749, he joined the South Carolina Independent Regiment and during the French and Indian War (1754–1763) commanded the garrisons at Fort Moore and Fort Augusta.[5] Given Bartram's curiosity about the southern frontier and the close quarters of the *Charlestown Packet*, the old soldier and the young explorer had much to talk about and time to do it.

As the vessel neared the shore, pleasant memories must have stirred. Charlestown represented some of Bartram's happiest times. He realized that he had disappointed his father when he found the printing business tedious and merchandising impossible, but the lure of exotic places, particularly Florida, constantly distracted him. In Charlestown he and his father, recently appointed the king's botanist, began their adventure. John Bartram, with his open and engaging personality, made friends easily. Dr. Alexander Garden of Charlestown knew both men, having visited John Bartram's garden in 1754.[6] In 1765 the Bartrams met others who shared their love of nature: Dr. John Moultrie, who later served as lieutenant governor of Florida; Henry Laurens, the wealthy merchant who thereafter exhibited a paternal attitude toward William; Dr. Lionel Chalmers, who won election to the Royal Society with his paper on the connection between weather and disease; Mrs. George Logan, whose garden in her widowhood served as a nursery for the sale of shrubs to the rapidly expanding wealthy class; John Stuart, since 1762 the superintendent of the southern Indians; and the Lambolls.[7] William referred to the latter as the "very Antient and honourable family" who invited him to lodge with them. Thomas Lamboll had achieved a certain antiquity; he celebrated his eightieth birthday on October 28, 1773. As for honor, he had been appointed judge in 1736 and served on the commission that regulated the important Indian trade. The Bartrams regarded Elizabeth, Thomas's second wife, as equally distinguished. She planted Charlestown's first extensive garden below Lamboll Street and adjacent to King Street. Like Martha Logan, she exchanged letters and seeds with John Bartram.[8] William cherished a warm memory of the Lambolls' daughter Mary, "Charming Polly" to her family. She had just turned 20 when he saw her last in 1765. When William decided to remain in Florida after his tour with his father, Mrs. Lamboll made it her business to send things she thought he needed. John Bartram suggested to his son that by way of thanks he might "draw some pretty thing" for Mistress Polly.[9] Coincidentally most of

John Bartram's friends happened to be Scots: Garden, Chalmers, Moultrie, Stuart, and Logan. Perhaps the Bartrams felt a special bond with the Lambolls, who shared their belief in the Quaker doctrine.

William came to Charlestown this time, not as a youth in the train of an imposing father, but as a man on an important mission. He acted as an emissary of the eminent Dr. John Fothergill of London, whose patients included Lord Dartmouth, the American secretary, and who kept one of the finest gardens in England on his estate five miles outside of London. William owed his appointment to the offices of Peter Collinson, like Fothergill, a naturalist and a Quaker who brought William's drawings to Fothergill's attention. Collinson informed John Bartram how it happened. Fothergill had come to breakfast with him and being "always thoughtful How to make Billy's ingenuity turn to some advantage," as he said, he showed some of William's recent drawings to the doctor and won him over immediately. "Billy may Value Himself in Having such a Patron who is Eminent for his Generosity and his noble Spirit to promote every branch in Natural History."[10] New and exotic plants enjoyed great demand among the British country gentlemen who competed with one another in adorning their estates. One observer of the scene reported how at that time a "horticultural fever" swept England, "where wealthy men were filling their gardens with curiosities and every physician a botanist, seeking cures in plants."[11] Fothergill, a successful physician, knew well the curative value of plants. A good Quaker, he shared the Bartrams' belief that a benevolent Providence endowed plants with marvelous powers and expected godly men to discover those secrets. Fothergill also reveled in the sheer beauty of nature: "I love the vegetable creation," he once said. "I love its variety and cultivate it as an amusement, every new plant is an addition to my pleasure."[12] Fothergill's interest in him had stirred William in his self-imposed exile at Ashwood and led him to write the good doctor that he would love to go botanizing for him.[13]

Now the adventure had begun, and William dutifully began his report to his employer even before the *Charlestown Packet* berthed. These cribbed notes would serve as a memory jogger for his later book of *Travels*. William observed the increased traffic in the harbor. Eight hundred vessels called at Charlestown annually, and the long wharves projecting out from the shore berthed dozens of vessels in the process of loading and unloading. The row of mercantile buildings lining East Bay appeared much as Bartram remembered, but a dramatic new addition altered the skyline. Beyond Champney's Wharf and blocking the seaward view of Broad Street stood a handsome brick building in the latest

Georgian style. Bartram learned that the edifice housed the Royal Exchange and Customs. A traveler from New England observed that the "New Exchange which fronted the place of my landing made a most noble appearance."[14]

II

Went to the house of a very Antient and honourable Family who received me friendly during my abode in this Town.

Harper, *Travels*

Disembarking, William found himself caught up in a crowd of sailors, longshoremen, mechanics, and merchants. Charlestown teemed with activity; its population numbered twelve thousand people, half of them black and most of those slaves. Charlestown, in fact, served as the entrepôt for the slave trade. In the two years 1772 and 1773, some sixty-five vessels unloaded ten thousand Africans for sale to Carolina and Georgia planters and merchants.[15] White persons who could afford to do so traveled the sandy streets in single-horse open buggies called "chairs." Wealthier individuals (Charlestown boasted that it was the wealthiest city among the colonies), rode about in four-wheeled closed carriages as handsome as any in London.[16]

William walked up busy Broad Street, passed the City Tavern on the corner of Church Street, which had been the center of heated political discussion since the Stamp Act, and soon confronted the statue of the hero of the repeal of that hated measure. The legislature voted to honor William Pitt in 1766, the year of the repeal; the statue, made in England, stood squarely in the center of the intersection of Broad and Meeting Streets. Bartram remembered the handsome St. Michael's Church, built after the style of James Gibbes's St. Martin's in the Fields, and the statehouse diagonally across the square. The other two public buildings were new. The treasury occupied the southwest corner with the guard house adjacent to it. On the northeast corner, in curious juxtaposition to serene St. Michael's across the street, stood the beef market, an open arcade surmounted by a belfry. A contemporary called it "a low, dirty-looking brick market house for beef."[17] Tame turkey buzzards strolled about this market, as well as the fish market at the foot of Queen Street. Both markets exuded an unpleasant odor. For Bartram the beauty of the early flowering shrubs more than compensated for the sand, the smell, the flies, and the swarming gnats.

At King Street, Bartram felt a spiritual connection with the old Quaker Meeting House and cemetery near the northeast corner of Broad and King. To his left, the Orange Garden of eight years ago had been divided into lots and Orange Street opened. The stately new frame house at Orange Street and Broad belonged to Henry Laurens's brother James. At the other end of Orange Street where it met Tradd Street stood an even more imposing residence erected in 1772 by Supt. John Stuart. In fact, Bartram could not help noticing that Charlestown had undergone a building boom. Vanderhorst Creek still penetrated past Church Street, but the other creeks and marshy lowlands bordering the Ashley River to the south of town had been filled and handsome residences constructed. Lamboll Street no longer marked the southern edge of the growing city.[18]

The old Lamboll residence on King, a typical Charlestown two-story single house with a double piazza running along the south side, once seemed large but now stood in the shadow of one of the most magnificent houses in America immediately above it on King Street. The London architect Ezra White designed the Palladian structure for Miles Brewton, a wealthy merchant who occupied the house on August 22, 1769, to the admiration of all and the envy of many. New Englander Josiah Quincy marveled at the elegance of the interior of Brewton's mansion, noting how a majestic peacock strode about, pecking at crumbs from the table. Bartram might have shared Quincy's amazement at this new Charlestown. "I can only say in general," wrote Quincy, "that in granduer, splendor of buildings, decorations, equipages, numbers, commerce, shipping and indeed almost everything, it surpassed all I ever saw or expect to see in America."[19] Such a statement from one who knew Boston might have surprised strangers, but not the smug Carolinians.

William met with a warm reception at the Lamboll house although elderly Thomas Lamboll, nearing eighty, showed his advanced years. He still mourned his wife, Elizabeth, who died in 1770 at the age of 45. Elizabeth had cultivated the extensive garden that John Bartram admired so much in 1765. Since her death Lamboll sold off most of his property to the south, including the frequently flooding low-lying areas where pirates and other criminals had been buried in the exciting days of Stede Bonnett and Edward "Blackbeard" Teach. All that property had been filled in, and in 1773 handsome houses overlooked the south bay. Of those, visitors regarded William Gibbes's residence as the finest.[20]

Daughter Mary's story is a combination of happiness and heartbreak. In 1769 at the age of twenty-four, she fell in love with a man her own age, the Reverend John Thomas, newly arrived in Charlestown to assume the pastorate of the Independent Church, known as the White Meeting House, the church that gave Meeting Street its name. Mr. Lamboll took a dim view of Polly's marriage, especially such a precipitous one, to a man of modest means and prospects. However, the doting parent came around and, as a wedding present, gave the new bride four female slaves for her lifetime. Evidently, in spite of her father's doubts, young John Thomas proved worthy of Polly. One who knew him described him as very handsome and eloquent, and another as cheerful and serene, "his conversation open, free, pleasant, and felicitous—much of the gentleman in him."[21] The well-matched couple had two children, Mary, born June 19, 1770, and Elizabeth, born August 14, 1771. Then tragedy struck. In addition to all the social graces, John Thomas must have possessed heroic altruism. He suffered a severe exposure while crossing the harbor to give a Christian burial to a criminal and contracted an illness that was complicated by a sea voyage to New York. Pneumonia set in, and he died in that city on September 19, 1771, at the age of twenty-six. He was buried in the Presbyterian Church on Wall Street.[22] Thus when she greeted William Bartram on March 31, 1773, Polly had become a widow at twenty-eight with two small children. William admired her more than any of those he favored with his correspondence and pronounced her "excellent in goodness beyond her sex." She displayed the same "affable and cordial friendship," which marked her father's attitude toward the Bartrams.[23] After her father's death the following year, she insisted that William continue to lodge at her residence on King Street when visiting Charlestown. William left a trunk with her, and she gave him a small prayer book to carry with him on his journey.[24]

Father and daughter expressed the same interest in William's new venture they had shown in supporting John and William's earlier exploration. William came to Charlestown with only a general idea of where he might go. For a start, he would retrace his previous route at least as far as Augusta in Georgia and southward into Florida. William did not know that a major Indian congress would meet in Augusta within a few weeks, but when he learned of it, the possibility of studying Indians more closely excited him. Flora and fauna interested him, but the study of the human condition concerned him even more. He wondered about the prevailing prejudice against Indians. Slavery also bothered him, and he deeply sympathized with the plight of the African slaves. However affable Mr. Lamboll might be, Bartram could not agree with his opinion that slaves constituted "the greatest curse that ever came to America."[25] Bartram believed that the enslavement of Africans threatened to bring God's judgment on America. Charlestown seemed obsessed with fears of slave risings ever since the Stono rebellion of 1739, when some slaves from the Stono region attempted to escape to Florida. The huge increase in the black population since then intensified those dark forebodings. The appeals to "Liberty" by the Stamp Act protestors had been taken to heart by slaves in Charlestown and throughout the South.[26] As he toured the region, William would notice signs of increasing discontent among African Americans. Bartram refrained from taking notes about slavery—Fothergill had not given him that task—and therefore the topic is conspicuously absent in *Travels*, but Bartram worried about it. Later, he wrote a heartfelt appeal addressed generally to his fellow countrymen regarding the injustice of slavery. If he felt that there was not much that he could write about slavery at the time, Bartram knew that he could shed light upon the condition of the American Indian. He resolved to go to Augusta and to extend his travel into the Cherokee and Creek country. Here, Lamboll could be of help. He once served on the commission that regulated the Indian trade after the late war with France and the French-allied Cherokees. The commissioners had met at Lamboll's house and entertained visiting Indians there. Lamboll became familiar with the licensed traders in the Cherokee country, particularly one Patrick Galahan, who once served as porter at Fort Prince George. Galahan had been of essential assistance to the 1768 expedition of Thomas Griffiths in search of fine white clay for the English pottery maker Josiah Wedgwood. He later would be a good guide for William from his village of Cowee in the middle settlements of the Cherokee country.[27]

As for local news, there were aspects of the new prosperity that did not please good Christians. When William and his father last visited Charlestown, the town contained about 70 taverns; in 1773, 115 did good business. The city jail just above the Lamboll's at King and Tradd held so many criminals that a new jail had to be built at the west end of Broad. The grand jury's complaints about thievery, disorderly behavior, and possible slave risings caused the authorities to increase the size of the town guard. Yet the conservative Charlestonians had more to worry about than random crime. Since the Stamp Act riots, those whites considered to be the lower classes adopted disorder as a means of political expression. Under the leadership of Christopher Gadsden, and in association with radicals in the northern colonies, they claimed credit for securing repeal of the Stamp Act and the most obnoxious of the Townshend Duties.[28]

The specter of mob rule might dispirit Mr. Lamboll in his declining years, but the irrepressible Bartram refused to entertain gloomy thoughts. An American Candide, he was anxious to begin his journey in this, the best of all possible worlds.

III

I waited on Doctor Chalmers . . . to whom I was recommended by my worthy patron.

Harper, *Travels*

Dr. John Fothergill won his medical reputation through his research on the link between weather and disease, published in 1754. He went on to build a lucrative London medical practice that subsidized his avocation as a collector of exotic plants, said to be second only to the collection at the royal gardens at Kew. In fact, he stated as much to Bartram's cousin Humphry Marshall: "Few other gardens, Kew excepted can show either so large or so healthy a collection," he wrote in 1775.[29] Lionel Chalmers's essay on fevers impressed him, and Fothergill managed its London publication in 1767. Chalmers's continuing research on the link between Charlestown weather and disease, eventually published in 1776,[30] linked him more closely with Fothergill. So it was that Fothergill asked Chalmers to act as fiscal agent for Bartram's expedition. Fothergill explained that William disliked merchandising, and although not a professional botanist "he knows plants and draws prettily." He instructed Chalmers to give any assistance he could to the young man and to start him with ten guineas and credit his account with fifty.[31]

So William called upon Dr. Chalmers the day after his arrival in Charlestown. Charlestown devoted much of its energy to the pursuit of money and of pleasure and had little left for intellectual activity and even less for religion. Its prestige in the world of science, such as it was, rested upon the reputation of John Lining, Alexander Garden, and Lionel Chalmers. Dr. Lining studied yellow fever and published a paper on the subject in the American Philosophical Society's Transactions in 1740. Dr. Chalmers became Lining's partner in 1737 upon his arrival from Scotland and continued to study weather-related diseases. After Lining's death in 1760, Chalmers became the "leader of scientific activity in Charlestown."[32] Dr. Garden took over Lining's medical practice and achieved a reputation as a botanist. He corresponded with Linnaeus of Sweden, Peter Collinson and John Ellis of London, as well as Fothergill.[33]

William Bartram realized that Chalmers's recommendations would open doors for him on his travels and welcomed the doctor's offer to contact the right persons. Chalmers invited some of his friends to greet William at his dinner table. Among them Bartram met a fellow Philadelphian in Dr. John Morgan, a 1756 graduate of the College of Philadelphia who went on to further study in London, Edinburgh, and Paris. Like Chalmers, Morgan had been honored by election to the Royal Society.[34]

Though Bartram shied from political controversy, he could not avoid political discussion, a favorite pastime in Charlestown. Dr. Chalmers and his friends, most of them Scots, felt increasingly alienated by the public mood. For years, especially since the Scottish rising in 1745 on behalf of Prince Charles, the Charlestown Scots regarded themselves as a group set apart. Peter Timothy's *South Carolina Gazette* carried anti-Scottish material, and therefore Robert Wells, a Scot and publisher of the *South Carolina and American General Gazette,* did his best to portray his countrymen in the best light. The local friction worsened after the ascendancy of James Stuart, earl of Bute, as the principal minister to King George III after 1760. Anti-Scottish sentiment in England flared with the publication of a journal called *The North Briton,* an undisguised attack on Bute and the Grenville, Egremont, and Halifax ministry that successfully concluded the Seven Years' War. Issue 45 of *The North Briton* reached new heights of insults to the king and the ministry. A hitherto obscure member of Parliament named John Wilkes authored the scurrilous piece and fled to France to escape prosecution for libel. He returned to England and imprisonment in 1768 but was reelected to Parliament. Wilkes, a rascal and a rake, thus became a champion of those in England and America who opposed the ministry of Frederick, Lord North.[35]

The controversy reached Charlestown in 1769 and fed into the smoldering anti-Scottish prejudice so offensive to Chalmers, Garden, Stuart, and others. Wilkes supporters in London asked Christopher Gadsden to drum up financial support for Wilkes in Charlestown. Gadsden attracted the attention of opponents of government by his management of the Sons of Liberty during the Stamp Act riots. The mob frightened conservatives such as Henry Laurens who perceived "the cloven hoof [of Christopher Gadsden]" among the agitators.[36]

Gadsden had his way, and in a rash vote on December 8, 1769, regretfully by many of its members, the House of Commons directed Isaac Motte, the treasurer, to send fifteen hundred pounds to the Wilkes fund. The ministry displayed understandable outrage at the donation. Not only had the Commons abetted a rogue, but it had done so illegally, without securing the concurrence of the governor and council. Lord Hillsborough, secretary for America, instructed Lt. Gov. William Bull not to permit expenditures authorized by the House alone. The House had been doing exactly that for years and was not in the mood to surrender its prerogative. A stalemate occurred when Gov. Charles Greville, Lord Montagu, returned to the colony in 1772 and attempted to enforce the ministry's directive. In a foolish move, Montagu called the House to meet in Beaufort, hoping the opposition leaders would not attend. They did, and he immediately dissolved the session. In fact, there were four dissolutions of the assembly in just over a year before the frustrated Montagu left Charlestown on March 10, 1773, prior to Bartram's arrival.[37] Though government was once again in the hands of the popular lieutenant governor William Bull, Bartram's hosts felt uneasy about the rise of radicalism. Bartram might prefer not to discuss politics, but he could not avoid noticing the gathering storm.

Chalmers assured Bartram that he would alert his acquaintances in Georgia and Florida to expect the botanist to call and to extend to him any needed assistance. He also suggested that William visit John Stuart, the Indian superintendent. Stuart knew the Cherokee country thoroughly; in fact, he had drawn a map of the region. Chalmers described Stuart as "an excellent painter and draughtsman and in many respects a Virtuoso."[38] Indian affairs appealed to Bartram much more than politics did, and he eagerly anticipated his meeting with so eminent an authority as John Stuart. Before retiring on his second day in Charlestown, he took pen in hand to acknowledge the ten guineas, seventy-three pounds Carolina money, received from Dr. Chalmers at the direction of Dr. Fothergill "towards defraying my charges in serch of Plants and other Natural Productions in No America for use of said Dr. Fothergill and have signed these receipts for the same." He dated the letter April 2, 1773, and posted it the next day.[39]

IV

With the consent of Dr. Chalmers, waited on the Hon. John Stewart, Esq. Superintendent for Indian Affairs, in order to lay before that Gentleman my designs of Traveling in the Indian Countries.

Harper, *Travels*

When William and his father traveled through the Carolinas and Georgia in 1765, they knew that a war with the Cherokees had recently occurred. Now,

William meant to go exploring through the Cherokee country, and he needed to know more about the history of the war, the location of the trails, forts and towns, the names of the friendly and not-so-friendly headmen and traders. In short, he had to know the state of the Cherokee Nation. No one was better equipped to educate him about the Cherokees than John Stuart, the royal superintendent for Indian Affairs in the Southern Department.

Chalmers offered to introduce Bartram to Stuart, but the Philadelphian needed no introduction. Stuart remembered meeting John and William on their earlier visit. Stuart entertained the traveler at his Tradd Street residence. Unlike the typical Charlestown single house, in which the real front door led onto a side piazza, Stuart's entryway faced the street and opened to a hallway. The formal drawing room occupied the front of the building on the second floor and reflected the classic trimmings popularized by Robert Adam. A large mirror with rococo ornamentation dominated the room.[40] Stuart's residence was a testimony to his comfortable circumstances. A recent onset of gout, commonly believed to be brought on by a rich diet, forced the superintendent to adopt a sedentary lifestyle. With the encouragement of Bartram's curiosity, he expanded at some length about his career and his experiences in the Indian country.

Stuart was born in Inverness, Scotland, on September 25, 1718, and claimed a distant relationship with the members of clan Chattan who settled Darien on the Georgia frontier. The Darien Scots had scattered by the year 1748, when Stuart arrived in Charlestown. His fame and fortune, such as it was, derived from his four years at sea under the command of Adm. George Anson, who himself owned extensive property in Charlestown. Stuart rose from cabin boy to captain's clerk and earned the good opinion of the admiral. More importantly, he shared in the prize money from a captured Spanish gold galleon. In 1748 the young Scot went to Charlestown to further his fortune, as so many of his countrymen had done. He married Sarah, whose last name is unknown, and the marriage produced four children. Daughter Sarah married James Graham, brother of John Graham, later Georgia's lieutenant governor. Daughter Christina, 21 when Bartram visited the household, planned to marry Edward Fenwick, a member of one of Charlestown's old families. A third daughter died in infancy. John, the only son, pursued studies in London in 1773; a brilliant army career and knighthood lay in his future. Persistent rumors held that Stuart had a son of mixed blood in the Cherokee country, which was likely. It seemed that almost every Indian village in America had youngsters with British names, mostly Scottish, in fact, and Stuart had opportunity to form liaisons with Cherokee women during his tour of duty at Fort Loudoun, deep in the Cherokee overhills settlements.[41] Bartram hoped to hear more about the Cherokee country.

Stuart told how he gladly accepted a captain's appointment from Gov. William Henry Lyttelton in 1756 because his mercantile business was going badly; besides, there was a war on and Stuart already served as a militia captain. With his provincial company of sixty men, he marched to recently built Fort Prince George on the Keowee River in the northwest corner of South Carolina, crossed the first range of mountains, moved north along the Little Tennessee River through the Vale of Cowee past several villages including the important town of Nikwasi, then through the Jore or Nantahala Mountains to the overhills town of Tellico, there to build Britain's outermost fort, named in honor of the British commander in America, the ineffective Lord Loudoun. Stuart had little good to say about the builder, a man Bartram met on his earlier tour, the engineer William Gerard De Brahm, who quarreled with everyone and left before the fort was finished. Capt. Raymond Demere referred the management of Indian relations mostly to Stuart.[42] Stuart took advantage of his situation to make a map of the Cherokee country. Bartram would make good use of the map.

Stuart formed a lasting friendship with Attakullakulla, who had accompanied Sir Alexander Cuming to London in 1730 and had since harbored a hankering to return to that marvelous place. The chief, known as the Little Carpenter by the English, accompanied Stuart to Charlestown in December 1756 to assure Lyttelton that rumors of his alliances with the French in Louisiana were untrue. His brother Willinaiva and Ustenaka (Judd's Friend) and more than sixty others went with him to Charlestown and were entertained by Governor Lyttelton for two weeks. The governor promised a bounty for French scalps, and Attakullakulla offered to collect some. True to his word, Attakullakulla led a raid on French-allied Indians on the Ohio River. In 1758 more than six hundred Cherokees went off to battle the French in Virginia under the command of Gen. John Forbes, successor to the unfortunate Edward Braddock, whose army was destroyed by the French and Indians in 1755. Disappointed by Forbes's inaction, the Cherokees drifted back to their mountains. In a display of arrogance too often characteristic of English officials, Forbes sent a party after Attakullakulla and had him arrested for desertion.[43]

Anglo-Cherokee relations deteriorated rapidly. On their way home some of the Indians skirmished with Virginia settlers with fatalities on both sides. The

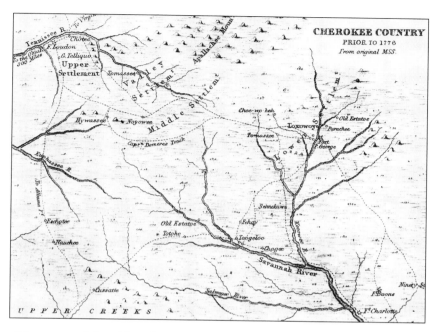

The map of the Cherokee country prior to 1776 shows the location of forts and trails but is vague about the middle settlement towns.
Courtesy of Special Collections Division, University of Georgia Libraries, Athens

important chief Ouconnostotah, known by the English as the Great Warrior, led a delegation to Charlestown, and Lyttelton, the governor, whose arrogance matched that of Forbes, made the visitors hostages, cut off trade with the Cherokee villages, and marched at the head of fifteen hundred men to Fort Prince George, the hostages in tow.[44]

Attakullakulla conferred with Lyttelton at Fort Prince George and learned to his dismay that the Carolina governor demanded twenty-four Cherokee lives for twenty-four English killed by the Cherokees. The Little Carpenter gave up two of the guilty Indians in exchange for the release of Ouconnostotah and the chief of Keowee, Tistoe. The governor and the headmen then signed a treaty by which the Indian culprits were to be handed over, as they could be found, in exchange for the hostages. Meanwhile trade would be resumed. Lyttelton returned to Charlestown as something of a hero.[45]

The governor and his smallpox-ridden army had scarcely reached Charlestown when Cherokee warriors besieged Fort Prince George in an effort to free the captives. At the beginning of February, Indians from the lower and middle settlements attacked settlers in the Long Canes region and raided down the Savannah River to the gates of Fort Augusta and Fort Moore on the Carolina side below Augusta. They caught and massacred about fifty white persons, including women and children. Farther north, on the Keowee River, the commander of Fort Prince George was slain in a parley with Ouconnostotah, and in retaliation the Cherokee hostages in the fort were killed. The war party, under the vengeful Ouconnostotah, laid siege to the remote Fort Loudoun on March 20, 1760.[46]

Bartram disliked war and talk of war, but he needed to know about the recent history of the Cherokees and the degree of danger facing him in his explorations. He noted the names of the great chiefs and the location of the villages as Stuart continued his narrative.

Gen. Jeffrey Amherst responded to Governor Lyttelton's plea for help by dispatching regulars under Col. Archibald Montgomery to Carolina. Montgomery moved quickly from New York to Charlestown, then to Fort Prince George. He destroyed the lower settlements in Carolina, then crossed the Chattooga River into Georgia to attack the middle towns along the headwaters of the Little Tennessee River. Just south of Echoee (the present site of Otto, North Carolina) some six hundred warriors staged an ambush, and a four-hour fight ensued before the attackers withdrew. Montgomery's casualties totaled twenty killed and seventy-six wounded. An estimated forty Cherokees lost their lives. Montgomery destroyed Echoee but decided against a farther advance. When he retreated to Fort Prince George, the Cherokees claimed victory.[47]

Montgomery's decision doomed Stuart and the Fort Loudoun garrison in the inaccessible Nantahala Mountains. Capt. Paul Demere, successor to his brother Raymond in command of the post, realized that his garrison had been abandoned. Neither Virginia nor North Carolina sent help as Ouconnostotah's warriors besieged the place. Stuart negotiated a surrender of the fort and its contents in return for the safety of the garrison. The soldiers marched out, but within a few miles of the fort, some seven hundred warriors under Usteneka attacked them. Captain Demere and about thirty others died in the assault; the other soldiers became prisoners and suffered frightful treatment. Stuart was lucky: Attakullakulla purchased him from his captor and escorted him to a camp of Virginians and to freedom.[48]

Two thousand victorious Cherokees gathered at the principal middle town of Nikwasi (site of present-day Franklin) and offered the Carolinians peace in return for the destruction of Fort Prince George. While Lieutenant Governor Bull temporized, Georgia's governor Henry Ellis, whose skill in diplomacy had kept the Creeks neutral, went to New York to urge Amherst to send another relief expedition. Amherst had already decided to do so, giving charge to Montgomery's second in command, Lt. Col. James Grant.[49] Bartram had met Grant in Florida when he and his father were guests of the then-governor James Grant.

Grant's force was twice the size of Montgomery's, with half of the 2,250 men Carolina provincials under Col. Henry Middleton. On June 7, 1761, the army marched out of Fort Prince George in a column two miles long. It threaded its way along the trail through the first ridge of mountains into the valley of the middle settlements. At the site of Montgomery's battle, the Cherokees attacked again and accounted for sixty-three casualties. Grant kept his force moving, again burned the deserted town of Echoee, the farthest point on Montgomery's march, and proceeded to Tassee and Nikwasi. Using Nikwasi as a base, the soldiers destroyed the neighboring villages Joree, Cowee, Watauga, and Burningtown. They burned fifteen middle towns in all and fifteen hundred acres of corn. Grant decided that he could not continue his march through the formidable Joree (Nantahala) range. He withdrew from the Cherokee mountains and waited at Fort Prince George for an expected peace delegation from the Cherokees. Stuart's friend Attakullakulla, shunted aside while Ouconnostotah held sway, now took the lead in the negotiations, which involved two long journeys from the overhills to Charlestown and resulted in a treaty on December 17, 1761. Stuart accompanied Attakullakulla on his tedious travels, and the small chief did his friend the favor of urging Lieutenant Governor Bull to make Stuart the royal agent to the Cherokees. In no better way could the governor ensure the peace.[50]

The timely death of the controversial Edmund Atkin, the first superintendent, paved the way for Stuart's appointment. General Amherst recommended Stuart for the position, and on January 12, 1762, the earl of Egremont, William Pitt's successor as secretary of state, informed Amherst that Stuart had the job. Egremont did nothing about America without the advice of former Georgia governor Henry Ellis, so it is likely that Stuart owed his appointment to Ellis, who was well informed regarding Cherokee affairs.[51]

All this was essential information for Bartram as he prepared to venture into the Cherokee country. How much of Stuart's story Bartram learned at the time of his visit to Tradd Street and how much he picked up from other sources can only be guessed. It is certain that when he finally went into the Cherokee mountains, he knew the names of the mountains, streams, and villages, and he knew the bloody history of the Cherokees. And it is certain that when, in an improbable coincidence, he came face to face with Attakullakulla himself, he could truthfully say, "Yes, I have heard your fame."[52]

Stuart explained how the Cherokee war led to the upcoming conference at Augusta, news of which appeared in the *South Carolina Gazette*. Stuart blamed the Augusta traders, particularly George Galphin of Silver Bluff, for taking advantage of the destitution of the Cherokees. As a result of the war, the lower and middle settlements fell behind in their payments to the traders who supplied them; the traders in turn ran up debts to the merchants in Augusta, Charlestown, and London along the line of supply. The solution to the problem was that Cherokee land would be exchanged for their debts. The traders insisted that the idea of swapping land for debt originated with the Indians; Stuart doubted it. British policy forbade private cession of Indian land, and Stuart vigorously opposed all such proposals. He had recently made a bitter enemy of William Henry Drayton for blocking his efforts to acquire a tract of land from the Catawba Indians. Stuart would have opposed this latest Cherokee scheme, but the traders and Gov. James Wright of Georgia had worked out an arrangement that secured the approval of Lord Hillsborough upon the condition that the Creeks, who also claimed the land in question, gave their approval. Governor Wright succeeded in persuading Hillsborough that there would be no private cession involved. The Indians would cede the land to the king, and the governor as the king's representative would sell the land to the "better sort" of settlers, namely those who could pay. Unfortunately, in Wright's opinion, the valuable region above the Little River on the Georgia side of the Savannah River was being overrun by vagabonds generally referred to as "Crackers."[53]

Stuart explained the details of the complex arrangement as he had learned it from Governor Wright upon the latter's return from London in February, fewer than two months previous. After the cession could be properly surveyed it would be sold for six shillings an acre, with a thousand acres maximum for each family. The proceeds would be used to repay the debt due the traders, estimated at forty-five thousand pounds sterling. Expenses of the conference, the survey, the construction of fortifications, the patrol of rangers—all would be defrayed from the sale of land. If the traders consented, Wright could apply the first proceeds to the expenses of the fort and rangers. Stuart thought that the traders would not agree to any postponement of payment.[54]

The success of the proposed land-for-debt exchange rested with the attitude of the Creek headmen. Their people had not suffered during the war. Their trade flourished; their debts were insignificant compared to those of the Cherokees. Stuart had been informed by his deputy, David Taitt, and others that the Creek leaders were most reluctant to approach Augusta, having heard rumors about losing their land. Stuart doubted whether they would give up as much as the Georgians wanted. He looked forward to the congress with concern, but he would do his best to carry out the directives of the secretary of state for America, a post now held by Lord Dartmouth. Stuart cordially invited Bartram to accompany him to Augusta, where the botanist would have a rare opportunity to meet influential traders and important headmen in both the Cherokee and Creek Nations. If Bartram wanted to wander in Indian country, he would need such acquaintances. Bartram welcomed the invitation, but because the conference would start at the end of May, nearly two months away, he told Stuart that he would use the intervening time for a quick excursion into coastal Georgia, where spring had already produced the flowering plants he sought. Bartram accepted Stuart's offer of a letter of introduction to Governor Wright though he hardly needed it. He and his father had been guests of Georgia's governor eight years earlier.[55] Thus thoroughly informed about the coming conference, Bartram took his leave of the superintendent, promising to rendezvous in Savannah on the way to Augusta.

Dr. Chalmers heartily approved of William's plans to spend his time productively before the Augusta conference. William pleased the good doctor with a gift of his drawing of a finch that the storm cast aboard his ship on the way to Charlestown. Chalmers chided his old friend John Bartram in a letter of April 7, 1773: "And indeed it surprises me, that you should not have encouraged this Genius of his as a Naturalist sooner, for, tho' you endeavour'd to cure it by putting him to be a Merch[an]t, etc, yet Nature prevailed so far as to disqualify him from Pursuits of this sort." Then he added a sentiment that must have made the aging father proud: "On the whole, John Bartram has a Son, who I hope will perpetuate his Father's and his own name, for the Advancement of Natural Philosophy, as well as of Science in General."[56]

William bade goodbye to his good friends the Lambolls and accepted their invitation to stay with them when he returned. He took a coastal packet boat and in twelve hours reached Savannah.[57]

V

Arrived in Savanna, the capital, where acquainting the Governor Sir J. Wright with my business, his Excellency received me with great politeness.

Harper, *Travels*

The new lighthouse, standing near the ruins of Oglethorpe's original wooden structure on Tybee Island, welcomed William Bartram to Georgia.[58] Charlestown and Philadelphia, with their hectic crowds and thriving commerce, prided themselves on their civilized amenities. Georgia seemed to William several degrees removed from that kind of bustling modernity. Georgia, he recalled with pleasure, remained mostly wilderness.

His vessel, the schooner *Savannah Packet*, with John Turner master, had no trouble crossing the bar off Tybee though heavier ships had to wait for high tide.[59] Beyond Tybee on Cockspur Island a small wooden structure euphemistically called Fort George pretended to guard the mouth of the Savannah River. Beyond Cockspur on Lazareto Creek a recently arrived group of slaves waited out a smallpox quarantine. The *Savannah Packet* picked up a Georgia pilot who guided the schooner up the fifteen mile channel with its shifting sandbar islands. The *Packet* slowly made its way up to the "Commerce row," the nine wharves that lined the riverfront. The warehouses behind the docks crowded into the slope of the bluff. Some of them reached the top of the bluff and overlooked the town.[60] The logic of the terrain demanded a road along the riverbank between the wharves and warehouses, but private owners of the river property could not be persuaded to give up a section of their lots for the general good or for any other reason. Riverfront traffic went by river, with small craft scuttling about among the larger vessels.

Savannah's main street, Bull Street, reached the public wharf on the river by a path down the face of Yamacraw Bluff. When he climbed the slope, ankle-deep in sand, William could see the entire southern face of Savannah, all 870 yards that ranged along Bay Street. Because the river ran from west to east and the town paralleled the river, Savannah sat southward of it. Many visitors expected the river to be flowing from north to south and had to learn that the Atlantic lay some miles due east.[61]

William could see why James Oglethorpe chose to plant his colony atop this bluff, the highest ground of the fifteen-mile stretch from the sea. And as William looked across Bay Street on the east corner of Bull, he gazed at the very house in which the general had lodged. Built in 1733, the house stood as an example of the modest aspirations the original Georgians were expected to have. Like the others constructed according to the trustees' specifications, it measured twenty-four feet long, sixteen feet wide, and eight feet from floor to ceiling.[62] Most of Savannah's houses had been added to, and recent prosperity introduced two-story brick buildings. But a town never loses its first character completely, and a number of simple hall and parlor houses survived. Just as Charlestown replicated and elaborated upon its Barbadian origins, Savannah's architecture reflected the town's humble beginnings. Oglethorpe's best idea, the organization of the town around squares each surrounded by forty lots, gave Savannah its unique character. In 1773 the town featured six squares, each with its well or a pump and most of them fenced in. The squares provided a spaciousness that the town did not really require because there was space enough surrounding the town, but the open areas in time proved a blessing.[63]

Each of the six squares with its forty lots constituted a ward, and the earth-works designed by Bartram's acquaintance William G. De Brahm surrounded the town. De Brahm's plans were implemented and improved upon by the capable Henry Ellis, the second of Georgia's royal governors. Now only Fort Halifax remained of the four bastions that once stood at each corner of the town in Ellis's day. Oglethorpe intended that the larger lots flanking each square be used for public buildings, but Savannah had fewer public buildings than lots to accommodate them. The old filature, or silk factory, in Reynolds Square, the Christ Church on Johnson Square, the Independent Church on Ellis Square, and the market in the same square were the principal buildings. The governor's house occupied a lot in Heathcote Ward facing the square. (The Telfair Academy of Arts and Sciences occupies the same lot today.) In 1773 the governor's house resembled a Charlestown town house, with its two stories above a basement and a piazza running along the side.[64]

Before visiting Governor Wright, William reserved lodgings in one of the town's boardinghouses. Later, when writing about his travels, he stated that the Georgia assembly was in session at the time and several members of the legislature lodged in the same building. As with a number of other details, his memory played tricks here. The assembly had adjourned on March 13, but some of its members lingered in Savannah, among them those who might have called themselves "the royal governor's loyal opposition." One of those legislators, Benjamin Andrew of St. John Parish, made a particular impression upon the Philadelphian. Andrew invited William to stay a while at his plantation near

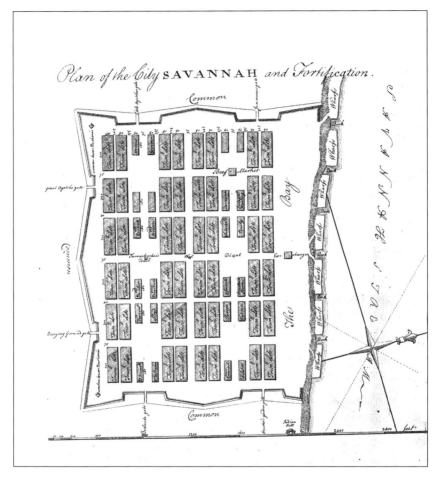

Savannah had not outgrown its original squares by 1773.
Courtesy of the British Library, London

Midway, and William gratefully accepted the invitation. Andrew acquainted the botanist with the state of Georgia politics. Most liked and respected James Wright, who had held the office of governor since Henry Ellis's departure in 1760, but they disliked the policies he enforced. Andrew was one of those who voted against an official congratulations to the governor upon his recent return from England. Andrew's party consisted mostly of low country planters and merchants Jonathan Bryan, Noble W. Jones, William LeConte, John Baker, and Henry Bourguine. Opposition to parliamentary taxation began with the Stamp Act and festered under the Townshend Duties. In 1771 the House of Commons elected Noble W. Jones its Speaker. Because Jones had opposed government measures too boldly, Governor Wright disallowed his election. The House resolved that the rejection of the Speaker subverted the rights and liberties of the people. Thereupon the governor dissolved the assembly and went off to England to be made a baronet for his good services.

Acting governor James Habersham convoked the assembly, which promptly elected Noble W. Jones again. Jones thanked the honorable members but declined the office. When Habersham learned that the House had elected Jones in spite of Habersham's stated objections, he dissolved the assembly. Habersham blamed South Carolina's insubordinate example as the reason for the opposition to royal government in Georgia.[65] He was partly right. Andrew and his neighbors in the Midway settlement maintained close ties with the neighboring colony. Many of them had migrated from Dorchester, South Carolina, in 1752, when the Georgia trustees gave up their ban on slavery.[66] James Habersham, who had grown old and irritable in public service and who drank excessively to calm his nerves, felt vastly relieved at the return of Sir James in mid-February 1773. Noble W. Jones's friends expressed their solidarity by voting against a public welcome for the returning governor. They lost the vote and joined in the welcome because, truth to tell, they liked the governor.[67]

In contrast to the St. John faction, the backcountry representatives had always rallied around the governor, especially since he helped secure the Ogeechee River boundary in 1763 and opened the region to settlement. When the governor obtained permission from the notoriously antiexpansionist earl of Hillsborough to treat with the Indians for the valuable land above the Little River and out to the Oconee, the governor's popularity achieved new heights. To show that they really harbored no ill will for the governor, the St. John crowd, through Benjamin Andrew, asked that the governor get an extension of the Indian line behind their parish while he was at it.[68] Sir James graciously replied that he would do his best to oblige.

To William Bartram, Georgia seemed far less hostile to the ministry of Lord North than Carolina had been. Nor was there the tension between radicals and conservatives he had observed in the other colony. In fact, everyone appeared to be genuinely excited about the big Indian congress and its possibilities. No one exuded greater enthusiasm for the proposed cession, Bartram discovered, than the good governor himself.

Governor Wright put his visitor at ease, recalled seeing him and his father in 1765, promised to write letters of recommendation for William, and launched into an exhaustive explanation of the benefits of the coming congress. As Wright portrayed the transaction, it would be a boon to British manufacturing and trade. Moreover, Georgia's population increase would render it more secure against future Indian attacks.[69] According to his calculations, there would be enough money after all debts were paid to raise two troops of rangers to patrol the region and to build forts, churches, schoolhouses, and jails. In Wright's utopian New Georgia, silk manufacture would at last become a reality.

The governor showed William a map he had prepared in anticipation of a successful treaty. A line marked "the present boundary line" ran along the Little River with the Wrightsborough settlement shown abutting the line. Above the boundary the caption read, "Cherokee Lands Proposed to be Ceded." Numerous exciting words such as "rich lands" and "very rich lands" interspersed. Below the Little River the Creek trail out of Augusta forked, the northern trail to the Upper Creek country along the Coosa and Tallapoosa Rivers, the southern fork leading to the lower villages on the Chattahoochee. The map extended the western boundary from the Ogeechee to the Oconee with the inscribed words "Creek Lands Proposed to be Ceded."[70] The governor became animated with the possibilities the new territory offered. With the Oconee as an additional avenue of commerce, a proper seaport would be necessary to handle the Oconee-Altamaha traffic. In fact, he had the plans for the new town of Brunswick in his possession, and he and his council had begun granting lots.[71] Thus coastal Georgia would benefit as well as the backcountry from the proposed treaty.

The one cloud upon the horizon of this brighter day, the governor admitted, was the reluctance of the Creek headmen to attend this congress. The earl of Hillsborough had given grudging approval of the transaction on the condition that the Creeks freely consent. To secure that cooperation, Wright turned to two giants of trade, George Galphin and Lachlan McGillivray. Galphin ran his trading empire among the Lower Creeks from his plantation at Silver Bluff, twelve miles below Augusta on the Carolina side of the Savannah River. William remembered the man and the place from his 1765 tour. McGillivray had retired from the trade to live as a wealthy planter and merchant in Savannah. Together with another trading partner, John Rae, Galphin and McGillivray had promoted

Georgia's most ambitious colonization scheme. They secured land on the Ogeechee and arranged passage for emigrants from Ireland for the township of Queensborough. Since 1768 a steady flow of prospective settlers from Ireland fil-tered into Georgia, but comparatively few remained in the Queensborough township.[72] McGillivray returned from a visit to his relatives in Invernesshire in October 1772, thus adding his prestige to lure the Upper Creeks to the bargain-ing table. John Stuart cordially resented the governor's practice of relying upon prominent traders to conduct diplomacy as distracting the Indians from proper attention to himself as the mouthpiece of the king.[73]

The governor expressed satisfaction at the prospect of seeing William again in Augusta and wrote a letter of reference for him:

> To all Persons to whom this May be Shown
>
> Know Ye that the Bearer Mr. Bartram, botanist, is come into this Province to Travel about in Search of, and to discover Trees Shrubs Plants etc—that may be Uncommon, usefull or Curious.
>
> I therefore Request the Favour of Such to Whom he may Apply that they will receive him kindly and assist him With their direction in Travelling from one Place to Another, and give him their Advice, the better to Enable him to Prosecute his intentions.[74]

William thanked the governor, bought himself a horse, and set out southward to see as much as he could before the great congress at Augusta.[75]

VI

"Bought a Horse and the day following set out for the town of Sundbury."
Harper, *Travels*

Benjamin Andrew urged William to tour Georgia's coast before the spring plants lost their bloom. They could ride along with several acquaintances returning to Sunbury. William gladly accepted the proposal. He knew the high road that ran behind the coastal islands and marshes; he and his father had trav-eled to Florida on that same road, and he fully intended to repeat that excur-sion when time allowed.

William and his companions rode thirty miles to Midway Meeting House, just in time to attend services presided over by Mr. William Piercy. William learned that Mr. Piercy had arrived in Georgia a few months before to assume direction of the Bethesda Orphan House. William and his father had visited Bethesda in 1765, when the "Great Itinerant," George Whitefield, presided over and dreamed of converting the orphanage into a college after the pattern of the College of Philadelphia.[76] Whitefield could not get a royal charter because he would not agree that the president must be a member of the Church of England. He willed the institution to Selina, countess of Huntingdon, and after Whitefield's death in 1770, the countess attempted to carry out Whitefield's plans for a college under a charter from Georgia. She named the Reverend Piercy as president and sent a staff of people to work under him. Piercy saw himself as another Whitefield and preferred traveling about, evangelizing to the less exciting work of administering the school. Though some objected to Piercy's style as overly "enthusiastic," Bartram commented favorably upon the preacher's zeal.[77] He noted in his journal to Fothergill that the "Religious and Pious Spirit throughout the whole Audience reflects a shining light on the Character of the inhabitants of Midway and Newport."[78] If these godly people found fault with the king's ministers on matters of principle, William felt sure they must be right.

The Midway Meeting House represented the soul of the forty or so Congregationalist families who moved from Dorchester, South Carolina, to Georgia in 1752. They had resided northwest of Charlestown after emigrating from Massachusetts long enough to learn how to plant rice successfully. Their Puritan doctrine assured them that those who were saved were blessed in this life, and rice provided many blessings. Of course, rice planting required slave labor, and the Midway settlers brought their slaves with them. William wondered how such pious people could reconcile slavery with their religion, and he worried that God would not continue to bless those who enslaved people. He kept these concerns to himself for fear of discomforting these genteel folk. Mr. Piercy preached only occasionally at Midway; the Reverend John Osgood served the congregation as its resident pastor and had done so since 1752. The parish flourished under Osgood's ministry and numbered more than 150 members at the time of Bartram's visit.[79]

William expressed delight at his first sight of Sunbury, some ten miles east of the meetinghouse near the mouth of the Midway River. He counted about one hundred houses, neatly laid out around three squares. Five wharves lined the riverfront. Sunbury basked in its greatest prosperity at the time of Bartram's visit; fifty-six vessels cleared the Sunbury customs house in 1773. Bartram described the inhabitants as "genteel and wealthy" merchants and planters who kept town houses in addition to their rice plantations and otherwise imitated Carolina gentry.[80]

William and Benjamin Andrew arrived there in the evening and enjoyed the gentility. "I supped and spent the evening in a circle of genteel and polite ladies and gentlemen," Bartram recalled.[81] The next morning William set about the business of which Dr. Fothergill had sent him, a search for interesting and curious flora and fauna. In his own expressive language he explained his motivation: "Obedient to the admonitions of my attendant spirit, curiosity, as well as to gratify the expectations of my worthy patron."[82] Fording a narrow shoal, he explored a neighboring island, hoping to find something exciting for Fothergill but instead found "nothing new, or much worth your notice."[83] If Fothergill might not have been interested, William certainly was because he filled three pages of his *Travels* with description of things he saw. Among the remains of a prehistoric settlement he found a nearly whole clay pot imprinted with intricate basket-weave design. He described magnolias, water oaks, pines, cedars, palmettos, and other trees and shrubs. Numerous deer inhabited the island along with "tygers," wolves, bears, foxes, raccoons, opossums, and a variety of snakes. He did not care much for the majestic bald eagle, an "excreble tyrant" who "supports his dignity and grandeur with rapine and violence." He much preferred the fishing hawk that caught its own meal rather than robbing others of theirs.[84]

William dined that evening at the plantation residence of one of the wealthier members of the Sunbury, noting that a hundred slaves worked the rice fields.[85] He lingered several days in the company of Benjamin Andrew and his family and on one occasion went to hear Dr. John Osgood's sermon at the meetinghouse. Andrew renewed his insistence that Bartram visit his plantation outside Sunbury. William did so and admired the efficient way Andrew managed his rice crop. In the evening they fished in the creek that ran through the property. William devoted a long paragraph of imaginative prose to describing a redbelly fish he had caught.[86] In his report to Fothergill, William devoted most of his attention to a plant called fly poison. Juice from the plant when mixed with honey attracted swarms of flies that promptly died "in incredible numbers," a most useful plant in this fly-infested region.[87]

Within a short time war would shatter the idyllic calm of the golden isles of Georgia. Bartram's host, Benjamin Andrew, would be in the thick of it, de-

nounced by one faction as too radical and by another as too conservative. Some
of those who disliked the way in which Andrew and his friends took their lead
from the ultra Whigs of South Carolina lived here in the village of Sunbury.
Most of the group adhered to the Church of England and would have disagreed
with the Congregational majority on the basis of doctrine alone. They had petitioned for a resident cleric as recently as 1771, but to no avail. As merchants,
they cordially disliked the St. John habit of joining boycotts every time Parliament did something disagreeable. When the final test came in 1776, many of
these minority members of St. John Parish declared for the king, notably Roger
Kelsall, Simon Munro, and John Simpson. Kelsall, proprietor of the largest
wharf and store in Sunbury, had entered into partnership with James Spalding
in 1763, and their firm expanded prodigiously. Spalding managed their five
stores in Florida, and Kelsall supervised the trade to the Cherokee and Creek
Nations. Both men had closer ties with St. Andrew Parish than with St. John
Parish. Kelsall married Barbara, daughter of Capt. James Mackay, a transplanted Scot, and James Spalding wed Margery McIntosh, one of the Darien clan.[88]
An advertisement in the *Georgia Gazette* of December 27, 1769, took an entire
page to list the wares available at their Sunbury store. The list included: cloths,
coats, jackets, breeches, buttons, silk knee garters, bed ticks, mattresses, Irish
linens, Russian and Irish sheets, knee buckles, silver thimbles, lamb gloves, sta-
tionery, shaving boxes and brushes, black Barcelona handkerchiefs, and a great
variety of hardware. The well-to-do inhabitants of Sunbury must have been
indeed "genteel" if they required Barcelona handkerchiefs and Russian sheets.[89]
The firm of Kelsall and Spalding played a major role in the ensuing frontier history, and William Bartram found himself caught up in those events.

VII

I took leave of this worthy family and set off for the set-
tlements on the Alatahama.

Harper, *Travels*

William had no way of knowing it, of course, and in his modesty he would not
have believed it, but his description of his journey southward would send major
British writers into flights of rhetoric and poetry. His *Travels* appeared at the
time the Romantic movement flourished in Europe. A literary historian noted
that America seemed "a strange and remote land and especially the section
described by Bartram, the Carolinas and the Floridas, and therefore wonder-

30

fully interesting."[90] Goldsmith, Coleridge, Wordsworth, and Carlyle, among others, revealed that they had read Bartram.[91] This region that Bartram approached, "the wild Altama" as Oliver Goldsmith called it, particularly caught their imagination.[92]

Traveling alone on horseback, he followed the high road south from Midway. After ten miles the plantations became fewer and the road worse. The thrifty people of St. John complained in the legislature that the inhabitants of neighboring St. Andrew neglected the upkeep of the road. The Scots had a reputation for not caring much for tidiness; John Bartram, when he and William passed this way in 1765, bluntly noted that "ye scotch highlanders is very lazy and careless making poor improvement where settled."[93] William would never have made such a remark. It was not that the Georgia Scots were lazy but that they had different traditions. The New Englanders practiced collective responsibility in their towns whereas in Scotland the Highlanders regarded roads as English intrusions. With the poor road and the gathering dusk, William managed to lose his way completely and blundered along through swamps and creeks, characteristically unafraid and trusting to Providence. Sure enough, he saw a light glimmering through the darkness and followed it to a house, where he stayed the night.[94]

If St. John represented a colony of transplanted New England Puritans, St. Andrew was little Scotland. In 1735 James Oglethorpe sent his most trusted aide, Capt. George Dunbar, to recruit Scots for his Georgia colony. With Dunbar went Hugh Mackay, son of the Mackay who commanded a garrison at Castle Ruthven in Invernesshire. Oglethorpe, anticipating trouble with Spanish Florida, wanted fighting men on his southern frontier, and Dunbar and Mackay knew that there was a surplus of fighting men in Strathnairn of Invernesshire, the land of the Mackintoshes of clan Chattan. Aeneas Mackintosh, South Carolina Independent Regiment brother to the chief William Mackintosh of Moy Hall, served as a captain in the South Carolina Independent Regiment and was subject to Oglethorpe's overall military command of both Georgia and South Carolina. It is likely that Aeneas promoted the scheme to bring over his clansmen, and as the eventual successor to the chiefdom, he had unusual influence in Strathnairn. The Mackintosh of Moy Hall entered readily into the project because a mass migration of his relatives would free up his lands for sheep raising. He mortgaged his property to pay the way of seventeen kinsmen. On behalf of the Georgia trustees, George Dunbar agreed to pay the passage of nearly 150 others. John Mohr Mackintosh (called Mohr for his great size) would lead the Highlanders in Georgia. A well-known story, embellished in the retelling, of his going off to fight in the Jacobite Rising of '15 with his uncle Brig. Lachlan Mackintosh, added to his authority. The "gentlemen" among the clan members, distinguished by their ability to speak English and by their disdain for manual work, recruited their Gaelic-speaking tenants, most of whom were related to them. Clan Chattan included smaller clans that over the years affiliated with the Mackintoshes: McGillivrays, McBeans, Macphails, Macphersons, McQueens, Gows, and Shaws. These families were represented among the Georgia contingent.[95]

The Highlanders settled where Oglethorpe wanted them, on the Altamaha, Georgia's southern boundary according to its charter. Oglethorpe concocted a map that showed a branch of the Altamaha conveniently flowing into the St. Johns, which gave him the pretext to extend Georgia's boundary to the St. Johns. Meanwhile, he acted as though he had a right to the St. Johns. There occurred a famous moment on February 22, 1736, when Oglethorpe put ashore at the Scots new town of Darien, clad in a tartan plaid. The Highlanders cheered Oglethorpe even if most of them could not understand what he said. They knew that he expected them to fight the Spaniards, and they liked fighting better than farming. Oglethorpe tweaked the nose of the Spaniards by putting a garrison of Scots on Amelia Island at the mouth of the St. Johns.[96]

While waiting for the expected war to start, the Scots occupied themselves by cutting timber for Oglethorpe's military town of Frederica, on nearby St. Simon's Island. They should have paid more attention to planting because within two years they did not have enough to eat. Many of the leaders wanted to quit Darien in favor of Charlestown, where a number of Scots were successfully employed in the Indian trade. John Mohr Mackintosh persuaded them to stay in Darien on the condition that the trustees establish a store there to supply their needs. The quid pro quo exacted by George Dunbar, Oglethorpe's factotum, was that the gentlemen of Darien disassociate themselves from the Savannah appeal for the removal of the ban on slavery. So from a mixture of motives the Scots went on record as declaring slavery a curse to mankind. The statement hindered them not at all in the acquisition of slaves when the trustees removed the prohibition.[97]

The Highlanders finally got their war in 1740, when they accompanied Oglethorpe's regiment, the 42nd, on the invasion of Florida, with their Indian allies coming and going, adding to the color of the occasion. Oglethorpe assigned John Mohr Mackintosh's men to Fort Mosa and told them to watch St. Augustine's back door. Instead they quarreled with the party of Carolinians under Col. John Palmer and went to sleep. The night attack by Capt. Antonio Salgado's three hundred Spaniards found Colonel Palmer's twenty Carolinians ready but utterly unable to hold the fort. The suddenly aroused Highlanders fought desperately but futilely. Some escaped over the back wall, but most of the eighty died or went to a Spanish prison. John Mohr Mackintosh wrote to a relative in Scotland that seven hundred Spaniards had attacked his eighty. He thought that probably three hundred of the enemy had been killed.[98]

The Mosa fiasco ruined Darien as a community. With Mohr Mackintosh gone, the venerable pastor John McLeod moved to Charlestown with several families, among them young Lachlan McGillivray, who joined the trading company headed by his relative Archibald McGillivray. Two of Mohr Mackintosh's children, Lachlan and Anne, went to the Reverend George Whitefield's orphanage at Bethesda.[99] The survivors of Oglethorpe's invasion, reinforced by additional recruits from Scotland, helped Oglethorpe repel the Spanish counterattack at Bloody Marsh on St. Simon's Island and thus helped to redeem the Highlanders' reputation, damaged by the disaster at Mosa. But Darien never recovered as a town during the colonial period. The remaining Scots scattered around the region and endeavored something they had never done successfully, farming, and rice farming at that.[100]

Mohr Mackintosh, back from prison, set an example by securing a grant on Black Island, planting crops and raising cattle. In 1758 Governor Ellis constituted the old Darien district the parish of St. Andrew, in honor of Scotland's patron saint. The governor and council honored Mackintosh with the title conservator of the peace. He died in 1761 at the age of sixty-three. His achievement was that he rooted his clan in Georgia and thereby stamped the district of Darien with its indelibly Scottish character. Eldest son, William, a survivor of Mosa and of Oglethorpe's victory on St. Simon's, acquired several plantations, including Fair Hope on the Sapelo River. His cousin Roderick McIntosh, known as Old Rory for his ferocious temper, had a neighboring plantation he called Mallow. Anne McIntosh, John Mohr's daughter, obtained a grant along the Sapelo River; she brought that property to her marriage to Robert Baillie, who commanded Fort Barrington on the Altamaha as a lieutenant in the Independent Company. After the disbanding of the Independents following the 1754–1763 war with France and French-allied Indians, Baillie settled down on his estate as a prosperous rice planter. From 1764 to 1768 he and George McIntosh represented St. Andrew Parish in the colonial house of assembly. George, whose upbringing had been the responsibility of brother Lachlan, profited from Lachlan's tutelage. He had accompanied Lachlan to Charles-town when he was eleven and Lachlan twenty-one.[101] George went to school while Lachlan worked in a countinghouse. The great merchant Henry Laurens took a liking to the tall, amiable Lachlan and hired him as a clerk. In 1756 Lachlan married Sarah Threadcraft, and he, Sarah, and George moved back to Darien. With credit supplied by Henry Laurens, both Lachlan and George prospered. In 1772 George married Ann Priscilla Houstoun, daughter of Sir Patrick Houstoun and sister of the second Sir Patrick Houstoun. George and his brother-in-law sat in the assembly as representatives of St. Andrew Parish.[102]

Lachlan managed to acquire fourteen thousand acres, more than his sixty slaves could cultivate. He maintained close ties with Henry Laurens, especial-ly when Laurens bought nine hundred acres of Lachlan's land on Broughton Island. Lachlan suggested that Laurens hire fellow Scot James Bailey to man-age the rice plantation.[103] Lachlan had a special regard for the deserted old town of Darien. On June 1, 1767, Governor Wright signed an order requiring the resurveying of the town. New lots were to be laid out "where the Old Town formerly stood."[104] Lachlan McIntosh, who had learned something about sur-veying, actually laid out the new town, covering thirty and one-half acres fronting the river. McIntosh then encouraged settlement by offering free ferry transportation across the Altamaha or across to the deserted town of Frederica and to St. Simon's Island. On March 3, 1773, he informed Governor Wright that he could no longer oblige the increasing number of travelers and asked for the right to charge passengers for the ferry crossing.[105]

When with his father, William Bartram had not wandered from the high road to Florida, and this incursion marked his introduction to McIntosh coun-try. The unknown host whose "glimmering light" rescued Bartram had his overseer guide the botanist through a dangerous swamp and point him in the direction of Darien. He rode through a forest of pines, crossed a branch of the Sapelo River and arrived at a small plantation on the South Newport River, the home of Donald McIntosh, one of the original emigrants from Inverness. Bartram described how the "venerable grey headed Caldonian" came out to welcome him to his home and hospitality. He admired the primitive simplici-ty of the household. A furious storm broke out while they were at a meal of venison; a bolt of lightning set a tree ablaze less than forty yards away. Typical-ly, Bartram used his time during the storm by taking notes on the appearance and behavior of a large male turkey with comparisons to the smaller turkeys of Europe and Asia. Although William may never have visited Donald McIntosh again, he never forgot him. Writing to Lachlan McIntosh in 1796, he said, "Give respects to Good Old Don'd McIntosh at the Swamp between Sapello and the great swamp where I had shelter during the tremendous thunder storm."[106]

William did not tarry at Strathlachlan, as Donald McIntosh called his farm, because he had a message to deliver from Governor Wright to Robert Baillie at Sapelo Main. Baillie, the one-time commander of the Fort Barrington garrison, urged Bartram to linger, but the explorer explained his desire to push on to Darien. His friend Benjamin Andrew had told him that he needed to secure the endorsement of Lachlan McIntosh, and Bartram carried a letter of introduction written by Andrew.[107]

Of the many people he met and friends he made, with the exception of Mary Lamboll Thomas, William Bartram liked Lachlan McIntosh best. They hit it off from the first. Many years later Bartram's heart filled with sentiment when he recollected that meeting: "When I came up to the door, the friendly man, smiling, and with a grace and dignity peculiar to himself, took me by the hand and accosted me thus, 'Friend Bartram, come under my roof and I desire you to make my house your home as long as convenient to yourself; remember, from this moment that you are part of my family, and on my part I shall endeavour to make it agreeable.'"[108] There were already ten in the McIntosh household so the invitation to Bartram represented a triumph of hospitality over housekeeping. The eight children paraded by to be introduced to their guest: John, at sixteen the oldest, then in chronological order, Lachlan, William, George, Henry, John Hampton, Hester and Catherine. William got along famously with them, and the warmth of their regard drew him to Darien for prolonged visits during his explorations. William later recalled "those happy scenes, happy hours which I enjoyed with your family." He especially liked the conversations he had with McIntosh in the evenings, the "improving Philosophic conversation," as he phrased it. The discussions touched on William's favorite theme, the working out of the designs of Providence. He exclaimed, "O my Friend, what a degree of intellectual enjoyment our nature is susceptible of when we behold and contemplate the Moral system impressed on the Human Mind by the Divine Intelligence."[109] In retrospect Bartram could readily understand how the divine plan dictated that America free herself from the confining connections to England; it was not so clear in 1773, either in his mind or in that of Lachlan McIntosh. None of the McIntoshes and few of their neighbors of St. Andrew burned with revolutionary zeal. Tradition required them to feud with the busybodies of St. John Parish, and if the St. John people advocated revolutionary measures, St. Andrew preferred to go slowly. A descendant of John Mohr McIntosh inherited the attitude of his forebears. To him the "perfervid celts" of St. Andrew represented the "moral antipodes" to the Puritans of Midway.[110]

William encountered so many McIntoshes that he had difficulty sorting them out. The Scots compounded the problem by insisting on using the names of fathers and grandfathers. For example, Lachlan and Sarah named their sons John, Lachlan, William, George, Henry, and John Hampton. Lachlan's older brother, William, and his wife, Jane Mackay, also named their sons John, William, Lachlan, and George. William had a decade head start on Lachlan in the production of offspring. His oldest son, John, twenty-five and still unmarried, would become celebrated in Georgia history as the defender of Fort Morris at Sunbury in 1778. William McIntosh's other children continued the practice of marrying fellow countrymen and women. Lachlan and Hester both married Baillies. Margery had recently married James Spalding, Roger Kelsall's partner, and the couple lived on nearby St. Simon's Island. William would soon become well acquainted with James and Margery Spalding. Barbara, the youngest daughter, compounded the confusion by marrying yet another William McIntosh.[111] Even Bartram, who knew them well, could get confused. Years later, when a young man approached Bartram at his home in Kingsessing, William recognized him as a McIntosh but could not place him. "Lachlan," the young man answered. That narrowed the possibilities but remained imprecise. "Lachlan's or William's?" "William's," came the answer. William Bartram paid him a nice compliment: "His countenance and manners bespeaks the Gentleman."[112]

William Bartram and Lachlan McIntosh discovered that they had mutual friends. William had become acquainted with Lt. White Outerbridge on his voyage down. McIntosh remembered Outerbridge as an officer in Oglethorpe's regiment stationed in nearby Frederica. In fact, the old soldier owned four hundred acres on the Newport River and had offered it for sale. If Lachlan could afford it, he would snatch the property. Meanwhile, Lachlan did his best to look after Henry Laurens's nearby Broughton Island plantation while Laurens was in England, overseeing the education of sons John and Henry.

Did William know Mr. Laurens? Indeed he did. He and his father visited Laurens in 1765 and admired his gardens. Later, Laurens figured in the most painful episode in William's career. When William decided to become a gentleman planter, against the objections of his father and his father's friends, Henry Laurens helped recruit six slaves for the venture and gave advice on setting up a plantation. Unfortunately, William selected a low-lying sandy pine barren for his farm, on a stagnant backwater of the St. Johns River. A nearby swamp might have afforded good rice land, but William lacked the skill to work the wetlands. When Laurens looked in on Bartram, the young man suffered from a fever and looked thoroughly miserable. Laurens expressed dismay at the hovel he lived in and the starvation diet that barely kept him alive. By temperament and inclination Bartram hated slavery and utterly lacked management skills when gentle suasion failed. "Six negroes that rather plagues than aids to him," Laurens reported to John Bartram, "one so insolent as to threaten his life, one a needless espense and one a helpless child in arms." After painting a woeful portrait of the failed farmer, Laurens felt he had not been bleak enough. "No colouring can do justice to the forlorn state of poor Billy Bartram," he concluded.[113]

Yes, William remembered Henry Laurens as a somewhat overbearing surrogate father. He owed much to Laurens, but he feared that he would always be "poor Billy Bartram" to the great merchant. Lachlan McIntosh understood. Laurens at times acted the parent to him too. Laurens once chided McIntosh for a tendency to pinch pennies, a fault many of McIntosh's countrymen were accused of. "Do for God's sake get the better of that foible," Laurens told McIntosh in his forthright manner.[114] Lachlan accepted the advice as he would from a loved relative. He owed much to Laurens. He had sent his oldest son, Jack, to school in Charlestown educated under Laurens's vigilant eye. When Jack tried to drop French because he could not possibly learn that and Latin at the same time, Laurens commanded him to stick to it. Jack did well enough in Latin and arithmetic and pleased Laurens very much in his ability to read and write.[115]

Sixteen-year-old Jack expressed keen interest in Bartram's expedition. The idea of exploring a vast and mysterious wilderness appealed to his sense of adventure. Would William permit Jack to accompany him on his trip to the interior of Georgia? William expressed his entire satisfaction at the idea. He remembered that he had accompanied his own father on a botanizing excursion into western Pennsylvania at about the same age.[116] Proud father Lachlan was all for it; Sarah McIntosh needed further gentle persuasion.

2

The Ceded Lands

I

We set off with the prayers and benevolent wishes of my companion's worthy parents.

Harper, *Travels*

While the eager young McIntosh, now referred to by Bartram as "my fellow pilgrim," prepared for his quest, Bartram explored the Altamaha, up one side to the ferry crossing at Fort Barrington and down the south side to the proposed town of Brunswick. On the way to the Barrington crossing, he had the satisfaction of seeing again the shrub he and his father discovered on October 1, 1765, the Franklinia. Francis Harper, the historical detective, located the actual spot of the fortuitous incident, 1.7 miles west of the community of Cox and four miles east of the fort.[1] Interestingly, William expressed greater wonder in another new shrub growing near the Franklinia. He described this plant in a letter to Robert Barclay, an English Quaker: "I was struck with surprise and delight when beholding its gaiety so very singular in its bloom. It grows from 15 to 20 ft. high perfectly erect and pyramidal." After other detailed descriptions, he suggested that if the British botanists deemed it a new plant that it be named *Bartramia bractiata* in honor of his father, "whose labours, travels, collections and communications to the curious in Europe hath contributed perhaps as much as that of any man of his time toward increasing the stores of Botanical knowledge."[2] In 1773 William believed that the Franklinia belonged to the gordonia family; only later did he and other experts realize its uniqueness. Bartram listed the plant in his catalog in 1785, and his kinsman Humphry Marshall published a description under the name *Franklinia Alatamaha*.[3] The other discovery that excited William proved to be a branch of the *Pinckneyta bracteata*, or "Georgia bark."[4] The improbable but actual fact is that the Franklinia, so named by John Bartram in honor of his friend Benjamin Franklin, at some point after Bartram collected its seeds, ceased to grow in the wild. The Franklinia trees today all descend from the seeds gathered by the Bartrams.[5]

Fort Barrington sat on the Satilla Bluffs, theoretically guarding the place where the high road crossed the Altamaha. Only because no enemy had challenged the crossing, the fort could be called a success. William G. DeuBrahm, the busy and contentious engineer who built the ill-fated Fort Loudoun, designed Fort Barrington in 1760 during the late war with France. Gov. Henry Ellis conferred the name in honor of his friend, Secretary at War William Wildman, Lord Barrington, and put in a troop of rangers commanded by Lt. Robert Baillie. An American officer who saw the fort in 1778 described it as "badly planned and wretchedly constructed."[6] One function of the fort consisted in the quasi-military task of serving as a landmark. Beyond lay Creek Indian territory. Lachlan McGillivray and Samuel Savery had marked the boundary line from Barrington across the fearsome Okefenokee to the St. Marys in 1768. Now in 1773 the expansionists of St. John and St. Andrew hoped that Governor Wright would extend the line and muted for the interim any impolitic and revolutionary expressions.[7]

John and William had visited the fort in 1765 when it was still garrisoned. Now abandoned and in need of repair, it had lost any military value and served only as a boundary marker. Within three years William would see it rehabilitated and put in a posture of defense against British invaders from Florida. He did not remain on the frontier long enough to know that Barrington failed its first test when Lt. Col. Thomas Brown and a hundred of his Florida rangers and Indian allies swam across the five-hundred-yard river and captured the fort.[8]

William crossed over the Altamaha in a "good large boat" manned by a Creek Indian. He scarcely met an Indian he didn't like, and he thought his ferryman an "active, civil, and sensible" person.[9] He mounted and rode alongside the river again, through forests of tall, straight, virgin pines, past green meadows and across marshy ground, noting the different varieties of plants in his journal. For the first time in his journey, he slept outdoors, savoring the balmy late April nights in this semitropical region. The next day he reached the coast and a plantation belonging to Henry Laurens and managed by Peter Nephew.

39

Curious about the proposed new town of Brunswick, he rode to the site of the town. He thought it a fine situation between the St. Simons and Turtle River sounds. Potentially rich rice lands spread to the Turtle River. Unfortunately, to Bartram's mind, absentee owners neglected the area.[10] This region below the Altamaha and above the St. Johns had been contested for by Britain and Spain since the founding of Georgia and even before that. The grant of Carolina by King Charles II represented the first intrusion into Spanish La Florida because it ignored the Spanish presence and gave the Carolina proprietors everything from Virginia to the middle of the Florida peninsula. Thus when Parliament established Georgia between the Savannah and Altamaha Rivers, South Carolina continued to claim the region below the Altamaha. Former governor Henry Ellis, working assiduously for Georgia as advisor to Lord Egremont, managed to write the extension of Georgia's boundary to the St. Marys into the Royal Proclamation of 1763. However, the eager speculators of Charlestown bought up huge estates below the Altamaha before they could be stopped. Henry Laurens cultivated his property, but most of the Carolina gentlemen waited to sell at a profit. "Thus," noted Bartram in his memorial to Dr. Fothergill, "one of the most valuable Parts of the Province lay as useless as any part of the Indian Country."[11]

The dearth of inhabitants had not prevented the region from gaining equal status with the eight older parishes. In deference to the historical importance of Frederica, St. Simon's Island became a parish unto itself, St. James. From the Altamaha to the Turtle River became St. David Parish; from the Turtle to the Little Satilla, St. Patrick; from the Little Satilla to the Great Satilla, St. Thomas; and from the Great Satilla to the St. Marys, St. Mary. For four years after the new parishes were created in 1765, they were not represented in the legislature because of the paucity of residents. With all the talk about taxation without representation much in vogue since the Stamp Act of 1765, it occurred to the Commons House that the four lower parishes should not be taxed, and in 1769 they were exempted. Governor Wright agreed that taxation necessitated elections but explained that he had to get permission from England in order to issue writs of election. This delay would not do; the fledgling opposition party argued that such a basic right should not require approval from Whitehall. In 1770 the Commons refused to pass any tax law at all, whereupon for this and other reasons the governor dissolved the assembly. Before the new assembly met in 1771, the ministry had given its consent and Governor Wright issued writs of election. Thus this sparsely populated region that William Bartram contemplated had already figured in a potentially revolutionary issue.[12]

Bartram's depiction of the Franklinia has been called his best drawing.
Courtesy of the American Philosophical Society, Philadelphia

William's hurried notes confused him when he sat down years later to write his epic, for he thought he traveled all the way to the St. Marys, but the dispatch he sent to Fothergill reveals that he returned to the McIntosh household immediately after visiting the site of "New Brunswick." By then Sarah McIntosh had given her consent to her anxious son Jack, and with this last obstacle (Bartram called it the "difficult point") finally settled, the adventurers set off for Augusta on May 1, 1773.[13]

Two days riding took them to Savannah where they learned that John Stuart had preceded them to Augusta. William delayed only long enough to forward his collection of dried specimens to Fothergill by way of Dr. Chalmers. Fothergill acknowledged receiving the material in a letter to William of September 4, 1773. He complimented William on his drawing of a bird but observed that the *starry annis* had been done in too much of a hurry. He expressed satisfaction that William meant to go to Augusta and beyond and reminded him to keep a journal noting the various shrubs and animals. Above all, "take care of thy health."[14]

William had traveled this road before with his father so he could point out familiar places and plants to his companion with some authority. They rode leisurely past the great Savannah River rice plantations. Vale Royal and Springfield belonged to Lachlan McGillivray and Rae's Hall to McGillivray's former partner in the Indian trade, John Rae. They passed Jonathan Bryan's Brampton estate on Pipemakers Creek, where Oglethorpe's intermediary with the Creek Nation, Mary Musgrove, kept a trading post.[15] Bartram would later visit Bryan's plantation as an honored guest, but for now he and his young companion continued until they reached Dacres Tavern, fifteen miles from Savannah in the vicinity of John Graham's extensive Mulberry Grove plantation. If William had nothing good to say about a person or a place, he said nothing, and public taverns on rural roads had deservedly poor reputations. William and Jack would have been lucky if they did not have to share their bed with booted strangers, snoring and snorting with drink. They had breakfast at a common table with everyone present digging into the large bowls of rice or hominy grits and the proprietor cutting huge slices of salted ham. William wrote nothing in his journal about Dacres Tavern.[16]

Beautiful springtime weather buoyed their spirits as they rode on through the nearly deserted village of Abercorn, past the turnoff to Zubly's Ferry and Purrysburg, to the village of Ebenezer. Oglethorpe's original agreement with the Creek Indians confined his colony to the tidewater, and Ebenezer sat on a bluff at the far reaches of the tide. Its inhabitants came from Salzburg, Austria, and professed the Lutheran religion under the strict discipline of their pastor, John Martin Bolzius. Bolzius died in 1765, the year John and William Bartram visited the place. Since then the Salzburgers had built a handsome brick church and had fallen to quarreling about the use of it. Rev. Christian Frederic Triebner's faction earnestly disputed with Rev. Christian Rabenhorst's followers about matters of ritual and procedure that seemed petty to outsiders. When our two travelers reached the village, they learned that the Reverend Henry Muhlenberg had been sent for to restore harmony to the fractured community.[17]

William, of course, ignored the bickering and commented favorably on the appearance of the town. The people were "very industrious and temperate, their little Plantations . . . well cultivated."[18] Orchards, cornfields, and pastures surrounded the town. Since the trustee era the people of Ebenezer had attempted to raise silkworms and to spin silk from the cocoons. Their indifferent success failed to discourage them, and Bartram observed that silk cultivation remained a communal activity.

The following day began hot and turned hotter as the sun rose. Bartram devoted more attention in his notes to the scenery than to the passage of Governor Wright's retinue on its way to the Augusta congress, only mentioning that several fine horses belonging to the governor's escort "died in the Road by reason of the Heat and drouth."[19] He described the herds of deer and flocks of wild turkey. He noticed how the hard clay prevented the pine trees from sinking taproots and how storms had knocked over a number of trees, a phenomenon that still happens in the red clay country. The travelers took the fork leading up the south side of Briar Creek, probably because William wanted to show his companion a place he and his father had visited in 1765. Francis Harper, who traced Bartram's route in 1936, described the site as "probably the most attractive spot along the entire route between Augusta and Savannah."[20] The pond of clear water, today known as Blue Springs, lies along a sparsely traveled side road between Newington and Sylvania, and still affords the wayfarer a cool retreat on a hot day.

Bartram's route from Blue Springs followed present Georgia Highway 24. He may have crossed Briar Creek at Millhaven Plantation and continued through present-day Girard to McBean, where they were ferried across the Savannah to George Galphin's plantation and trading post at Silver Bluff. The fact that Bartram and McIntosh tarried there for two days and possibly longer, in spite of the fact that a "number of people" were already there, says much for the hospitality of this extraordinary man, George Galphin.[21]

Galphin left a wife in Ireland to come to America in 1737 and entered the Indian trading company headed by Patrick Brown and John Rae. For a decade he resided in Coweta, the principal town of the Lower Creeks. He lived with an Indian woman, then another; both produced children that he candidly acknowledged. By virtue of these living ties to the Creek Nation and by the honesty of his conduct and decency of his character, he gained an ascendency among the

Lower Creeks, unrivaled by any white man before him. Before the last war with France and Spain he retired from the Indian country and built a handsome brick two-story residence at Silver Bluff on the Carolina side of the river twelve miles below Augusta. He acquired well over a hundred slaves, had three children by two of them, and had two others by a white woman named Rachel Dupre.[22]

Edmond Atkin, the first Indian agent for the Southern Department, complained bitterly that the Augusta-based company constituted a law unto itself and that Indians paid more attention to the company than to him. Indeed the surviving partners of the company represented by Galphin, Lachlan McGillivray and John Rae, exercised a virtual monopoly over the Creek trade. The era before 1763 constituted a golden age of the trade compared to the ten years following. The employees of the company understood just how far they might cheat the Indians, and the Indians knew the limits of their ability to palm off green and damaged skins.[23]

The inefficient governor John Reynolds left Indian affairs to the traders, and Gov. Henry Ellis worked with the traders to secure Creek neutrality during the 1754–1763 war, when even the Cherokees joined the French. Governor Wright expected Galphin and McGillivray to summon the Indians to Augusta in 1763. They obliged, and they worked out the terms of a cession before the arrival of Governor Wright and the governors of Virginia and both Carolinas. They exercised such influence that John Stuart agreed with Atkin, his predecessor, that these traders interfered in his ability to control Indian affairs.[24]

Since the peace of 1763, Galphin, McGillivray, and Rae acquired vast estates and had endeavored to increase land values by populating the Ogeechee frontier. As a member of the legislature, McGillivray secured the necessary legislation creating the Queensborough township, and Rae wrote to relatives in Ireland about how prosperity awaited all who would come to Georgia. By 1773 nearly nine hundred Irishmen had answered the invitation, but they scattered about rather than establishing a town. In Georgia the pull of the plantation negated experiments in town planning. Bartram would encounter the one place where community prevailed in the Quaker settlement of Wrightsborough.[25]

Silver Bluff resembled a town itself, or rather a manorial village, with Galphin as father figure and his many slaves as villagers. In surveying the slave population of Silver Bluff, Bartram realized that Galphin encouraged the practice of Christianity, unlike some masters who worried that baptism might lead to manumission. Itinerant preachers proclaiming the new doctrines of the Great Awakening had begun to filter down to Georgia. Daniel Marshall and his brother-in-law Shubal Stearns established a Baptist Church on Kiokee Creek the year before Bartram's tour. At the request of some of his slaves, Galphin permitted one Wait Palmer, a preacher from Connecticut, to start a church at Silver Bluff in 1773. The moving spirit of this congregation was David George, whose story was replete with adventure. He had escaped from a cruel master and fled into Indian country only to be captured by a friend of the English, a Cusseta chief named Blue Salt, and returned to Augusta for the reward. The courageous David ran away again, deeper into Indian country only to be captured again and sold to John Miller, Galphin's agent. David worked as a cowboy on that far frontier until he brought back a caravan of deerskins to Galphin and obtained permission to stay at Silver Bluff. An experienced cattleman, David proved a useful hand at Silver Bluff. On his first visit William Bartram had observed black cowboys at work, herding and branding. William marveled at their ability to train horses to work the cattle. Although the rodeo events are associated today with the nineteenth-century West, the Georgia frontier had its cutting horses, its roundups, its brands, and its cowmen.

Galphin's children of their varying ethnic origins learned to read from a tutor, and David George learned to read from the children. In Mr. Palmer's absence David preached to the growing Baptist congregation at Silver Bluff. Bartram would have been astonished if he had been told that these humble Christians constituted the first African American church in the United States.[26]

II

Set off with a number of People and a Party of Indians. . . .
Bartram, "Report to Fothergill"

If William Bartram became an authority on southeastern Indians, as he did, he owed part of his education to George Galphin. Bartram had sat at Galphin's feet as an impressionable youth in 1765, and in addition to this visit in 1773, he would call upon the veteran trader twice again before returning to Philadelphia. Because he left the South at an early stage of the American Revolution, he believed that Indians acted differently than they actually did. He later wrote to Washington's secretary of war, Henry Knox, about the Creek Indians: "Amidst all their difficulties they stood firm to our advocate Mr. Galphin even to the termination of the contest."[27] They did not stand nearly as firm as Bartram believed or as Galphin wished they might.

Galphin influenced another authority on Southeastern Indians, a man intimately associated with the Muskegans, better known as Creeks, the flamboyant and controversial James Adair. Galphin and Lachlan McGillivray urged Adair to write an authentic account of Indian life and history to counteract the superficial stereotypes that passed for knowledge in London and even in Charlestown and Savannah. Adair dedicated his book to Galphin and McGillivray, expanding upon their wisdom in Indian diplomacy and reciting their virtues. His book, he said, owed more to their encouragement than to any desire of his own. He shared their hope that the book would shape a humane Indian policy. He believed that, within limits, Indians should manage their own affairs. Lord Shelburne's direction to John Stuart to persuade the various tribes to stop fighting each other, the two traders regarded as muddleheaded as well as futile. However, coexistence between Indians and whites was a realistic possibility. Adair, Galphin, and McGillivray had coexisted quite happily among the Musgogulges. If the tribes could be induced to practice a more diversified economy, they could become self-sufficient instead of relying on imported trading goods. Above all, this recent policy of flinging the trade open to every unscrupulous character had to be ended and order introduced once more.[28]

William Bartram took up the same theme in his advice to the government. He would urge that the benefits of civilization be explained to the southern Indians and then coexistence would be possible. After the Revolution, and with Bartram back in Kingsessing, Benjamin Hawkins, the able United States agent, enthusiastically promoted the "plan of civilization," as he called it. He reported to President James Madison that hunting had been reduced in importance to an amusement for the young men: "We shall in future rely on stockraising, agriculture and household manufactures. Warfare and talk of warfare had been banished from the Indian country; Tell Mrs. Madison that we are all Quakers in the Indian agency."[29] Presumably, Dolly Madison approved, and certainly William Bartram would have. Expansionist Americans delayed the "plan of civilization" by preempting the basis for acculturation, the land itself. However, after removal, the Creek Nation worked out its own adaptation, realizing the vision of Galphin, Adair, Jefferson, Hawkins—and Bartram.

On May 14 Bartram and Jack McIntosh set off for Augusta in the company of "a number of people and a party of Indians."[30] Galphin either accompanied them or followed soon after. Noon found them at the site of historic Fort Moore on a high bluff overlooking the Savannah River. Earlier in the century South Carolina traders kept their warehouses here and outfitted their caravans, and from here they reached out to the Creeks on the Chattahoochee and to those on the Coosa and beyond to the Chickasaws. They called the settlement Savannah Town. After the Yamassee War, Carolina signed a treaty with Emperor Brims of the Creek Nation, acknowledging that the Savannah River marked the boundary between them, and erected Fort Moore to emphasize the agreement. The French countered by erecting Fort Toulouse at the junction of the Coosa and Tallapoosa and claimed everything their friends the Creeks claimed. An official French map in 1719 showed Louisiana stretching all the way to the Savannah River, demonstrating the height of French ambition.[31]

When Oglethorpe established Augusta across the river from Fort Moore in 1736, he required Georgia licenses for trade west of the Savannah. Carolina officials immediately lost their good opinion of Oglethorpe and protested vigorously to the Board of Trade, but the pragmatic men of Fort Moore simply moved to Augusta and became Georgians. The decrepit fort sheltered refugees from the Carolina upcountry during the Cherokee War. After the 1763 peace settlement, the government abandoned the site in favor of a new stone fort farther upriver named Fort Charlotte.[32] Bartram would become well acquainted with Fort Charlotte.

With the decline and disappearance of Fort Moore, the district, properly known as the New Windsor township, began to be called Beech Island. The origin of the term is uncertain and confusing because the bluff was not an island. Some explain that beech trees grew there and "Island" is a corruption of "Highland."[33]

Bartram's party crossed on the ferry to a sandbar created by the river, changing its bed and cutting into the New Windsor bluff. The road leading to Augusta today is still called the Sandbar Ferry Road though the old river bed has long since been filled in. Bartram recorded his first impression: "The village of Augusta is situated on a rich and fertile plain on the Savanna River, the buildings are near its banks, and extend nearly two miles up to the cataract of falls, which are formed by the first chain of rocky hills, through which this famous river forces itself, as if impatient to repose on the extensive plain before it invades the ocean."[34] Augusta was and is located at the fall line, the place where the rock of the Appalachian plateau meets sedimentary stone. The ancient ocean reached this far into the interior, and sandhills above Augusta were dunes of the prehistoric coast.

The last rocky ledge forced the river into a west-to-east direction as it flowed by the town, resuming its southerly course at the New Windsor highlands. Bartram's "fertile plain" was river silt, deposited over the millennia since the recession of the sea. A long, narrow lagoon paralleled the river a few hundred yards inland perversely flowing from east to west, emptying into the river after slicing across the main road and dividing the town. The road continued over a gully and forked; the road along the Savannah River led to the Cherokee country and the left fork led to the Creek Nation. Even before the coming of humans, animals followed those trails to cross the river on the rocks of the fall line. Bartram understood why Oglethorpe put his town and garrison here where the land trails met the water, for below "the cataract of falls" the river flowed unobstructed to the Atlantic and was navigable by small boats laden with deerskins from the Indian country. Perhaps he had read William Stephens's description of the river at this point. Stephens predicted in his 1736 report to the Georgia trustees that the Savannah would become as famous as any river in America. The Savannah at Augusta, he said, "Glides smoothly on as the River Thames at Putney."[35] There had been two Kings Forts in Augusta when John and William visited in 1765. The old fort stood near the church west of town. The newer fort on the eastern edge of town was abandoned when the Royal Americans were recalled northward in 1768. The forts soon fell victim to vandals and termites.[36]

During their brief stay in 1765, the Bartrams lodged in Lachlan McGillivray's "White House" where the main road forked into the Cherokee and Creek trails. McGillivray built the house when he left his trading post at Little Tallassee in the Upper Creek country on the eve of the war with the French. McGillivray's Indian friends visited the White House frequently, camping at Indian Springs, a short distance up the Creek trading path. McGillivray moved to Savannah after the war, leaving the storekeeper, William Trevin, in charge of the White House with its supply of Indian trading goods.[37] It was Trevin who entertained the Bartrams in 1765.[38] Now in 1773 Robert Mackay was master of the house. Mackay's son recalled that Augusta was still "a small town, the houses standing far apart from each other, being few in number, but occupied by very worthy and respectable people."[39] Mackay's White House would become the scene of an important battle during the American Revolution.[40]

On the occasion of his 1773 visit, Bartram and his young friend lodged with one of the "genteel" residents of the town, Dr. Humphrey Wells, who with his wife, Abigail, lived on a plantation off the Cherokee road northwest of town. Dr. Wells, a Marylander by birth, had friends in Charlestown and undoubtedly was one of those recommended by Dr. Chalmers.[41]

This enlargement of a portion of British lieutenant colonel
Archibald Campbell's 1780 map of Georgia is
the earliest depiction of Augusta.

Courtesy of Special Collections, University of Georgia Libraries, Athens

Bartram could hardly make out Oglethorpe's original plan for Augusta,
intended to be forty lots around a square similar to Savannah's units. The
square coincided with the main road, and the inhabitants preferred living
along the road rather than filling in the neat pattern of lots. Oglethorpe's road
from Savannah intersected the main east-west road and crossed the Savannah
River on a ferry to Martintown Road, where Squirrel King's Chickasaw band
lived in Oglethorpe's day. William counted about a hundred houses compared
to the eighty he had seen on his last visit. A few were of brick, most of wood,
built in the Charlestown fashion but facing front rather than sideways, with single and double porches, or piazzas. The rising gentry competed with Savannah
in the emulation of Charlestown so there were the occasional riding chairs and
chaises, the drinking clubs, the horse races, and the social affairs. One of
Augusta's gentlemen, Edward Barnard, displayed a competitive one-upman-
ship by donating an organ to Savannah's Christ Church. Barnard, like most

Augustans, made his money in Indian trade and intended to continue doing business with the Indians, a fact that put him at odds with the growing number of settlers who viewed Indians as obstacles to their possession of land and dreams of planterdom. The Creeks trusted veterans such as Barnard, so he and George Galphin accompanied the surveying party that marked the upper boundary line following the cession of 1763. Lachlan McGillivray and James Mackay marked the lower reaches of the boundary.[42]

The evening of his arrival in Augusta, William rode with Jack two miles upriver to see the falls, or cataracts, at the head of navigation just as he had done with his father. William noted in his report to Fothergill that only canoes could ply the river above the falls.[43] The following day, May 15, Bartram called upon John Stuart. Stuart received him warmly, promised again to assist him in any way, and explained that the Upper Creek delegation had not yet arrived for the conference. Bartram no doubt took advantage of the opportunity to learn more from Stuart about the Muscogulges. Though Stuart had not lived among those people as he had among the Cherokees (a fact that added to his jealousy of Galphin, who had spent many years in Creek country), he could tell Bartram about the current state of affairs. More important, he could give Bartram the official British opinion of the principal headmen. The lower Creek towns on the Chattahoochee and Flint Rivers had different interests from the Upper Creek villages on the Coosa and Tallapoosa Rivers, but the intricate clan system united the various towns in a loose confederacy. The traditional leadership of the nation came out of Coweta on the right bank of the Chattahoochee at the fall line. The legendary "Emperor" Brims and his successors Chigilli and Malatchi were Cowetans. Malatchi's son Togulki shrank from the responsibility of leadership, and Coweta had lost standing as a result. The current headman, Sempoyaffe, seemed unable to control his unruly warriors. Escochabey, known as the Young Lieutenant, gave Stuart particular concern because of his flirtation with the Spanish in Havana. Spanish fishing boats put in on the northwest coast of East Florida and traded openly, though illegally, with the Lower Creeks. The most notable chief of the Florida Creeks, or Seminoles, Ahaya the Cowkeeper, however, would have nothing to do with the Spaniards.[44]

Leadership among the Creeks had shifted to the upper towns, and Stuart most admired Emistisiguo of Little Tallassee. More than any other, this leader had brought the Upper Creeks to an acceptance of the 1763 Treaty of Augusta that granted the king all the land east of the Ogeechee and below the Little

River. Stuart relied on Emistisiguo to do the same at this congress. Emistisi-guo's policy was based on the realization that his people required trade goods that only the British could supply. He devoted his considerable energies to upholding the treaty agreements despite the aggravation caused by traders' abuses and settlers' encroachments. A radically different policy was espoused by an equally talented leader, Wolf of Okchoy, known as the Mortar. Because he remembered that early in the century the English under James Moore had enslaved hundreds of Muscogulges and sold them to sugar planters in the West Indies, the Mortar tried to avoid dependence upon Charlestown and Augusta. He played the French against the English until the French lost Louisiana in 1763, and even then he did not give up hope that French officials in Spanish New Orleans might help his people. At the moment of Bartram's visit he had gone off on some mysterious mission to the Cherokees, and Ouconnostotah thought it important enough to wait for him instead of going to Augusta. Stu-art feared that the worst that might happen would be the formation of an anti-British confederacy.

Another headman, Handsome Fellow of the Okfuskees, occupied a mid-dle ground between Emistisiguo and the Mortar and behaved unpredictably though his loyalty generally lay with his trader, Richard Rae of Augusta. Two venerable headmen, Gun Merchant of Okchoy and the Wolf of Muccolossus, could not come to Augusta because of age and ill health; meanwhile they loaned moral support to Emistisiguo. Stuart, James Wright, and all Georgians who gave any thought to the matter believed that the Creeks could easily over-whelm the whites if they chose to. Therefore, Stuart and his agents, David Taitt among the Creeks and Charles Stuart in the Choctaw country, devoted their efforts to stoking the simmering Creek and Choctaw War in the certainty that as long as the Creeks warred against the Flats, as the Choctaws were called, they would remain at peace with the British. The policy permitted the traders to enjoy the profitable business of furnishing ammunition to both sides.[45]

Bartram decided to make use of the delay caused by the tardy Upper Creeks to accept an invitation to visit the town of Wrightsborough upon the Lit-tle River, the edge of the area open for legitimate settlement. No one knew exactly how many wanderers had already crossed over the Little River into Indi-an territory, but in 1772 acting governor James Habersham estimated three thousand. British officials from Savannah to Whitehall denounced those tres-passers as vagabonds and crackers, the latter an invidious term for half-savage Scots borderlanders. George Galphin had no use for most of these people; they seemed determined to antagonize the Indians who came and went along their traditional trails. To his mind they behaved worse than the Indians.[46]

As William set out for Wrightsborough along the Creek trail, he knew that the way had its perils. Whites and Indians went armed, and each complained about the other. An Indian who went down to visit the trader James Grierson in 1771 was murdered and the culprit never caught.[47] On the other hand, as Governor Wright reported to the earl of Hillsborough, the wayfaring Indians "often rob and plunder his Majesty's subjects of their property and sometimes murder them."[48] Wrightsborough residents Thomas Jackson and George Beck had been killed outside their town, and their killers remained at large. If Bartram was concerned about his safety, he did not mention it. In fact, he started out in the evening to avoid the heat of the day even though that meant sleeping on the roadside with unknown brigands of various races lurking about. The excursion marked his first venture beyond the limits of his previous journey into Georgia. He marveled at the hills and plains of pine forests and on the abundance of buffalo grass.[49] He said very little to Fothergill about Wrightsborough; however, in his *Travels* he commented favorably about the elderly, energetic, and public-spirited Joseph Maddox, who led a group of Quaker families from Hillsborough, North Carolina, to the 1763 Georgia cession. In gratitude to Governor Wright, they named their township Wrightsborough. By the time of Bartram's visit 124 Quakers held title to more than 30,000 acres of land. Non-Quakers moved in also and by 1773 constituted a majority of the population.[50] Bartram must have applauded the peaceable principles of the people of Wrightsborough, but it would be difficult to practice peace on a frontier among adversaries bent on violence.

On his return to Augusta, Bartram noticed an unusual mound of soft white stone, weirdly eroded and broken. He took refuge among the rocks as a storm broke and remained there during the night. At daybreak "I scrambled up the craggy sides of this Pile of Rocks, heaped and placed on one another to the height of 50 feet and bout 200 yards in length; from their highest summits had a pleasant Prospect of the extensive Forests and green Savanahs below and all around me but could see no other Rocks any where about."[51] Francis Harper photographed the diminished mound of rocks in 1936, and soon after that the rocks were quarried for tombstones. A depression in the ground marks the spot, and a nearby Methodist church is still known as The Rocks Church.[52]

The Rocks lay beside a cutoff that connected the Creek trail, or Wrightsborough Road, to the Cherokee trail. Bartram followed the cutoff to the Wells's residence.[53] People hereabouts, Dr. Wells no doubt explained, were not so much concerned with British trade policy and taxation as they were about relations with the Indians. He had heard that the Upper Creeks objected strenuously to yielding their land and were coming to the congress in a surly mood. With so many Indians in Augusta and so many Indian haters in the countryside, he feared the worst.

III

The chiefs and warriors of the Creeks and Cherokees
being arrived, the Congress and the business of the treaty
came on.

Bartram, "Report to Fothergill"

Not since the 1765 congress at Picolata, Florida, had Bartram seen so many Indians in one place. The Upper and Lower Creek delegations numbered more than three hundred, the Cherokees about one hundred. This was not as grand an occasion as in 1763, when nine hundred Indians gathered in Augusta to hear talks from John Stuart and the governors of Virginia, North and South Carolina, and Georgia, then to sign away the Ogeechee strip. Meetings in Augusta had become commonplace since then; the 1768 congress that celebrated the marking of the boundary was especially impressive. But this congress, in retrospect, was the most crucial in that it launched a chain reaction that led to the American Revolution in Georgia. William Bartram's account of the Augusta negotiations is the best available. For once, the marvelous resources of the British Public Record Office fail. Only the terms of the treaty survive—none of the details, no names of the participants. Fortunately, Bartram acted as historian for the occasion.

Stuart's friend Emistisiguo led the Upper Creeks, Alleck the Lower. The veteran Attakullakulla spoke for the Cherokee party in the absence of Ouconnostotah, the Great Warrior, who sent his excuses by way of his brother, Otacite Oustenaka (Judd's Friend). Stuart interrogated Attakullakulla privately to learn what was going on at the simultaneous meeting at Chote. The Little Carpenter explained that the congress had nothing to do with the English. Rather, it had as object the formation of a confederacy of northern and western tribes against the Indians of the Ohio Valley who engaged in sporadic raids against the overhills towns. The Chote gathering included Shawnees, Iroquois, and Canadian Indians as well as Chickasaws and delegates from the Arkansas.

Attakullakulla assured his old friend Stuart that he would be alerted to any sign of impending trouble.[54] As far as the Cherokees were concerned, the meeting in Chote was fraught with greater consequence than that in Augusta. A confederacy of northern and southern tribes, anticipating Tecumseh, might have slowed American expansion.

Bartram returned from his visit to Wrightsborough around May 19, and the conference began soon after that, "continuing undetermined many days," as he observed.[55] In the first part of his *Travels* Bartram suggested the cause of the prolonged negotiations: the young warriors among the Creeks refused to accede to the governor's demand for the Ogeechee-Oconee strip. They "betrayed a disposition to dispute the ground by force of arms." In Part Four of *Travels* Bartram returned to the subject in greater detail. He indicated that the congress drew a number of whites, the "principal men and citizens of Georgia, Carolina, Virginia, Maryland, and Pennsylvania." Some of these people were merchants, but most were land speculators and settlers, the first of the thousands Governor Wright hoped to lure to these fertile new lands. As Bartram explained, Governor Wright would not get the Oconee and was lucky to get anything. When the governor's interpreter referred to the area above the Little River as already ceded by the Cherokees, the Creek chiefs rose up in wrath, and one "with an agitated and terrific countenance" demanded what right the Cherokees had to give Creek land away? The Savannah River and its tributaries marked the natural boundary of Creek territory. The Cherokees were old women and should wear petticoats. This and other humiliating strokes the Cherokee chiefs had to bear passively, even when some whites (in an incredible display of bad manners) joined in the jeering.[56]

Bartram revealed his own attitude by referring to the Creek chiefs as "arrogant bravos and usurpers" who "carried their pride and importance to such lengths as even to threaten to dissolve the congress and return home."[57] The governor had to abandon any hope of extending Georgia's boundaries to the Oconee, then acknowledge that the Creeks rather than the Cherokees had the rightful claim to a portion of the region above the Little River. Liberal distributions of presents pacified the most unruly, and the older headmen finally concurred on boundaries of the new cession. The new line would follow a ridge dividing the waters of the Ogeechee River from those of the Oconee until it reached a certain tree marked by the Cherokees. From there the boundary cut across from the ridge to the point where the Tugaloo River joined the Savannah. Bartram must have been amazed that headmen and the chief

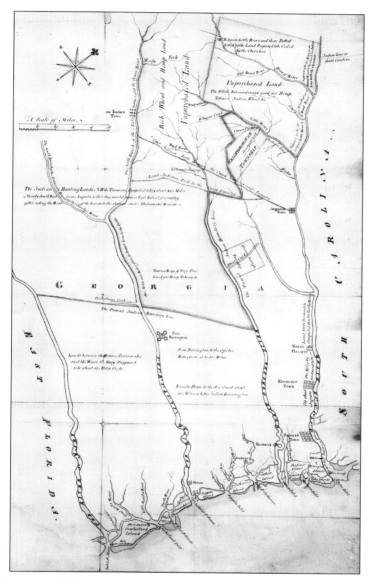

This map of Georgia in 1773 shows the "unpurchased lands" that
Governor Wright hoped to obtain at the 1773 congress in Augusta.
Courtesy of the British Public Record Office, London

traders seemed to know exactly where these places were. George Galphin persuaded the Lower Creeks to agree to the extension of the line behind the coastal parishes.

Governor Wright made the best of it. He set about surveying the new lines immediately, appointing a team headed by Edward Barnard to accompany an Indian delegation commissioned by Stuart. Wright hired Philip Yonge to draw up a map of the region. LeRoy Hammond, a leading merchant and land speculator who resided on the Carolina side of the river, acted as Barnard's second in command. Joseph Purcell, whose maps would make him famous, seconded Philip Yonge. Wright returned to Savannah to prepare a proclamation opening the new cession but confided to Lord Dartmouth, "I must confess that I am very anxious" about the temper of the Creek chiefs.[58] He and Stuart heard a rumor that the Creeks planned trouble after the Green Corn Dance, sometime in the fall. Stuart had a great deal of difficulty after Wright left Augusta. He intended to withhold some of the promised supplies, he told the chiefs, until after the Green Corn Dance. This bad news threatened to destroy the fragile agreement already made and would have if Emistisiguo had not come to Stuart's rescue. Stuart worried, as he reported to Lord Dartmouth, that the Creeks had grown "very insolent and troublesome."[59]

Stuart also felt responsible for the welfare of his botanical friend. He could not guarantee William's safety if he traveled into the Creek country just then and advised against it. William expressed disappointment. If it had been up to him, he would have gone on with his faith in Providence and in the goodness of his fellow man, regardless of the danger. Now, as he wrote to Fothergill, "I was at a stand how to pr-ceed [sic] on my Botanical discoveries."[60] It occurred to him to approach Edward Barnard with the request to go along on the surveying expedition. Barnard had heard about Bartram and his mission, and he made the explorer feel welcome. Young Jack McIntosh pleaded not to be left behind. He had come this far in their venture, and the best part lay ahead. With the small army of surveyors, gentlemen speculators, and hunters, Bartram decided that the risk would be minimal, and he agreed that the eager youth could join the expedition. Delegations of Creek and Cherokee warriors accompanied the Georgians to make sure they drew the line correctly.

The large contingent assembled quickly, a credit to Barnard's leadership. In his memorandum to Fothergill, Bartram estimated as many as eighty persons (in his *Travels* he said ninety), set out on June 7, 1773. Though not "the middle of the month of May," as he recalled in *Travels*, nature's exuberance matched his as he rhapsodized about the "arbustive hills, gay lawns and green meadows which on every side invest the villa of Augusta."[61] He permits his reader a revealing insight by confessing that no matter how rich the present delights, "I was restless to be searching for more, my curiosity being insatiable."[62]

The ponderous caravan traveled at packhorse pace, making fifteen miles the first day along the main Creek trading path. One reason they stopped, as Bartram observed, was that "the Young Warrior Chief of the Creek Party being drunk . . . was not able to move a foot farther."[63] Nor could they set out early the next day. Colonel Barnard prudently deferred to Young Warrior's ritual priorities. As Bartram explained, "They never rise from Sleep till after the Sun, then Smoke the Pipe and give out the Talk which is their Plan of pr-ceedings [sic] for the day delivered by the chief: He rises his left hand bearing on his Gun, his Right armed with his Tomahoc their ensign of Authority, with a Heroick air and action, a loud and determined Voice speaks, then marches a head with his Party."[64] Young Warrior clearly realized the importance of the occasion in case the Georgians might have missed it. Though the chief and the botanist communed with nature in different ways, they were kindred spirits.

Bartram, and presumably McIntosh, rode ahead of the Indian party. He explained that this practice allowed him to escape the dust of the caravan and provided more time for his observations. It also permitted him to do what he loved, to be the vanguard of civilization, to view the undisturbed wilderness, to discover plants not known by even the great men with whom his father corresponded, Linnaeus, Gronovius, or his own patron, Fothergill. He did make discoveries. One "curious little Shrub" that he described to Fothergill is known today as yellow root. Bundles of yellow root may be bought nowadays at any number of roadside stands in the southern Appalachians. According to a writer whose grandmother learned the recipe from a Cherokee woman, "Boiled it makes an extraordinary bitter yellow tea, which can be led to salvation by a little mountain honey and some lemon, giving it a pleasant, hardy, sweet citrus taste."[65] Mountain people take it to purify the blood and cure any number of miseries. Yellow root was one of Bartram's unrecorded discoveries, as was another plant he found on the journey to Wrightsborough, a "very curious shrub" with large yellow berries called an oil nut.[66] That he did not receive recognition for these and other discoveries bothered him not at all; the experience counted as reward enough.

Barnard's little army took two days to wend its way to Wrightsborough. The trail led over gently rolling hills among tall pine forests. The clay of the Georgia piedmont turned into an orange bog when it rained, but the weather this June stayed hot and dry. The riders crossed Ogeechee Creek and the headwaters of Kiokee Creek. Along the Great and Little Kiokee Creeks new settlers staked out claims in increasing numbers. Itinerant preachers Daniel Marshall and Shubal Stearns brought the Great Awakening to Georgia when they established the first Baptist Church in Georgia on the Kiokees a year before Bartram's tour of Georgia. Bartram's leader, Edward Barnard, acting for the vestry of St. Paul Parish, had Daniel Marshall arrested for preaching without a license. Tradition has it that Barnard, impressed by Marshall's evident piety, became a Baptist on the spot; he did not, but he allowed Marshall to go on preaching with the result that the Kiokees experienced an awakening of religious fervor on this rude frontier.[67]

When they crossed Germany's Creek, named after Galphin's veteran employee James Germany or one of his kinfolk, the travelers entered the township of Wrightsborough. The town traced its origins to a request by Joseph Stubbs in 1767 for a grant of two thousand acres of land on behalf of several Quaker families originally from Pennsylvania and more recently Orange County, North Carolina. In the following year Joseph Maddox and Jonathan Sell asked for an additional grant of fifteen thousand acres on behalf of sixty-one heads of family. Ninety-nine lots were laid out in the town before July 3, 1770, and eighty-two of the lots were taken up. Historian Alex M. Hitz, who once served as Georgia's surveyor general, expressed annoyance at Bartram's statement that Joseph Maddox had obtained a grant of forty thousand for himself and his followers. But Hitz made a larger mistake, as Robert S. Davis showed, by assuming that all of Wrightsborough's inhabitants adhered to the Quaker sect. Actually only about one-fifth of the men belonged to the monthly meeting inaugurated in 1773.[68]

A map of the original town depicts an imaginative arrangement of lots laid out around three squares. Bartram might have been interested in the fact that the central square bore the name Galphin while the other two honored Lachlan McGillivray and Joseph Maddox. Galphin and McGillivray acted as founders of nearby Queensborough, but their role in the establishment of Wrightsborough is less evident. However, the two men had been instrumental in obtaining the 1763 session in which Wrightsborough stood, and both played important roles in marking the lines in 1768, the year of Wrightsborough's founding, and for those reasons, at least, the good people of Wrightsborough honored them.[69]

The arrival of Colonel Barnard's impressive brigade with its colorful collection of Indians, surveyors, and gentlemen marked the grandest event in the history of the town. In fact, the town suffered greatly during the Revolution, and soon afterward the Quaker inhabitants moved to Ohio and the others wandered to the West, so it had an abbreviated history. No one would have guessed such a fate in 1773. Despite several Indian alarms and the actual killing of George Beck and Thomas Jackson, the population grew steadily.

While Barnard's party tended their horses and stocked up on provisions, Bartram scouted the neighborhood with his usual enthusiasm. "Mills are erected on the swift flowing streams," he wrote Fothergill, "the flowery Meads smile in their Vernal Robes and the fruitful Hills and Vales already team with Plenty of Corn and Grapes."[70] The industrious inhabitants, he explained, followed the same farming practices as in the northern colonies, tilling small farms rather than plantations worked by slave labor. They planted wheat, barley, flax, hemp, oats, corn, cotton, and indigo. They bred cattle and manufactured cheese. Fruit trees did especially well. Joseph Maddox showed William apple trees bearing fruit supposedly only two years from seed, and grapes only two years from cuttings. Bartram must have known the impossibility of such precocity, but he entered the statement in his report without comment. His worthy patron in London must have wondered about the accuracy or credulity of his agent. Governor Wright continued the long and futile quest for silk cultivation by sending Maddox mulberry seeds as preparation for the introduction of silkworms. The mulberry trees grew, and some still mark the place, but before they reached maturity the town itself entered its decline. However, the future seemed bright for the little Quaker colony in 1773. The Augusta Treaty set aside two hundred acres on a branch of the Ogeechee for a square fort of one hundred feet to be garrisoned by an officer and twenty men. The governor and council declared the road to Augusta a public thoroughfare with Wrightsborough's John Stubbs and Issac Lowe as overseers of road repair. Wrightsborough expected to share the benefits of the rapidly populating ceded lands, a future always depending on the shifting mood of their neighbors of the Creek Nation.[71]

IV

Having provided things convenient in the best manner we possibly could. 21st June We set off for the great Buf- falo lick. . . .

Bartram, "Report to Fothergill"

The old Cherokee trail led west below the former boundary of the Little River through "a country agreeably diversified with gentle rising Hills and shady Vales," as Bartram described it.[72] He noticed outcroppings of rock, the result of the ancient tectonic collision that created the Appalachian range and its plateau. The leisurely moving caravan made camp at Williams Creek, only about eight miles from Wrightsborough, itself an important landmark because of a near-critical event that happened there during the 1768 mark- ing of the boundary. Edward Barnard could have told Bartram the story because he and George Galphin were involved. In addition to Barnard and Galphin, John Stuart had named his countryman Roderick McIntosh of Darien as commissioner and Samuel Savery as surveyor. Three Creek chiefs—the Young Lieutenant, Salechee, and Blue Salt—led the wary Creek contingent. The Indians argued that Upton Creek at the proposed town of Wrightsborough should be the boundary set by the 1963 treaty. "Old Rory" contended with increasing vehemence that the south fork some twenty-five miles upstream should be the source of the line. One of the chiefs took a decided aversion to McIntosh, pointed his gun at the Scotsman, and pulled the trigger. Fortunately for the cause of peace along the frontier and to the enormous relief of Galphin, Barnard, and presumably McIntosh, the gun misfired. Galphin calmed the hot heads, and they settled on Williams Creek by way of compromise.[73] So Williams Creek became part of the old bound- ary, now erased by the 1773 treaty.

After caring for his horse and pitching his tent, Bartram liked to roam about in hopes of discovering new plants, a joy shared by few others as he admitted. At times the agreeable young McIntosh would go along. They found the yellow root plant at the Williams Creek camp. The next morning after Young Warrior's daily ritual, they saddled up and resumed their deliberate pace along the south side of the Little River. They crossed numerous small streams, thought by Bartram to be branches of the Ogeechee but most likely tributaries of the Little River. The Yonge-Purcell map shows the trail crossing several of these creeks.[74] Francis Harper's remark that Bartram's supposition that he crossed streams leading to the Ogeechee shows "how thoroughly con-

Bartram accompanied the surveyors who mapped
the ceded lands, 1773.

Courtesy of the British Public Record Office, London

fused he was concerning the Ogeechee and Little Rivers."[75] But if Bartram had veered slightly to the south, he would have run into the waters of the Ogeechee. Most likely he noted what the surveyors Yonge and Purcell told him and was no more confused than they. The branches of the two rivers so intertwined that the caravan could not find a continuous ridge between them. Colonel Barnard called a halt that evening at the south fork of the Little River.

The next day they crossed the north fork of the Little River and entered a region described by the surveyors as heavily timbered in oak, hickory, walnut, chestnut, and tulip poplar, interspersed with pine and canebrakes. The dark topsoil of six to seven inches covered a bed of red clay. Bartram expressed awe at the most magnificent forest he had ever seen. He measured several oaks that had a circumference of thirty feet. Not many of those giants remain today, but a few still stand as reminders of the pristine past.[76]

In his *Travels* Bartram referred to ancient mounds and "tetragon terraces" and other evidences of prior civilizations. However, he did not mention anything of the sort in his report to Fothergill, and no traces of such structures have been found in that part of Georgia; the nearest are on the Ocmulgee near present-day Macon, Georgia, which Bartram saw on a later journey.

They passed a buffalo lick noted by the surveyors but not by Bartram on the way to their destination, the Great Buffalo Lick. Bartram called the latter "an extraordinary place" several acres around. In his more accurate Fothergill report, the lick shrinks to an acre and a half with some depressions five and six feet deep. Buffalo had roamed this region as recently as Oglethorpe's time. By 1773 they were gone, leaving behind as memorials the names "buffalo grass" (a substance that the horses relished), "Buffalo Creek" near the lick, and the name of the lick itself. Deer and other animals kept the ground clear. When Francis Harper visited the site in 1934, he could make out some of the depressions noted by Bartram.[77] Today the ground is covered with thick grass and young pines, and no obvious depressions can be seen. One huge skeleton of a dead oak gives the meadow a melancholy appearance. Bartram tasted the soil and observed that it did not contain salt. Harper subjected a sample to a more scientific analysis, however, and learned that sodium sulphate in the soil appealed to animals. The little town of Philomath lies alongside the old lick, and the residents preserve the memory of Bartram's passing. As in the case of Wrightsborough, there have been few events in the area's history to equal the importance of that June day in 1773, when Colonel Barnard's explorers pitched camp.

The significance of the Great Buffalo Lick, as Bartram's contemporaries knew, was that it lay at a gap of the ridge that divided the waters of the Savannah River from those of the Oconee-Altamaha basin. Bartram referred to it as the Great Ridge, probably because of its cartographical importance rather than its topographical elevation. In truth, there is little to distinguish this ridge from the innumerable long hills of the piedmont. However, the treaty writers regarded the ridge as a crucial dividing place. From the lick the line went southward down the ridge to the "source of the southernmost branch" of the Ogeechee. Facing the opposite direction, the line proceeded from the lick northward "in a straight line to the tree marked by the Cherokees near the head of a branch falling into the Oconee River."[78] The immediate problem for Colonel Barnard and his surveyors was how to ascertain just where that particular marked tree might be so that a straight line could be drawn to it. The question led to a lively dispute between Young Warrior and Philip Yonge that must have reminded Barnard of Rory McIntosh's near-fatal dispute. Bartram witnessed the surveyor pointing in one direction and the chief in another. The surveyor insisted that he knew the route; his little instrument, the compass, showed the way. The chief replied that the little instrument lied, and he would have nothing more to do with it. The angry Creeks said this was a trick to cheat them out of their lands and that they would go home and break up the treaty. Barnard proved that he had learned the art of conciliation and that he respected the Native Americans' intimate knowledge of the region. He decided to follow the direction of Young Warrior rather than that of his professional. Bartram approved the decision and praised "the complaisance and prudent conduct of the Colonel."[79]

The party split into two teams, Barnard's following the northern line and LeRoy Hammond's the southern. Bartram and McIntosh went along with Barnard's party because that route offered promise of being "more extensive and varied." Young Warrior, pleased with his victory over the little instrument, led the way. Although the treaty clearly stated that the boundary ran straight from the lick to the Cherokee tree and although Bartram recalled in his *Travels* that "the Indian Chief, heading the party, conducted us on a straight line . . . to the desired place," the map of the cession shows that the line became contorted in an effort to separate the Savannah basin from that of the Oconee.[80] Bartram rode out with the hunters and within three miles came upon the banks of the Oconee. A little farther and they reached the famous tree that marked the line dividing the Cherokee hunting grounds from those of the Creeks. At this point the proud Young Warrior and his crew turned back and left the rest of the business to Barnard and the Cherokees.

From the tree the boundary left the ridge and followed a line to the junction of the Tugaloo and Keowee Rivers.[81] Bartram loved this pioneering and burst into poetic imagery in his ordinarily prosaic message to Fothergill. "A pleasant morning attended by the feather'd inhabitants of these shady retreats, with joyful song invites us forth, the elevated face of this Hilly country breathes an elastic pure air, inspiring health and activity." As always, nature's beauty reminded him of its Creator. "I arose and joyfully contributed my aid in the contemplation of the wonderful Harmony and perfection in the lovely simplicity of Nature tho naked yet unviolated by the rude touch of the human hand." And as always, he realized that inevitably progress with all its advantages and shortcomings must encroach upon nature. He ended his brief apostrophe with a remark much like a sigh, "What a beautiful scenery is Vegetable Nature!"[82]

The route to the Buffalo Lick followed an old Cherokee trail, then the Great Ridge, but thereafter no natural boundary guided the surveyors. Surveyors had to sight more carefully, the axmen had to blaze the trees, and yet Colonel Barnard's men made better progress than before, covering about fifteen miles the first day. Perhaps it had something to do with the absence of Young Warrior and his morning ceremony. They camped on what Bartram assumed to be a branch of the Broad River. The next day they made only three miles to another tributary of the Broad River and paused for the Cherokee hunters to bring in fresh provisions.

As usual, Bartram employed his time in search of new plants. While exploring a rocky hillside, he lost his footing and slid down, grabbing at shrubs to break his fall. He related the story to Fothergill, not to draw attention to his daring, but to explain that his accident led to a discovery. A plant he grasped came up by the roots "and filled the air with animating scents of cloves and spicy perfumes." He judged the plant to be a species of *Cariophylata*. He discovered another shrub, if discovery can be used to describe a plant long known by the Native Americans. Indian hunters prized the root of the plant, believing that it attracted deer. Bartram reported that the smell and taste were quite disagreeable but the plant might prove to be of benefit to mankind. Francis Harper noted that botanist André Michaux later gave the name *Pyrularia pubera* to this plant, commonly called the oil nut, and that Bartram again missed an opportunity for receiving recognition for the find.[83]

Returning to camp, he found Jack McIntosh, his "philosophic companion," raptly engaged in the study of little hills of gravel here and there in the shoals of the swift, flowing stream. He thought that the hills were made by crawfish as tiny citadels against the numerous predatory goldfish. The swift, darting, beautifully colored goldfish so fascinated Bartram that he drew a picture of one. He even caught several and took them into camp. Colonel Barnard, a man of intelligence and good humor, professed to be greatly interested, and the delighted naturalist led him to the stream to show him the continual fish war going on there. The same scene can be observed in some of the Broad River tributaries today. The little hills in the water are made by minnows hatching their eggs, and goldfish still dart about in the shoals looking for prey.[84]

The hunters brought in three deer and several large turkeys, and the next day the expedition continued along the line as best they could. In fact, the waters of the Savannah refused to be neatly divided from those of the Oconee; Bartram noted their occasional interlocking. He also observed signs of ancient habitation, arrowheads, broken pottery, and piled rocks. His Cherokee companions had no idea who the original inhabitants were. Groves of fruit-bearing trees, black walnut, mulberry, wild plum, and chestnut grew thickly around the remains of old Indian settlements, and Bartram assumed that the trees had once been deliberately planted and cultivated.[85]

Colonel Barnard sent the surveyors down the Broad River to map it while he rode along the ridge to the Tugaloo. Bartram and McIntosh went with him. Bartram commented on the pleasant appearance of the high ground with its open vistas of distant hills. This region of Georgia, north of present-day Hartwell, is a quietly prosperous corner of the state with scenic views of rolling hills. The Cherokees demonstrated their appreciation of the region by calling it Ah-Yeh-Li A-Lo-Hee, the center of the world. As the caravan neared the Savannah River, Bartram caught a view of the Cherokee mountains, a serrated silhouette, purple against the pale blue sky. In the foothills nestled the village of Bartram's Indian companions, the town of Tugaloo. Somewhere in the recesses lay the places he had heard about from John Stuart—Fort Prince George and the ruins of the ill-fated Fort Loudoun. The mountains cast their spell on him, and he meant to explore their fastnesses.

The entire company, gentlemen adventurers, surveyors, and Cherokee Indians, celebrated their arrival at the junction of the Savannah and the Tugaloo Rivers. With appropriate ceremony, the Georgians carved "GR" (for George Rex) on a tree, and the Cherokees put their mark alongside.[86] Bartram scoured the banks of the Savannah, accurately estimated by him to be a quarter mile wide at this point, and commented on the various kinds of shrubs. Rhododendron and mountain laurel flourished, as they do over the entire Appalachian Range. Hydrangeas also grew plentifully. Two of his young Indian friends treated him to a display of their fishing skills. They found strong reeds growing near the river, broke off several, and took a position in a stream flowing into the river. They allowed for the distortion of light caused by the water and with a swift movement let fly the reed harpoon; then they chased after the impaled fish. One trout measured two feet, and Bartram put its weight at fifteen pounds. The young Indians caught dozens of trout and bream and brought them back for a barbecue at camp. Bartram's contribution consisted of a snake. He called it "an admirable creature" but noted that no one in camp seemed to share his admiration. The fishermen presented the largest trout to Colonel Barnard for his supper. This last meal celebrated a successful end of the expedition.[87]

The next day, sometime in mid-July, the Georgians began their return to Augusta. Bartram mentioned a new plantation on the Broad River without comment. In this part of his journal as in other sections, the omissions are significant. What Bartram does not say tells us as much about him as what he says. There should not have been a plantation on the Broad River, and yet there were hundreds of trespassers upon the new cession. Their presence indicated a disregard of the law on the part of the settlers. Some of these people lived on a level scarcely removed from savagery. Historians such as David Hackett Fischer and Grady McWhiney trace the proclivity to violence of the Appalachian Scotch-Irish to the perpetual wars of the Scottish borderlands.[88] Many of these new settlers came from Scotland by way of northern Ireland. Their migration can be traced from New York and Pennsylvania down the Great Wagon Road of the Shenandoah Valley into North Carolina and in the decade before the Revolution into the upcountry of South Carolina and the backcountry of Georgia. The Reverend Charles Woodmason vividly described the depraved behavior of some of those rude Carolinians.[89]

Those who did business with Indians, such as George Galphin and Edward Barnard, deplored the unreasoning hatred these people harbored against Indians, and increasingly, so did William Bartram. While still camped on the Broad River, two of Bartram's former companions, one nineteen and one twenty, called at the house of one of these new settlers. The woman of the house happened to be alone. The Indians indicated that they would like something to drink. The woman let them in, sat them down at the table, brought out milk and something to eat. The unarmed, unsuspecting youths might have been the same clever fishermen whom Bartram admired. While the two sat eating, the woman's husband, Hezekiah Collins by name, appeared at the door. Without warning he leveled his rifle at one visitor and pulled the trigger, killing him instantly. He struck the other with his rifle so savagely that the barrel broke away from the stock. While the injured Cherokee crouched in pain, Collins picked up an ax and finished the bloody work. John Collins, father of the murderer, arrived in time to drag the bodies to the river and sink them. They scalped and mutilated the corpses first because Indian scalps were prized among men of Collins's ilk.[90]

The tragic incident must have happened immediately after Barnard and Bartram left the Broad River. Barnard hurried to Savannah to take his seat in the assembly on July 14.[91] Bartram accompanied him, and it was on this occasion rather than his earlier visit to Savannah that he lodged with members of the legislature. On July 21 Wright received notice of the Cherokee murders from Barnard's deputies, Thomas Waters and Edward Keating.[92]

John Stuart heard the grim news a few days later in Charlestown and dashed off a letter to Lord Dartmouth reporting the "unprovoked and atrocious murder of two of the party I sent to mark the boundary line." When the Cherokees reported the two men missing, Waters and Keating searched the Broad River area. Under their questioning, Collins's wife related the sad story. They arrested John Collins for his part in the affair, but Hezekiah eluded them and remained at large.[93]

Barnard's men found the bodies in the shallows of the river and returned them to their people. A wave of anger swept through the Cherokee country as the deed became known. White traders in the mountain villages quickly left for the lowlands. Stuart sent Alexander Cameron into the settlements to promise that the guilty would be punished. Governor Wright's exasperation matched Stuart's. He deplored the brutal murders, and the possibility of the incident ruining his plans for the ceded lands added an edge to his anger. He immediately issued a proclamation promising a reward for the seizure of Collins and sent word to acting governor William Bull of South Carolina to broadcast the alarm.[94]

Bartram mentioned none of this, either in his dispatch to Fothergill or later in his *Travels*. He chose not to admit the serpent into his paradise. By ignoring evil, he portrayed the world as he would like it to be. Nevertheless, running like a refrain through his journal and his letters is the message that Indians deserved better treatment than his white contemporaries gave them.

V

Soon after my return from the Tugilo journey to Savanah
the country was alarmed by an express from Augusta,
that the Indians were for war. . . .

Bartram, "Report to Fothergill"

No one had worked harder for the cession of 1773 than Governor Wright. The upper house thanked him profusely, citing the "Fatigues and Difficulty's you underwent upon that Occasion."[95] As soon as he returned from Augusta to Savannah he issued a proclamation advertising the opening of the highly desirable new lands for sale. Heads of families might purchase up to two hundred acres at five pounds sterling for each hundred, with the option of purchasing an additional fifty acres for each member of the family, including servants. The proclamation assured prospective purchasers that Georgia enjoyed a healthy tranquillity, with none of the demonstrations against British efforts to raise revenue that characterized New England.[96] Wright intended to charge the busy Edward Barnard and his surveyors with the task of evaluating the land as they divided it into convenient grants. He attempted to preserve the uncertain tranquillity by appointing John Stuart's deputy, David Taitt, justice of the peace for the province west of St. Paul Parish. Taitt's jurisdiction included the entire Creek country. Wright hoped that Taitt would dissuade the Creeks from any rashness resulting from their displeasure about the recent cession.[97]

Wright worried about the reaction of the Creeks because of the surliness they had displayed in his presence and still more because of the persistent rumors of trouble after the harvest. He hoped to avoid war by filling up the new territory with enough settlers to overawe the Indians. However, he avoided mentioning in his proclamation that the new settlers would constitute a buffer for the protection of the older Georgians. They might be far from the tumult in New England, but a different kind of tumult threatened to engulf the Georgia frontier. The petitions for land came pouring in; "great numbers have already applied," Wright informed Lord Dartmouth on June 17, 1773.[98] A group of families from the Long Cane region of South Carolina asked for a reserve of sixteen square miles at the headwaters of the Ogeechee. As "Families of Character," they preferred to live together because they had heard about the villainy of the Georgia Crackers and intended to avoid living among such "a promiscuous crowd."[99] A party of Presbyterians from North Carolina and Pennsylvania asked for land on the Oconee, not realizing that the cession did not include the Oconee strip. The Long Cane people received a grant of seventy-five thousand acres and the Presbyterians fifty thousand in the new cession.[100]

On June 28, 1773, as the House prepared an effusive message of congratulations to the governor, the members voted on a resolution of thanks to George Galphin and Lachlan McGillivray. The motion thanked the veteran traders for "exerting their Influence with the Indians and being very Instrumental in assisting the Governor to obtain the late Cession of Lands." Bartram's friends Jonathan Bryan and Benjamin Andrew voted for the resolution, as did ten in all. However, the motion failed passage by one vote.[101] Historian Alan Gallay suggests that the pro-Galphin, McGillivray resolution amounted to an effort to detract some of the credit from Governor Wright, and perhaps that explains the vote.[102] However, its failure could have resulted from a disappointment that Galphin and McGillivray failed to get the Oconee strip. For the time being, Georgians concerned themselves more with the near frontier and less with constitutional differences with the mother country.

The July slaying of the two young Cherokees threatened to escalate into a general frontier war and to disrupt Wright's careful work of the past three years. David Taitt, from his house at Little Tallassee on the Coosa River, reported that traders were leaving the Creek country. Two new reports added to the unrest among the Creeks. The Mortar returned to Okchoys with dire warnings about a proposed white settlement on the Tennessee River. An Indian from the Appalachicola region in Florida came up to Coweta bearing a Spanish commission for Escochabey the Young Lieutenant and a message that the Spanish authorities in Cuba would supply ammunition and other trade items. When this man, the Alligator, carried the report into the Upper Creek towns, Emistisiguo rebuked him sharply, saying they should have nothing to do with the Spanish.[103]

Although the Augusta traders refused to allow the first proceeds from land sales to be used for defensive measures, Governor Wright decided that he needed a troop of rangers immediately. He commissioned Edward Barnard, Thomas Waters, and Edward Keating as officers. All three had a stake in making the land-for-debt plan work; they had affixed their names to the original petition to him to purchase the territory, as had George Galphin and James Spalding.[104] By August the surveyors finished their map of the new cession, and Wright learned that he had bought 1,616,298 acres instead of the 2,000,000 he had counted on in the region above the Little River. With the traders claiming outlandish sums as legitimate debts, he wondered if land sales would suffice.

Wright scribbled notes on the Yonge-Purcell map; one indicated that he intended to straighten the zig-zag line between the Great Buffalo Lick and the Cherokee line, thus adding another 30,000 acres.[105] He dated his notation August 12, 1773, and included it with his August 10 letter in a dispatch to Lord Dartmouth. Because Bartram's Great Ridge did not extend to the Savannah River, Wright would have preferred a "natural boundary" to the one the surveyors drew at the northern end of the cession. He issued a proclamation commanding trespassers such as the villainous Collins to leave the ceded territory, but proclamations had failed before. His advisors urged him to undertake a tour of the cession with an entourage large enough to chase off the banditti. The same people in the legislature who had thanked him for his "strenuous exertions" on behalf of the province urged him to undertake even more strenuous exertions. His decision to go on the tour indicated the firmness of his determination to make his plan work.[106]

Meanwhile, Alexander Cameron had the nearly impossible task of quieting the Cherokee towns from the lower settlements to the overhills villages. Stuart also charged him to find out the result of the potentially threatening recent gathering at Chote. Cameron learned from the Great Warrior at Torquah that the Cherokee elders had kept their young men from rash reprisals while they waited for justice; no less than a life for a life. By chance a chief called Second Man caused the death of a white man. Even though an accident, the Cherokees counted that against the murder of one of the boundary-marking party. Satisfaction for the second murder resulted from an unusual circumstance. It seemed that a warrior named Cold Weather had too much to drink at John Walker's trading house in the overhills town of Chilhowie. He became quarrelsome and threatening, and Walker turned him out of the house. Instead of leaving, he grew more belligerent. Finally he let out a war whoop and tried to break into the house. Walker's mother-in-law, an Indian war woman and according to Cameron "the greatest conjurer in the nation," tried to appeal to the warrior. He turned his wrath on her and struck her dead with a blow of a heavy stick. Her daughter, Walker's wife, set up a cry and her relatives caught Cold Weather and killed him with a tomahawk. With ceremony befitting her status, they carried the war woman to the top of a hill, sat her upright, and entombed her body with stones. The Great Warrior said that her death compensated for the second young Cherokee. Even though a Cherokee, he would count the war woman as a member of a white man's family. His willingness to equate her death with that of Collins's victim indicated his desire for peace.[107]

As for the Chote conference, the Mortar had attempted to persuade the Cherokees to enter into a coalition against white encroachment, but Ouconnostotah refused to trust the Creeks. His decision must have pleased Attakullakulla and the others who endured ignominious taunting from the Creeks at Augusta. As a token of good will, Ouconnostotah made the long journey to Charlestown to assure John Stuart that he would have no part in any conspiracy.[108] Cameron had a message for Stuart from his friend Attakullakulla. No white man who entered the mountains would suffer, he said. Should any meet him in his way he would take care of him like a brother.[109] Unfortunately the great chiefs, esteemed though they were by the Cherokee people, could not guarantee peace. The relatives of the slain Tugaloo youths, not satisfied that justice had been done, vowed vengeance. Several of them rode down to Coweta to seek allies, and John Stuart feared that the fragile peace would soon be shattered.[110]

Governor Wright spent the month of November and part of December touring the new cession. He followed the Quaker road from Augusta to Wrightsborough, and again the little town bustled with excitement. His party crossed Williams Creek, found the Great Buffalo Lick, and followed the blazed trail along the ridge to the Cherokee line, then went down the main branch of the Broad River to its confluence with the Savannah. He ordered a town to be laid out there and named Dartmouth in honor of the American secretary. The new fort, Fort James, honored himself. Wright believed that he had demonstrated that the king's governor was not to be trifled with, and he hoped that those vagabonds still remaining would be cleared from the valuable lands by Barnard's rangers. He reported to Lord Dartmouth that at last he had reason to hope for success; applications for land grants totaled 300,000 acres, and 55,000 acres had actually been granted. Legal residents of the ceded lands numbered 1,413 whites and 300 blacks. He wrote his report on December 27, 1773.[111] He did not know at the time that men in Indian guise had dumped a shipload of tea into Boston Harbor on December 16, and only after he finished his letter he learned that a war party of Creeks had attacked Wrightsborough on Christmas Day. A band of Cowetas massacred William White, his wife, and his four children. For the next three weeks war parties terrorized the frontier and cleared the ceded lands of stragglers and squatters more effectively than anything Wright had done. People flocked into Augusta, and even there in the comparative security of a town, those who could afford to do so built stockaded fences around their residences.[112]

Only later, after the alarm sent tremors of fear throughout the frontier, did David Taitt learn the details of the White massacre. The guilty party came from a detached Coweta village called Pucknawheatly by the Indians and Standing Peach Tree by the whites. A warrior named Oktulgi killed another Indian and convinced his tribesmen that White had done the deed. Oktulgi's story incited other Cowetas who already harbored resentment about the recent cession.[113]

On January 14 a party of Cowetas and Tugaloo Cherokees struck again, attacking William Sherrill's fortified house west of Wrightsborough. They killed Sherrill and six others in the first surprise. The survivors took refuge in the stockade and waged a battle with the painted riders circling around. The skirmish lasted from nine in the morning until three in the afternoon. At least one Indian fell, shot through the eye by a black defender. Four others suffered injuries.[114] Wright immediately ordered out Barnard's new troop of rangers. Barnard's militia subordinate Lt. Col. James Grierson called up 101 men and marched them out through Wrightsborough to Williams Creek, where they encamped. On January 23 Lt. Edward Keating escorted several survivors back to the Sherrill plantation. Returning to camp the next day, they ran into an ambush and reported that a large number of Indians, as many as sixty, opened fire on them. Lt. Daniel Grant and two others were killed then or later by the Indians. In any case, they were abandoned. One other ranger died of his wounds at Wrightsborough. When the militiamen learned what had happened, they promptly deserted. The *Georgia Gazette* heaped scorn on them, saying that they raced back to Augusta "with this silly speech in their mouths, that their families were dear to them, that they were in danger, and that they were wanted at home to protect them."[115] Governor Wright explained ruefully that the militiamen were "struck with such a Panick that neither fair means nor threats could prevail on them to stay."[116] Capt. William Goodgion's company of fourteen men salvaged some dignity by marching back in good order instead of a panicky rout.

John Stuart related a grisly story about the way Lieutenant Grant met his death. His horse stepped in a hole, and Grant fell to the ground. The Indians tied him to a tree and tortured him. They cut off his ears and his genitals, and scalped him. Then they thrust a red-hot gun barrel down his throat. After he died they used his body as a target. They left thirteen arrows protruding from his chest and a tomahawk in his skull.[117]

After celebrating in Coweta the exultant raiders traveled to Tugaloo, distance meaning nothing, to exhibit their trophies, including the scalp and wig of Daniel Grant. The villagers hooted and jeered at the sight of the "false hair." Grant's friends in Augusta, not willing to risk their own lives, hired two hunters to lay an ambush for the war party. The men waited outside Tugaloo for the raiders to ride out. From ambush they shot and killed the warrior Big Elk and retrieved the wig he carried.[118] For good measure, they took the dead Indian's scalp and had their own celebration in Augusta. The *Georgia Gazette* made much of the incident; even a minor victory helped morale.[119]

The panic spread to Florida, where three people were killed by a roving band of Lower Creeks at St. Joseph's Bay near the mouth of the Appalachicola River at the boundary between the two Floridas.[120] Wright, Stuart, William Bull, Peter Chester of West Florida, and acting governor John Moultrie in East Florida realized that they faced the imminent danger of a general Indian war. Wright begged for a troop of regulars; so did Moultrie. Bull of South Carolina, with greater manpower to call upon, immediately raised three detachments of rangers. The members of the Georgia legislature had never been so loyal to His Majesty as they professed to be in this emergency. They estimated that the situation required a thousand soldiers as long as the war lasted and then a permanent force of five hundred just to patrol the frontier.[121] (In less than a year they would change their minds about soldiers.) James Habersham expressed the chagrin most Georgians felt; he related how the happy prospects for the ceded lands had been blasted by this unexpected Indian war and "reduced us from a State of increasing Security and Opulence to a state of distress and imminent danger."[122]

Wright did not know how to account for the rising. He blamed "runagate" Indians who wanted to stop settlement on the ceded lands.[123] Runagate they may have been, but they were men of standing in their villages. Oktulgi, who instigated the attack on the White family, belonged to the Tiger clan. So did Escochabey the Young Lieutenant, a chief of importance in Coweta whose unpredictability added to his reputation. The nominal headman, Sempoyaffe, had lost control of his young people and dared not chastise the guilty. Another of the raiders, Houmachta, was thought to be a witch, an excellent reason for leaving him alone. The gang of raiders had grown so bold that they beat a headman who objected to their conduct.[124] They declared that if the whites demanded satisfaction they would kill every white they met.[125]

Wright agreed with John Stuart, who hurried over from Charlestown at the height of the crisis to confer, that the traders shared the blame for the disruption. When these men of business discovered that they might receive less from the land sales than they expected, they cut the supplies promised to the Creeks. Stuart accused Galphin of being the worst offender. In fact, Stuart himself had caused part of the problem by withholding a portion of the promised goods until after the Green Corn Dance. Stuart cited the recent cession as a reason for resentment; nothing annoyed the Indians more than what he called "our incessant requisitions for land."[126]

The redoubtable Governor Wright refused to give up his dream of a colony of the better sort of settlers, or at least the middling sort, who tilled their farms, paid their obligations, and obeyed the law. He told the House that as soon as peace could be restored, he expected that the migration to the new cession would be resumed and then the larger population would "secure us against all future attempts of those Faithless and Cruel Savages."[127] Wright proposed to embargo the Creek trade, thereby punishing the entire nation for the errant behavior of the few. For this he had to obtain the approval of Lord Dartmouth and the cooperation of John Stuart and all of the governors who granted licenses from Dunmore in Virginia to Moultrie in Florida. It seemed an impossible task.

The trade embargo would take time to implement though the general panic would hasten the process. Meanwhile, Wright and Stuart could think of nothing better than to instigate attacks on the Creeks by the Choctaws to distract them from warring upon frontier people. Stuart sent his cousin and deputy, Charles Stuart, then in Charlestown and about to embark on an errand to England, back to his post in Mobile with incentives to the Choctaws to press their war against the Creeks. The zealous deputy asked for a warship to ferry Choctaws across Mobile Bay to facilitate their raids.[128] Even the usually judicious governor Wright suggested bringing the Chickasaws down upon the Creeks.[129]

Fortunately, David Taitt kept a cool head in the crisis. To gain time he convened the Creek headmen and advised them to go down to Savannah on a peace mission. The chiefs appeared to be on the verge of agreeing when emissaries from the Cherokees arrived and reminded them that on a similar occasion in 1759 Governor Lyttelton of South Carolina had taken a Cherokee delegation hostage and at Fort Prince George they met their death. Only Emistisiguo, recovering from a Choctaw wound, and the second man of Little Tallassee consented to accompany Taitt to Savannah. Their errand bought valuable time.[130]

Though Stuart and Taitt had nothing good to say about George Galphin, the veteran trader used his considerable influence to keep the peace. He asked his friend the Young Lieutenant to disclose who had started the trouble. The whites did, he told Galphin. Even so, said Galphin, "You must take care to tell the Young People not to be frightening the traders and telling them they will knock them in the head as they often do when they are drunk."[131]

The hope for peace also suffered a setback when Mad Turkey, a chief of the Upper Creeks who had not been involved in the disorders, came into Augusta as the guest of William Goodgion. Goodgion, a veteran of the important Campbell and Macarten trading company and Edward Barnard's son-in-law, as well as the only officer to maintain discipline in the recent disgraceful retreat from Sherrill's fort, should have had the clout to guarantee safe passage to his Indian friends. Particularly so in this case because Mad Turkey had come bearing a peace offering. Unfortunately for the cause of peace, Augusta had become a place of refuge for many who preferred an all-out war as the best means of driving Indians away, especially if others fought the war for them. As the unarmed, unsuspecting Mad Turkey accepted a friendly drink in a tavern, Thomas Fee, a blacksmith, crushed his skull with an iron bar.[132] The fact that Fee escaped, that he was allowed to escape, says much about the attitude of backcountry Georgians. Again, Wright expressed outrage: "As inhuman and shocking as the murder is," he wrote to Lord Dartmouth, "there are many in this province as well as in South Carolina who look upon it as meritorious and who threaten to do the same."[133] Wright offered a reward for Fee's arrest. However, when the magistrates in the Ninety-Six District of South Carolina seized Fee and put him in jail, a mob broke into the building and set him free.[134]

William Bartram learned a great deal about white-Indian relations during the interim while the crisis delayed his explorations, but he refrained from chronicling the events of that fall and winter season while writing his report and finishing his drawings. One wonders how he felt about the sequence of hostilities that began with the assassination of the Cherokee youths near the Broad River, for that was the impetus for the rest of the ugly business. When Alexander Cameron bluntly asked the Raven of Tugaloo why he had raised the hatchet, the Raven replied that he was thinking of his brothers that the English killed near Fort Charlotte last summer.[135]

3

East Florida

I

*As the lower Creeks in east Florida were not openly con-
cerned in the mischief I imagined I might with safety
turn my discoveries in that quarter.*

Bartram, "Report to Fothergill"

If William Bartram lodged with the legislators during a session of the Georgia assembly, it must have been on his return from the surveying expedition rather than on his first visit to Savannah, as he noted in his *Travels*. Considering the acrimony in neighboring South Carolina and the fact that half the members of the House would soon be listed by the royal authorities as rebels, a surprising tranquillity prevailed. The apparently successful enlargement of the public domain followed by the threat of an Indian war caused Georgians to rally around their governor with unusual unanimity. The only bickering during the sitting of the assembly concerned the oversensitivity of the lower house to questions of prerogative. Edward Barnard, for example, might have expected accolades for his important public service. Instead, on his return to take his seat on July 14, he found himself in trouble because he had absented himself without permission. It did not matter that his party had left Augusta before the House met—he had to pay a fine.[1] Such an ill-tempered attitude on the part of the members might be construed as a slap at the governor, Barnard's militia commander, except that the House routinely dispensed such penalties. Indeed, Jonathan Bryan, frequently a leader of the opposition, got himself expelled because he left the province without first obtaining leave of the House.[2] An unlucky individual named James Muter complained that he had received notice to open his private road to Thomas Netherclift, a member of the House, and asserted that the ruling deprived him of his constitutional property rights. The indignant legislators resolved that the memorial constituted a "most insolent and daring attack on the dignity and privileges of this House" and ordered that it be burned. Muter abjectly apologized for his brashness.[3] Clearly this House was not to be trifled with, even by its friends. On September 7, 1773, the House gave grudging approval to Barnard's resignation so that he might begin his duties as captain of the troop of rangers.[4]

William did not tarry long in Savannah. He had to escort Jack McIntosh home to the embrace of an anxious mother and a proud father. He is more casual than usual, both in Fothergill's report and in *Travels*, about his movements during the time the Indian scare lay on the land: "I spent the remaining part of this season," meaning the last part of the year 1773, "in botanical excursions to the low countries between Carolina and East Florida."[5] He remembered this interval with particular fondness; writing to Lachlan McIntosh many years later, he described "the happy hours which I enjoyed in your family."[6]

Bartram borrowed a canoe from James Bailey, manager of Henry Laurens's Broughton Island plantation, for a botanizing expedition up the Altamaha. He had gone by land to Fort Barrington earlier in the year; he would see how the valley had changed with the onset of fall. He paddled upstream for a distance, then drifted downriver with the current, taking copious notes on all he saw: the sharp-sighted cranes, the defoliated cypress, the solitary wood pelican, the crying bird, the Spanish curlews, and the wonderful charms all around. Again he meditated on the beauty of primitive nature, as yet unspoiled by civilization.[7]

He slept outside under the spreading branches of a live oak. Remarkably, an eclipse occurred while he watched. Francis Harper's experts say that this event must have happened in July 1776.[8] If so, Bartram would not have witnessed it in such a tranquil setting because the violence of war racked the Altamaha region in 1776. Bartram referred to the eclipse as an "annual" occurrence, and perhaps it did happen in 1773, experts to the contrary notwithstanding.

A sudden morning storm made him think how difficulties arise in one's life and how for the moment we lose sight of the guiding hand of Providence, but then the trouble passes and God is once more in His heaven. The thought frequently occurred to him, and he noted it almost as often. The Altamaha was not all poetry, and he added some geography to help his readers locate his route. The river originated in the headwaters of the Oconee in the Cherokee country, a river whose upper reaches he had visited. The Ocmulgee joined the Oconee to form the Altamaha, which flows broadly for a hundred miles and enters the sea through different branches. The northern channel passes the bluff at Darien, where Lachlan McIntosh then resided, and enters the ocean between Sapelo and Wolf Islands. The south channel flows between Broughton and McIntosh (now Colonel's) Islands and then into St. Simon's Sound.[9]

Bartram made reference to an ancient fortification on the west bank of the south branch with discernible remains of bastions and surrounding ditch. He supposed that the French or the Spanish might have constructed the works and historians have wondered about it ever since. William G. DeBrahm also speculated about Spanish ruins near the site Bartram mentioned. Historical geographer Louis De Vorsey believes that in this area Lucas Vazquez De Ayllon located his short-lived colony in 1526.[10]

The resentment on the part of the Cherokees because of the murders of the two youths deterred him from traveling in the Carolina mountains just then. However, the Florida frontier beckoned. Lt. Gov. John Moultrie of East Florida, with whom Bartram was acquainted, had toured the northern part of his province earlier in the year and boasted about the fertile dry land and rich swamps in the hope of bringing settlers to that sparsely populated region.[11] Moultrie's letters read like a chamber of commerce promotion; he reported to Dartmouth that in September "this colony continues to be in its progressive state of improvement."[12]

Knowing of his friend's interest in Florida, Lachlan McIntosh introduced William to James Spalding of nearby St. Simons, whose firm maintained two stores along the St. Johns River. William liked most people he met, and he formed a good opinion of James and Margery Spalding. James came from Scotland, where his father had fought for Prince Charles in the 1745 rising. He had worked in a Charlestown countinghouse before settling on St. Simon's, and after the last war he opened a trading house at Fort Barrington. When his first partner, Donald McKay, died, Spalding joined Roger Kelsall of Sunbury in the successful business described earlier. Bartram thought of the Spaldings as family because Mrs. Spalding happened to be a McIntosh, the daughter of William and niece of Lachlan. Forty-year-old James Spalding had taken eighteen-year old Margery McIntosh as his bride in 1772.[13] James made Bartram welcome, expressing lively interest in his visitor's estimation of the value of the land in the new session. James had a vested interest in those lands because the Cherokees owed his firm a great deal of money, and he hoped to be reimbursed from the land sales. In fact, he and Kelsall had acted as prime movers in bringing about the cession, along with George Galphin,

Edward Barnard, and other leading traders.[14] Bartram might have mused about how interconnected events were. Apparently, isolated places such as St. Simon's were enmeshed in the web of trade. It made good business sense for James Spalding to keep abreast of the unfolding Indian excitement.

James Spalding's trading boats plied the inland waterway to his stores on the St. Johns, and Bartram could travel to Florida on one of those vessels. William thanked him and left his trunk and a specimen box to be sent ahead in care of Charles McLatchy, Spalding's superintendent. Spalding's notification to McLatchy bore the date August 15, 1773. William still had some exploring to do around Darien, and he had not completed the report of the surveying expedition for Dr. Fothergill so he would not follow his luggage until later.[15]

Plans go awry, as William reflected in his *Travels*. "We are, all of us, subject to crosses and disappointments, but more especially the traveller."[16] William's "cross and disappointment" in this case consisted in an illness that confined him for the better part of two months and left him weak. He could not impose on the hospitality of the McIntoshes for that long and rented a house for himself. In a letter to his father he referred to "my home" on the Altamaha.[17]

By November he had recovered sufficiently to pack up his specimens and bring them to Savannah to be forwarded to Dr. Fothergill. The members of the House had departed a month earlier, but William located his friend Benjamin Andrew, who volunteered to convey the collection to Dr. Chalmers in Charlestown, to be packaged and shipped from there. After delivering the parcel to Chalmers, Andrew called upon the Lambolls, father and daughter, to give them news about William, that he was quite well now and that he intended to proceed to Florida to follow up on the discoveries he had made there with his father. The venerable Lamboll expressed his great relief in a letter to William. He and Mary had worried, not hearing anything for so long. They had asked Dr. Chalmers about William, only to be told that William might not be alive for all he knew. Not liking that opinion, they inquired of Superintendent Stuart, who took a more optimistic view. William must have gone up into the Cherokee country, and Stuart assured them that the botanist would be perfectly safe there. Stuart expected to hear some news at any moment.[18]

Bartram might as well have sent his papers and paraphernalia by slow packet because Dr. Chalmers did nothing with them for a month. On December 15 he acknowledged that "your drawings have come to hand." He seemed disappointed that Bartram had not colored them or included a complete description. Chalmers sent word to Florida's lieutenant governor John

Moultrie to expect the botanist and to be obliging. As Fothergill's financial agent, Chalmers paid John J. Zubly twelve pounds sterling on William's behalf.[19] William had a habit of meeting prominent people wherever he went, people whose names were etched in history—John Stuart and Henry Laurens in Charlestown, Lachlan McIntosh and Benjamin Andrew in coastal Georgia, Edward Barnard and George Galphin in Augusta. Zubly matched their caliber, making his own mark on history. He and William had in common the good friendship of the Lambolls. Zubly preached in Lamboll's Congregational Meeting House before accepting the pastorate of Savannah's Independent Church. His pamphlet on theology earned him a doctor of divinity degree from the College of New Jersey. A philosopher and polemicist, Zubly loved controversy. He had to contend with a schism within his own church led by Lachlan McGillivray and other prominent Scotsmen. Henry Mulhenberg asked him to help sort out the factional issues at Ebenezer. But his favorite debate concerned the constitutional rights of colonists, and his essay on the subject would gain him fame and election to the Continental Congress.[20]

Doctor Fothergill appreciated William's drawings, but he had hoped for living plants that he might introduce into his garden. To that end he sent William specially made boxes for the transportation of plants.[21] Chalmers assumed that William had gone off to Florida by December and forwarded the letter from Fothergill to acting governor Moultrie. However, William remained in coastal Georgia during December, and the repercussions from the Indian attacks on residents near Wrightsborough kept him there during January and February. The general alarm caused Florida's John Moultrie to mute his advertisements about the safety of his province, especially since the Nineteenth Regiment had been withdrawn from St. Augustine at the height of the crisis.[22]

William told his father that he turned back from his second attempt to journey to Florida because of the Indian outbreaks. He learned that the outlying Florida planters had fled to St. Augustine and that Spalding's stores had been plundered. So he remained in the southern part of Georgia waiting, not idly because in the interim he "discovered and collected many valuable and new vegetables."[23] It may have been during this waiting period that he had one of the most dramatic encounters in all his travels. He related the story out of place in his book, putting it in spring 1773. His Fothergill journal reveals that he had no time for a trip to the St. Marys then.

Alone and on horseback, he rode along the high road to the Satilla River, passing successively through St. David and St. Patrick Parishes, described by him as "an uninhabited wilderness." He preferred it a wilderness. Along the way he discovered a new species of Annona and an elegant diminutive kalmia, both of which thrilled him so that he did handsome drawings of them, now among the treasures of the British Museum of Natural History. He marveled at the *testudo polyphaemus* and the heaps of soil they pushed out from their burrows. Georgians called the animal the gopher turtle. He lodged that night at a cowpens, identified by Francis Harper as belonging to Arthur Carney, a prominent planter in that sparsely settled region, later recruited by Lachlan McIntosh to raise a company in defense of the Georgia borderlands.[24]

He continued through St. Thomas Parish to the Satilla the next day, noticing herds of cattle and horses. Within two years these herds would be contested for by belligerents on both sides of the border. He reached the Satilla on the evening of the second day, lodged at the ferry operator's hut, and crossed the river the next morning. He noted that he "had now passed the utmost frontier of white settlements," but actually he had entered St. Mary Parish, a fertile region for land speculation. He might have been surprised at how many of his friends had filed for land grants between the Satilla and the St. Marys: Lachlan, George and William McIntosh, Edward Barnard, Jonathan Bryan, James Spalding, John J. Zubly, Lt. White Outerbridge, and the Lambolls' Charlestown neighbor Miles Brewton. More than 130 grants had been recorded. Governor Wright and his relatives did well. The governor's 4,000 acres were dwarfed by the more than 20,000 awarded to his brothers Charles and Jermyn. The brothers Wright presided over prosperous plantations and cattle herds, but most of the grants had not been taken up at the time of Bartram's visit, and he had the impression of traveling out beyond civilization.[25]

Nearing the St. Marys at the close of the day, his "happy moments of evening contemplation" ended abruptly at the appearance of an Indian armed with a rifle. Startled, he turned his horse behind a screen of trees. Too late. The warrior saw him and spurred his horse toward him. William had never been afraid of Indians before, but this time he confessed that "my spirits were very much agitated." As usual, he had no weapon but his trust in the Almighty, and he decided to act upon that trust. He urged his horse toward the fierce stranger with his best affectation of a cheerful smile. He thrust out his hand and hailed the Indian as "brother." That approach disconcerted the warrior, who intended, Bartram firmly believed, to kill him. Bartram imagined the thoughts that ran through the Indian's mind as he considered his next move: "White man, thou art my enemy, and thou and thy brethren may have killed mine, yet it may not be so, and even were that the case, thou art now alone, and in my power, live; the Great Spirit forbid me to touch thy life; go to thy brethren, tell them thou sawest an Indian in the forests, who knew how to be humane and compassionate."[26]

The two men shook hands, and the warrior pointed the way to the trading house. Except for two bouts of serious illness and some perilous adventure with alligators, Bartram never again came so close to mortal danger. Francis Harper commented on the Indian's behavior: "Little did this son of the wilderness realize how the world of science and literature was destined to benefit by his forbearance!"[27] Only when he reached the trading house did William realize the full danger of the encounter. The lone Indian, he learned, had murdered a man and had been outlawed by his people. He had been beaten by whites at the trading house and his gun broken. However, he stole another rifle and escaped, vowing to kill the first white man he saw.

The dramatic confrontation probably occurred during the early part of 1774. Florida's lieutenant governor John Moultrie assured Lord Dartmouth that despite the alarms from Georgia, he thought he could keep the peace. However, he acknowledged that Indians lurked about, stealing horses and killing cattle in the woods.[28] Moultrie's successor, Patrick Tonyn, arrived on March 1, 1774, and confirmed the unease Floridians felt: "The Indians had been very troublesome to the planters, had taken away whatever they pleased, had threatened and menaced so they were in great fear of their lives."[29] A precarious peace prevailed on the Florida borderlands. The assassination of William Bartram likely would have ignited a general war. The incident might have suggested to Bartram the advisability of securing a weapon. Instead he drew the lesson that the moral sense, implanted by the Creator, is universal.

He proceeded no farther south on this occasion than to the St. Marys. He remained on that border long enough to record fanciful stories about the great swamp in which the St. Marys originated, the mysterious Okefenokee. When Lachlan McGillivray led a survey team across a section of the swamp, his Indian companions told frightening stories about a race of immortals who lived in the bottomless depths and haunted intruders. Samuel Savery put their name on his map of the Okefenokee, "Este Fatchasicko."[30] Bartram chose to remember a different version. A peculiar race of Indians inhabited the swamp, whose women were incomparably beautiful. These "daughters of the sun" had rescued lost hunters, but when the hunters tried to follow them to their home, an enchanted island, the island disappeared. Bartram also heard another story, not nearly so romantic, that the remnants of the defeated Yamassees had taken refuge in the impenetrable swamp.[31]

With that adventure out of the way, he made his way back to Darien. His neighbors there had another portentous topic to discuss other than the Indian alarms. The *Georgia Gazette* of January 10, 1774, reported that a party of men dressed like Indians had dumped tea into Boston Harbor almost a month earlier.

II

I went on board a small boat for Fredericka on St. Simons Island, arrived safe there and waited on J. Spalding Esq.

Bartram, "Report to Fothergill"

The killings at Wrightsborough and St. Joseph's Bay in early winter set off petty raids by parties of disgruntled Creeks and Seminoles, as the Florida Creeks began to be called. The raids and rumor of raids kept William Bartram on the Altamaha longer than he liked. At last he heard that the new governor of East Florida, Patrick Tonyn, had summoned the local chiefs to a conference at St. Augustine, set for March 9, 1774.[32] Bartram made up his mind to risk an excursion through East Florida.

Patrick Tonyn acted quickly in calling the Indians to meet him. He assumed office on March 1, 1774, and made peace his first priority. He owed his education and much of his character to the military, having attained the rank of lieutenant colonel. He thought and acted like a military man, and at the age of fifty he had fixed notions about subordination and democracy, much preferring the former. The Proclamation of 1763, which created East and West Florida, promised a representative government modeled on Georgia's. Tonyn found one excuse after another for postponing elections to an assembly.[33]

Tonyn's self-assurance embroiled him in quarrels with Chief Justice William Drayton, Supt. John Stuart, Gen. Augustine Prevost, and other officials during his Florida tenure, but it became an asset in dealing with his Indian guests. Nearly a hundred visited St. Augustine in March, the Oconee King and the Long Warrior with their retinues first and then Ahaya the Cowkeeper, and his followers on March 13, 1774. Tonyn had his commission read to them and thought that it impressed them greatly. He told them he was sorry to hear that some of the Great King's children in Georgia had been killed by some Creek Indians and that the path between the white and red people was bloody. He complimented the chiefs for coming, letting them know that they acted wisely and he hoped to tell the Great King that the black cloud was gone. The headmen of the nation must go talk to Governor Wright; their guilty people must be punished. The Cowkeeper denied having anything to do with the troubles. He and his warriors intended to go off and fight the Choctaws; he would visit the governor again on his return. In fact, the Cowkeeper proved to be Governor Tonyn's most loyal auxiliary during the war of the American Revolution.[34]

William recalled in his *Travels* that he set out for Florida in March, a time that corresponds to Tonyn's conference with the Lower Creeks. In stating that he left from Savannah, his memory probably failed him, a fault that troubles only the purists among his readers. He had been in Savannah in August and in November but said nothing about visiting that place in his letter to his father in which he outlined his movements, nor in his report to Fothergill. He left the place he had begun to think of as home near the McIntoshes at Darien and boated down the Altamaha to Broughton Island, there to be hospitably entertained by James Bailey, Henry Laurens's agent, before proceeding down the sound to St. Simons. Again, as in August, James Spalding promised to help in any way he could. He offered transportation to Florida on one of his trading boats; he wrote letters to his agent to provide Bartram with horses, guides, and whatever supplies he needed. Bartram later confided to Fothergill that he owed his success in the Florida expedition to "the generous assistance" of James Spalding. The merchant cautioned Bartram about the dangers of wandering about Florida just then, stating that his upper store on the St. Johns had been looted. Having recently faced up to a hostile warrior, Bartram would not be deterred by vague warnings of plundered stores.[35]

While waiting for the trade boat, Bartram indulged in botanizing around St. Simons Island. The memory of Georgia's founder, James Edward Oglethorpe, lay heavily on the land. In fact, James Spalding owned the fifty acres Oglethorpe set out for himself, and his orange trees had been planted by the general. Oglethorpe's modest house lay just southeast of the garrison town of Frederica, once Britain's proud southern bastion where the Forty-second Regiment had paraded. Then a wall of cedar puncheons and a ditch that could be flooded at high tide surrounded the town of one thousand people. Charles and John Wesley each served a brief and unhappy ministry there. An explosion destroyed the magazine and most of the barracks, and the regiment dissolved in 1749. People drifted away, and the place decayed into the condition Bartram saw in 1774, "almost in ruins."[36]

Bartram followed Oglethorpe's military road, already overgrown. He noted a "venerable grove of wild oaks" that led to Harrington Hall, the estate of one of colonial Georgia's most important military figures, Capt. Raymond Demere.[37] Bartram had heard about the brothers Demere from John Stuart. The names conjured visions of the Cherokee mountains, Fort Prince George, and the tragic fate of Fort Loudoun. Raymond and his younger brother Paul, Huguenots from Guienne, France, went to England early in life, probably to avoid the religious wars. Both bought commissions in the British army and served in the Twenty-fifth Regiment of Foot at Gibralter. Raymond named his St. Simon plantation after his commanding officer there, William Stanhope, Lord Harrington.[38]

When Robert Walpole reluctantly agreed to give James Oglethorpe a regiment to defend Georgia, Raymond Demere happened to be in England and helped organize the Forty-second Regiment of Foot with himself a lieutenant. The Twenty-fifth Regiment from Gibralter was incorporated into the Forty-second, and so young brother Paul came along to Georgia as an ensign. Both took part in the failed invasion of Florida. Both defended against the Spanish counterattack in 1742, Raymond in command of a company at Frederica and Paul with a lookout watch at Fort William on Cumberland Island. Raymond's company formed part of Oglethorpe's front line at an opening along the military road and engaged the advanced guard of Spanish troops there. In the melee Demere's men broke and ran, but Oglethorpe, galloping from Frederica at the sound of the guns with fleet-footed Highlanders and Indians keeping up, turned the retreat. When they reached the battlefield, they found it quiet. The gallant few who stood their ground had turned back the Spanish force. The place, called Bloody Bend and later Bloody Marsh, has been venerated ever since by Georgians. The engagement, minuscule in numbers, loomed large in importance because the three thousand or so Spaniards declined to renew the fight and went back to St. Augustine.[39] If Bartram pondered the significance of Bloody Marsh as he walked down the military road, he did not write about it. He declined to write about battles among humans.

Raymond Demere, promoted to captain, signed up in the South Carolina Independent companies when the forty-second disbanded. So did Lt. Paul Demere. Governor Glen gave Raymond key assignments, emissary to St. Augustine, builder and commander of Fort Prince George in the Cherokee lower settlements, and finally the construction of Fort Loudoun on the Little Tennessee in the remote overhills country. Governor Glen sent Paul Demere's company to Virginia; they suffered defeat under Braddock and experienced victory under Forbes. Then Paul returned to Carolina to replace Raymond in command at Fort Loudoun and to die with the garrison in 1760.[40] John Stuart, who survived the massacre, had told Bartram about it because Bartram intended to follow the Little Tennessee through the mountains. If Bloody Marsh symbolized victory, Fort Loudoun represented the worst aspect of an Indian war. Fort Loudoun still, in Bartram's experience, struck terror in the souls of backcountry people.

When Raymond Demere died on St. Simon's in 1766, he left half his possessions to his son, Raymond Jr., and half to Paul's son, Raymond II. Raymond II farmed land nearer Savannah and would distinguish himself during the American Revolution as an aide to Gen. George Washington. Raymond Jr., "born and bred" on St. Simons in Margaret Davis Cate's expression, inherited Harrington Hall and the Grove, a plantation on the south end of the island. The island seemed world enough to this Raymond; the highest military distinction he achieved was the rank of ensign in Capt. Arthur Carney's militia. He felt better suited for his other role, that of justice of the peace for the southern parishes.[41] It was almost certainly this Raymond Demere whom Bartram met in his walk about the island.

Bartram's description of his tour is a hymn to the glories of nature and to their Creator. When he came upon a view of the ocean, he exclaimed, "O thou Creator supreme, almighty! how infinite and incomprehensible thy works! most perfect and every way astonishing!"[42] He continued along the beach and rounded the south point of the island. In a cove of the sound he beheld a house and farm, "situated in the midst of a spacious grove of Live Oaks and Palms." Old maps of the island show the plantation known as the Grove located here, belonging to Raymond Demere Jr.[43] The scene is painted in prose with the same skill Bartram employed to draw his flowers.

As he neared the house, the owner greeted him: "Welcome, stranger, I am indulging the rational dictates of nature, taking a little rest, having just come in from the chace [sic] and fishing." Bartram remembered the salutation because it fit his creed exactly. Here he saw a model for Americans, a man guided by reason in communion with nature. A servant (Bartram followed the tradition of southern gentry in avoiding the term "slave") brought out honey diluted with water, a most refreshing liquor to Bartram. After a companionable chat Bartram rose to go, but his host would not hear of it. The visitor must stay for lunch, a picnic under the trees. Bartram loved it: "Our rural table was spread under the shadow of Oaks, Palms, and Sweet Bays, fanned by the live salubrious breezes wafted from the spicy groves. Our music was the responsive love-lays of the painted nonpareil, and the alert and gay mockbird." All the while the "solemn sound of the beating surf" provided a background rhythm.[44] Such scenes delighted the English Romantics.

However, his modern readers might wonder at the omissions. Why not mention Bloody Marsh when he walked by the site along the military road? Why not mention the name of his accidental host? Instead of battle, the botanist gives us flowers, a glossary of them. Instead of a specific Raymond Demere, with his baggage of heritage and context, he gives us "my sylvan friend," first seen smoking his pipe and reclining on a bearskin. The reason must be the same that caused him to omit the murder of his Cherokee friends—he intended to describe an ideal America, an America as he wished it to be.

He returned to James Spalding's place near Frederica later that day, stayed the night, and next morning set out at last for Florida. However, the wind turned against them and they lost the tide so they got no farther than the south end of St. Simon's, probably Gascoigne's Bluff. Capt. James Gascoigne of His Majesty's ship *The Hawk,* who escorted Oglethorpe's transports to Frederica in 1738, used the high ground for careening and repairing his vessel and thereby gave his name to the place.[45]

Bartram went out with the captain of the vessel to hunt for game and came back with three raccoons, which they had for supper. With better wind and weather they sailed by Jekyll and along Cumberland next morning. They hailed an approaching ship, another of Spalding's trade boats, and asked what news. "Bad," they were told, "the Indians have plundered the upper store and the traders have escaped, only with their lives."[46] The factor at Spalding's lower store had taken the precaution of hiding the supplies, including Bartram's trunk, on an island in the river. When the captain of his vessel decided to return to Frederica because of the danger, Bartram asked to be put ashore on Cumberland. He had waited long enough to get to Florida and would not be deterred now.[47] Bartram knew something about Cumberland before he landed. He had been invited to visit Amelia Island just below Cumberland by a gentleman he met at Spalding's who happened to be the supervisor of Lord Egmont's estate on Amelia. He knew that people lived on Cumberland and trusted that someone would ferry him across the narrow sound to Amelia.

The memory of Spanish missions along the Georgia sea islands had already dimmed in the collective mind of Georgians. They would have remembered only that Cumberland lay in the region contested by Britain and Spain. Oglethorpe's charter clearly stated that the new colony extended only to the Altamaha. The founder attempted to improve upon the charter by fabricating a branch of the Altamaha that ignored geography and flowed into the St. Johns River.[48] His colleagues in Parliament took his word even if the Spanish officials did not. With this dubious authority Oglethorpe established a chain of little forts below Frederica, on the southern end of St. Simons, the northern shoulder of Cumberland, the southern coast of Cumberland, and in an excess of brazenness, even on the north side of Amelia. These incursions annoyed the Spanish, and the severing of Robert Jenkins's ear bothered the English so the two countries went to war in 1739, featured by Oglethorpe's victory at Bloody Marsh sandwiched between his two failures to capture the Castillo de San Marcos and St. Augustine. The Treaty of Aix-la-Chappelle in 1748 ended that war but did not settle the question of sovereignty over the debatable lands.

During the ensuing Seven Years' War (in America the French and Indian War) William Pitt attempted to keep Spain neutral while fighting France and therefore refrained from contesting the borderlands. When a group of Georgians led by a colorful character named Edmond Gray settled on the Satilla, Pitt became nervous and ordered Carolina's governor William Henry Lyttelton and Georgia's Henry Ellis to break up the settlement. Ellis had met Edmond Gray on his tour of the southern region and had taken a liking to him; nevertheless he carried out Pitt's instructions. Gray and some of his people moved to Cumberland, where Gray obtained a trading license from Ellis's successor, James Wright.[49] Henry Ellis, back in England, found himself adviser to Pitt's successor, William Wyndham, Lord Egremont. When Spain entered the war on the side of France, Ellis advised attacking Cuba and, in the subsequent peace treaty, swapping Cuba for Florida. Egremont agreed and it was done. Ellis's advice about drawing the boundary at the St. Marys and creating two Floridas with a representative government modeled on Georgia's was written into the Proclamation of 1763. With the end of the war in 1763 the coastal fortifications began a decline, and the last garrisons were gone by 1768. A map of Amelia Island that William H. DeBrahm did for Lord Egmont in 1770 showed Fort William on the tip end of Cumberland, but the 1775 map by Jacob Blainey bears the caption, "Ruins of Fort William built by Gen. Oglethorpe."[50] William Bartram caused confusion for historians by referring to the "commandant" of Fort William. In a fine history of the fort, William Ramsay wondered about Bartram's reference. The best check on Bartram, the author of

Travels, is Bartram, writer of the report to Dr. Fothergill. In the latter he makes it clear that the pilot who conducted vessels on the St. Marys lived at the point of the island, evidently in what was left of the fort.[51]

A fellow passenger went ashore on Cumberland with Bartram with an intention of "sharing my adventures," as Bartram expressed it. They reached the fort—such as it was—by evening to find "the commander" out hunting. Bartram seemed surprised that his tired companion decided not to go off hunting novelties just then. After walking a mile along the beach, the botanist came upon a deer slain by the hunter and decided to wait for him, meanwhile enjoying the "fine prospect of the rolling billows and foaming breakers."[52] The pilot—Bartram called him the "Captain of the fort"—soon appeared, and they returned together to the former military outpost with an ample supply of venison. The next morning the pilot ferried the two men across to Amelia Island.

III

Being now in readiness to prosecute our voyage to St. John's we set sail in a handsome pleasure-boat.

Harper, *Travels*

Bartram lingered on Amelia Island for several days in mid-April as guest of Stephen Egan, agent for the second Lord Egmont. The first Lord Egmont figured prominently in Georgia's history as the assiduous chairman of the Board of Trustees. The second lord used his position as member of the Board of Trade to secure the grant of Amelia Island as soon as the Treaty of 1763 made the island available. Egmont ordered a village laid out on the north end of the island, and Egmont Town is the only habitation shown on DeBrahm's 1770 map. A cluster of houses and huts surrounded three wells, one of which is still in use in the city of Fernandina.[53]

Bartram referred to Egan as "a very intelligent and able planter" and enjoyed his company. As they rode about the island, Bartram admired the flourishing indigo and noted the variety of other crops on the self-sufficient plantation. Several Indian mounds intrigued Bartram. Egan explained that locals called them Ogeechee Mounds, supposing that the same Indians who left their name on the Ogeechee River in Georgia built them. Egan did not know what to make of other ruins. Bartram noted to Fothergill that these were "vestiges of great Towns and square of the antiant [*sic*] Indian Natives."[54] Every

Spanish mission had a square or plaza as well as a church, a *convento* for the friars and huts for the people of the mission. Amelia Island had two such missions in succession. Santa Maria de Yamassee, established some time after 1650, lasted until about 1680, when the Yamassees moved north to join their cousins and in 1715 engaged in a war against the Carolinians. A second mission followed when Santa Catalina de Guale suffered an attack by the Carolinians in 1680. The mission on Amelia retained the name Santa Catalina and until 1702 served as the northernmost Spanish outpost. In that year Gov. James Moore's Carolinians and Indian allies destroyed the mission and everything else in La Florida outside St. Augustine's Castillo de San Marcos.[55] So William Bartram inspected the site and noticed that there had been a settlement there, with a plaza. In 1985, when George and Dorothy Dorison decided to build a house in a clearing of their property, they discovered skeletal human remains caught up in the roots of a tree. They alerted professional archeologists and even subsidized the excavation of the site. The dig uncovered the remains of Santa Catalina and by 1990 produced an enormous amount of data, according to Prof. Rebecca Saunders, one of the archeologists.[56] Thus, Bartram's unstated question about ancient villages and squares required more than two hundred years to answer fully.

Stephen Egan had to go to St. Augustine to transact business with Governor Tonyn. He intended to visit friends along the way, and he welcomed the company of the Philadelphian. They found that the planters in the area, though much shaken by raids and rumors of raids by renegade Indians, felt more secure because Tonyn had recently dispatched British regulars to patrol the area, making "an appearance of readiness" as the governor explained to Lord Dartmouth. Tonyn credited the availability of troops with nothing less than saving the province.[57]

The crossing from Amelia to the mainland went well. Egan shot a pelican for Bartram's inspection. They pitched tents on a bluff thick with orange trees and feasted on an abundant supply of oysters near at hand. Bartram seldom complained, but he did note that the swarms of mosquitoes, the peculiar roaring of alligators, and the continual flapping about of innumerable seabirds roosting nearby rendered repose "incompleat."[58]

He devoted careful attention to the palmetto royal, or yucca plant, which formed an impenetrable barrier "as if they were a regiment of grenadiers with their bayonets pointed at you." In his *Travels* he went on so about the yucca that he neglected to mention that he and his fellow travelers enjoyed the hos-

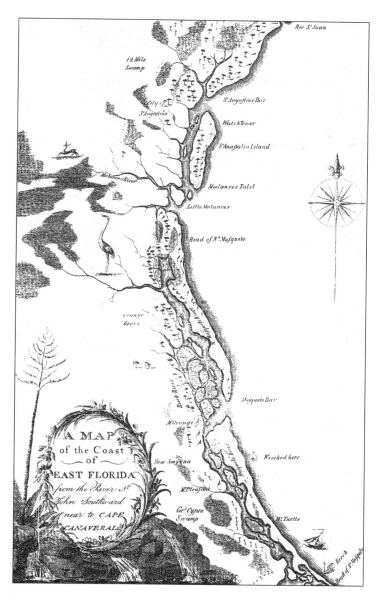

Bartram's map of the coast of East Florida reveals his skill as a draftsman.

From the 1791 edition of *Travels*

pitality of Francis Philip Fatio, a Swiss gentleman who had established a plantation on the St. Johns River. Fatio showed his guest his garden with its grapevines; olive, orange, lemon, and fig trees; and a glorious assortment of flowers. Fatio later achieved modest recognition for his service as army commissary during the Revolution and almost unique distinction by choosing to remain in Florida after the transition to Spanish rule.[59] After their stop at the hospitable Fatio's, William and Egan parted company. Egan pursued his errand to St. Augustine by land while Bartram continued his explorations by boat. Deciding to travel up the St. Johns, he purchased a sailboat for three guineas, bought a gun, and laid in a stock of provisions. The young man who had joined him at Cumberland Island and accompanied him this far would go no farther; he had lost his nerve. "I suppose not relishing the hardships and dangers which might befall us, [he] chose rather to stay behind amongst the settlements," Bartram noted.[60] In light of the explosive situation throughout the Indian country, the young man cannot be faulted for exercising prudence. Bartram, "impelled by a restless spirit of curiosity," was the rash one, plying up the broad river in his little vessel. In fact, as he later commented in his Fothergill report, "I found the Inhabitants greatly alarmed at the hostile disposition of the Indians and were generally on the flight or fortifying themselves by Stockadeing in their houses."[61]

The weather became an important factor now that he went by water. He made seven miles the first day and five the second, as the wind failed. Putting in at shore, a huge alligator came at him as if to upset his craft, then plunged underneath, surfacing on the other side. Bartram's casual references to such life-threatening episodes are the more remarkable for their understatement. Bartram camped on shore, went hunting, and met a lone Indian. "I saluted him with 'It's well brother,'" Bartram recalled. The Indian worked as a hunter for a planter named Abraham Marshall who had established an estate in the area the previous year. Marshall, on meeting the visitor, made much of him, treating Bartram as a celebrity. He conducted Bartram over the property, an already thriving indigo plantation. His neighbors came upon invitation to meet the botanist. The next morning Marshall loaded Bartram with provisions and saw him off.[62]

The third day of his journey since setting out alone went well; a lively breeze propelled his vessel, and plunging alligators provided excitement. This part of the St. Johns brought back bittersweet memories for the explorer. At Florence Cove on the right bank, he had tried to do what Marshall and others had done so well, but he failed miserably. In 1766, he had remained in Florida while his father returned to Philadelphia, and he had attempted to grow rice and indigo. He might have died of malnutrition, made worse by a depression of spirit, had not Henry Laurens rescued him.[63] He expressed pleasure that others had been successful in establishing plantations since 1766. That evening he stayed with an acquaintance of his earlier sojourn and inquired about the state of Indian affairs.

The informed answer to that question was that the frontier from Carolina to the Mississippi continued to be as tense as ever. Gen. Frederick Haldimand, in command of the military in America during Gen. Thomas Gage's temporary absence, thought seriously about sending troops south despite the Boston Tea Party furor in that city and in fact had written home for authorization. Rumors of Indian massacres caused consternation in West Florida. Gov. Peter Chester ordered fortifications thrown up around Pensacola because he expected "a sudden stroke from the merciless hands of the cruel savages."[64] Virginia governor Lord Dunmore complained to John Stuart that Cherokees had been involved in the deaths of some of his people.[65]

Fortunately for the cause of peace, Emistisiguo decided to accompany David Tait to Savannah even though most of the headmen stayed away for fear of being taken hostage. With him came the second man of Little Tallassee and a few followers. Alleck represented the Lower Creeks. Governor Wright received them with enormous relief on April 14, 1774. John Stuart hurried over from Charlestown, not to be left out of the negotiations. Wright and Emistisiguo had settled the main issues before Stuart arrived. Emistisiguo agreed on the necessity of an embargo on trade as perhaps the only way to restore order even though the Creeks already suffered from a shortage of ammunition in their war against the Choctaws, a shortage made more acute by the recent aggressiveness of the Choctaws. Because of the brutal murder of Mad Turkey in Augusta, which the headmen only learned about in Savannah, Wright could not demand the life-for-life satisfaction he wanted. He compromised by insisting on the execution of the four leaders of the early winter Wrightsborough raids. When Stuart joined the meeting, he added that another life must be sacrificed for the whites killed at St. Joseph's Bay. The Indians agreed, but Emistisiguo had a question for his good friend Stuart. What was the truth of the report he had heard from the Cherokees that Stuart had solicited their help against the Creeks? Did he intend to start a war between the nations? Stuart denied any intention of such, but in fact Cameron had volunteered to lead Cherokees against a Creek village, and the word had reached Emistisiguo through the amazingly efficient Indian grapevine. Then Emistisiguo wondered why the Cherokees had called a meeting of so many tribes to Chote, including the Arkansas, the Chickasaws, Shawnees, Delawares, and the Six Nations. Did they intend to make trouble for the Creeks? Those people called Stuart their father; he should know what this meeting meant. Stuart assured him that he had the word of Ouconnostotah, the Great Warrior, that these meetings were meant to establish peace and to bring the belligerent Wabash and western tribes to reason. Emistisiguo commented that the Cherokees resembled mocking birds; they changed their tunes as the situation required.[66]

Neither Wright nor Stuart felt optimistic about the chances for peace as the Indian delegation left Savannah. Would the traders abide by an embargo? Would the guilty Cowetas be punished? Governor Tonyn in St. Augustine reflected the general opinion in Florida: "Indian affairs in Georgia are not as favorable as expected, though a few Indians have been in Savannah."[67] Stuart advised Taitt not to return to his post in Little Tallassee but to linger in Augusta, where he could receive reports from the Indian country and at the same time monitor the conduct of the traders. Wright gained an important point when Lord Dartmouth subsequently agreed to a trade stoppage and instructed the various southern governors to enforce it.[68]

Some of the bolder young Seminoles had taken advantage of the general alarm caused by the Creek raids in Georgia and plundered the traders' stores in Florida. However, the Cowkeeper had promised Governor Tonyn that restitution would be made.[69] Bartram's friend thought that the Seminoles, at least, would keep the peace, even if the Creeks did not give satisfaction. Bartram needed no further encouragement to resume his long journey.

A flower that Bartram found growing near his old property and named *ixia coelestine* still grows in the same area today. The delicate flower blooms in late April, but the watcher must be up early to see it. The purple flower opens at dawn and closes at sunrise.[70]

About noon Bartram arrived at another familiar site, Fort Picolata. He and his father had attended one of John Stuart's great Indian congresses here in 1765. William became something of a hero on that occasion by killing a huge rattlesnake, to the amazement of the Indians and to the satisfaction of Gov. James Grant, who had the snake for supper.[71] Bartram said nothing about the congress in his report, just as he had said nothing about his short-lived homestead. Instead he revealed some of the information he garnered in his previous stay by explaining how the fort was built and that the porous coquina stone came from the nearby islands. Continuing a short distance, William camped on the bank of a little lagoon. He shared with his readers his meditation on the beauty of the swarming insects.[72]

After a night's rest under the stars and a sail along the gradually narrowing river, Bartram arrived at the site of a failed experiment much more elaborate than his own. Denys Rolle, a member of Parliament from Barnstaple in Devonshire had convinced himself that misfits in England might be rehabilitated in the Florida wilderness. He obtained land on the St. Johns and made several attempts to establish a settlement called Charlottia by Bartram and Rollestown by most others. He demonstrated that persons of low character and indifferent morals fared no better in the New World than in the old.[73] Bernard Romans, a person very different in temperament and opinion from Bartram but on a similar mission of chronicling the natural history of Florida, called Rollestown "the sepulchre of above four hundred such victims."[74] He cited Rollestown as a tragic example of the mistake of using white labor in the southern latitudes. He instead advocated enslaved African labor as the necessary factor in successful planting. Efforts to settle Florida with white labor he called foolish and cruel. Bartram vehemently disagreed though his most impassioned denunciations of slavery did not appear in print.[75] In his 1775 publication Romans probably expressed the general opinion of the gentry in the plantation South as he did in his evaluation of southeastern Indians. In his characteristically blunt language he said that Indians were "a people not only rude and uncultivated, but incapable of civilization, if they had always studied to be in contrast with us, they could not be more so than nature has made them."[76] Bartram wrote his book to refute such ideas.

As Bartram considered the nearly deserted "Charlottia" with its dwellings in a state of decay, he merely commented on poor planning and "a bad choice of citizens."[77] An overseer and his family still lived there with a blacksmith's family nearby. One of those persons told Bartram the location of the island where the traders had secreted their goods, a fact that causes one to wonder how many shared the secret. Bartram somehow surmised that his chest, sent ahead months ago, would be among the trade goods. A seven-mile sail upriver and a measure of good luck in choosing the channel brought Bartram to the right place, today's Murphy Island. He might have sailed by except that one of the traders called out to him. He found several men camping in a thicket. Sure enough, they had his precious chest, and he found everything intact.[78] If he had come any later no one would have been there to greet him because the traders were engaged in moving Spalding's goods to the lower trading house. Bartram got directions to the store and went on ahead of them. He found the store without incident at the site of today's Stokes Landing on the west bank of the St. Johns. Charles McLatchy, chief trader at the store, greeted him warmly; he had been expecting Bartram since getting Spalding's letter of last August 15. It had been a long eight-month wait.

IV

I found out from frequent conferences with Mr. McLatchie that I might with safety extend my journeys every way, and with prudence, even into the towns and settlements of the Indians.

Harper, *Travels*

At Spalding's lower store, William Bartram found himself, quite by accident, at the crucial testing place that determined the fate of the frontier. British policy decided that trade would be the means of restoring order in Indian relations. The policy would succeed or fail, depending upon the cooperation of the great traders such as George Galphin and the Spalding-Kelsall Company. David Taitt monitored trade from Augusta, the most important backcountry post, with Edward Barnard's rangers to enforce the ban. How well the stoppage would be enforced in Florida remained to be seen, and Bartram happened to be at the right place to observe the result.

During May, while Bartram had his base at Spalding's store, the trade embargo took effect. Wright and Stuart appealed to the southern governors immediately after Emistisiguo's April meeting in Savannah, without waiting for Dartmouth's approval, asking for their cooperation in stopping the Creek trade.[79] Bull of South Carolina readily agreed, as did Chester of West Florida.[80] East Florida's Tonyn had already recognized a de facto stoppage in February, when the traders fled from their posts, but as Bartram arrived, the traders were about to resume their business.[81] Before the end of the summer, however, Tonyn joined the other governors in prohibiting trade, thus completing the strangulation of commerce, in theory at least.[82]

Historians of the American Revolution have quite rightly focused attention on the colonial reactions to Lord North's Coercive Acts, culminating in the convening of the Continental Congress in Philadelphia in September. Many on the southern frontier regarded Indian relations as more immediately relevant and anxiously awaited the results of meetings beginning in May and climaxing in October. Emistisiguo called a crucial meeting at Tallassee to talk peace. An indication of his influence is that twenty-six towns sent delegations. The congress began on May 23, 1774, with the security of the frontier's people depending upon the outcome.[83]

Ironically, James Spalding's plans, if carried out, might well undermine Emistisiguo's position that trade depended on compliance with Governor Wright's demands. A clandestine Florida trade would certainly undermine the British embargo. Spalding intended to stock three satellite stores during May and June. An upper store, sixty miles upriver from the main house, a second at Alachua, fifty miles west by Bartram's reckoning, and a third at Talahasochte on the Little St. Johns, today's Suwanee River. Bartram intended to go on each one of the expeditions though in his retrospective *Travels* he confused the sequence. His report to Fothergill indicated that on his first excursion in late April and early May he accompanied some traders to Alachua to round up company horses that had been abandoned in the general alarm. In his *Travels* Bartram wrote that the traders intended to reestablish the trade.[84]

Charles McLatchy, Spalding's superintendent of Florida trade, introduced Bartram to a veteran trader named Job Wiggins. Wiggins, a one-time ferry operator at Rolleston, fathered six children by his black wife, Anna Gallum, and earned a reputation for honesty and reliability.[85] Bartram grew to like Wiggins, and the feeling seemed reciprocal. Of all the traders, he considered Wiggins "the most intelligent and willing to oblige me." Most of the traders, a hardened and dissipated lot, must have wondered about their fellow traveler who preferred drawing pictures of birds rather than shooting them and who spent so much time scribbling in his ledger. Scribble he did, filling his pad with descriptions of birds, lizards, snakes, fish, turtles, and all manner of plants, in short enjoying himself immensely. Emotion he could not reveal to his companions he put in his book, as he did on the first morning of the expedition: "Hark! The musical savanna cranes, ere the chirping sparrow flirts from her grassy couch, or the glorious sun gilds the tops of the Pines, spread their expansive wings, leave their lofty roosts, and repair to the ample plain."[86]

Bartram's description of the Cowkeeper's town of Cuscowilla provides students of Indian life valuable insights. Young people greeted the traders, led them to the chief's house, one larger than the rest and flying a flag. The Cowkeeper greeted them with the usual Creek hospitality, sat them down, and passed the pipe and drink. After McLatchy explained the purpose of their mission to the chief, he introduced Bartram and his reason for being part of the entourage. The Cowkeeper grasped the idea immediately and gave Bartram the nickname Pug Puggy, or the Flower Hunter. Another person might not have rejoiced at the name, but Bartram seemed delighted.[87]

Bartram noticed that some of the villagers showed the influence of Spanish civilization, even to the point of wearing Christian medals, and speaking Spanish. The fact should not be surprising, given that Spanish occupation of Florida ended only a decade earlier. More unusual was the presence of Yamassee slaves—unusual because the Yamassees had been driven into Florida by the Carolinians almost six decades ago. Once proud warriors, these people waited upon the chief "with abject fear."[88]

The traders camped that night at one of Bartram's favorite places, the Alachua Savanna, an open plain on which cattle, horses, and deer grazed, intermingled with flocks of turkeys, communities of cranes, and a myriad of other birds and where a clear little lake with its golden blossoms nearby added contrast. Bartram expressed awe at the sight: "How is the mind agitated and bewildered, at being thus, as it were, placed on the borders of a new world."[89] Bartram's sensitivity to and appreciation of the natural world is one of his most attractive qualities and has inspired some members of later generations to regard nature with greater respect. (The Alachua Savannah is now Payne's Prairie State Preserve. Although turkeys still inhabit the place, almost impenetrable palmetto growth crowds out most wildlife.)

The next morning the party encountered a group of Indians rounding up the Cowkeeper's cattle for a grand barbecue celebrating the traders' meeting with the headmen of the region. The conference took place on the main square and turned out to be heavier on ceremony than substance, but with the practical consequence of the resumption of regular trade.

Bartram had time to look about him and describe the town with its thirty families or so, each with two huts, one divided into a kitchen and a bedroom, the other an apartment for receiving guests and a storeroom. Their buildings ranged around a square, carefully swept, and the village itself was clean of litter and filth. The people deposited their trash away from the town. That evening, while Bartram worked at his drawings in camp, the traders consorted with their women friends in the town. These liaisons served economic as well as amorous ends. The temporary wives became partners in commerce and protected the interests of the traders.[90]

The traders spent another day near Cuscowilla rounding up horses. Bartram and Wiggins explored the area, Wiggins regaling him with stories of the

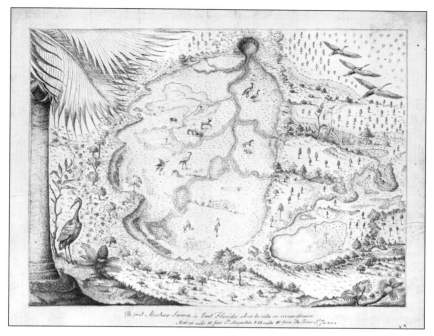

The small Alachua Savana in East Florida above 15 miles in circumference. Near 60 miles W from St Augustin. V 44 miles N from the River St Juan.

Bartram's representation of his favorite place in Florida, the Alachua Savannah, now Payne's Prairie, south of Gainesville.

Courtesy of the American Philosophical Society, Philadelphia

happy times when many people inhabited the region and the villages competed with each other in rough and tumble ball plays. They came upon a herd of deer, and Wiggins instinctively reached for his rifle. Bartram argued briefly to spare the animal, but as he said, the hunter "would not yield to my philosophy."[91] Wiggins brought down a splendid buck with one shot.

The main attraction of the locale for Bartram, the Great Sink, so astonished him that he achieved new heights of hyperbole in describing its "infundibuliform cavities."[92] Various streams flowed into this lake and sank into the vast underground caverns honeycombing the Florida peninsula. Swarms of alligators feasted on the fish congregating there.

With their herd of horses the traders returned to Spalding's lower store. Bartram learned that he had received letters from Charlestown, but because the letters had been addressed to Lieutenant Governor Moultrie, they were being held for him at Governor Tonyn's plantation some forty miles upriver. Bartram immediately set out on a two-day voyage in his little sailing vessel, met neither Moultrie nor Tonyn, but collected his letters. The September 4 note from Fothergill, which Chalmers held for two months until he learned of Bartram's whereabouts, pleased him greatly. It confirmed the fact that the good doctor had actually received the first shipment, never a certain thing, and that Fothergill seemed satisfied with his work. The doctor suggested that William keep a journal noting shrubs and animals.[93] William had thought of that himself. Another Fothergill letter by way of Chalmers, written January 7, 1774, accompanied a large box with tin canisters for Bartram to use for his specimens and paper for his drawings.[94] If Dr. Fothergill meant for William to forward seeds of living plants in the box, he should have said so more plainly. Bartram would continue to send drawings and dried plants in the happy conviction that the doctor approved. "These letters gave me great satisfaction," he noted in the journal intended for Fothergill's eyes. A follow-up letter from Chalmers, dated May 17, 1774, did recommend that William pay more attention to using proper botanical terms and to collect more seeds.[95]

When Bartram returned to Spalding's store he found the place excited about the latest news, brought down by runners from the Lower Creek country. Headmen had been summoned to Tallassee by Emistisiguo. Great confusion prevailed, but it seemed that most of the leaders made up their minds that the Cowetas must give up their guilty warriors in order to restore the trade. The same runner, and the Seminoles who came south with him, said that the murderers of the Magee party had been put to death to satisfy the governors and superintendent.[96]

Bartram's reference to the intense interest stirred by the news reveals that he traveled in a coherent frontier, where events in one part had an impact on all the others. The infrequency of his references to contemporary events obscures the reality of his daily communication with persons caught up in these happenings. If he chose not to discuss the concerns of his companions, except by allegory, it was not because he was isolated or uninformed. He knew about troubling events that surrounded him; he preferred to describe more edifying and enduring subjects of natural history.

Emistisiguo effectively dominated the important meeting at Tallassee. The Mortar, who might have challenged his authority, acquiesced in the necessity of sacrificing the leaders of the Wrightsborough raids. Coweta caused the trouble and Coweta must suffer, no matter how important their guilty men were. If Oktulgi, the culprit who initiated the attack on the White family, belonged to the Tiger clan, so did Emistisiguo, and the clan would not protect him. Blue Salt, the Cusseta King, caused one of the perpetrators, a man of his own village, to be put to death. A party of Cussetas, together with warriors of other villages, apprehended the three Cowetas who had been marked for execution. Even as they prepared to put all three to death, the White King of Euffalies intervened with the dramatic statement that a runner from Galphin's Old Town on the Ogeechee had just brought word that the death of Oktulgi would be retribution enough; no more lives need be exacted. The assembled headmen decided that Oktulgi must die and that the other two, Houmachta and Sophia, be banished. One of the Cussetas shot defiant Oktulgi, an unfortunate, misplaced shot that fatally wounded the warrior but caused him to linger in agony for four days. The dying man called upon his relatives to avenge his death upon the "Virginians," the white intruders, and not to rest until all had been killed.[97] The warrior's last message demonstrates his motivation. He did not choose to die as a renegade; he preferred to give his life as a nativist. He meant that his death should be a protest against white encroachment and in particular against the cession of 1773.

Emistisiguo notified Wright of the execution of the one and the banishment of the other two. If they did further mischief, Wright should not hold the nation responsible.[98] Other headmen pleaded for the resumption of trade. Wright received a talk from the Pumpkin King of Eusitchees, signed also by the headmen of Hichitas, Palachicola, Oconees, and Okmulgees, stating that they had put to death "one of our great warriors" as well as another man for the murders at St. Joseph's Bay. Was that not satisfaction enough?[99]

No, Wright declared, one death would not give satisfaction; seventeen whites and two blacks had been killed by the raiders. Wright reminded his visitors that in Savannah, Emistisiguo and Alleck had agreed on four lives as well as one other for the Florida killings. Any fewer would encourage reckless young men to take up the hatchet. Wright agreed that John Stuart should make that reply to the Creek headmen. Stuart did so, as tactfully as he could, in a talk to Emistisiguo. He took the precaution of sending another talk to the Mortar, thanking him for his role in containing the crisis.[100] Stuart had expected the Mortar to lead the opposition to the recent cession. Perhaps because Ouconnostotah had declined to form a Cherokee-Creek alliance, the Mortar deferred to Emistisiguo and the pro-British party. However, he remained suspicious of the land-hungry whites and sought allies among his French friends in Spanish

New Orleans.[101] He hoped that they would help bring the Choctaw war to an end, then provide an alternate source of trade. The plan might have worked, and at least it showed a bold, creative mind at work. Unfortunately, as he and eighty Upper Creeks, most from his Okchoys town, made their way down the Alabama River on their way to secure peace with the Choctaws, they were ambushed by thirty warriors of that nation. David Taitt reported that the Mortar had been wounded and ungraciously added, "I heartily wish it would carry him out of this world."[102] In far-off Boston, with his own myriad of troubles, Gen. Thomas Gage echoed Taitt's wish: "If the Mortar's wounds should carry him off you will be saved much trouble."[103] From the perspective of his own people, the Mortar died a hero, desperately seeking innovative ways to stem the tide of Anglo-Americans.

The execution of Oktulgi had other repercussions. His relative Escochabey the Young Lieutenant openly consorted with the Spanish, even traveling to Havana in an attempt to increase the clandestine trade to the gulf coast of Florida.[104] A disgruntled band of Cowetas, possibly including the outlawed Houmachta and Sophia, went to the Cherokee town of Tugaloo, a restive village since the murder of the two youths by Hezekiah Collins. They threatened the life of Alexander Cameron, whom they accused of sending bad talks to Stuart.[105] Just as white authorities could not bring Collins to justice, the Creeks could not apprehend Houmachta and Sophia. The breakdown of order portended a bloody ethnic war.

In this context of frontier tension, Bartram pursued his Florida explorations.

V

These accounts were agreeable and enlivened my hopes
of having yet an oppertunity of travelling with safety in
this wild savage part of America.
Bartram, "Report to Fothergill"

The report of Emistisiguo's May 23 congress encouraged Bartram to set out for Spalding's upper store on the west side of the river five miles above Lake George, described by a Florida historian as "the southernmost outpost of British East Florida."[106] In his little vessel Bartram followed the larger traders' boat laden with supplies for the store, innocently or deliberately in violation of the trade ban. The journey began pleasantly as they passed Mount Hope, so named by John Bartram when it was an orange grove, now an indigo plantation. They stayed the first night with a former trader named Kean at Mount Royal. Bartram mused about the contrast between the wild appearance of Mount Royal when he and his father visited the place and its present cultivated state, and he regretted the change. He prayed that his fellow men would have the necessary wisdom and charity befitting those who had dominion over all creatures.[107]

The river opened into wind-swept Lake George, and the travelers had to seek shelter on a convenient island. While the traders fretted, the busy botanist explored the island and listed the "many curious shrubs," including a variety of lantana, a rambling vine he called a "convolvulus," several species of hibiscus, and others. The next morning he set sail, trailing the larger craft across Lake George and reentering the river without incident. They camped at Cedar Point, a bay in the river. He went wandering while the traders gathered firewood. Again he fell under the spell of "these sublime enchanting scenes of primitive nature." Later he went hunting with "his companion, the trader" Job Wiggins and returned to an evening meal of trout and turkey. Bartram loved it: "Our situation was like that of the primitive state of man, peaceable, contented, and sociable, the simple and necessary calls of nature being satisfied. We were altogether as brethren of one family, strangers to envy, malice and rapine."[108] Reading such scenes, no wonder the European romantics found fodder for their glorification of natural man.

The next day they completed their journey to the remote upper store, where Bartram lodged for several days and witnessed a curious case of spousal harassment. The resident trader lived with a beautiful young Seminole woman, the daughter of a chief named White Captain, who camped nearby. Bartram described the trader as genteel, well bred, amiable, honest, and industrious—in short as something of a paragon. He had fallen hopelessly in love with "this little charmer" who gradually drained him of all his possessions and distributed them among her relatives. Now poor, emaciated, and distracted, he attempted to drown his sorrows in liquor. Not even her father, White Captain, could reform her conduct toward the unfortunate man. Bartram learned the sad story from Job Wiggins, who heard it from the chief himself, with the trader present and both of them, father and son-in-law, shedding tears. The fact that her own people condemned her dishonesty demonstrated to Bartram that the same divine principle operated in Indian society as in that of so-called civilized people. Wiggins succeeded the distracted trader as chief factor at the store.[109]

Bartram met a Mr. Bernard, agent to Lord Beresford, who invited him to visit him at the plantation where he worked as overseer. The place lay sixty miles farther upriver. Bartram readily agreed and made most of the trip alone.[110] The second evening brought him to the shore of Lake Dexter. As he pulled his boat up on the shore of the promontory where he intended to camp, he noticed that a crowd of alligators swarmed about the entrance of his little harbor and, to his dismay, that he had no provisions with him. Bartram decided to risk paddling his boat through the milling reptiles to the open water of a lagoon, where he could fish for trout. He did not take his gun "lest I might lose it overboard in case of a battle" and went armed only with a club. Paddling furiously, he broke through the first line of alligators, but then several huge ones attacked his boat, attempting to overset it. They lifted their heads above the water, "roaring terribly and belching floods of water," and the snapping of their jaws so near his face nearly stunned him. Those crushing jaws might pull him from the fragile boat at any moment. He flailed about with his club, striking animals on one side and the other and winning just enough space to regain the shallow water and the shore.[111]

Relieved that the beasts did not follow him on land, he recovered his confidence and did his fishing in a cove. But then he had to run the gauntlet again to return to his original camping place, keeping close to shore. One twelve footer followed him closely as he pulled his boat up on land. Even a gentle Quaker can stand just so much harassment. Bartram retrieved his gun and shot the monster. Feeling somewhat secure then, he began cleaning his fish. A sound caused him to look up, and almost in his face a huge alligator swung open his jaws. He darted back, and in another minute he would have been dragged off into the water. He pulled his boat farther up on land and started a fire, prepared to watch all night if necessary. With a swamp behind him, he could retreat no farther.[112]

That night, as he revised his notes, he heard a noise from the marsh. He took his gun and advanced toward the sound. Two large bears a hundred yards away came toward him, drawn by the smell of his barbecued fish, and they began to sniff in anticipation of a feast. Bartram fired his flintlock, but it merely flashed. With bears on one side and alligators on the other, the botanist might well have reevaluated his avocation, especially the safety factor involved. To his immense relief the flash of his musket frightened the bears, and they shuffled off through the marsh. Understandably, Bartram slept only fitfully that night.[113]

Next morning he wondered whether or not to hazard a ride through the alligators again. He compared that prospect to running the gauntlet between two rows of Indians armed with knives and firebrands. He decided to give it a try. If proof of the explorer's courage is necessary, these incidents certainly provide it. He admitted to a twinge of fear as he approached the "battle lagoon" and more than a twinge when a huge alligator rushed out of the reeds straight at his boat, dived under the craft, and surfaced with gaping jaws and a frightful noise. Bartram beat it on the snout with his club, and after snorting and plunging furiously, the big beast swam away.[114]

Another person might feel that he had had enough of alligators for a while. Not Bartram. On the shore he saw a cluster of mud hills that he took to be alligator nests. He worded his reaction this way: "These nests being a great curiosity to me, I was determined at all events immediately to land and examine them."[115] His careful investigation allowed him to go on at length in his book about the breeding habits of alligators. After gratifying his curiosity he continued his journey with somewhat less peril until that night, when he camped on the edge of a marsh only to be pestered by more alligators and swarms of mosquitoes. Worn out by lack of sleep and exhausted from working his boat, his enthusiasm for botanizing reached a low ebb.

One more test of his stamina awaited. As he entered Lake Beresford with his destination in sight, a storm struck and quickly gained the force of a hurricane. "What a dreadful rushing and roaring there is everywhere around me," Bartram wrote.[116] He headed for an oak grove only to see it blasted by the wind, huge limbs ripped off and flying about like leaves. He managed to tie his boat to a low hickory tree overhanging a bank. His boat filled with water, and his precious box with its books and specimens floated but to his relief did not leave his flooded vessel. At last the storm subsided, and he could clean out his boat and make his way across the lake to the plantation. Mr. Bernard, agent to Lord Beresford, expressed astonishment that anyone could have crossed the lake in that storm.[117] The plantation itself suffered terribly, most of its outbuildings and slave quarters leveled, its great oak trees blasted, its indigo crop ruined. Bernard proved a good host in spite of the calamity; the next day he escorted Bartram four miles to see the warm, sulphurous waters of Blue Springs and provided a hunter to accompany him part way of his return downriver on the following day.[118]

After parting from his hunter companion, Bartram seemed perfectly recovered from the vexations of his journey upriver and happily collected plant specimens along the way downstream. When he arrived at the upper store, he found his friend Job Wiggins, cheerful and in good health, in charge of the store. A party of Indians "had lately arrived with their hunts to purchase goods."[119] If Bartram failed to comment on this commerce, it must have been because he did not realize that Job Wiggins was guilty of disregarding the frontierwide prohibition of trade. If this had been the only trade violation perpetrated by Spalding and Kelsall, it might well have gone unnoticed. Unfortunately for the company's reputation, it was not an isolated incident.

Bartram's descent of the St. Johns River went almost serenely compared to the trials of the voyage upriver. He experienced a nervous moment when camped on the shore of Lake George. His broiled trout, the remains of his supper, he had placed safely on a nearby bush, then had fallen asleep beside the bush. He awoke suddenly at midnight, startled by the movement of a large animal. He realized with a start that a wolf had snatched his fish from just over his head. He thanked his guardian angel for directing the wolf to the fish instead of his throat.[120]

Francis Harper dates Bartram's return to the lower store early June 1774. When Charles McLatchy, Spalding's superintendent, announced that his caravan would leave for Talahasochte on the Little St. Johns in the Appalache district of Florida's west coast, Bartram readily agreed to go; he had heard about "the delightful fields and groves of Apalatche."[121] He may not have known that the expedition represented a more flagrant violation of the trade embargo than the small-scale business carried on at the upper store. Their route took them past the now-familiar Alachua Savannah. Bartram commented on the snakes, birds, and shrubs along the way. The hunters shot a crane measuring six feet from toes to extended beak with an eight-foot wing span. Bartram sketched it for Fothergill, and then the bird served as an evening meal for the group. Bartram thought it tasty enough but said, "I shall prefer his seraphic music in the etherial skies."[122]

Within ten miles of Talahosochte they came upon a curious sight, a herd of horses obedient to the shepherding of a single black dog. If one strayed, the dog would head him off and bring him back to the others. In the evening the dog visited his master in Talahasochte, then returned to horse herding. The Little St. Johns River delighted Bartram. Its clear stream flowed out of the mysterious Okefenokee and into the gulf a few miles distant. Bartram soon recorded another violation of the restriction on trade. The Cuban-based Spanish fishermen dried their fish along the west coast. Bernard Romans, in his book about Florida, exaggerated by stating that "the whole of the west coast of East Florida" was covered with fishermen's huts and stakes for their nets.[123] The thirty or more Spanish vessels that came here annually brought trade goods for the Lower Creeks and Seminoles though such commerce violated the British navigation acts. In fact, a white trader at the Indian town frankly admitted to Bartram that he stocked his store with goods from the Spanish fishing boats and bought them more cheaply than he could get similar things from Augusta or St. Augustine. The Indians of Talahasochte in their big cypress canoes stroked by as many as thirty men, traveled to the Bahamas and to Cuba to obtain supplies. A crew had just returned from such a voyage with liquor, coffee, sugar, and tobacco. One of these adventurers gave Bartram a plug of tobacco that he claimed to have received from Cuba's governor.[124]

Bartram's description of the extent of the Spanish trade in the region would have alarmed officials such as Wright of Georgia and Stuart, the Indian superintendent. At first they seemed unaware of the scale of these clandestine operations. The potential for increased trade with Cuba explains Escochabey's dalliance with Spanish authorities, including his visit to Havana. However, it is unlikely that the Spanish would have risked any extensive overt trade with Britain, master of the seas.

While waiting for the arrival of the chief of Talahasochte, the White King, Bartram inquired if he could explore the river to the coast. An old chief warned him against it. He said that because matters between the whites and Indians had not yet been resolved, the Creek Nation "lately forbid the white People travelling on that coast."[125] Hunting parties of Lower Creeks frequented the region, and the chief could not answer for their conduct. Bartram heeded the advice and limited his exploration to Manatee Springs, some four miles downriver. This natural wonder retains the name today though the manatees are long gone. The clear depths, the subterranean currents, and the myriad of colored fish delight today's tourist, as they did Bartram.[126]

Bartram returned by land to the Indian village, passing vestiges of Spanish occupation. The dinner prepared by the White King proved to be an elaborate affair with three fat barbecued bears as entree. The men feasted in the square, and only when they had finished were women allowed to distribute the remains to the rest of the village people. After passing around the pipe and the black drink, a cassina tea, the company watched dancers go through their rituals by way of entertainment. Then the business of the evening came on, and again Bartram recorded trade illegalities as assiduously as if he were a witness for the prosecution. The White King stressed the fact that all but two of the guilty warriors had been killed, and he hoped that now trade would be resumed. That is precisely why we are here, said McLatchy, or words to that effect. In fact, he had brought goods with him. So the evening ended in a mellow mood of good fellowship. The White King regarded Bartram benevolently and called him one of his own children. The traders departed the next day, after more feasting, with the Indians urging them to hurry back with more supplies.[127]

On the evening after leaving Talahasochte, the traders encountered seven young warriors, elegantly painted and decorated, under the leadership of one of the young headmen of the village. Bartram quoted the chief as calmly stating that one of his favorite wives had gone off with another young warrior, and he intended to cut off both their ears. He was not in such a hurry as to decline an invitation to food and drink. The evening ended in song, some of it with a note of longing indicative of the young chief's mood. Bartram felt moved; "There is a languishing softness and melancholy air in the Indian convivial songs," he wrote, "especially of the amorous class, irresistibly moving, attractive, and exquisitely pleasing, especially in these solitary recesses when all nature is silent."[128] One wonders if the maiden in question would have shared his opinion.

The return to the lower store took them by the Alachua Savannah again. Bartram predicted that those twenty acres or so would one day become one of the most populous and delightful seats on earth. Nearby Gainesville, Florida, represents the reality of his prediction. By July 15 the company had completed the trip because Bartram's letter to Lachlan McIntosh from the lower store bears that date.[129]

In late July, Bartram braved the heat, mosquitoes, and alligators for his second visit to Mr. Bernard at Lake Beresford.[130] When he returned to the lower store sometime in August, he witnessed a scene described by one Florida historian as "undoubtedly one of the most unrestrained bacchanalian revels ever to take place on the shores of the St. Johns River."[131] Bartram used even stronger adjectives to describe the revelry. Readers of his *Travels* might raise eyebrows at his account of the unbridled license of the gathering, but a more astonishing aspect of the event was the sheer boldness of the trade violation.

Forty Lower Creeks under their leader, the Long Warrior, camped near the store. They had visited Tonyn at St. Augustine with promises to fight the Choctaws and had brought away with them kegs of rum as the governor's tokens of friendship. Even these gifts by Tonyn represented a breech of his agreement not to do business with the Indians. The carousals began when some of the traders and packhorse men persuaded the visitors to open their kegs in exchange for trifles. When Indians and whites began drinking, they kept at it for most of ten days until the liquor was gone. Seminole women joined in the festivity; as Bartram observed, they "act without constraint or shame such

Of the many chieftains he met, Bartram's only drawing
is that of the Long Warrior.
Courtesy of the American Philosophical Society, Philadelphia

scenes as they would abhor when sober. . . ."[132] When the rum supply ran low,
the "dejected lifeless sots" would pawn everything they had to get more drink.
This is where the shrewder women profited. The drunken men, each clasping
his own bottle, offered the women a swallow. Some of these females would dis-
charge a mouthful of rum into their own jars that they concealed beneath their
mantles. They later traded their supply of rum for anything the still-thirsty men
possessed. So these women ended the frolic reasonably sober and in possession

of most of the visitors' belongings. Seminole women must have been well known for this ploy because Bernard Bomans described exactly such a scene in his treatise on Florida.[133]

When the Indians sobered sufficiently, their meeting with McLatchy began. The Long Warrior, who remained aloof from the revelers, took a seat along the bench that ran the length of the trading house, his warriors next to him in order of rank. McLatchy, Job Wiggins, the other traders, and Bartram sat on the chief's left, with the botanist sitting next to Wiggins. The Long Warrior began by saying that they could have obtained goods in St. Augustine, but they preferred to get them from their old friend Mr. Spalding. They had nothing to barter for at the moment, but because they were such good friends, the chief assumed that his credit was good. They needed blankets, shirts, and other supplies and would pay after the hunting season. McLatchy observed that he could not extend credit for that length of time; he would need to refer the matter to his employer, Mr. Spalding. The Long Warrior fell into a tantrum, threatening to bring down thunder and lightning as a token of his displeasure. Job Wiggins whispered to Bartram, asking if he understood what the chief said. Bartram replied that he could see that the great man was displeased.[134]

McLatchy, used to these negotiations, said that he knew that the Long Warrior was a great man, terrible to his enemies, and if he wanted to display his marvelous powers, perhaps he should blast that large oak tree just there, pointing. After considering the proposition for a while, the chief became calmer and announced that in view of their long friendship he would withhold his power for the present. McLatchy then struck a bargain: if the visitors could pay for half the goods they wanted, he would extend credit for the rest. As he suspected, the Indians had secreted skins enough to meet this condition. Trading negotiations of this kind usually involved a tacit mutual cheating. The meeting broke up in a general display of satisfaction, marked by feasting and dancing.[135]

A huge rattlesnake interrupted the conviviality by boldly slithering into the Indian camp. Job Wiggins told Bartram that people were asking for Pug Puggy to take the snake away. Modestly, as well as prudently, Bartram declined the invitation. Then three young fellows entered his hut and argued that if Bartram liked to collect natural things, here was a splendid opportunity. Unable to refuse, Bartram picked up a heavy stick and approached the coiled snake as the silent Indians watched. Coming close as he dared, Bartram hurled the stick, luckily striking its head and stunning it. He quickly cut off the head to the applause of his audience. Later the same young men came to thank him and to scratch him, arguing that he was overly heroic and needed to lose some blood, something done to warriors who acted recklessly. Bartram appreciated their concern, but declined the bloodletting. He proceeded to draw the snake's head for Dr. Fothergill. The incident prompted him to write a chapter about snakes, frogs, and birds that he had observed.[136]

He did not say anything about McLatchy's violation of the trade embargo.

VI

The company being busily employed in forming their
packs of leather and loading the vessel. . . .
Harper, *Travels*

The illicit trading so innocently recorded by Bartram created a firestorm of recrimination reverberating around Wright in Savannah, Stuart in Charlestown, Tonyn in St. Augustine, Gage in Boston, and Dartmouth in London. It began in June, when James Spalding shipped a cargo from Frederica to his lower store. Governor Tonyn learned about it, secured a warrant from Chief Justice William Drayton, and dispatched Captain Moncrief to seize the contraband. Accordingly, Moncrief removed 24 rifles, 554 pounds of gunpowder, and 700 pounds of musket balls and deposited the items in the magazine in St. Augustine. On June 27 Governor Tonyn reported the action to Governor Wright with this assurance, "I shall prevent supplies being carried to them [the Indians] and have issued a proclamation for that purpose."[137] As a result, Wright and Stuart assumed that their embargo was being enforced in Florida. On July 7, however, David Taitt wrote Stuart that Spalding and Kelsall were smuggling goods out of Augusta.[138] On August 24 Col. James Grierson of the Augusta militia reported that George Galphin informed him that the value of Spalding's goods amounted to fourteen hundred pounds sterling and that the company had sent seventeen kegs of rum into the nation.[139]

A worried Wright, on September 9 informed Gage that he had received intelligence that private trading was being conducted from the southern part of Georgia to a store on the St. Johns and that "Indians were flocking from all parts of the nation to that store." In no uncertain terms he blamed Tonyn for not enforcing the ban. He felt anxious because he had not heard from the nation and despondent because of the trade infractions. People had been leaving the province ever since the winter alarms; no one dared settle the ceded lands. The entire militia numbered only twenty-six hundred whereas the Creeks had at least four thousand gunmen; "In short, we are in a very dangerous, ticklish situation."[140] Wright convened his council and presented the alarming information to them for their advice. After due consideration that body voted to direct Att. Gen. Anthony Stokes to look into the offenses committed by Spalding and Kelsall and determine to what extent they were liable. Stokes should also advise on a suitable punishment for violating the governor's proclamation.[141]

John Stuart's degree of irritation matched Wright's. In his letter to Gage he used strong language in reference to Spalding and company. "Our efforts have been rendered ineffective by the villainy and avarice of some traders who by the way of the St. Johns River found means of furnishing the Lower Creeks with £1400 worth of goods." Governor Tonyn had merely blocked the shipment of guns and ammunition.[142] David Taitt, still at Augusta, reported that Robert Rae had engaged in illicit trade and had been heard to say that he had no regard for anything Governor Wright might do. These reports caused Capt. Edward Barnard to station his rangers at Wrightsborough and along the Creek trail and to give orders to seize skins or goods that came that way.[143]

Against this background of fear and uncertainty about Indian intentions, a group of those opposed to Lord North's Coercive Acts gathered in Savannah on August 10, 1774. The meeting culminated a month of organizing and agitating that began when South Carolina radicals elected delegates to a Continental Congress on July 8. On July 14 four Savannah residents signed a broadside in the *Georgia Gazette* inviting all parishes to send delegates to a meeting on July 27 to decide on Georgia's course of action. At this session, held in the Tondee Tavern, a committee of thirty was assigned to write a set of resolutions to be voted on by another general meeting on August 10. In spite of Governor Wright's proclamation that such assemblies were unconstitutional, the delegates met and adopted eight resolutions defending Americans' right to petition and to be taxed by representatives only. They declared the closing of the Boston port and suspension of government in Massachusetts unconstitutional acts by the British Parliament. Historian Kenneth Coleman has called these resolutions "the first real statement of revolutionary sentiment in Georgia."[144]

However, revolutionary ardor burned only faintly in Georgia. The delegates to the August meeting, perhaps the most radical of Georgians, unanimously declared their loyalty to the king and could not bring themselves to send representatives to the Continental Congress, a fact that guides at Carpenters' Hall in Philadelphia never fail to mention to this day. The August meeting represented parishes closest to Carolina and farthest removed from the

Indian country, namely St. Johns and Christ Church. The most interesting aspect of the incident is that so many Georgians completely disassociated themselves from the Tondee Tavern resolutions. The *Georgia Gazette* printed counter resolutions from the town and district of Augusta, St. Paul Parish, Kiokee settlements, Broad River settlements, St. George Parish, Queensbor-ough, and the township of Wrightsborough. The St. Paul's resolutions typified the others: "Because the persons who are most active on this occasion are those whose property lies in or near Savannah and, therefore, are not immediately exposed to the bad effects of an Indian war, whereas, the back settlements of this Province, and our Parish in particular would most certainly be laid waste, and depopulated, unless we receive such powerful aid and assistance as none but Great Britain can give. For these and many other reasons, we declare our dissent to all resolutions by which His Majesty's favour and protection might be forfeited."[145] These contra-Savannah resolutions clearly reveal the state of mind of many, perhaps most, Georgians only a year before the violence of the Revolutionary War began. The attitude, and the change in attitude, were inextricably linked to Indian relations. The transplanted Carolina Puritans of St. John Parish understood the attitude of the other Georgians, and their committee, chaired by Lyman Hall, printed a notice in the *Georgia Gazette* chiding their neighbors for worrying about Indians when "the grand question is whether the Parliament has the right to tax the Americans."[146] After a series of comments and responses by each side, a "lover of liberty" had the last word in the December 21, 1774, *Gazette*: "But some will say we should sacrifice everything for the purpose of Boston. When the Indians were cutting our throats, did Boston offer to assist us?"[147]

During this anxious time the Indians broke their silence and relieved the tension. Nine Okfuskee braves walked into Robert Mackay's trading house at the Augusta junction of the Creek and Cherokee trails. Remarkably they had not been observed by any of the outlying residents, by the people at Wrightsborough, by the rangers or any militiamen though they came armed and painted, the exact portrait of a dreaded war party. They walked to within forty yards of Mackay's house before being seen. Their arrival interrupted David Taitt's dinner. He knew several of them and felt suspicious of their motives. One, Cusseje Mico, nephew of the murdered Mad Turkey, asked when his uncle's killer would be punished. Taitt told him that Fee would die when he was caught, a lame excuse by now since no one knew Fee's whereabouts. Two other warriors had been in the party responsible for killing two Wrightsborough residents in 1771. Despite their appearance and Taitt's suspicions, they came bearing a talk for Governor Wright. The nation wanted peace; they would meet the governor's demands and kill Houmachta and Sophia.[148]

The Indian initiative had a galvanic effect. Governor Wright seized upon the opportunity and invited the headmen of the Creek Nation to Savannah for a formal treaty. Nervous backcountry people took heart and began to revert to pre-1773 land schemes. With the Indians suing for peace, would not this be a splendid opportunity to extract the Oconee strip? The rumor that the Indians would be asked for the additional land and that they came prepared to give it up gained currency with surprising speed. The prospect made Governor Wright even more popular in the outlying parishes. John Stuart, greatly relieved by the breaking news and unwilling to leave the denouement to Wright, came over from Charlestown on September 27, 1774. He admitted to General Gage that he had harbored the fear that in an open rupture the Cherokees would have joined the Creeks.[149]

On October 5 Governor Wright dispatched Capt. Samuel Elbert's Grenadier Company to escort Emistisiguo and seventy Upper Creeks into town. The Pumpkin King and the Chiaha King brought fifty Lower Creeks with them to Savannah. On October 18 the talks began. The Indians readily agreed to kill Houmachta and Sophia if they ever found them; the names of the two outlaws thus became part of the formal treaty. They also agreed to return any runaway slaves and to break up the Creek town on the Oconee. Because they had agreed to these terms at their May meeting in Tallassee, and in fact had already burned down the Oconee town, it is difficult to see the treaty as a capitulation. If they came willing to give up the land between the Ogee-chee and Oconee, they were not asked to do so. On his part Governor Wright announced the opening of trade. He and Stuart rejoiced at their diplomatic triumph.[150] Wright's announcement of the good news to Lord Dartmouth contained no hint of the nagging doubts of the past months: "Thus your lordship will see that I was right in my plan and that firmness and perseverance blessed and assisted by the Hand of Providence have obtained the wished for success."[151]

But the jubilation did not extend to the more aggressive backcountrymen who had hoped for a land-for-peace agreement. Instead of relief they felt anger. A hothead who pretended to be a "practitioner of physick" by name of George Wells represented those people. Wells was such a colorful character and so influential in shaping backcountry opinion that a word of introduction is in order. George happened to be brother to Bartram's friend Humphrey Wells, who lived near Augusta; both were sons of Dr. Richard Wells of Queen Anne's County, Maryland, and both had studied medicine and went by the title of doctor. However, they differed radically in temperament and personal history. George Wells deserted his wife, Marian Boyd Wells, in Chowan County, North Carolina, and by 1771 acquired property in St. George Parish, Georgia.[152] His deserted wife's father took care of her financially but stipulated that George Wells would not get a penny of her property.[153]

During the Revolutionary War, George Wells would become as obnoxious to the McIntoshes as he was to his father-in-law. His enemies accused him of biting off a neighbor's ear and carrying away another man's wife, leaving her two children to the care of her hapless husband.[154] Wells continued to accumulate property. As the owner of four slaves, he acquired 100 additional acres in St. George Parish and 150 acres in St. Paul, including a lot in Augusta.[155]

He seems to have been attuned to the pulse of the people generally, even if indifferent to the practice of medicine. His name led the list of petitioners of St. George Parish disavowing the Tondee Tavern resolutions and declaring loyalty to the king.[156] Wells accurately sensed the disappointment felt by many of his neighbors who were upwardly mobile in their aspirations, with land as the great object of their ambitions. He expressed this disappointment in another remarkable petition that he organized in 1776. On behalf of persons living on the frontiers of Georgia who were exposed to the "barbarous attacks" of the Creek Indians, he objected to the Indian trade. He argued that the trade "tends to bring those savages down into the settlements," and (in a wild exaggeration) the Indians "seldom return without either committing murder or robbery, and generally both." Furthermore, only a few profited from the trade; most opposed it. Worse still, his petition argued, the traders selfishly interfered in Sir James Wright's conference with the Indians in October 1774. The Indians came to Savannah ready to cede the Oconee strip and even made a "certain offer." The backcountry Georgians badly needed the Oconee with its connection to the Altamaha and the newly laid-out port town of Brunswick. In their view the Oconee had been formed by nature "for the benefit and advantage of the inhabitants." The Indian offer was rejected by the governor, Wells believed, because the selfish Indian traders objected to pushing the Indian boundary farther west and losing the trade to Pensacola and Mobile. The petition ended by recommending that an attempt be made "to exterminate and rout those savages out of their nation." He and his fellow petitioners stood ready to help in "so desirable a purpose." The letter was addressed to Gen. Charles Lee, then commander of the Continental troops in the Southern Department.[157]

Governor Wright's October treaty represents a crucial watershed in the history of the American Revolution on the southern frontier. Backcountry people had been loyal as long as the royal government seemed to be the agency for the acquisition of land and even more so when the governor had rangers out interdicting Indian trade. With the dawning perception that the royal government preferred maintaining the trade to acquiring land, the people turned to an alternative authority. Perhaps the new Continental Congress would help dispose of the Indians and make the land available. Such was the gist of the Wells's petition.[158]

One of the Savannah opponents of the British ministry explained the critical shift in public opinion to a member of Congress. The colony had reasons to be cautious in its opposition to Parliament because many officials had been appointed by Parliament. Added to that, the Indian war threatened and "we had just applied home for Troops." Now that obstacle had been removed, and "Two of our back parishes which made the most noise, are now come over to us." He had no doubt that the delegates scheduled to meet in Savannah in January would vote to join the Continental Association banning trade with Britain.[159] Wells's opponents accused him of following the prevailing winds, stating that his name led those of the loyal petitioners against the Tondee Tavern resolutions, but "finding the patriotic party prevail, he put about and apparently changed sides" because he could personally profit from the change.[160] The significant point here is not so much that Wells changed but that he reflected the popular shift in backcountry attitude.

Were the Creeks willing to cede the Oconee strip? Probably not, because the bitterness of the 1773 cession still lingered so strongly throughout the Creek country. However, a bizarre aftermath of the October 1774 treaty lends some credence to the rumor. Jonathan Bryan entertained some twenty of the Creek visitors in Savannah for the treaty and persuaded them to cede an enormous tract in northern East Florida to him. The land in question happened to coincide with that lately explored by William Bartram, from Alachua to the west coast. In fact, Bryan went to Florida to survey the region during the same November 1774 that Bartram left Florida. They might have crossed each other's path coming and going.[161] Bartram knew Bryan, even lodged at Bryan's Brampton plantation. He knew about Bryan's "grand diversified schemes" for land development, an apparent reference to the bold bid for most of northern

Florida.[162] Bryan had been a major actor in colonial Georgia since his services to Oglethorpe, and his acquaintance with the Lower Creeks began even before the arrival of Oglethorpe. Bryan had become a champion at the gentleman's game of land acquisition, and he had his sights on the Florida region since at least 1770. Bryan's biographer, Alan Gallay, treats the attempted acquisition as a deliberate attempt on the part of the Creek Nation to acquire an alternative source of trade to the British.[163] There are problems with this interpretation, however. The Creeks would have to know that there would be a revolution and that Bryan would not be on the British side. The supposition credits them with a perspicacity most Georgians did not have. It also assumes that Florida's Tonyn could not have prevented Bryan from trading. Finally it argues that Bryan's Indian friends spoke for the nation. Emistisiguo, who had represented the nation in Savannah, did not dicker with Bryan, nor did the Pumpkin King of the Lower Creeks. The Mortar (whose fatal encounter with the Choctaws had not yet happened) would certainly have opposed another cession. Like the Mortar, Escochabey searched for alternative sources of trade that did not involve land cessions. Nor were the Seminoles represented at Bryan's gathering though Bryan hoped to get the Cowkeeper's consent. Wright reported that the signers said that Bryan deceived them; they thought he only wanted a bit of land to live on and raise cattle.[164] After repudiating their agreement with Bryan, some of them were persuaded by Bryan to repudiate their repudiation. As the historian Kathryn Braund puts it, "When later confronted with Bryan's deed, those who had signed the lease claimed to have been hoodwinked. When they returned and signed a second lease, after receiving more presents and rum, perhaps they intended to hoodwink Bryan."[165]

David Taitt expressed the opinion of most British officials that "Bryan must certainly be mad."[166] According to Taitt, Bryan had bragged that he would soon have Wright sent back to England. The Indians involved in Bryan's schemes urged Governor Wright to hurry and warn the Cowkeeper that Bryan wanted his land.[167] Tonyn in Florida seemed even more exasperated than Wright and Stuart, especially because Wright hinted that members of Tonyn's government were involved in the scheme. Tonyn called the plot a "monstrous imposition" and a "gross violation of the Majesty's Proclamation." He assured his superior that if he had known about the complicity of Florida officials, he would have put a swift end to the affair. He issued a proclamation condemning Bryan's lease, then directed his attorney general to make out a writ for Bryan's arrest.[168] Tonyn then blamed Drayton for his reluctance to sign a warrant for Bryan's arrest and next for warning Bryan that an arrest was impending. Bryan escaped to Georgia. The feud between Florida's governor and attorney general grew heated. Tonyn suspended Drayton; London reinstated him; Tonyn found other reasons to suspend him again whereupon Drayton gave up the contest and resigned.[169]

The strangest twist in this curious episode is that Bryan's initiative gave Governor Wright a new idea. If the Indians were willing to give Bryan land, perhaps they would be willing to yield the coveted Oconee strip in exchange for a pardon to Houmachta and Sophia. He went so far as to suggest to Stuart that Taitt arrange to have the Indians announce the plan as their own. Wright thought so well of his notion that he began to plan another Indian congress.[170]

In retrospect Wright's proposal seems wild, and even at the time Stuart thought it a terrible idea for the excellent reason, as he confided to Gage, that the "Indians can have no such powerful motive of quarreling with us as our insatiable avidity for land."[171] However, the plan would have been welcomed by the George Wells crowd in the unlikely event that they knew about it. From deep in the Flint River country, Stuart's deputy, Samuel Thomas, indicated that the idea of land for the lives of the troublesome two Indians had support among the Lower Creeks. Meanwhile the prince of outlaws, Houmachta, conveyed his own declaration of war to Governor Wright. He intended to kill every white man who used the upper trading path out of Augusta.[172] Gen. Thomas Gage, with his own troubles in Boston mounting to a climax, put a stop to any further discussion about land cessions. Wright's proposal about land for lives would set a bad precedent, he said, and that was that.[173]

The October treaty and its aftermath provided the context for Bartram's return to Georgia in November 1774. As a thoughtful, sensitive person, he might have reflected on how history seemed to follow him about: the cession treaty in Augusta in June 1773, the marking of the line in July followed by the tragic deaths of the Tugaloo youths, the Coweta retaliation at Wrightsborough, the trade embargo and Spalding's violation of that policy, the resumption of trade as a result of the October 1774 treaty, Bryan's effort to obtain the same Florida lands Bartram explored and described—all these events linked together and leading to what? Perhaps he would learn the answer from the McIntoshes of Darien. He loaded four large boxes of specimens with his precious trunk aboard Spalding's trading vessel, bade farewells to Job Wiggins and Charles McLatchy, and made his way to Sunbury.[174]

Coincidentally, Sunbury and St. John Parish formed the core of the revolutionary movement in Georgia.

118

VII

On my arrival at Frederica I was again, as usual, friend-
ly received and accommodated by the excellent J. Spald-
ing, Esq.

Harper, *Travels*

Governor Wright or Superintendent Stuart would not have characterized
James Spalding as being excellent in anything but mischief making. His clandestine trade nearly wrecked the governor's peace strategy. William Bartram
knew about the troubled course of Indian relations; he waited until the October treaty between Wright and the Creeks to resume his botanizing in the
interior. However, by principle and disposition, Bartram refrained from judg-
ing the motives and even the conduct of his associates. Although he encountered many scoundrels, he named none. So he perceived James Spalding,
presently in disfavor with the royal government and soon to be proscribed by
the Whig revolutionaries, as "the excellent James Spalding." Like the other
Darien Scots, Spalding regarded the Philadelphian as one of the clan, and
Bartram felt so much at home among them that he did not consider his interludes at Darien part of his adventures. Bartram returned to Frederica in
November 1774. On March 26, 1774, Margery McIntosh Spalding had presented James with their first child, Thomas. So the healthy bairn cheered the
household.[175]

Bartram took up his old quarters in Darien after greeting the rest of the
McIntoshes. He had plenty to do catching up on the notes that later became
the raw material for his *Travels*, and he had the leisure to improve upon his
sketches of birds, alligators, snakes, and sinkholes for the collection of Dr.
Fothergill. If he had hoped for the tranquillity of his previous winter sojourn,
however, he was disappointed. For the next decade, and even longer, the Georgia low country remained a troubled region.

Nearby, St. John seethed with revolutionary fervor. Their hotspurs had
grown increasingly impatient with the Indian obsession that gripped the rest of
Georgia. A spokesman for the Liberty Society, a radical revolutionary group,
later accused St. Andrew Parish of weakness in the cause of liberty.[176] A defender of St. Andrew stated that the Scots need apologize to no one for their love of
liberty. He argued that the people of St. Andrew thought for themselves whereas the men of St. John followed a party line, "for it is pretty well known that
they are unanimous upon every occasion, though it should be to plunder and

rob the best friends to the American cause, and distress women and chil-dren."[177] On December 1, 1774, St. John voted to join the continental ban on trade with England.[178] The parish elected Lyman Hall to the Continental Congress and collected two hundred barrels of rice for the people of Boston suffering from the closing of their port.[179] During the same month Button Gwinnett of St. John and George Wells of Augusta began to organize a coalition in opposition to the more conservative gentlemen of Savannah's Christ Church Parish.[180]

If Bartram liked "philosophical discussions," he must have loved St. Andrew. Men and women of that parish had to deliberate on their course of action as the crisis loomed. From conviction and tradition the Scots opposed attempts by English monarchs to rule arbitrarily. Lachlan McIntosh called himself a "mad Republican."[181] If fate had not placed William Bartram in a nest of republicans who counted him a colleague, would he have cast his lot with the revolutionary faction? It is an interesting question in light of his opposition to war and violence.[182] Like all such historical ifs, it is unanswerable. The fact is that he did follow the McIntoshes into military action in 1776 and he did become convinced that the Revolution represented the unfolding of a grand providential plan for the betterment of mankind.

The Darien debate about liberty inevitably touched upon the issue of African slavery. Although Bartram once owned slaves and as recently as 1773 had accepted a slave and paid off a debt by selling her, he disliked the whole business of slavery.[183] Later he scribbled a passionate antislavery appeal to the American people, warning that the perpetuation of such injustice would forfeit the continuing blessings of Providence upon this country.[184]

Slaveholders lived in a state of constant concern about the possibility of a slave rising. Bartram's penchant for happening along just as events of historical importance occurred held true yet once again. Soon after his return to Darien, the most serious slave revolt in colonial Georgia took place in St. Andrew Parish. The *Georgia Gazette* of December 7, 1774, reported that some slaves belonging to a Captain Morris killed their overseer, his wife, a carpenter named Wright, and an unnamed boy. Then they attacked the plantation of Angus McIntosh, appealing to his slaves to join them. When McIntosh tried to stop them, they left him seriously wounded. At least one of McIntosh's slaves joined the party and marched upon Roderick M'Leod's house with deadly intent. M'Leod's son saw them coming and challenged them. A scuffle ensued; the lad broke the arm of Angus McIntosh's slave, but the others killed the boy.

They left Roderick M'Leod a casualty near death and continued on their way. By that time the militia of the parish responded to the emergency and apprehended the runaways. Unlike murders committed by Indians that required death for death, the magistrates of St. Andrew demanded two lives for the five whites killed and two severely hurt.[185]

Nothing like it had happened before. The people of the parish worried about it and talked about it and finally determined to draft a resolution. They remembered that in January 1739 the founders of Darien addressed a petition to the trustees taking issue with the Savannah request for the introduction of slavery. "It's shocking to human Nature," they declared, "that any Race of Mankind and their Posterity, should be sentenced to perpetual Slavery; nor in Justice can we think otherwise of it, than they are thrown among us to be our Scourge one day or another, for our sins; and as Freedom to them must be as dear to us, What a scene of Horror it must bring about."[186] Despite their firm statement, they acquired slaves, and now they had their horror. It is impossible to imagine William Bartram haranguing a public gathering on course of action and equally impossible to picture him mute in private discussions.

The result of the prolonged parochial discussions was the adoption of a resolution drawn up by a committee headed by Lachlan McIntosh. His brother-in-law George Threadcraft sat on the committee as did his nephew John McIntosh. Such a compatible committee would not have disagreed with the chairman on any major point. The resolutions, adopted on January 12, 1775, expressed sympathy with the people of Boston, objected to the absentee ownership of parish lands by British speculators, opposed the payment of salaries of local officials by Parliament, and agreed with the resolutions of the Continental Congress. Those sentiments, in the general climate of the time, might have been expected. The fifth resolution must have surprised many and delighted William Bartram. The parish, by its approval of the resolution, declared its "detestation and abhorrence of the unnatural practice of slavery, a practice founded in injustice and cruelty, and highly dangerous to our liberties, debasing part of our fellow creatures below men." Therefore the parish resolved to "use our utmost to end slavery."[187]

The resolution rang like a clarion call equating freedom from servile work with freedom from British tyranny. Such a forthright denunciation of slavery was seldom voiced by an individual in the plantation South let alone by an entire district of planters. But the Darien resolution did not speak for the hundreds of new Georgians who coveted Indian lands for the express purpose of establishing plantations worked by slaves. The biographer of Lachlan McIntosh, Harvey H. Jackson, and the historian of slavery in colonial Georgia, Betty Wood, agree that McIntosh and his committee might have had a less altruistic motive for their declaration. Alarmed by the recent slave rising, the Darien petitioners worried that slaves might take advantage of the political turmoil and stage another revolt. In that light the statement might be seen as an attempt to retain the allegiance of the slaves. Coincidentally, within a few months the rumor that the Crown meant to enlist the slaves against rebellious masters swept through South Carolina and Georgia, and in Virginia, Gov. Lord Dunmore gave credence to the rumor by appealing to slaves to enlist in a loyal regiment.[188]

Still it is difficult to imagine William Bartram as party to a conspiratorial scheme to maintain slavery by a pseudodenunciation of slavery. Although he could overlook failings in his companions, he would not likely have retained his admiration for his father figure, McIntosh, nor would he have described their philosophic discussion in such rapturous language. In the discussions he so warmly remembered, his voice would have upheld idealism. If the discussion turned to the issue of slavery, as it must have in January 1775, Bartram would have favored its extinction.

There is little doubt that the slaves of St. Andrew Parish would have embraced the antislavery resolution. William Bartram would have become acquainted with two of the workers; according to McIntosh, "they are the most valuable I own." The two, Ben and Glasgow by name, were skilled carpenters, shingle makers and boatmen, the type of master workmen essential to the smooth operation of a plantation. Ben, a stout, strong fellow of forty, had learned Spanish as well as English. Among his other duties Ben made the barrels for the rice harvest. Glasgow, a tall, slim individual of about twenty-five, neat in his habits, learned the same skills. Both men were natives of the Congo country. Within a few weeks of Bartram's departure from Darien, the two tried to escape only to be captured in Charlestown.[189]

John Houstoun, a neighboring planter and future governor of Georgia, wrote to McIntosh in June 1775 that his "Negroes were up to their old pranks." He determined to "ship off" Jacob and Pompey. Houstoun had a brand made to mark his slaves, the better to recognize them when they ran away.[190] Clearly the white inhabitants of St. Andrew were not the only ones having thoughts of freedom.

Antislavery rhetoric did not extend to Savannah, where delegates gathered for the January 18 opening of the assembly. Every parish sent its delegates to the session. However, the extralegal Provincial Congress, scheduled to meet the same day, drew only five delegations. The St. John group attempted to prod the others into a more radical stance by circulating a resolution calling upon other parishes to emulate the example of St. John and declare for the Continental Association ending trade with England. Until they should do so St. John would remain aloof. Two days later, on January 20, Lyman Hall, on behalf of St. John, chided the others for not replying to the first message. A committee of the Provincial Congress replied that each parish delegate had to answer to his own constituents "and therefore ought not to let any other man or set of men judge for him."[191] Rebuffed, the St. John people resolved that the congress did not represent Georgia and certainly did not represent St. John and they would have nothing more to do with it.

Without St. John the congress proceeded to the adoption of a watered-down version of the association. The resolution delayed the effective beginning of the ban on imports from Britain until March 15 and exports until December 1, 1775. Goods for the Indian trade were specifically exempted from the general boycott. Before adjourning, the congress elected Archibald Bulloch, Noble W. Jones, and John Houstoun to the Continental Congress. The three later wrote to the Continental Congress, explaining why they felt they could not attend that body. Members of the Provincial Congress hoped that the sitting house of assembly, where all the parishes had representation, would ratify their resolutions. However, Governor Wright, who, "either treacherously informed or shrewdly suspecting the step," adjourned the assembly before it could take action. Whether the House would have adopted the association they could not be sure because the "importers were mostly against any interruption and the consumers very much divided."[192] Therefore, because they could not speak for a united province, they would not go to Philadelphia.

Robert Mackay and other Indian traders went to Savannah to protect their interests. Mackay informed his wife that he had attended a meeting of merchants in Savannah who voted to continue shipping goods to Britain until their debts had been paid. He had a poor opinion of the radicals in the Provincial Congress who favored an immediate boycott: "We have had strange doings here among the delegates who I believe will break up greater fools than they met."[193] Mackay and his friends who did business with the Indians had reason to be concerned. The trade, so recently renewed after the October treaty, could be curtailed by the Continental Association. Another interruption of the supply of goods would certainly be interpreted by the Indians as an unfriendly act.

The South Carolina revolutionary General Committee intended to force Georgia's compliance with the association. In a severe reprimand of February 8, 1775, Carolina deemed Georgians "unworthy of the rights of freemen" and even "inimical to the liberties of their country." Therefore, Georgia would be punished by a trade embargo.[194] Even before receiving Carolina's condemnation, Lyman Hall spoke for St. John in begging Carolina to regard his parish "as a distant Parish of your own Province" and to continue trading with Sunbury.[195] The Carolina committee commiserated with St. John's unhappy situation but pointed out that St. John was part of Georgia and, like it or not, would have to suffer with the rest of the province.[196] St. John completed its own isolation by cutting off trade connections with other Georgia parishes, and it sent Lyman Hall as its delegate to the Continental Congress. Congress proved to be kinder than Carolina; it welcomed Hall on May 13, 1775, without a cavil.[197]

In its general prohibition of trade with Georgia, the Carolina committee took care to exempt produce from Georgia plantations owned by Carolinians. That exemption meant that Henry Laurens might collect the harvest from his New Hope and Broughton Island plantations. Not surprisingly, Henry Laurens sat on the Carolina committee.

4

The Cherokee Country

I

Learning that the honourable Henry Lawrens, Esq had
a large ship loading at Sunbury for Liverpool, I deter-
mined to embrace so favourable an offer for conveying
my collections to Europe.

Harper, *Travels*

Henry Laurens, a man of moderation, returned to Charlestown on December 11, 1774, after a thirty-nine-month sojourn in Europe to find the city caught up in a frenzy of political fervor. His advice to his son John, "Don't take either side," he found impossible himself to follow.[1] Elected to the first Provincial Congress, which convened in Charlestown on January 11, 1775, he observed that "Reins are not in the hands of Towns Men as formerly."[2] Radical delegates from the upcountry argued that adherence to the Continental Association required a ban on the export of rice, an idea unwelcome to Laurens. Others who never sat in the Common House of Assembly now voted in the congress, "So it is now that certain persons who are themselves great Debtors and Some who have no visible Estates have the Reins committed to them."[3] These people welcomed the association as a means to avoid payment of just debts. The Provincial Congress adjourned January 18, the same day the Georgia congress began, and appointed a "general committee" to enforce the association. Laurens sat on that committee.

Laurens walked a tight rope, radical enough not to lose the position of leadership while opposing the extremes proposed by the faction of mechanics and artisans led by Christopher Gadsden. Privately he trembled for what might happen. "What is worse than kingly tyranny?" he asked his son, then answered,

"Popular tyrany."[4] He anguished over the way in which silent men were suspected of a lack of patriotism. He painted a sad picture of creditors coming before the General Committee to ask permission to collect money owed them while committee members who were debtors themselves mocked the petitioners.[5]

Laurens announced his intention of going to the Georgia coast on February 4, but the press of business and his service on the General Committee kept him in Charlestown until February 25.[6] On February 28 he negotiated some business with James Spalding's partner, Roger Kelsall, and left for his Broughton Island plantation the same day on his schooner. Lachlan McIntosh had arranged to meet Laurens at Broughton, and Bartram accompanied him, bringing his accumulation of specimens and drawings, expecting to ship them to London with Laurens's cargo of rice.[7]

It had been almost ten years since Laurens rescued "poor Billy Bartram" from his disastrous experiment in farming along the St. Johns. Now Laurens saw a mature William Bartram who had braved Indian alarms and survived the wilderness. Not only that, but Bartram worked for the eminent Dr. John Fothergill, whose patients included Lord Dartmouth and Benjamin Franklin. Laurens knew that even then Fothergill worked with Benjamin Franklin to find a compromise modifying the British Declaratory Act's claim to parliamentary supremacy in all matters.[8] Henry's brother James Laurens insisted on being treated by Dr. Fothergill during his London illness[9] so there was a note of respect in Laurens's message to his factor in London: "Mr. Bartram who is employed by Dr. Fothergill of London has put on board several boxes of plants and shrubs collected in the woods of this and the neighboring province of East Florida."[10] Laurens invited him to share his cabin on the return to Charlestown. Bartram gratefully accepted. He wanted to see Superintendent Stuart before going off into the Cherokee mountains. Then too he wished to express his sympathy to Mary Lamboll Thomas, whose father, Thomas Lamboll, had died last October. Bartram said his goodbyes to the McIntoshes, or as he phrased it, to his "friends and liberal patrons in these parts," and left Broughton.[11] Laurens loaded his bumper rice harvest on Capt. Joseph Yowart's *Mermaid*: 887 barrels and 72 half barrels. There would have been even more if Peter Nephew had managed the New Hope plantation as well as James Bailey supervised Broughton.[12]

Laurens and Bartram had time and opportunity for the "philosophic discussions" Bartram loved. The older man revealed that he keenly felt the seriousness of the role into which he had been thrust. "I am one of those who perceive Errors on both sides and am for conciliatory measures," he had written prior to leaving Charlestown, adding, "these Doctrines are unpalatable to the Majority."[13] Laurens had a poor opinion of crowd pleasers such as Christopher Gadsden and William Henry Drayton. He clung to the hope of a reconciliation with the mother country.

At some point, probably Sunbury, Laurens lingered to do more business while Bartram continued to Charlestown, arriving there on March 25, 1775. He found the town in turmoil with little sign of Laurens's hoped-for reconciliation. The latest news from England that Parliament approved the king's reference to "rebellious colonies" angered people and an impending British embargo played into the hands of the radical element. Carolina's delegates prepared to leave for the Second Continental Congress in a grim mood. Henry Laurens, who reached the city on April 4, lamented the dangerous escalation of radicalism but accepted its inevitability: "There appears a general determination against a tame submission," he wrote.[14] The option for moderates was clear—join the movement and attempt to control it, or oppose it and risk the anger of the popular faction. Laurens chose the former course and was elected to the chair of the General Committee on May 1, 1775. Alexander Innes, secretary to Gov. Lord William Campbell, preceded the governor to Charlestown and expressed surprise that Laurens served on the revolutionary committee. He observed that the gentry had to appear more radical than they really were in order to maintain leadership over the demagogues.[15]

William Bartram meant to get out of this contentious town as soon as possible. Charlestown in 1775 was not a congenial place for a peaceable man—too much violent rhetoric, too much uncertainty, too much civilization. There were necessary errands first. He had to write home, having not done so for the past two years; he had to settle accounts with Dr. Chalmers; he had to interview John Stuart about the situation in the Indian country; and he had to collect letters of introduction to persons of influence in the Cherokee country and out in the far reaches of West Florida. His base in Charlestown was again on King Street at the Lambolls. There he commiserated with his dear friend Mary Lamboll Thomas. Her father, the venerable Thomas Lamboll, patron of John and William Bartram, died the previous October, rich in years and the respect of his townspeople, and was interred in the Meeting Street churchyard.

The letter to his father turned into a major production, covering all that had happened in the past two years. He reported that he had arrived safely at the house of the late Mr. Lamboll and that he intended to stay only a few days before setting out again. He had sent Dr. Fothergill a first shipment of drawings and plants after his 1773 tour of Georgia's ceded lands. Since then the good doctor expressed appreciation of his work and asked for more of the same. Prevented from returning to the Indian country by the outbreak of hostilities, he turned to Florida. Bartram's narration of his Florida adventures is detailed, giving rein to occasional rhetoric such as "the face and constitution of this country is Indian, wild, new and pleasing." He noted with some satisfaction that he had recently loaded four large boxes for Dr. Fothergill at Sunbury before coming to Charlestown. He had called upon Dr. Chalmers already, though only in town for two days, and was happy to learn that his parents were alive and well. He resolved to explore the Cherokee and Creek country the next year and "please God" reach the Mississippi.[16] The letter represented an unusual effort; Bartram seldom wrote home. But then, as he noted, his parents had not written him since he began his journey.

Next came the interview with John Stuart at his Tradd Street residence. They had not seen each other since the Augusta congress, and Stuart had lost track of the wandering botanist. Bartram described his Florida adventures. Bryan's land grab was on Stuart's mind. In fact, Jonathan Bryan happened to be in Charlestown while Bartram was there and had not given up hope of somehow securing the vast tract in Florida. Stuart hated to see more of these illegal deals between private individuals and Indians. He had just learned from Alexander Cameron that a man named Richard Henderson had gone to the overhills country to dicker with Attakullakulla for lands on the Holston River.[17]

Since the October treaty the Indian country seemed safe enough for Bartram to explore. Stuart had received news that the Mortar, thought to be a troublemaker for his unwillingness to be shackled to British trade, had succumbed to his wounds. Stuart considered that good news. Other tidings bode less well. Escochabey continued his flirtation with the Spanish in Cuba. The outlawed Houmachta and Sophia remained at large, and Stuart suggested that the Cherokees protected them. Other than that, the Cherokees and Creeks seemed well disposed. Stuart had heard from General Gage in troubled Boston that some disaffected people there tried to poison the minds of the Indians against the king. Therefore, Stuart wrote to his deputies to alert the Indians to any attempts of that nature. He so informed Lord Dartmouth of his action on March 28, within days of Bartram's interview, pledging to keep all the Indians in love and attachment to the king "and in a temper to be always ready to act in the Service."[18] Stuart carefully copied all his letters into a ledger. He had no idea that the Carolina committee would seize his ledger and infer from his words that he engaged in a conspiracy to launch an Indian war upon them. Stuart would be forced to flee Charlestown under a storm of vilification. Neither Stuart nor Bartram could have guessed that such an interpretation would be placed upon the letters Stuart gave to Bartram to be delivered to Alexander Cameron at his residence, Lochaber, on the Cherokee line.[19]

Bartram discussed with Stuart the best route to take to Lochaber. The shortest way was by the trading road to Ninety-Six. However, as Bartram explained in his *Travels*, the way "led over a high, dry, sandy and gravelly ridge, and a great part of the distance an old settled or restored part of the country, and consequently void of the varieties of original or novel productions of nature."[20] He decided to take the highway to the Three Sisters Ferry on the Savannah River and follow the road to Augusta he had traveled twice before.

At least one Charlestown horticulturist heard that Bartram intended to go botanizing in West Florida and ordered plant samples to be shipped from Pensacola.[21] Bartram solicited letters of reference from Stuart, Chalmers, and Laurens. Laurens's friend John Lewis Gervais wrote a letter of introduction for him to Andrew Williamson. Both Gervais and Williamson had plantations in the same district as Cameron's Lochaber, and Williamson's Whitehall seemed a logical stopping place.[22] On April 20 Bartram sent a brief note to Dr. Fothergill asking him to reimburse Dr. Chalmers £53 for his expenses.[23]

While Bartram completed his business in Charlestown, an incendiary letter from Arthur Lee in London was en route to Carolina's General Committee. The letter purported to tell about a secret conspiracy on the part of British agents to arm slaves and enlist them as well as Indians against rebellious Americans. Normally such hearsay reports would have been ridiculed, but in the poisoned climate of the day, the rumor spread like wildfire and gained credibility as it grew. As chairman of the General Committee, Henry Laurens forwarded the report to the Carolina delegates at the Continental Congress on May 8, 1775.[24] Coincidentally the news of Lexington and Concord further inflamed angry emotions. A week later the forty-eight members of the General Committee approved a resolution that the commencement of hostilities in Boston together with "the dread of instigated Insurrections at home" were sufficient reasons to take up arms whenever the Continental Congress or Provincial Congress would so declare.[25] "It was given out," John Stuart reported to

Lord Dartmouth, "that the Negroes were immediately to be set free by Government and arms given to them to fall upon their Masters."[26]

The alleged conspiracy referred to by Stuart began even before Bartram left Charlestown. According to later testimony, a free black harbor pilot named Thomas Jeremiah spread the word that slaves should be ready to join the redcoats, "that the war was come to help the poor Negroes."[27] Jeremiah's brother-in-law accused him of collecting guns in preparation for the coming battle. Jeremiah was arrested, tried, and condemned under the Negro Act of 1740 though one judge expressed doubt that the law applied to free blacks. Jeremiah's cause was not helped by the intercession of Gov. Lord William Campbell, who arrived aboard the *Scorpion* on June 1, 1775. Rumors raged that the governor brought guns to arm the rebellious slaves. Despite his firm denials of guilt, despite the retraction of accusations by key witnesses, despite the appeals for clemency by clergy who attended him, Jeremiah was hanged and burned on August 17, 1775. Henry Laurens had trouble convincing himself of Jeremiah's guilt, but he realized that a pardon, in the inflamed climate of the times, would have incited mob violence. Lord William, though convinced of the pilot's innocence, sadly agreed.[28]

During the turmoil Henry Laurens managed to retain a leadership role even though he remained conciliatory in his private sentiments. On June 1, 1775, the Carolina Provincial Congress met and elected him president. The congress required all inhabitants to subscribe to the association. In addition the congress created a Council of Safety to act as an executive authority while the congress was not in session, and on June 16 Laurens became president of that council.[29]

John Stuart wrote to General Gage on May 26, 1775, that the party in power intended to make him a prisoner and force him to work for them.[30] Stuart subsequently left Charlestown for Savannah with agents of the Council of Safety chasing after him. There Stuart sought refuge on a British schooner bound for East Florida with his enemies paddling canoes in hot pursuit. "I had a narrow escape," he wrote Gage from St. Augustine.[31]

Laurens's council then went after Alexander Cameron, Stuart's deputy and the alleged coconspirator in the plot to bring on an Indian war. On June 26 the council instructed Andrew Williamson to pay a visit to his upcountry acquaintance and offer him a bribe or a threat, whichever would do the most good. Cameron indignantly denied any intention of inciting Indians and spurned Williamson's offer of money. His denials had no effect in quieting the animosity against Stuart. Soon Cameron had to take refuge in the Cherokee country for fear of his life.[32]

Nothing of this perturbation of events found its way into William Bartram's notebook. With letters from Stuart to Cameron that might have made him accessory in the suspected conspiracy in his knapsack, he set off from the Lambolls' house on King Street on April 22, 1775. He would travel light so he left his trunk in Mary's care, and she gave him a prayer book, a gift he cherished throughout his coming adventures.[33]

It may not have been a chance coincidence that Bartram's departure occurred at the same time a group of men, including Henry Laurens, broke into the armory on the second floor of the statehouse and took away eight hundred stands of arms and two hundred cutlasses.[34] The escalating violence hastened Bartram's departure from Charlestown.

II

It was agreed that my future route should be directed West and South-West, into the Cherokee country and the regions of the Muscogulges or Creeks.

Harper, *Travels*

William Bartram avoided Savannah on his return to Georgia. By now the Charlestown frenzy had affected Governor Wright's town. Wright wrote General Gage on April 24 that he had heard that Carolina threatened to invade Georgia if any blood was spilled in Massachusetts.[35] Bartram had to stay away from the Indian country for fear of violence in 1774. Now in 1775 he had to venture into the Indian country in order to avoid violence in the "civilized" region.

Bartram noted that he followed the Savannah high road to Jacksonborough on the Ponpon River the first day, rode thirty miles the second day, and reached the Three Sisters Ferry on the Savannah River the third day. Here he found the wilderness he luxuriated in and commented on the "ancient sublime forest," "extensive savannas," and "far distant Rice plantations," all of which "agreeably employs the imagination and captivates the senses by their magnificence and grandeur."[36] The region he described, just east of the hamlet of Clyo, Georgia, is mostly wilderness today and requires someone of Bartram's creative imagination to find wonder and excitement there.

He rode twelve miles and stopped for the night at a plantation he described in some detail. His host and hostess, "though educated as it were in the woods," he found to be "no strangers to sensibility and those moral virtues which grace and ornament the most approved and admired characters in civil society."[37] After surveying their stock of cattle, he went with his host to observe the slaves cutting timber to be floated to Savannah, singing as they worked. "Contented and joyful, the sooty sons of Afric" forgot their bondage and praised their master in songs of their own composition. What is the reader to think of this idyllic depiction of slavery, an institution Bartram privately deplored? Perhaps, by portraying an idealized plantation, he wished to elevate the standards of plantations generally. In any case many of these apparently contented "sooty sons" would soon take protection behind British lines, preferring the risks of freedom to the security of slavery.

This sylvan paradise he had discovered had its Adam and Eve in his host's son and daughter-in-law: "As we approach the door conducted by the young man, his lovely bride arrayed in native innocence and becoming modesty, with an air and smile of grace and benignity, meets and salutes us."[38] Bartram remarked on the goodness of this family because such virtue was rare on the southern frontier. He perhaps wrote about them in order to nourish the flickering hope that the new Americans, born of the wilderness and proven by the Revolution, would be like them.

Early the next morning he set out on the familiar Augusta road, and as before, crossed the river at Silver Bluff to visit George Galphin, who ranked high among his heroes, John Stuart's opinion to the contrary notwithstanding. Bartram described Silver Bluff as "a very celebrated place" and predicted that Galphin's buildings would be lasting monuments to him. Not so. Silver Bluff declined after the Revolution. Its people moved away, but as previously mentioned, its African American church lasted. After a wartime interlude in Savannah, Jesse Peters established the church in Augusta as Springfield Baptist Church. By the time of the Civil War, Galphin's fine brick house was a ruined shell. Nothing is left today; the wilderness has reclaimed Silver Bluff.[39]

At the time of Bartram's visit George Galphin had every reason to be pleased with himself. Land sales on the 1773 backcountry cession had resumed after the scare of 1774, and Galphin expected to recoup nearly ten thousand pounds sterling from the proceeds. He followed the example of his partners, Lachlan McGillivray and John Rae, and retired from the trade business to live the life of a gentleman planter. He turned over his profitable Creek trade to his nephew David Holmes, and to his sons, George, John, and Thomas, under the name Galphin and Company. He expressed the hope that he would live "Easey the remainder of my Live."[40]

Galphin's lack of formal education deterred him from following his colleagues into town and up the social ladder. Despite his shrewdness for business, his writing remained barely legible and marginally literate. However, no one dared mock his style. He gave his endorsement to his friend Bartram on April 30, 1775: "To Messrs. Graham, Germany, Mosley, Cornell, Cussins or any other gentleman of my acquaintance in the Creek country, The berer M. Barteram is a gentm I have none a lange time, he is an onest worthey man he is imployed by some of the first people in England to procure flowers, seeds and roots of the different spasemens that is in Amaraca to send home to them any serves you can do him or any sevelty shown him I shall esteme it as a faver don me."[41] Bartram continued his way to Augusta, following the same route as in 1773, and crossing into Georgia on the ferry at historic Fort Moore Bluff. He embellished on his previous praise of Augusta, calling the location "perhaps the most delightful and eligible of any in Georgia for a city. I do not hesitate to pronounce as my opinion [that Augusta] will very soon become the metropolis of Georgia."[42] By the time Bartram published his *Travels* Augusta had become the state capital. Thus flattered, Augusta has always had a good opinion of William Bartram, and his prediction is carved in stone on the city's riverwalk promenade.

At the time of this visit, early May 1775, Augusta still resisted the infectious impulse to change governments. The veterans of the Indian trade dominated local society. Edward Barnard and his son-in-law William Goodgion, James Grierson, Martin Campbell, Robert Mackay, Andrew McLean, and others had done very well in the Indian trade, and they looked askance at roughnecks such as George Wells and Robert Hamilton, who talked about exterminating Indians. Others, though less committed to the Indian business, who did not choose to be associated with Indian haters, included Bartram's friend Dr. Humphrey Wells, Dr. Andrew Johnston, Parson James Seymour, and schoolteacher John Daniel Hammerer. It would have been a shame if Bartram had not met Hammerer; the two were kindred spirits. Hammerer, exiled in London because of religious persecution in his native Strasbourg, conceived a plan for assimilating American Indians by teaching them crafts. Bartram would have been interested in the coincidence that he and Hammerer had a patron in Dr. John Fothergill. Fothergill liked Hammerer's ideas and wrote letters of recommendation for him to friends in Carolina and Georgia.[43] Hammerer met the Cherokees who traveled to London with Lt. Henry Timberlake in 1765 and returned to America with them. Attakullakulla endorsed Hammerer's plan, and Hammerer started a school near Fort Prince George in 1766. Meeting with indifferent success, he moved to the Long Canes region and set up another school. That failed also, and Hammerer tried again in Augusta.[44] Because both were idealists sympathetic to a benevolent Indian policy, they would have enjoyed each other's company.

Wealthy trader Robert Mackay described the mood in Augusta to a friend in Edinburgh: "There is nothing new in this part of the country. The Indians are all quiet, and the Ceded Lands are selling fast."[45] Despite the heavy deductions Governor Wright exacted from the land sales, Mackay expected to retrieve the trading debts due him. He hoped that Parliament would not give in to American demands. "If you yield an inch in this matter, adieu to Great Brittan's power over America."[46]

A recent addition to Augusta society was a wealthy young Yorkshireman named Thomas Brown, who had arrived in town in November 1774 with an impressive train of indentured servants, English horses, and wagon loads of baggage. He had read Governor Wright's glowing description of the new cession, recruited servants from his native Whitby and others in the Orkneys, and had packed them aboard his father's ship, the *Marlborough*. Governor Wright expressed his delight in seeing one of the better sort come over to Georgia, and he made Thomas Brown a justice of the peace for the Kiokee District. Robert Mackay, Andrew McLean, and other Augustans had welcomed Brown as enthusiastically as Wright. While his people worked at establishing the settlement of Brownsborough, Brown made his residence at LeRoy Hammond's house, New Richmond, overlooking the Savannah River above Augusta on the Carolina side.[47]

The timing of Brown's arrival and his unusual affluence caused the radical faction to begin to whisper that he was the illegitimate son of Lord North, sent over by the ministry to spy upon them. In June, when the Georgia Provincial Congress established local committees to enforce the association's prohibition of trade, Brown became a marked man. He stoutly refused to swear to obey the restrictions set by the Continental Congress; instead he spoke out in favor of associating for the king. For that reason a crowd of Liberty Boys marched out to New Richmond, and after a dramatic confrontation they made an example of him by fracturing his skull, scalping him, and applying a burning brand to his feet, then hauling him through the streets of Augusta, all in the name of liberty.[48]

By then William Bartram had entered the more peaceful domain of the Cherokee Indians. He set his course in May for Fort James at the junction of the Broad and Savannah Rivers. On the first day he got as far as the Little River, the former boundary of the Indian country. His spirits rose as he distanced himself from fractious civilization and melded with the wilderness. "How harmonious and sweetly murmur the purling rills and fleeting brooks, roving along the shadowy vales, passing through dark, subterranean caverns, or dashing over steep rocky precipices, their cold, humid banks condensing the volatile vapours, which fall and coalesce in crystalling drops, on the leaves and elastic twigs of the aromatic shrubs and incarnate flowers."[49] He was alone and happy.

Bartram's mention of finding bones of elk in what is today Lincoln County marks the southernmost elk habitat, according to Francis Harper.[50] Of the myriad plants the botanist encountered, the one that thrilled him most was the fiery azalea, which grew in profusion in early May. "This is certainly the most gay and brilliant flowering shrub yet known," Bartram exclaimed.[51] The hills seemed on fire with them. On the evening of the second day, he reached the recently constructed Fort James, a square stockade with bastions at each corner enclosing the commandant's house, a house for officers, and barracks for the garrison of fifty men. The fort dominated a ridge between the Broad and Savannah Rivers. Somewhat to the south and across the Savannah on the Carolina side stood Fort Charlotte, a stone fort that superseded Fort Moore after the last war.[52]

Col. Edward Barnard, captain of the troop of rangers at Fort James, welcomed Bartram as an old friend. Lts. Thomas Waters and Edward Keating also remembered Bartram from the tour of the 1773 cession.[53] Dr. Francis Begbie, a resident of the Kiokees and surgeon to the garrison, took Bartram to see some Indian mounds near the bank of the river. Bartram guessed that they had been constructed to provide higher ground in case of a sudden flood. The largest mound had a spiral path leading to the summit. The Georgia historian George White visited the mounds in 1848 and corroborated Bartram's description of them.[54] However, a century later, when Francis Harper looked for them, they had been eroded by successive floods. Bartram commented that a proposed town called Dartmouth had been laid out near the fort. After the Revolution a settlement did develop. Called Petersburg, it flourished for a while as the market for the farmers along the Broad River. Petersburg boats, long, narrow, shallow craft propelled by poles, plied the river between Petersburg and Augusta, risking disaster in the rapids.[55] The town declined as people followed their fortunes west. Few houses remained after the Civil War. Today the ground is inundated by the Clarks Hill Lake.

Bartram noted that he set off on May 10 from Fort James with the Cherokee town of Keowee as his destination. He followed the river road northward
for seven miles and crossed the river near today's Calhoun Falls. He soon came
upon the high road, corresponding to the present South Carolina Highway 81.
After a few miles northward on that road, he turned east and followed a path
that paralleled the Cherokee boundary line that is equivalent to the present
line between Anderson and Abbeville Counties.[56] The terrain is unexciting
today, and it was made worse for Bartram because of a torrential downpour. For
once the ebullience disappeared from his prose. "The season being uncom-
monly wet," Bartram wrote, "almost daily showers of rain and frequently
attended with tremendous thunder, rendered traveling disagreeable, toilsome,
and hazardous, through an uninhabited wilderness, abounding with rivers and
brooks."[57] The soaked and weary traveler expressed relief to find Alexander
Cameron at home at Lochaber, his residence on Penny Creek, a tributary of
the Little River. Cameron had no trouble prevailing upon the explorer to bide
a while until the rain stopped and the flooded streams fell.

After the Cherokee War others settled along the Little River and its tribu-
Alexander Cameron played a major role in the history of the area. He had
come to Georgia in 1738 as a private in Oglethorpe's Forty-second Regiment.
When that unit dissolved in 1749, he volunteered for service in the Independent Companies serving in South Carolina and Georgia. Cameron served in
the Cherokee War, made the rank of ensign in 1761, and was stationed at Fort
Prince George in the Lower Cherokee country. As a result of that service he
claimed and received two thousand acres on Penny Creek. He took as his wife
the daughter of the important chief of the Estatoe village, Saluy. She bore him
two children, George in 1767 and Susanna in 1770. Another girl, Jane, was
born in 1776 after Bartram's visit to Lochaber. Since 1768 Cameron had served
as John Stuart's deputy.[58] He had the Scots' gift of easy assimilation with the
Indians; the Cherokees loved him and called him Scotchie.

After the Cherokee War others settled along the Little River and its tribu-
taries. Some who lived in this upper part of Ninety-Six District included
William and Hugh Calhoun, Aaron Alexander, Andrew Williamson, and John
Lewis Gervais. The larger plantations, like Cameron's, had names: Cameron's
Lochaber, Williamson's Whitehall and Gervais's Herrenhausen. In the course
of his conversation about these distant neighbors, Cameron imparted a useful
bit of information. George Whitfield, who purchased Fort Charlotte when the
Royal Americans abandoned it in 1768, happened to be nephew of the famous
evangelist, Rev. George Whitefield, whose Bethesda School near Savannah

Bartram had visited with his father in 1765. Whitfield married Frances Tyler of Virginia at Herrenhausen, the residence of John Lewis Gervais, and Gervais performed the service in his capacity as justice of the peace for the Ninety-Six District. Miss Tyler happened to be sister to Mrs. Andrew Williamson and sister to Mrs. LeRoy Hammond, who lived near Augusta. All this was of passing interest to Bartram, who did not plan to record social activities in his report. He had in his pocket a letter from Gervais recommending him to Williamson, but Bartram decided that he would proceed directly to the Cherokee country and not call at Whitehall. LeRoy Hammond he knew as a distinguished officer in Col. Edward Barnard's surveying team who marked the lower portions of the cession of 1773. Of more relevance was Cameron's statement that Mr. Whitfield planned to organize an expedition to Mobile later that summer. Bartram intended to go to Mobile although he was uncertain how long he would be in the Cherokee country. He asked Cameron to recommend him to Whitfield in case he decided to join the caravan.[59]

Though the site of Lochaber seems isolated today, it had a busy history. Stuart and Cameron hosted a thousand Cherokees there in 1771 to set the boundary line between the Cherokees and Virginia-North Carolina in the Treaty of Lochaber. Since then various groups of Cherokees had come to call on Cameron. Cameron's main problem at the time of Bartram's visit concerned the apparent willingness of the Cherokees to barter away portions of their land. They had tried to give him a substantial tract on the upper Saluda River, contrary to Carolina law and the Royal Proclamation of 1763. Even though the Treaty of Lochaber stipulated that no more cessions be made without consent of the government, Richard Pearis had obtained a twelve-mile area on the upper Saluda some miles to the northeast of Lochaber. Despite the illegality of the transaction, the British government compensated Pearis for his loss of the land after the Revolution.[60]

More recently Cameron had been unable to stop the Cherokee chiefs, including Stuart's great friend Attakullakulla, from ceding a huge tract between the Kanawha and Tennessee Rivers. The chiefs signed away that territory to a company headed by Richard Henderson at Sycamore Shoals on the Watauga River on March 17, 1775.[61] Cameron's attention had been focused on the Indian country to the exclusion of the political turmoil in Charlestown. Events caught up with him when he served as foreman of the 1775 grand jury of the recently created Ninety-Six District. The jury passed on a routine critique of the British Coercive Acts, much to the displeasure of John Stuart when he learned about it. Cameron's embarrassed explanation was that he and the other jurors had consumed so many bottles of port (estimated at one hundred) that he did not know what they passed on.[62]

Bartram spent several days cataloging plants, including an aromatic root with the taste and smell of the anise seed. Called the *Angelica lucido*, or *Nondo*, it tasted like ginseng, and perhaps because people supposed it had the same aphrodisiac properties of ginseng, it was greatly esteemed by whites and Indians alike. Undoubtedly, Bartram used his time at Lochaber to learn more about the geography and culture of the Cherokee people. He had to plan his route carefully because a wanderer could easily get lost in the confusion of mountains with their swift-running rivers, precipitous slopes, and dense forests. As an added element of danger, Cameron could not guarantee the temper of the Cherokee warriors. He knew that they felt angry at the encroaching "Virginians." William Bartram would take his chances. This is what he had been waiting for.

III

The weather now settled and fair, I prepared to proceed for Fort Prince George Keowe, having obtained of the agreeable and liberal Mr. Cameron, ample testimonials and letters of recommendation to the traders in the nation.
Harper, *Travels*

William Bartram left Lochaber on May 15, 1775, a week after the news of Lexington and two weeks after the rumor of the Stuart-Cameron conspiracy alarmed Charlestown.[63] The report must have reached Cameron while Bartram lingered and learned all he could of Cherokee lore. Cameron would soon follow Stuart into exile. Bartram's friends Laurens and McIntosh regarded them as fiendish for plotting an Indian war. Long before he transcribed his notes, Bartram knew of the allegations. Yet he did not see fit to change his original opinion. Cameron, in retrospect, remained "the agreeable and liberal Mr. Cameron."[64]

Nor did Bartram mention anything about the Indian-hating settlers on the frontier, some of whom were involved in the skirmishing in 1768 called the Regulators War.[65] Increasing banditry caused settlers to form vigilante patrols and make examples of some of the worst of the marginally civilized. Alexander Cameron shared George Galphin's opinion of these people: they were more dangerous than the Indians. Thomas Fee, murderer of Mad Turkey, was a hero to the mob that released him from the Ninety-Six jail.[66] Even now as Bartram followed the trail from Ninety-Six to Seneca, the notorious Fee lurked in the settlements, sheltered by friends. Hezekiah Collins, who killed the young Cherokee companions of Bartram on the New Purchase survey, remained at large. Radicals in Charlestown, notably William Henry Drayton, would play upon the fear of Indians, characteristic of frontier people, and on their desire for Indian land to gain their support.[67]

A young black slave belonging to Cameron escorted Bartram as far as Seneca on a tiring, uneventful journey of about forty-five miles. Bartram admired the setting of the town, situated on the southern section of the Keowee River that is now called the Seneca. The settlement occupied both banks of the river, easily forded at that point. From his vantage point on the east side of the river, he looked across to the council house on the opposite plain. A range of hills "seem to bend" over the green fields and the river. Bartram commanded a wide view of the "plantations" along the river.[68] Seneca occupied a broad valley; the pleasant hills beautified but could not protect the village. Bartram knew Seneca's fate when he revised his notes for publication. Almost exactly a year after his visit an army under Andrew Williamson invaded the Cherokee country in retaliation for an attack on frontier settlers. A fierce fight occurred at Seneca's ford, and Francis Salvador, a prominent Jewish planter, was killed in the fray. The Carolinians drove the Cherokees at Seneca and other villages out and put their houses to the torch. The six thousand bushels of corn destroyed by Williamson's troops demonstrated the productivity of the Indian farms.[69] Bartram chose not to discuss the destruction; he preferred to report on the production of the typical village farm.

The town of Seneca, as example, shared the best lands, with each family marking out a separate plot. The entire community engaged in planting, men and women, old and young. Women tended the crops of corn, squash, pumpkins, melons, and the rest, and the village turned out again for the harvest. Each family kept the product of its own plot. Every family contributed to the town granary, available to the headman for entertainment of guests and for a reserve supply in case of famine.[70] Bartram might have just missed the planting, but he could see the fields sprouting in the rapid spring growth. Spring comes late to the mountains; flaming azaleas that bloomed in March in Savannah appeared on the hillsides in May. As Bartram made his way into the interior and May lapsed into June, spring unfolded before him, laying its lush green carpet over hills and valleys recently bare. On the highest mountains winter still lingered into June.

Though Bartram disliked war and avoided the subject in his journal, he could not ignore it completely. He knew that he followed the great military highway into the interior, and he had learned from Stuart the bloody history of the trail. He noted simply that Seneca was a new town, rebuilt since the last war, with about five hundred inhabitants living there in 1775. Curiously, he wrote that "General Middleton" commanded the late expedition. Bartram had met the actual commanding officer, Col. James Grant, when Grant presided over the Indian congress at Picolata, as governor of East Florida in 1765. Perhaps Bartram had heard Henry Laurens denounce Middleton's role in the 1761 invasion so vehemently that he wrote Middleton instead of Grant. In Laurens's opinion Middleton deserved no credit for the success of the expedition. Middleton, as colonel of the Carolina provincials, grumbled that Grant did not pay him enough attention, and went home before the campaign terminated, not even bothering to inform his second in command, Henry Laurens. When Grant returned to Charlestown, Middleton challenged him to a duel. Grant spared Middleton's life when he could have taken it. The dispute became public when Christopher Gadsden criticized Grant's military management in the press and Laurens had to defend the commander. Historian George Rogers Jr. noted that the affair fanned anti-Scottish feelings in Charlestown.[71] Laurens's feud with Gadsden still festered.

Leaving Seneca, Bartram's black companion returned to Lochaber, and the botanist rode alone to Keowee and the historic Fort Prince George he had heard so much about. The ground rose gradually, the air cooler, the hills steeper, and the scenery more dramatic as he neared the mountain country of the Cherokees. He felt apprehensive as he approached Keowee at the end of the sixteen-mile journey upriver. The warnings repeated by Stuart and Cameron troubled him more than he would have liked. He knew that the Cherokees had reason to quarrel with the encroaching "Virginians." Uncharacteristically he referred to the Indians as "the savage vindictive inhabitants" of this country, who were "extremely jealous of white people traveling about their mountains," poking into private places and digging up plants. He confessed for the first time to feeling lonesome, a thousand miles from his home, among strange people, white and red.[72]

However, there was and is a curative quality about the mountain country, and Bartram felt it at his first sight of the village of Keowee. He paused at the top of a hill to take notes. The steep hills crowded close, confining the swift-flowing river. In the distance to the north a "conical" mountain closed the valley. White blossoms of wild strawberries adorned the landscape. The village lay beneath him, and across the shallows on a stretch of bottomland stood the historic fort.

The Raven of Toxaway, a headman of the valley in 1755, gave the land to Gov. James Glen so he could build a fort to protect the Cherokees from the French. The chief told the governor he could have all the land he could see, an offer not as generous as it might seem because the hills on each side severely limited vision.[73] Bartram could picture the month-long encampment of the fifteen hundred men under Governor Lyttelton, who bivouacked on the plain across the river. Lyttelton intended to punish the Cherokees for taking the lives of twenty-four persons on the Yadkin and Catawba Rivers but had to settle for a vague promise by Attakullakulla and Ouconnostotah to deliver up the guilty persons as they could be found. An outbreak of smallpox forced Lyttelton to return to Charlestown, leaving twenty-two hostages at the fort.[74]

In late January 1760, shortly after the departure of Lyttelton's disease-racked army, a general war broke out. Cherokee raiding parties terrorized both sides of the Savannah River even to the gates of Augusta and Fort Moore and took the lives of forty to fifty men, women, and children. Fort Prince George, like Fort Loudoun in the overhills, was cut off and besieged. Warriors hid on the Keowee hills overlooking the fort while Ouconnostotah lured Lt. Richard Cotymore outside. The Great Warrior stood on the Keowee side and called across the narrow river. He wanted a horse to ride to Charlestown, he said. Cotymore believed him and came down to the river on his side, whereupon the warriors rose up and mortally wounded Cotymore. The angry soldiers in the fort killed all the Indian hostages, an act that infuriated the middle and overhills settlements and doomed Fort Loudoun.[75]

In response to South Carolina's appeal for troops, Gen. Jeffrey Amherst in New York dispatched twelve hundred men under Col. Archibald Montgomery with orders to strike quickly and return for the campaign against the French in Canada. Montgomery marched his British regulars at a killing pace, surprising the inhabitants of Keowee after a sixty-mile march. Montgomery's second in command, James Grant, wrote the following account of what happened to Lt. Gov. William Bull. The soldiers killed about eighty people and took forty prisoners. The rest escaped to the hills; "some of them had just time to run out of their beds." Some left food on the table. At Keowee and other villages the invaders torched the houses and "astonishing magazines of corn." Grant observed that the "correction" had been "pretty severe."[76]

Montgomery struck hard at the middle settlements but failed to rescue the distant garrison at Fort Loudoun. It fell to James Grant to improve upon the "correction" after the fall of Loudoun. Grant destroyed all the lower settlements that Montgomery had missed in 1760 and revisited the middle settlements, returning to Fort Prince George to negotiate peace terms with Attakullakulla and Ouconnostotah. That event marked the last of the historic military moments at the outpost. The glory departed with the gore. Gen. Thomas Gage withdrew the garrison in 1768, and a deterioration set in. When Bartram arrived in 1775 the once formidable fort served as a trading house for "Mr. D. Home," the principal trader in the village.[77]

Bartram's Keowee had never recovered from the successive destructions wrought by British soldiers. The traders told the botanist that once the Cherokees had farmed the entire valley from Kulsage a mile above Keowee down to Seneca. The same river plain now exhibited "a very different spectacle," Bartram mused. The present generation represented "the posterity and feeble remains of the once potent and renowned Cherokees." At the site of the village on the right bank of the river, no Indian structures stood except for ancient mounds and terraces. No wonder Bartram was disappointed. He had heard so much about this place since his first arrival in Charlestown in 1773. He must press on if he wished to see how Cherokees lived outside the baleful influence of Charlestown.[78]

Bartram waited three days in Keowee expecting an Indian guide to meet him and lead him over the mountains to the middle settlements. Waiting had never been a problem before because nature produced an inexhaustible supply of flora and fauna to inspect, but Bartram grew impatient at Keowee, a charming situation but a depressing place. Finally he decided "to set off alone and run all risks."[79] Maps, if he had any, would have done no good because none were detailed or exact enough. He had to rely on the traders' instructions. Fortunately the old trail followed by Grant's two-mile-long caravan, including packhorses and cattle, showed clearly, but side trails and shortcuts could lead astray. He began to feel better as he climbed the ridge and looked back at Keowee with its clear swift river running through. The trail led him along the ridge by the east side of Stamp Creek to the present hill town of Salem. Bartram regained his enthusiasm as he cataloged the spring bounty about him: silver bells, mock orange plants, rosebay, mountain camellia, storax, trumpet vine, and honeysuckle. It took a sharp eye to detect some of those plants, but even amateurs delight in others he listed: flowering dogwood, yellow jessamine, newly sprouting ferns in dark places, and everywhere banks of mountain laurel. With nature so entertaining, Bartram forgot that he was alone in a dangerous wilderness.[80]

He crossed the Little River below its junction with Fiddlers Creek, climbed a gentle rise and from the crest viewed the great wall of the Oconee Mountains with the conical Tomassee Knob looming dramatically in the foreground. A year later a party of Andrew Williamson's force, including Capt. Andrew Pickens, fought a sharp battle at Tomassee and took sixteen Cherokee scalps.[81] A portion of the trail followed by Bartram may be seen today at the Oconee Station Historic Site near the 1792 blockhouse, built there to protect the advancing Carolina frontier.[82] Bartram continued past the ancient village of Oconee and climbed Station Mountain. The casual manner in which Bartram mentions such climbs belies the actual difficulty of accomplishing the feat. The trails avoided the highest peaks so the explorer would have to leave the trail to follow his romantic impulse. His reward was "a view inexpressibly magnificent and comprehensive." The terrain he had crossed since leaving Augusta spread beneath him, "appearing regularly undulated as the great ocean after a tempest." The nearest hills showed a rich green, the more distant waves gradually turning blue and blending with the far horizon. While he rested he scribbled a detailed description of the abundant mountain laurel thereabouts.[83]

Bartram descended the west side of the mountain and regained the rough, rocky road. He noted the "incomparable forests" and the fertility of the soil, speculating on the variety of plants that might be growing there: figs, olives, pomegranates, almonds, and peaches. In fact, the trees that did grow there resembled those he recognized in the Pennsylvania mountains. He crossed the headwaters of the Chauga River, commented on the open meadows and majestic forests as the trail led him along Whetstone Creek and through Rocky Gap, one of the infrequent easy passes through the mountains. The trail merged with today's Earl's Ford Road, sloping gradually down to the Chattooga. Highway engineers, for reasons of their own, have chosen to cross the Chattooga at much more difficult locations, with steep descents and hairpin turns.[84]

Earl's Ford as it crosses the Chattooga is a comparatively calm shallow section of this wild and beautiful river. The road continues on the Georgia side under the same name and follows the course of Warwoman Creek, the gradient more difficult than on the Carolina side. One of the soldiers in Andrew

Williamson's 1776 expedition complained that Warwoman Creek was "so crooked that we crossed it above sixteen times in the distance of eight miles."[85] Unfortunately for the travelers the trail became increasingly difficult as it followed Warwoman Creek to its source on Pinnacle Mountain. Benjamin Hawkins, a meticulous measurer of distances, counted nine crossings of Warwoman Creek before he reached its source.[86]

Bartram must not have taken notes as he rode along Warwoman Creek. He remembered it, though. In 1788 he responded to Benjamin Smith Barton's query about the place of women in Indian society. "When I was passing through the Cheroke country," he answered, "we came to and crossed a very fine rivulet, a branch of the Tugelo which is called Warwoman Creek." He said that he asked his companion, "an antient Trader," about the name. The trader replied that an Indian woman had helped her people win a battle on this creek and as a result had been made chief of her village.[87] (Thus the war woman mentioned earlier who met her death by the club of Cold Weather of Chilowee did not give her title to this stream.) It is passing strange that Bartram indicated that he went along the creek with "an antient trader" because in his *Travels* he stated that he traveled alone after leaving Keowee. He probably asked Patrick Galahan the origin of the name when he later met that gentleman.

The exhilaration he felt on the Oconee heights diminished as he made his way along the canebrakes of Warwoman Creek. The weather was unusually warm for late May. His horse, "my faithful slave and only companion," showed signs of stress. The trail climbed the southeastern side of Pinnacle Knob, and Bartram welcomed the cooler elevation. The sound of the creek cascading down the mountain attracted his attention. He crossed the creek stepping from rock to rock and following the right bank upward to a magnificent waterfall, not the most spectacular in the region but the best he had seen in his southern journey. "I have seated myself on the moss clad rocks, under the shade of spreading trees and floriferous fragrant shrubs, in full view of the cascades," he wrote.[88] Nature restored his spirits again, and he collected some plant specimens for Dr. Fothergill.

Francis Harper expressed equal enthusiasm for the falls when he found them in 1939. "In this wondrously enchanting scene, only a few hundred feet above the hot valley, one finds himself suddenly in a fairly boreal environment." He marveled that only one other person to his knowledge had recognized the place as Bartram's Falling Creek, and that was Benjamin Hawkins who followed the Warwoman Trail in 1796. The "boreal environment" looks today much as it did in 1775 and 1939, and the path that leads to the falls, now Martin's Creek Falls, is appropriately named the Bartram Trail.[89]

Bartram resumed his "lonesome pilgrimage" with his valuable specimens. Leading his horse, he scrambled down the steep slope of Courthouse Gap, following the old route. He emerged into the valley of Stekoa Creek, above today's Clayton, Georgia. The old road is impassable today, except for hikers. In Bartram's day the wayfarers used the path routinely. When crossing the ridge from the headwaters of Warwoman Creek to the head of Stekoa Creek nearly two decades later, Benjamin Hawkins met two Indian women driving "ten very fat cattle" to Oconee Station.[90]

A sudden storm, not unusual in the mountains in late spring, drenched him with rain and deafened him with thunder. Even his faithful horse showed uneasy nervousness; "my horse sinks under me at the tremendous peals," he wrote. Fortunately he came upon a trader's hut, empty except for bats and birds, struck a fire, and dried himself. He had never been so long away from an available food supply, and his provender consisted of a little biscuit and dried beef. He saved a piece of cheese he had brought all the way from Charlestown, possibly a parting gift from Mary Lamboll Thomas.[91] He intended to rely upon the reputed hospitality of any Cherokees he encountered, and he had letters of introduction to Galahan, head trader at Cowee, some thirty miles away.

He believed that the ruins he saw were the remains of the village of Stikoe, perhaps because Hunter's crude map of 1730 shows "Sticoe" at the point where the lower trading path meets Stekoa Creek, the headwaters of the Savannah River. Bartram mentions the trail dividing, the left fork leading westward to Hiawasee and the overhills towns, and the other going northward through Rabun Gap. (Today the town of Clayton occupies the divide; Highway 76 represents the only thoroughfare through the north Georgia mountains and the last until today's traveler arrives at Franklin and Highway 64.)[92]

Bartram continued several miles "over very rough, stony land," the low eastern continental divide at today's Mountain City, Georgia, and camped upon "a delightful brook, water of the Tanase." From this point the waters drained into streams and rivers that somehow found their way through the formidable Nantahalas down the Tennessee River and into the Father of Waters. A mile or so farther the beautiful "vale of Cowe" opened before him. There are still the "green turfy beds . . . parterres, vistas and verdant swelling knolls" along the Little Tennessee at Rabun Gap. As he marveled at the rich and cheerful scenery, the mountains receded on the right and "behold high upon the side of a distant mountain overlooking the vale, the unparalleled water fall appears as a vast edifice with crystal front, or a field of ice lying on the bosom of the hill." Estatoah Falls has never been so poetically or so aptly described. The falls are especially majestic after the kind of rain Bartram experienced the day before.[93]

Bartram forded the river near the present state line between Georgia and North Carolina and rode along the trail on the west side of the Little Tennessee. As he neared the site of the present town of Otto, he saw the many heaps of stones marking the graves of Indians killed in the battle of June 10, 1761. If he confused Middleton with Grant, the real commander, he clearly understood the importance of the event. The battle weakened the Cherokee Nation, "terrified and humbled them insomuch that they deserted most of their settlements in the low country, and betook themselves to the mountains as less accessible to the regular forces of the white people." Bartram had heard about the Cherokee War in the civilized environs of Charlestown. Now, standing at the battle site, the reality of the war and its aftermath sobered him as he contemplated "the gloomy shades and scenes of death."[94] He visualized those scenes as Henry Laurens might have described them.

Lt. Col. Henry Laurens was in the thick of those battles. After a grueling march from Oconee Mountain through Warwoman Valley, Grant's army of some twenty-six hundred camped at Estatoe Old Fields. Hunter's map shows Estatoe a short distance above Sticoe.[95] On June 10 the army set out in a column two miles long. Capt. Quentin Kennedy's Indian Corps, made up of Chickasaws, Catawbas, and Rangers garbed in forest green, marched in front and guarded the flanks. British light infantry followed and after them the Royal Scots and Burton's battalion. Middleton's South Carolina Provincials formed the rear except for the mile-long train of six hundred packhorses and a herd of cattle. Henry Laurens remembered the exact moment the firing began, 7:20 in the morning. Cherokee warriors, hidden on the hills on either side, kept up a rain of bullets and arrows. Grant pushed ahead, choosing not to fight on such disadvantageous grounds. British armies preferred to line up and shoot it out on level fields. Grant ordered his column to ford the river and form a battle line on an open plain. Meanwhile the Cherokees had infiltrated the supply train, and disaster threatened. Grant dispatched the Carolina provincials just in time to save his baggage. Grant held his formation while the Indians kept up an ineffective fire for two hours longer. By Laurens's precise reckoning the battle ended at 1:30 in the afternoon.[96]

A year earlier Grant, as Montgomery's second in command, had experienced the ignominy of a retreat after just such a battle near the same place. This time he buried his dead, took care of his wounded, and marched on. Bartram had seen the result in the sad condition of Keowee and the abandoned villages in the lower settlements. As he followed in the footsteps of Grant's army, he must have wondered what he would find in the middle towns.

IV

Set forwards again for Cowe which was about fifteen
miles distance, keeping the trading path. . . .
Harper, *Travels*

Bartram shook off the reverie occasioned by the sight of Indian graves and continued along the trail, following the twists and turns of the clear-flowing Little Tennessee. As evening approached he saw a hut at the base of a hill to his left, and at the same time a man in a canoe caught his eye. Bartram expected no trouble and usually none happened to him. The white trader banked his canoe and invited Bartram to stay the night. The man lived with an Indian woman and kept a stock of cattle. Bartram, who had not enjoyed a good meal since Keowee, pronounced the trader's helpmate "an excellent housewife and a very agreeable good woman." He had a pleasant surprise in the appearance of a group of Cherokee girls who brought baskets of strawberries.[97]

After a good night's rest he enjoyed a breakfast of barbecued venison, hot cornbread, butter, and cheese. Thus fortified for the road, he set out for Cowee. Trails led off from the main path to settlements in the hills, a clear indication that he had entered a more prosperous neighborhood than he had encountered since leaving Seneca. The town of Echoe at the junction of Cartoogechaye Creek and the Little Tennessee had recovered from Grant's devastating visit in 1761, and Bartram commented on the number of well-built houses. White travelers excited little curiosity along the busy road, and Bartram rode on without stopping. The town of Tassee at the junction of the Cullasaja and the Little Tennessee did not rebuild after Grant, nor did the ancient town of Nikwasi, two miles up the Little Tennessee. Forty-five years earlier the eccentric Sir Alexander Cuming met the assembled headmen of the Cherokees at Nikwasi and pronounced Moytoy "emperor" of the nation, a foreign notion to the Indians, but they agreed nonetheless. Cuming, representing only himself, demanded and received the nation's submission to King George and celebrated the treaty by taking a delegation to meet the king. Attakullakulla went along as one of the "ambassadors."[98] Fourteen years before Bartram, Grant used the village council house as his hospital, then destroyed the house as well as the town. Thomas Griffiths, on his mission to the clay pits near Cowee in 1768, noticed no settlements at the old site.[99] However, the mound on which the council house was built remained, and against all odds still remains in the busiest part of the town of Franklin.

Bartram mentions Nikwasi only as a place he passed, probably a reference to the mound and the site of the old village. Three miles down the road he came to Watauga. The path led to the council house and to his surprise stopped there. Noticing Bartram's quandary, the chief of the town stepped out of his house and beckoned Bartram to come. The chief, Will of Watauga, had been at the Augusta congress in 1763. Now in his sixties, he impressed Bartram with his posture and appearance. He commanded two young men to take Bartram's horse and feed it corn, then he conducted the visitor to an airy apartment, where the woman of the house brought out venison, "corn cakes," and a large bowl of hominy and milk. Next came the pipes and tobacco. Bartram marveled at the chief's four-foot-long pipe, sheathed in snakeskin and adorned with feathers and strings of beads. After the chief did the ritual honors to the sun and the four points of the compass, he handed the formidable instrument to his guest, who proved equal to the challenge of a four-foot draw. Only then did the host ask Bartram his business. Did he come from Charlestown? Did he know his good friend John Stuart? This was not the time for Bartram to reveal any ugly reports he might have heard about John Stuart's standing in Charlestown. He could say that he had spoken to Stuart before leaving Charlestown and received Stuart's approval of his expedition and that he merely wished to roam the countryside, perhaps as far as the overhills, searching for new flowers.[100]

This explanation pleased the chief, who demonstrated his pleasure by offering to escort Bartram to Cowee. Bartram's pleasure exceeded the chief's. "O divine simplicity and truth," he wrote, "friendship without fallacy or guile, hospitality disinterested, native, undefiled, unmodified by artificial refinements."[101] This prince of Watauga with his cheerful countenance and eagle eye bolstered Bartram's faith in the natural goodness of man, a faith shaken by the signs of the last war. The noble chief escorted Bartram to the trail and accompanied him two miles on foot before letting him go on by himself.

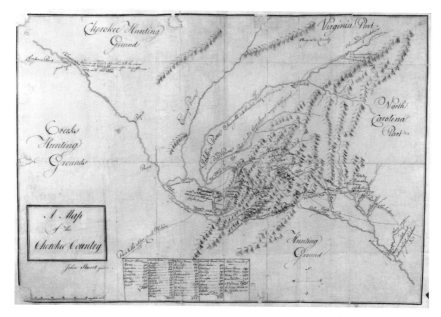

John Stuart's map of the Cherokee country demonstrates
his familiarity with the region.
Courtesy of the British Library, London

Around noon Bartram arrived at Cowee, the principal town of the middle
settlements. The great ridge of the Cowee Mountains closes the valley of the
Little Tennessee to the east, and on the west the Jore (Nantahala) Mountains
rise so that Cowee sat in a semicircle of mountains, its houses occupying both
sides of the Little Tennessee, which at this point is wider and swifter flowing
than before. Bartram considered the prospect "one of the most charming natural mountainous landscapes perhaps anywhere to be seen."[102]

He rode into the town and saw several white traders who directed him to
Patrick Galahan. Bartram had a letter of introduction from John Stuart, and the
trader received him kindly. Bartram found Galahan to be "something of a
prodigy," an honest trader. Never one to criticize, Bartram admitted that the
conduct of most of the traders he met left much to be desired. Galahan invited the explorer to share his house, and Bartram made good use of his opportunity to further his education about Cherokee culture. Cherokee houses con-

sisted of one large rectangular log construction divided into several apartments. Near this residence stood a round house that served as a "hot house" for winter lodging. Cowee's splendid earthen mound (which still rises beside the Little Tennessee) held a rotunda or council house in which a fire was maintained during the cold seasons. Winters tended not to be as severe in this sheltered fertile valley. The surrounding mountains acted as a buffer against winds from any direction except the south.[103]

Bartram heard the Cherokee language only through translation. He thought it sounded harsher than the Creek tongue, loud, with a frequent repetition of the letter *r*. The Creeks did not use the *r* sound. He pronounced the Cherokees "the largest race of men I ever saw," with bright complexions and an Asiatic cast. Bartram treated Cherokee women kindly in his several descriptions of them. They were "tall, slim, of a graceful figure, and have captivating features and manners."[104]

Bartram experienced a happy encounter with a group of Cherokee maidens the day after his arrival in Cowee. The adventure began as something of a lark. A young trader, who kept horses across the Cowee range, mentioned "some curious scenes among the hills," rousing Bartram's ever-lively imagination. As he climbed Cowee Mountain northeast of the village, he might have known that he again followed the path of Grant's destructive army and tried to visualize that scene. On June 25, 1761, while Lt. Col. Henry Laurens remained in the village with the Carolina provincial troops, Grant pushed on with fifteen hundred regulars and Quentin Kennedy's Indian Corps. Capt. Christopher French called Cowee Mountain "Stickowe Mountain" and wrote that it was more than two miles to the top "and extremely steep which made it a fatigue beyond description to get up to it."[105] Even the commander worried that his men might not be equal to the task: "No troops were ever in so dangerous a position and they continued so till we got to the top of the Catouche [Cowee] Mountains, one of the highest and perhaps steepest in America."[106] The soldiers then descended into the Tuckasegee Valley and destroyed the towns there.

It was this mountain with its cruel memories that Bartram decided to climb one sunny afternoon. Compare his description with that of his military predecessors. After following Cowee Creek for two miles through pleasant vales, they "then mounted their steep ascents, rising gradually by ridges or steps one above the other, frequently crossing narrow, fertile dales as we ascended; the air feels cool and animating, being charged with the fragrant breath of the

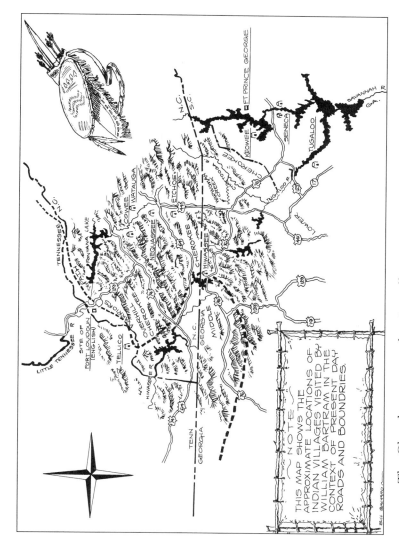

The Cherokee country showing village sites in present context.

Drawing by Bill Blackard

mountain beauties, the blooming mountain cluster Rose, blushing Rhododendron and fair Lily of the valley; having now attained the summit of this very elevated ridge, we enjoyed a fine prospect indeed; the enchanting Vale of Keowee, perhaps as celebrated for fertility, fruitfulness, and beautiful prospects as the Fields of Pharsalia of the Vale of Tempe."[107]

The present narrow gravel road, verging on precipices and winding steeply and dangerously up through Leatherman Gap, is only a degree improved from the trail Bartram followed and requires an hour of hard riding in a four-wheel-drive vehicle. One comes away with a greater admiration for the stamina of Bartram and a better understanding of how his appreciation of nature virtually levitated him up the mountain that challenged hardened soldiers. The view still rewards the climber. To the north across the Alarka Valley loom the Great Smokies; to the west the Nantahalas pile one upon the other; and the shoulder of the Cowee Mountain obscures the view to the east. Below, the meadows and vales of the Little Tennessee Valley stretch down toward the Georgia line. Bartram saw many villages along the hills to the south, an observation that suggests that the valley contained more people then than now.

If further demonstration is needed to establish Bartram's physical fitness, consider that he next descended the even steeper northern flank of Cowee. Finally the two adventurers reached the lowlands watered by Alarka Creek. Up and down they rode across open fields, then on foot through a forest. They found the trader's horses and treated the animals to salt he had brought with him.[108]

Mounting again, they ascended a ridge and viewed a scene surpassing even that of the Alachua Savannah of Florida, "parterres of flowers and fruitful strawberry beds; flocks of turkeys strolling about them; herds of deer prancing on the meads or bounding over the hills; companies of young, innocent Cherokee virgins, some busily gathering the rich fragrant fruit, others, lay reclined under the shade of floriferous and fragrant native bowers."[109] Without question this was one of the "curious scenes" his companion had promised him. Some girls bathed in the stream; others chased after their companions threatening to paint their cheeks and lips with ripe strawberries. This "sylvan scene of primitive innocence" proved "too enticing for hearty young men long to continue idle spectators." With "nature prevailing over reason" the two invaders stepped out into the open. The older matrons gave the alarm and attempted to gather the girls around them. However, a few of the bolder ones allowed themselves to be cut off from the others and captured. Bartram put it this way, allowing future disciples of Freud to interpret as they wished: "They confidently discovered themselves and decently advanced to meet us, half unveiling their blooming faces, incarnated with the modest maiden blush, and with native innocence and cheerfulness, presented their little baskets, merrily letting us know that their fruit was ripe and sound."[110]

The other girls and even the suspicious matrons then joined the party. The young trader spoke Cherokee, and so there followed animated conversation punctuated by much giggling and nibbling on strawberries. Bartram enjoyed it immensely and left "these Elysian fields" with happy memories. Men such as Will of Watauga and women such as these innocent maidens proved to Bartram the goodness of humans in a state of nature. The recrossing of the difficult Cowee Mountain caused no trouble, and the two adventurers managed to be back at the village before nightfall.

It is one of the interesting coincidences of history that today, just above Alarka Creek and near the place of the strawberry party, a portion of the Cherokee Indian Reservation is located, detached from the larger reservation in the Great Smoky Mountains National Park. On a May afternoon, when the strawberries are ripe, perhaps the visitor might come upon the same curious scene that delighted William Bartram.

V

I resolved to pursue the journey alone, though against the advice of the traders; the Overhill Indians being in an ill humour with the whites.

Harper, *Travels*

The Overhills Cherokees were in a particularly disturbed state because aggressive "Virginians" continued their encroachment. Their settlements, though twice protected by the Nantahalas from invasions by Montgomery and Grant, lay dangerously exposed to an army coming along the backside of the Appalachian chain from the northward. In October 1774 the Virginians defeated a coalition of northern tribes under the Shawnee chief Cornstalk at Point Pleasant. The Cherokees worried that they might be next. Worse, as far as the young hunters were concerned, was the recent cession of millions of acres of central Tennessee and Kentucky at Sycamore Shoals on the Watauga River in March 1775. The protracted negotiations fractured the Overhills people. Attakullakulla and the elders signed the treaty, but Dragging Canoe and many young men left the meeting in anger rather than sign.[111] Some of these disgruntled warriors subsequently killed two Virginians carrying messages to Carolina.[112]

Veteran traders such as Galahan were usually well informed about the mood of the people among whom they lived and carried on their business, for their lives depended on it. They were right in their advice to William Bartram not to go wandering in the hills just then, but Bartram could be foolhardy on occasion, and in this case he decided to ignore the good advice. If he could not dissuade the botanist, Galahan would at least show him the way. The first few miles of the trail across the Nantahalas followed the pleasant valley of Iotla Creek with its swelling hills and spacious meadows. Bartram called them "lawns," and the new May grass looked freshly mowed like modern lawns. At a ridge they lost the Iotla but encountered the swift-flowing Burningtown Creek that cascaded down the defile between Wildcat Knob and Wayah Bald. Galahan turned back at this point, unwilling to try the difficult crossing of the high ridge. Bartram had mixed feelings as he said goodbye to the older man: "I was left again wandering alone in the dreary mountains, not indeed totally pathless, nor in my present situation entirely agreeable although such scenes of primitive unmodified nature always pleased me."[113] He seemed surprised at his own reactions to being left alone. He remembered how comfortable he felt "in the society of the aimable and polite inhabitants of Charlestown" and understood how an outcast might feel, deprived of human company. He hurried on, eager to get over the Nantahalas and bring the Cherokee exploration to an end. He set no particular destination other than to see what the country looked like.

The path wound up steeply, crossing and recrossing a creek. Near the ridge he stopped to rest. Suddenly a young Cherokee man, armed with a rifle, with two dogs following, came down the path. He looked surprised, then came up and shook Bartram's hand. Bartram assumed that the man asked about his coming and going, but could not understand the language. Bartram's offer of a plug of tobacco eased the need for speech, and after a good deal of gesturing relative to trails and directions, the two parted. The Indian, on this occasion more Bartramlike than Bartram, went off singing.[114]

The meeting shook the botanist out of his lonesomeness and fatigue, and he recorded dozens of mountain plants in his notebook. To complete the cure he left the path to climb to the summit of Wayah Bald, higher even than Cowee Mountain across to the east, and his spirits soared. On this most elevated peak "I beheld with rapture and astonishment, a sublimely awful scene of power and magnificence, a world of mountains piled upon mountains."[115] (At the summit of Wayah Bald today, the Bartram Trail crosses the Appalachian Trail. Less adventuresome latter-day Bartrams may drive up to a parking lot and view the same magnificence from a lookout tower.)

He regained the path, made his way around the mountain, and began a gradual descent down the western side into the valley of Wayah Creek. He commented on the minerals he saw in the crumbling cliffs, isinglass and kaolin. He knew about Thomas Griffiths's excavation near Cowee "for the purpose of making Porcelain or China ware" for Josiah Wedgwood. Wayah Creek winds through a narrow defile, thick with rhododendrons and ferns; the lofty mountains shade out the sun. Here Bartram found the going much easier. He camped for the night near Wayah Gap, the opening to the overhills.[116]

The next day the path took him along Jarrett Creek to a ford in the Nantahala River, "a large branch of the Tanase." He picked up the Choga Creek and crossed over Old Road Gap to Junaluska Creek. In the vicinity of the present town of Andrews, there occurred a memorable incident. Descending the path came a company of Indians riding rapidly toward him. At their head Bartram recognized the famous Attakullakulla, about whom he had heard so much from Stuart, Cameron, and the traders. The reason he recognized the chief, now in his seventies, was that he had observed him closely at the great congress at Augusta in 1773. When the troop reached him, he turned his horse off the trail to let them pass. He meant it as a gesture of respect, and Attakullakulla understood it as such. The little chief paid Bartram the return compliment, clapping hand to breast, then offering it to Bartram saying, "I am Ata-cul-culla." He gave the botanist an opportunity to gain favor by inquiring in English if Bartram had ever heard of him. Instead of a pedestrian response to the effect that he had seen him in Augusta, Bartram showed that he could be diplomatic if disingenuous. "The Good Spirit who goes before me spoke to me," Bartram replied, "and said, that is the great Ata-cul-culla." He added, without the same finesse, that he belonged to the Pennsylvania tribe of white men who love the Cherokees and the name of Ata-cul-culla was dear to all the Pennsylvanians.[117] Perhaps Bartram had heard that the Little Carpenter was particularly fond of compliments.

The chief, obviously pleased, asked about John Stuart, whom he had once rescued at Fort Loudoun. Yes, Bartram happened to be a friend of the superintendent and had visited with him the day before he left Charlestown on his friendly journey to the Cherokees. Bartram asked the Little Carpenter to give Stuart his regards should they meet soon.

Bartram's account of his meeting with Attakullakulla raises questions, as does his passing reference to a coming Indian congress at Seneca in June.[118] It is certain that the Indian party did not find Stuart because at that same time, the end of May, Stuart prepared to take his leave of Charlestown. Stuart's correspondence is filled with his own problems, but there are clues to Attakullakulla's reason for seeking a meeting in the letters. The chief knew that Stuart adamantly opposed the Sycamore Shoals Treaty. In fact, the superintendent scolded the Cherokees for "giving away land to every white man that asks for it."[119] The protracted controversy about the elusive Houmachta and Sophia continued to annoy Stuart, and he and Cameron badgered the Cherokees about sheltering the refugees.[120] More recently Stuart ordered Cameron to call the headmen to Seneca to demand satisfaction for the two Charlestown-bound Virginia messengers recently killed. Bartram had heard about the meeting at Seneca from Cameron, and he assumed that the conference would ease tensions in the Cherokee country.[121]

After leaving Attakullakulla's party Bartram continued his journey, but as he went he wondered why he did so. He had crossed laboriously difficult ranges to get this far, the Oconee and the Cowee, and had just taxed his endurance by climbing the Nantahalas. Now if he wanted to continue on the path to the site of Fort Loudoun, another massive range reared beyond the pleasant broad valley of the Nantahala River. He had sampled the vegetation of this part of the overhills region and thought it unlikely that the distant ranges and valleys would produce different plants for his collection. Besides, if he went on he might miss the potentially important conference at Seneca. All things considered, he made up his mind to turn back. He would simply list the towns not visited, Chote, Tellico, Hiawassee, and the rest—towns on maps he had from John Stuart, towns he had heard about from Galahan. After a good night's rest he retraced his route without comment, arriving at Cowee late in the evening. Galahan had not expected him back so soon.[122]

On his last day in Cowee, Bartram witnessed a festival of music and dancing that may have been a farewell party for him, but which he said was a kind of pep rally for a ball game the next day. These ball games were a rough-and-tumble version of lacrosse that pitted every able-bodied male of one village against those of another. The games were played with the same testosterone-charged passion of modern college football, without the protection of padding, and they excited the same fervor among the spectators. Bartram's description of the evening provides an intimate glimpse of one aspect of Cherokee social life.[123]

The people of the town gathered in the council house atop the ancient mound that still stands at West's Mill, the site of Cowee. None of Bartram's contemporaries among the villagers knew the mound's age, origin, or purpose, but they honored it and put their town house upon it. Sitting inside and waiting for the show to begin, Bartram had an opportunity to record a thorough description of the building. The three-tiered circular structure had banked seats along the walls. One door permitted access and allowed smoke from a small fire to escape.[124]

The ceremony began with an aged warrior reciting the heroic play of athletes of old, not omitting his own, with a spirited challenge to the youth of Cowee to live up to the tradition. The musicians came next, and to their beat the young women shuffled in, keeping time to the music. Bartram complimented their appearances and the "gentle, low and sweet" sound of their voices. Then with a sudden whoop the young men leaped into the circle brandishing their webbed rackets and formed a line facing the girls. They executed complicated movements in perfect order. After the ball-play dance others followed. The men's dances tended to be exaggeratedly martial or lascivious, the women's more decorous. Even when engaged in "amorous interludes," Bartram admired the way they blushed modestly. There must have been some unlovely and cantankerous women in the Cherokee country, but Bartram does not mention them.[125]

William Bartram's explorations of the Cherokee country lasted only about a month, but for posterity his brief passage meant more than any other travel account—Cuming's, Griffiths's, Timberlake's, Michaux's, Hawkins's, and far more than the military annals of Montgomery and Grant at the end of the French war and Williamson's at the beginning of the Revolution. Because of the enthusiasm, sensitivity, and excitement with which Bartram wrote, future travelers and residents regarded the mountains with greater wonder and respect for having read his journal. Yearly, thousands of nature-starved city folk set out along the Bartram Trail in the hope of savoring the same emotions he felt. Many return satisfied.

Bartram's account of his return from the Cherokee country lacks the anticipation and excitement of that he felt on his journey into the middle settlements. Serious business lay ahead. Cameron had called the traders as well as the headmen to meet him at Seneca. Patrick Galahan intended to make the trip but had to take care of some business first so Bartram decided to set out alone and wait for Galahan at Keowee. He returned by the same route he had come, but there were no stops at huts of friendly Indians, no maidens bringing strawberries, no waterfalls, and no mountaintop views as he followed the Little Tennessee to Warwoman Creek, crossed the Chattooga, climbed Oconee Mountain, passed the familiar Tomassee Knob, and on the second day entered the unexciting village of Keowee. While waiting two or three days for Galahan, he scouted around the hills and came upon a number of curious structures consisting of four flat stones—one base, two for the sides, and one across the top. No one knew what they were, and Bartram left it at that. Galahan and the other traders arrived in Keowee, and Bartram went with them to Seneca. Cameron and some of the headmen had begun discussions that seemed likely to continue for some time. Unfortunately, Bartram neglected to record the subject under discussion, only that the Indians appeared unsettled and in ill humour.[126]

They had good reason to be disgruntled. John Stuart had been forced to leave Charlestown. Cameron himself, their good friend Scotchie, felt that his life was in danger. The Provincial Congress had met in Charlestown on June 1 and listed as one of its grievances that "There are just grounds for to apprehend an insurrection of the slaves, and hostilities from the Indians, instigated by the tools of a wicked Administration."[127] The congress ruled that anyone who failed to sign the association against trade with Britain would be treated as an enemy to the colony. It further resolved to raise fifteen hundred troops.[128] On June 14 the congress elected a Council of Safety to act as a plenipotentiary standing committee. Henry Laurens was chosen to head that body. On June 23 the council named as Cherokee commissioners Andrew Williamson, Edward Wilkinson, and John Bowie. At the same time new Creek commissioners were appointed in the persons of George Galphin, LeRoy Hammond, and David Zubly, brother of John J. Zubly.[129]

Bartram lingered in the backcountry during June. There is no indication in his *Travels* that he felt concerned about the deterioration of the social and political fabric, but he should have been concerned. He did not hide the fact that he had conferred with John Stuart, now an archenemy of the revolutionary council in Charlestown. He had carried messages from Stuart to Cameron. More suspiciously he had then gone into the Cherokee country carrying messages from Stuart and Cameron to the traders, and now he returned with traders and Indians for the mysterious Seneca congress. In the poisoned atmosphere of the day, when friends suddenly became enemies, William Bartram might easily have been suspect, and if he were accosted and made to take the oath to abide by the resolutions of the Continental Congress, would he have done it? An indication that he might have wanted to defer that decision is the fact that he retired to Fort James in Georgia rather than going to a more settled area. He had decided to accompany the company of adventurers under Captain Whitfield on their expedition to West Florida.

Meanwhile rumors filtered back to Charlestown of dark goings on at Cameron's Seneca congress. Veteran trader Robert Goudey of the overhills town of Great Tellico testified in a sworn deposition that he had heard Mankiller of Keowee say that Cameron sent for the Overhills Cherokees, gave them plenty of rum, and then Cameron allowed John Vann to tell the headmen that they must "fall upon the white people on this side of the river and kill them" but not to molest the people on the Georgia side.[130] If that happened while Bartram attended the session, one can understand why he went to Georgia. That he did not mention such an important matter is another indication that he deliberately ignored the fractious world of humans and focused on the ideal world of plants, animals, and a few selected good people.

5

The Creek Country

June 22nd set out from fort Charlotte in company with
Mr. Whitfield who was chief of our caravan.

Harper, *Travels*

Bartram is vague about his actions prior to setting out for Mobile on June 22, 1775. After the Seneca meeting he crossed over to Fort James in Georgia to wait for the departure of Whitfield's "company of adventurers," probably gentlemen interested in West Florida land. At the fort he renewed acquaintance with its commander, Edward Barnard, and with Dr. Francis Begbie, the garrison surgeon who enjoyed botanizing with Bartram.[1]

Bartram teases his readers with explanations of how he spent his days. Although he had "little time" to equip himself for the long journey, he made "little botanical excursions" along familiar Broad River. We might wonder why he spent as much as two weeks in the Georgia backcountry instead of going to Augusta, the logical place to secure equipment. The obvious answer is that he wanted to avoid possible confrontations. The rumor of a Stuart-inspired Indian war alarmed people in Augusta, especially the newcomers who disliked Indians from a distance. Agitators George Wells and Robert Hamilton found ready listeners when they urged a strict enforcement of the Continental Association. Few friends of government, with the striking exception of brash young Thomas Brown, dared oppose the radicals. In Savannah the confusion worsened. A radical group spiked the cannon on the battery on June 2, 1775, to prevent the guns firing in celebration of the king's birthday on June 4. On June 5 the same persons erected a liberty pole in defiance of Governor Wright.[2] "We have had the devil to pay in town," John Houstoun wrote to Lachlan McIntosh.[3] Houstoun warned McIntosh that Wright might try to raise a regiment of Darien Highlanders to defend himself.

Capt. Edward Barnard died while Bartram dallied at Fort James Dartmouth. The *Georgia Gazette* of June 21, 1775, carried the notice that Barnard's death occurred at the fort he commanded. Barnard had a distinguished record of leadership in the Augusta community and in the Georgia assembly. He had earned universal respect for his character, sound judgment, and dedication to the public good. He would be sorely missed in the coming crisis. One cannot doubt that a person of Bartram's sensitivity felt keenly the death of the leader of the ceded lands survey and his host at Fort James. The fact that he did not choose to record it in his journal is another clue to the kind of book he wanted to write. He would not write about death, not Barnard's or any others. He intended his message to be one of birth, hope, optimism, and the future in a divinely ordained world.

Capt. George Whitfield had set June 22, 1775, as the departure date for his Mobile-bound company. Bartram joined the expedition at Fort Charlotte on the South Carolina side of the Savannah River and left with them on that date. The troop traveled leisurely to New Bordeaux, a recent settlement of French Huguenots some ten miles downriver from Fort Charlotte. They were entertained that night by the community's founder and most prominent citizen, Jean Louis de Mesnil du St. Pierre. M. St. Pierre displayed considerable enterprise in establishing the settlement in 1768 and in starting a wine industry. In 1771 he went to London to secure financial backing for the wine business and succeeded in persuading Lord Hillsborough to give him a grant of five thousand acres. Henry Laurens happened to be in London then and gave his blessing, if not his money, to the project.[4] St. Pierre made the most of his grant. Bartram admired the way the French gentleman had built his mansion on a hill and developed neat vineyards on one side and well-cultivated fields of corn, rice, wheat, oats, sweet potatoes, and indigo on the other. St. Pierre speculated in land in Georgia and probably shared Whitfield's interest in West Florida property.[5]

Here another omission occurs in Bartram's narrative. Neither Whitfield nor St. Pierre got to leave New Bordeaux. Both men had come under the scrutiny of the South Carolina Council of Safety, presided over by Henry Laurens, and whose most zealous member was William Henry Drayton. On June

26, 1775, the council ordered one of its three new regiments under the command of Col. William Thomson to proceed to Fort Charlotte and assume command in the name of the council. If Whitfield proved cooperative, he and his family should be allowed to remain in the fort, but in a subordinate position. Laurens had a second thought: "It occurs to me that Captain Whitefield however chearfully he may shew an inclination [to] serve the Colony by a resignation may not be Content with a sub-command if he is a man of Spirit he will not."[6] Because the council doubted Whitfield's commitment to their party, Laurens thought it a good idea for him to come to Charlestown, hat figuratively in hand and profess his loyalty. A commission might be forthcoming. In any case Whitfield could not be entrusted with possession of such a strategically important place as Fort Charlotte even if it happened to be his property.

M. St. Pierre's loyalty came into question also. St. Pierre had returned to Fort Charlotte with Whitfield after seeing Bartram's party off. St. Pierre and possibly Whitfield had been observed talking with one Joseph Coffell (sometimes spelled Scophol). Coffell had an unsavory reputation as a leader of the lawless crackers during recent Regulator Wars when groups of vigilantes had imposed order by shooting some people. The council regretted that Coffell escaped with his life. Whitfield innocently mentioned Coffell's visit to area resident John Lewis Gervais, who promptly alerted Laurens and alarmed the council.[7] The council authorized Colonel Thomson to arrest Coffell, St. Pierre, or any person suspected of being an enemy of the colony.

On June 26 the council dispatched Andrew Williamson, one of the province's newly appointed Indian commissioners, to interview Alexander Cameron. Because of Cameron's influence among the Cherokees, he would be a valuable recruit to the patriot cause. Williamson reported in the first place that the Long Canes people were greatly disturbed and divided, and more to the point that Cameron had heard that he was in danger and had withdrawn from the town of Seneca to Keowee, a safer refuge for him. Good soldier Williamson decided to follow him there, accompanied by another district resident and fellow commissioner John Bowie. They approached Cameron as the friend he had always been. Williamson showed Cameron copies of the Stuart correspondence, but Cameron vehemently disagreed that Stuart intended to foment an Indian war. Even if Stuart commanded such a terrible thing, Cameron said he would never carry out the instruction. Williamson quoted him as saying that God forbid that he should be so void of humanity as to bring the Indians on the province. When Williamson asked what Cameron might want in return for his services, the deputy answered that he held any kind of bribe in contempt.[8] Cameron stood on the moral high ground and apparently embarrassed his visitors.

John Lewis Gervais then tried his hand at friendly suasion. He had seen Stuart's letters, and he worried about his good friend's complicity: "Resign and live admired, beloved and I make no doubt I may say rewarded among your friends."[9] The wooing of Cameron, like the proffer of a commission to Whitfield, provides an insight into the effective recruiting tactics of the gentlemen of the Council of Safety. The ploy failed to work in Cameron's case, partly because of his loyalty to Stuart but also because he knew that some of the same gentlemen wanted him dead. Cameron informed Stuart that William Henry Drayton ordered Richard Pearis to arrest Cameron or to kill him. Cameron knew that to be true because Pearis himself told him that his life was in danger.[10]

Even earlier in May, when he lingered in Seneca after his conference with the headmen and traders, Cameron learned that the council intended to arrest him. The word quickly spread from Seneca to other villages. The Good Warrior of Seneca, working in his fields, threw away his hoe when he heard about the threat to his friend Scotchie. He set up a whoop and, according to Cameron, in five minutes every man in Seneca fit to bear arms gathered around him. The headmen sent painted runners to the villages in the lower and middle settlements with the news that they might have to rally about Scotchie. It was then that Cameron retired to Keowee, where Williamson and Bowie found him.[11]

Adding to the turmoil and confusion in the Carolina upcountry was the arrival of Gov. Lord William Campbell, to the great relief of Lt. Gov. William Bull, who had by now abdicated responsibility in the crisis. Almost immediately upon his landing on June 18, Lord William realized that he had no control over the city and his only hope lay in the loyalty of the country people. He confided to Lord Dartmouth that several "reputable" people from the upcountry dared the wrath of the American party by calling upon him in Charlestown. They suggested organizing a counterassociation, one by people pledged to support the king. Campbell encouraged them to do so, promising protection and rewards.[12] Lord William came late to the game of handing out commissions but managed to retain the loyalty of leaders such as Thomas Fletchall, Joseph Robinson, Robert and Patrick Cunningham, and the fiery young Yorkshireman Thomas Brown. Campbell assumed that most of the outlying residents preferred the king to the Charlestown gentry, but they needed the support of redcoats to embolden them.[13] Out of these furtive meetings between the belea-guered governor and his informants grew the plan sometimes called the "south-ern strategy." Let the loyal Cherokees frighten the frontier people and the redcoats subjugate the city so that peace might be restored.[14]

It would have been impossible for William Bartram not to have observed that the Carolina upcountry had become a tinderbox about to explode. One of the chief incendiaries, William Henry Drayton, proclaimed "Peace, peace is not even an idea. A civil war in my view is absolutely unavoidable."[15] Bartram left Carolina before the explosion, but just barely. He discovered that Georgia lagged only a month behind South Carolina in the march toward revolution. Carolinians broke into their powder house on April 21. Georgia's Liberty Boys followed the example on May 11, the day after the news of Lexington and Con-cord reached Savannah. On June 1 Georgians of St. John Parish sent sixty-three barrels of rice to the distressed people of Boston. By the end of June, South Carolina's Barnard Elliott roamed the Georgia backcountry recruiting Georgians for the new Carolina regiments, playing upon the hatred of Indians and the frontier's fear of a Stuart-instigated war.[16]

Moderates had not completely given up hope of compromise. Savannah's leading citizens gathered at the liberty pole on June 26, with future loyalists and future patriots almost equally represented and Lachlan McGillivray in the chair. They resolved to do all they could do constitutionally to redress grievances against Parliament.[17] On July 4 Georgia's Second Provincial Congress gathered in Peter Tondee's tavern and listened to a stirring oration by Rev. John J. Zubly. Basing his text on the unjust Rehoboam of Israel, Zubly made the point that subjects need not obey an oppressive king, but the solution lay in an appeal to the king rather than separation from his rule.[18] The congress proceeded to the formal adoption of the Continental Association and to the election of delegates to the congress in Philadelphia. The adoption of the association marked the turning point for the colony and a crucial victory for the radical element. Enforcement of the association depended on local committees made up of per-sons new to politics who disliked the ruling faction, whether Whig or Tory. Power passed from the elected legislative to local committees of "liberty boys."[19]

No action of the Georgia Provincial Congress disturbed the Indians more than the July 8, 1775, seizure of the gunpowder intended for the Indian trade. The news of that action, together with the confusing reports that George Gal-phin had superseded John Stuart, agitated the Creek country even as William Bartram prepared to enter that country.

Someone from Georgia told someone in Charlestown that the government supply of powder and ammunition was en route to Savannah on board the *Magnacharta*, recently rechristened the *Philippa*, Richard Maitland, master. The Carolina Council of Safety resolved their moral qualms about purloining private property, such as they were, by saying to themselves that the king's servants intended to use the powder against them so the issue became one of self-defense. Besides, if the Georgia governor and the superintendent in exile were deprived of the powder they had promised at the October 1774 congress in Savannah, the Indians might well turn against them.[20]

A contingent of Carolina Liberty men hurried over to the "Bloody Point" at the mouth of the Savannah River. Georgians outfitted a schooner, named it the *Liberty*, and entrusted command to Oliver Bowen. The *Liberty* had no trouble taking over the *Philippa* despite the protestations of Capt. Richard Maitland that the powder he carried belonged to individual merchants, not the king or the governor or the superintendent.[21] Carolina took 5,212 pounds consigned to Carolina and East Florida merchants and persuaded Georgia to give up 5,000 pounds more to support the Continental army.[22]

The Carolina Council of Safety coached the fledgling Georgia Council of Safety in all important matters. On July 24, 1775, the Carolina council informed Georgia that George Galphin had asked for a present of powder for the Indians. If he had powder to distribute, he was certain that he could win the Indians away from Stuart. Meanwhile, Galphin instructed his traders to counteract Stuart's influence. The Carolinians cautioned the Georgians not to permit traders to supply powder as they usually did in return for deerskins. It would be better to give the headmen a small quantity of powder in the name of the province.[23]

Even before receiving this advice, the Georgia Provincial Congress decided to send two thousand pounds of the confiscated powder as a present to the Creek Indians. Governor Wright lamented that the powder was intended to be a gift not from the king, governor, superintendent, or traders but from the people of the province; "this will raise strange ideas amongst the Indians," he thought.[24] Thoroughly discouraged, Sir James asked to be allowed to return to England. The Georgia congress adjourned on July 17 and entrusted the conduct of affairs to the Council of Safety.

Bartram and his new traveling companions, not named by him, followed a road that took them to the great trading road from Augusta to the Creek country. They camped on a well-known rendezvous, Flat Rock, near present-day

Camak. Like other once-famous places such as Buffalo Lick, the Great Ridge, and The Rocks, Flat Rock has lost its importance as a landmark and lapsed into obscurity. When Bartram's party stopped there, it was a convenient place for the final organization of trading caravans.[25]

The campsite was familiar territory to Bartram; he had passed by it on his way to and from Wrightsborough. Middle Creek watered Flat Rock and connected it with Wrightsborough. Having previously satisfied his curiosity about the Quaker settlement, with its plant and animal life as well as human, he remained with his fellow travelers rather than visit the Wrightsborough people. If he had, Bartram would have noticed the general consternation about the worsening political climate. Community leader Joseph Maddox, elected as a delegate to the Provincial Congress, declined attending.[26]

There were optimistic signs of progress, however, in this back part of St. Paul Parish. Daniel Marshall's Kiokee Church attracted new members. Two other Baptist churches spilled over from Kiokee. According to Marshall's son Abraham, the church grew rapidly before the Revolution, "breaking forth on the right hand and on the left."[27]

Additionally, the village of Brownsborough was new since Bartram first passed this way. The seventy or so indentured servants brought over by Thomas Brown in November 1774 worked diligently in their fields. Most of them came from the Orkney Islands north of Scotland, and the adjustment to the Georgia climate absorbed their energies. One young Orcadian felt awed by his experience: "This is a good poorman's country when a man once gets into a way of living," he wrote home, "but our country people knows nothing when they come hear, the Americans are smart. Industrious hardy people, and fear nothing. Our people is only like the New Negroes that comes out of the Ships at first when they come amongst them."[28] Their young leader, Thomas Brown, spent his time in Augusta and New Richmond with surreptitious trips to Lord William Campbell in Charlestown.

Before the end of the year another village, called Friendsborough, would be laid out in the Kiokee neighborhood by an Orkney Quaker named William Manson. The other backcountry "borough," Queensborough on the Ogeechee, had already dissipated into a scattering of Irish people along the river. George Galphin, one of the promoters of the Queensborough project, kept two trading posts on the Ogeechee, one at Old Town, some twelve miles below present-day Louisville, and a newer post at Galphinton, about seven miles above the site of Louisville. A well-traveled cutoff called Tom's Path connected the two trading places to the Lower Creek path.[29] An indication of the growth of population is the fact that Governor Wright signed 358 grants averaging more than 250 acres in St. Paul in 1774 and the first months of 1775. An equal number of other squatters neglected to apply for grants.[30]

While Bartram and the gentlemen speculators were encamped at Flat Rock, two companies of Indian traders from Augusta rode into camp. They offered to escort Bartram's party to Mobile. Bartram mentioned that the traders had spare horses and that those of his companions were "jaded," thus joining the traders seemed a good idea. If their horses were worn already, the company of adventurers must have been poor planners. Bartram did not mention a much better reason for accepting the traders' offer, namely that Indians never attacked a trading caravan even though the Creeks were likely to be surly, especially when the traders had to explain their lack of gunpowder. Traders had always been the primary intermediaries with their Indian clients, and George Galphin expected his employees to persuade his Creek customers to accept rum in lieu of powder and to heed his talks instead of John Stuart's. If William Bartram's journal reflects George Galphin's views, it may have been because of the company the botanist kept as he traveled the Indian trails.

When the riders crossed the Ogeechee, Bartram chronicled a primitive country inhabited by peaceable people and adorned with pleasing plants. He neglected to mention, however, that it was also a testing ground in which agents of the king struggled against those of American Congress for the allegiance of the Creek Nation.

II

Our caravan consisting of about twenty men and sixty
horses, we made a formidable appearance, having now
little to apprehend from predatory bands or out-laws.
Harper, *Travels*

The traders Bartram traveled with included some hard characters, similar to those described harshly by Creek agent David Taitt in his report to John Stuart in 1772. They stand accused of flagrant cheating and general flaunting of trade regulations. One of them told Taitt bluntly that he would not obey the governor, the superintendent, or anyone but his employer.[31] The disintegration of the trade stemmed from an unfortunate clause inserted by the idealist Lord Shelburne into the otherwise sensible Proclamation of 1763 opening trade to all comers thus effectively destroying the discipline exercised by the great trading houses. Bartram met some rascals along the way, notably Adam Tapley, but he had a knack of seeking out respectable veterans such as Job Wiggins in Florida, Patrick Galahan in the Cherokee country, and James Germany among the Upper Creeks. Much of the information he recorded he gleaned from these friends.

In the crisis of 1775 the traders had a new role. They acted as emissaries for one side or the other in the contest for the allegiance of the Indians. George Galphin's people, including James Germany, worked for Galphin and therefore for the Continental Congress. The Spalding and Kelsall employees, in contrast, cooperated with John Stuart and the royal government. The coincidental deaths of Edward Barnard, Robert Mackay, and Martin Campbell in 1775 deprived John Stuart of influential traders who would likely have been auxiliaries. With the rise of radicalism in Augusta, Stuart attempted to transfer his base to West Florida. He persuaded the prominent Augusta merchant Andrew McLean to open a house in Pensacola. McLean's journal, recently acquired by the Georgia Historical Society, shows a "deerskin account" and a "beaver account" at Pensacola.[32]

Forward-looking traders such as Lachlan McGillivray had already opened houses in Mobile or Pensacola. Lachlan's cousin John McGillivray became an important person in Mobile's economic and political life, and served as lieutenant colonel of the loyal militia during the Revolution.[33] Bartram used the services of the firm of McGillivray and Swanson to ship his specimens.

The traders generally acted as couriers of the latest news, and those with Bartram had significant stories to tell. George Galphin's messenger, Benjamin Steddiman, might have been one of the party because the news of Stuart's flight from Charlestown and Galphin's appointment as the agent of the Continental Congress reached the Creek country about the time Bartram's entourage did. Bartram arrived at the Chattahoochee on July 11, 1775. Four days later David Taitt at Little Tallassee in the Upper Creek country first heard the news.[34] As a result the Creek country was thrown into confusion for the duration of Bartram's stay on the far western frontier.

Taitt immediately sent runners off to Mobile with the disturbing information. Thus alerted and alarmed, Dep. Supt. Charles Stuart hurried to tell Gov. Peter Chester in Pensacola about John Stuart's predicament.[35] Meanwhile, Taitt called together the Upper Creek headmen and told them the bad news. The Indians were sorry about Stuart's problems but outraged by the taking of powder intended for them. In their view they had fulfilled the terms of the

October treaty by delivering up thirteen fugitive slaves and sending a party of warriors into the Cherokee country looking for the notorious and still defiant Houmachta and Sophia.[36]

The simmering Choctaw war aggravated the tense situation. Six Choctaws recently ambushed and routed a party of twenty-five Creeks on the path to Mobile.[37] Some Creek leaders suspected that the British supplied the Choctaws and deliberately encouraged them to assault the Creeks. They were not far wrong; the traders supplied the powder, and British policy encouraged the war. Now the expected powder from Augusta had been stopped. Taitt warned that the road to Augusta, the road just traveled by Bartram, was no longer safe.[38]

Taitt also sent Emistisiguo and the second man of Little Tallassee to the Lower Creek towns to ascertain the mood of those people. They returned within the month of August with news that a Cusseta man had brought a talk from Galphin saying that he and the Augusta merchants were sending a supply of ammunition. The governor and Mr. Stuart, Galphin said, wanted to bring the Indians to poverty, but he and the Augusta merchants intended to supply the Indians. Jonathan Bryan, "that infamous villain" as Taitt called him, sent another talk explaining that the reason the governor withheld the Indian supplies was that he meant to ask for another cession of land before releasing the stores. Of course, Bryan had not given up his own scheme of securing a vast tract of Florida land. Taitt assured Charles Stuart that only the duplicitous Sempoyaffe and some other Cowetas listened to Galphin and Bryan. Adding to Taitt's concerns was his speculation about the intentions of Escochabey the Young Lieutenant, who kept to his house at Coweta since his return from visiting the governor of Havana. The Spanish might be up to some mischief. Most of the Lower Creeks, swayed by Emistisiguo's prestige, promised to heed only Stuart and the governors. However, they were much confused, and Taitt intended to visit the lower towns again himself.[39]

If William Bartram had thought to avoid trouble by going west, he discovered that trouble followed him, as it had from the beginning of his journeys. Though his instructions linked him to the products of the wilderness, his destiny seemed to be intertwined with the people of the frontier. From the congress of Augusta on, events in the Indian country influenced his mission. Typically he made no mention of the critical condition of the Indian country, and most of his readers have been led to believe that the frontier was no more dangerous than his father's garden on a larger scale. He declined even to complain of the heat of a southern summer except to express sympathy for the manner in which the swarms of horseflies made the packhorses miserable.[40] The only hint of discomfort was a certain absence of cheerfulness in his chronicle as he crossed Georgia. He commented, disapprovingly one suspects, on the way the traders got the attention of stubborn horses by biting their ears.

Francis Harper did his best detective work in tracing Bartram's route into the Creek country with the help of David Taitt's 1772 map. The old Federal Road coincided with the trading road to the Lower Creek town, but no modern road follows it except for brief stretches. The Mayfield Road from Warrenton, Georgia, to Mayfield is one such, and except for the pavement the country retains much of the primitive. Bartram crossed the Ogeechee at the site of Mayfield. For such a historic waterway—the Ogeechee remained the Indian boundary until 1790—the river has a modest appearance: trees shroud its thirty-foot span from both banks. The village of Mayfield sits forlornly on the Ogeechee; prosperity, like history, has left it behind.[41]

His route cut across country to the site of Sparta, a larger version of Mayfield. A cluster of antebellum houses testify to the vanished wealth of the antebellum cotton country. Many people of Hancock County are descendants of the county's plantation slaves.

Bartram's party camped at Rock Landing on the Oconee, a favorite resting spot for the trading caravans. Bartram regarded it as "a delightful grove of forest trees" on the edge of an open field. Of particular interest to him was that his Seminole friends of the Cowkeeper's town of Cuscowilla came from this place. When the trespassing "Virginians" bothered them, these Indians moved first to the Upper Creek country, then to Florida, where Bartram encountered them.[42]

From Rock Landing the path corresponded with modern Highway 49 as far as Macon. The "swelling hills and levels" are still there as are "the expansive illumined green fields," but gone are the "sublime forests" of Bartram's day. At the Ocmulgee he viewed "the famous Ocmulgee fields" with the "wonderful remains of the power and grandeur of the ancients."[43] The fields with their mounds are a national park today, and a fine museum relates the history Bartram had to guess at. (Although archeologists have found artifacts left by nomadic hunters of ten thousand years ago, the mounds date from about 1000 A.D. A huge funeral mound shows seven stages of construction; more than a hundred burials have been uncovered, many with shell and copper ornaments. A reconstructed earth lodge displays the original clay floor with sculpted seating places for the headmen around the circular sides. The site gives silent testimony to a long period of peace that allowed such elaborate architecture to be built.)

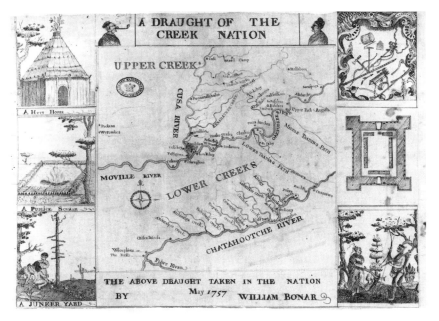

William Bonar's map of the Creek country, 1757.
Courtesy of the Public Record Office, London

Bartram did not mention a contemporary village on the Ocmulgee, but there was one. Before he returned along this road, the village would be raided by outlying Georgians, looking for horses.[44] The botanist commented favorably on the land west of the Ocmulgee. He venerated the primitive wilderness but was realist enough to realize that American civilization would work its inexorable way west. This part of Georgia, he thought, "promises a happy, fruitful and salubrious region when cultivated by industrious inhabitants."[45] He did not envision the kind of prosperity brought by the plantation system and could not have foreseen the long post–Civil War depression.

Bartram's route from the Ocmulgee to the Flint approximates today's Highway 80; his Tobosochte is today's Tobesofkee Creek, a surprising consistency of pronunciation, if not spelling. Francis Harper concluded that Bartram's beautiful Sweet Water Brook is today's Culpepper Creek. Here Bartram found a shrub new to him, a species of hydrangea, and did a careful drawing of it. Route 80 passes the adjacent small towns of Knoxville and Roberta and crosses the Flint River. There is no indication that this was the trail the Indians and their traders called the "great white road," no sign that later the Federal Road came this way. Nor is there today any evidence that Benjamin Hawkins located his Creek agency here near the river.[46]

After fording the Flint the heat began telling on the travelers. The horses suffered most, and the traders had to slow their progress, moving only early in the day and later in the evening. There was little opportunity for relaxation at midday because of the swarms of stinging, droning horseflies that tormented man and beast. "We fall into a kind of torpor, rather than a refreshing repose," Bartram wrote. A fierce thunderstorm—Bartram compared it to a hurricane— shocked the heat-stricken party. The storm cooled the temperature, and he recovered his enthusiasm: "indeed all around us appeared reanimated, and nature presents her cheerful countenance." The vegetation smiled and the birds sang merrily in the groves. The trail took a more southerly direction, following Upatoi Creek, and at last brought them to the Chattahoochee across from a Yuchi Indian village. The Yuchi people ferried the traders across the river in canoes while the horses swam the broad stream. Bartram considered the town "the largest, most compact and best situated Indian town" he ever saw. The well-built houses were plastered inside and out with a mixture of reddish clay and roofed with cypress shingles. Bartram realized that the Yuchis constituted a separate tribe from the Creeks and spoke a different language.[47]

After refreshing themselves at the Yuchi town, the travelers continued downriver to Appalachicola, an important peace town of the Lower Creeks. Headmen gathered there when they had to talk peace. By contrast, Coweta town some twelve miles up the Chattahochee was the traditional war town. Coweta, where George Galphin resided and fathered several children with two women and where the Wrightsborough raiders lived, must have seemed a dangerous place to Bartram. Even now no one could count on the disposition of Sempoyaffe, the headman of Coweta, and still less of Escochabey the Young Lieutenant. Bartram preferred to linger at the peace town.

The chief trader of Appalachicola entertained Bartram out of consideration for the botanist himself or for George Galphin, whose letter Bartram carried. They walked a mile or so downriver to view the site of the former town marked by mounds and terraces. The inhabitants abandoned the town about twenty years before because of flooding and also because blood had been spilled and the place became haunted by vengeful spirits. Some of its people scattered to other towns, but most settled the new town of Appalachicola on its high bank. A few merged with the Oconees in East Florida as Seminoles.[48]

Bartram learned about the current state of affairs of the Creek Nation and recorded some of it. According to his information the proud Muscogulges compelled the Chickasaws to enter an alliance with them, and then, by a series of raids, they humbled the Cherokees. Now they intended to break up the Choctaw Nation and extend their hunting ground. In Bartram's telling, the Creek and Choctaw War had little to do with British provocation and everything to do with the empire-building aspirations of the Muscogulges. This motive, he thought, compared favorably with the reasons so-called civilized nations went to war. He rejected the notion that the Indians warred capriciously or over trifling objects.[49]

Bartram had more to say in defense of the Indians later in his private correspondence with Benjamin Smith Barton. Bartram explained, when Barton inquired about the Indians' conception of property, that although the entire extent of the Creek territory was collectively owned, within villages they observed individual ownership of property. Here he cited a remarkable example of private enterprise on the part of one of the principal men of Appalachicola. Because he kept trading boats on the Altamaha and carried goods to Frederica, Sunbury, and Savannah, the traders called him Bo'sun (for Boatswain). Rather than rely on traders he carried skins on his own packhorses to his boats, delivering them himself. He had acquired wealth enough to live comfortably, as Bartram could testify by personal experience. Bo'sun invited Bartram and the veteran trader to breakfast in an open pavilion in front of his house, a "delightful place" to Bartram. He wrote, "We had excellent Coffee served up in China Dishes by Young Negro Slaves—We had plenty of excellent Sugar, Honey, Choice Warm Corn Cakes, Venison Steak and Barbacued."[50] Bo'sun had fenced in about a hundred acres, tended by his own family, including fifteen slaves. Bartram noted that when the slaves married Indians, they became free citizens. Bartram went on at length about this man's achievements, even drawing a diagram of his house and buildings to make a point. He explained to his friend Barton, in language harsher than he used in *Travels*, that he hoped this example among many that he could give would "serve to convince those prejudiced, ignorant, obstinate people, that attest it is impossible for the Cricks to be brought over to our modes of civil society." In fact, Bartram suggested that our society might be bettered by an imitation of theirs.[51]

The traders left the adventurers at Appalachicola, each one proceeding to a different town, and the company of speculators left the town on well-rested horses along the path to Mobile. Bartram gives the date as July 13, 1775. Their route took them through present-day Fort Mitchell and Uchee to Society Hill, where the path followed today's Highway 80. The Upper Creek town of Tallassee was located below the falls of the Tallapoosa River, near the mouth of Euphapee Creek and a short distance below the site of the present town of Tallassee. Atasi, another important town, lay several miles west on the Tallapoosa with Kolumi about five miles farther along the river. Bartram brought letters from George Galphin to James Germany, the resident trader at Kolumi, and visited Germany for two days, consulting with him about "my affairs and future proceedings."[52]

The old town of Kolumi and Germany's plantation occupied a site south of the westward flowing river. The mounds, fields, and commons mentioned by Bartram are still there while a later town site across the river has suffered erosion. A golf course and a grass farm protect the older site.[53] The ridge of hills north of the river that hemmed in Kolumi of Bartram's day still guards the Tallapoosa Valley.

Bartram described James Germany as an "elderly gentleman, but active, cheerful and very agreeable," who received him hospitably. His wife, though "industrious, prudent and affectionate," disappointed the trader in one respect. She refused to permit their children to be educated in Savannah or Charlestown. In her stance this mother simply adhered to the customs of her people, a matriarchal society. The children belonged to the clan of the mother, and the mother had the final word in their upbringing. The patriarchal Scots traders had to contend with this cultural clash in their liaisons with Creek women. Lachlan McGillivray, who sent his son Alexander to be educated in Charlestown, was a notable exception.[54] As for Germany, "this affair affects him very sensibly, for he has accumulated a pretty fortune by his industry and commendable conduct."[55] The clan of his woman and children would profit by his industry.

We can imagine that James Germany listened attentively to Bartram's news. Bartram merely hints that they discussed his "future proceedings." The turmoil and confusion accompanying the rapid drift toward revolution, especially Stuart's exile and Galphin's new status, must have occupied their attention. Only a few miles away, above the junction of the Tallapoosa and the Coosa, David Taitt used Little Tallassee as his command post, sending runners to all the towns in the Creek Nation on behalf of John Stuart. Bartram and his fellow adventurers held a unique position in this period of conflicting talks and rumors. As recent arrivals they could speak with some authority about current events. Bartram, for one, could be impartial. His dilemma stemmed from his Quaker commitment to peaceful solutions to problems and the fact that he knew and respected men on both sides of the argument, John Stuart and Alexander Cameron on one side and Henry Laurens and George Galphin on the other. For the present the adversaries carried the same message to the nation: this is a white man's quarrel—stay out of it! As the still incipient British plan of bringing the Indians into the conflict became a reality, Bartram would have an excellent reason for preferring Galphin's policy of neutrality.

III

Being now recruited and refitted, having obtained a guide to set us in the great trading path for West Florida, early in the morning we set off for Mobile.

Harper, *Travels*

Now, without the protective convoy of the trading caravan, the company of speculators regained the path leading to Mobile. During the last days of July while they made their way, Indian couriers traveled the same path. After David Taitt's first meeting with local headmen on July 15 at Little Tallassee to tell them about Stuart's misfortune, he made a quick trip to the Chattahoochee towns and back by August 1, 1775. His messenger to Mobile returned to Little Tallassee by the same date, as did another runner carrying messages from John Stuart in St. Augustine.[56] William Bartram certainly understood the reasons for all this excitement even if he did not write about it.

The road followed by Bartram passed through the present Mt. Meigs, a depopulated place just outside the thriving environs of Montgomery, and took a southwesterly direction through present Snowdoun.[57] A deluge of rain forced the travelers to stand on a flooded plain the first night out. Their guide left them the next morning and returned to Kolumi, having set the men on the clearly marked trail. Bartram's companions flushed out a litter of young wolves and chased and caught one. One man held the animal by its hind legs while another beat out its brains with the butt of his gun. "Barbarous sport," commented Bartram.[58] One suspects that the botanist had a poor opinion of his companions, none of whom he named.

Bartram demonstrated his acute perception and powers of description on the road to Mobile. A modern traveler near Greenville, Alabama, might not observe anything unusual about the soil, but Bartram commented that black, rich, and "soapy" topsoil lies on a deep bed of white limestone and is slippery after a rainfall.[59] Indeed it does. He seemed to notice every specie of tree growing along the way: oaks, magnolias, various pines, black locusts, basswoods, red mulberries, elms, hickories, walnuts, crab apples, redbuds, and sweet gums. He commented on the unique forest of dogwoods and imagined what a show it made in spring. He noticed how the ground gradually changed composition—pebbly, brown soil on a bed of red clay.

As he neared Mobile Bay in present Baldwin County, he mentioned the highest land as "somewhat encumbered with pebbles, fragments and cliffs of rusty ferrugineous rocks."[60] His description of the place, identified by Harper as Gopher Hill, is accurate today.[61] An abundance of gopher turtles in the vicinity gave the place its name. Except for Bartram's passing and the gophers, the hill is utterly undistinguished, rendered more so by a paper company's clear cutting of the area.

In 1939 Frances Harper photographed a portion of the old road five miles east of Midway where it corresponded to the Monroe-Conecuh county line. The road, now paved, betrays its origins by its narrow, winding course and by the old buildings scattered along the way, some dilapidated. Locals at a country store confirmed that indeed this was the old stagecoach road and that an abandoned house used to be an inn, but strangers should be careful about the rattlesnakes. Like so many other places along the old trading path, the area is sparsely populated. Except that country music icon Hank Williams came from there, travelers on Interstate 65 would have no reason to turn off.

Bartram's party reached Tensaw Bluff, where the trail met the Tensaw River. Francis Harper believed that Tensaw Bluff was located at the mouth of Hall Creek at today's upper Bryant Landing.[62] However, Davida Hastie, Baldwin County historian, has gone through deeds at Baldwin County Courthouse and concluded that Tensaw Bluff was at today's lower Bryant Landing, just above the point where Interstate 65 crosses the Tensaw River. The old trading path, approximated by Highway 59, makes its closest approach to the river at this point.[63]

In addition to fixing the location of Tensaw, or Farmer's Bluff, Davida Hastie secured the cooperation of other friends of William Bartram who, in 1976, formally established the Bartram Canoe Trail commemorating the naturalist's exploration of the Tensaw.[64]

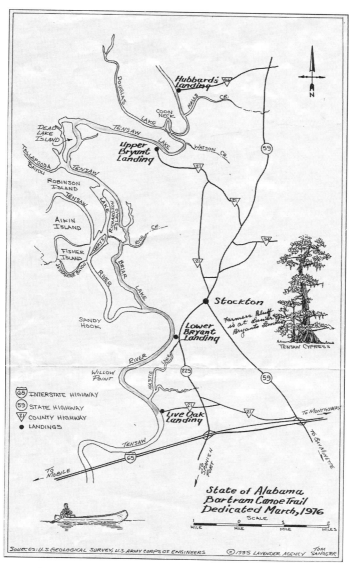

The Bartram Canoe Trail memorializes Bartram's
upriver expedition from Farm Hall.

Courtesy of Davida Hastie

Bartram and his companions paid their respects to Major Robert Farmer, whose plantation occupied Tensaw Bluff, and the major invited Bartram to spend a few days with him upon returning from Mobile. Presumably the unnamed adventurers lingered at Tensaw because Bartram used the first person singular in referring to his departure: "Next day early in the morning, I embarked in a boat, proceeded for Mobile."[65] He must have had a guide because the Tensaw confuses strangers as it divides into different channels and meanders toward Mobile Bay.

In the evening he arrived at Mobile, his long-anticipated destination, but there is little of the celebratory in his description of the town. Once occupying twenty-eight blocks along the bay, the town lay "now chiefly in ruins, many houses vacant and mouldering to earth."[66] However, there were a few good houses, and the big trading firm of John McGillivray and company made some improvements on the waterfront. Bartram's comments seem complimentary compared with other descriptions of Mobile. On first sight Gov. George Johnstone expressed dismay: "The state of the town in filth, nastiness and brush wood running over the houses is hardly to be credited."[67] Gen. Frederick Haldimand toured Mobile in 1770 and reported that the town appeared deserted and that old Fort Conde, renamed Fort Charlotte, might as well be torn down for its bricks.[68]

Founded in 1701, Mobile had the distinction of being second only to Biloxi in the history of Louisiana and seventeen years older than New Orleans. Successive French governors from Bienville to Kelerec used Mobile to entertain Indian visitors in an effort to counter British influence. French influence extended up the Alabama River to the junction of the Coosa and Talapoosa, where stood Fort Toulouse of the Alabamas, the embodiment of the claim of France to the southern frontier. When the French gave up that claim in 1763, the Alabama Indians destroyed Fort Toulouse rather than let the hated British have it and moved to the Mississippi. Most of the French "habitans" of Mobile chose to leave their town rather than remain as British subjects, giving Mobile the decaying look that William Bartram described a decade later. In 1766 Mobile's population numbered 500 whites (300 men and 200 women) and 360 black men, women, and children.[69] By 1774 the town consisted of 330 whites and 410 blacks.[70] Thus, Mobile's growth remained stagnant during the decade while the western parts of West Florida grew steadily. In 1774 the province numbered 4,900—3,700 whites and 1,200 slaves. Three-fifths of those lived near the Mississippi.[71]

William Bartram remained in Mobile for five days by his own account. He does not say what he did. One can assume that John Stuart, who gave him messages for Alexander Cameron, must have given him letters of introduction to Charles Stuart. Charles Stuart retired from the British army in 1763 to join his cousin John, the superintendent of the Southern Indian Department in Charlestown. John made Charles his commissary to the several small tribes on the Mississippi. Like so many Scots, Charles Stuart easily accommodated to tribal life and customs. In 1776 John promoted Charles to deputy superintendent and stationed him in Mobile. Good soldier Charles Stuart followed the shifting policies of the British ministry as they were relayed through John Stuart. When the idealist earl of Shelburne advised bringing the warring tribes to the peace table, Charles invited leaders of the Choctaws and Creeks to Mobile. He was on the verge of success when in 1770 Shelburne's successor, Lord Hillsborough, decided on a policy of nonintervention. In the words of John Stuart's biographer, John Richard Alden, Charles Stuart "then proceeded to undo his own labors and to foment discord so adroitly . . . that the war was continued."[72]

Charles Stuart obtained a leave of absence in 1773 and went to Charlestown, intending to visit his married sister in Paris, but the Wrightsborough raids of 1773 and early 1774 forced a change of plans. John Stuart sent Charles back to Mobile "with presents to manage the Choctaw war."[73] The deputy reached Mobile on April 26 and urged the Choctaws to keep up the pressure on the Creeks.[74]

Any messages Bartram might have for Charles Stuart, other than a letter of introduction, were made obsolete by events since Bartram's April 22, 1775, meeting with John Stuart. Charles Stuart heard the astonishing news of John's exile by a runner from David Taitt only a week before Bartram's arrival in Mobile. When Stuart alerted Gov. Peter Chester of West Florida about recent alarming events, he was able to borrow a token amount of powder for Taitt to use in the emergency. Before Bartram left West Florida, Charles Stuart would be called upon to reconcile the Creeks and Choctaws and to unite them for possible military action against the rebellious Americans.[75] Meanwhile, Bartram found Mobilians in a state of nervous anxiety about how their colony might be affected. Boston was far away, but the Indian nations were close, dangerously so if they could be won over by George Galphin and his friends.

Another person Bartram must have called upon was the merchant John McGillivray to make arrangements for the shipment of his specimens. McGillivray had come to America at the urging of his cousin Lachlan McGillivray in 1756 and had gone to work for the partnership of Lachlan McGillivray, George Galphin, and John Rae. He took up residence in the remote Chickasaw country and fathered two mixed-blood sons, Samuel and William.[76] When the British acquired Mobile in 1763, McGillivray opened a store there in partnership with Lachlan's former partner, William Struthers, and Peter Swanson. Maj. Robert Farmer, the military commander at Mobile, took exception to the typically rowdy behavior of a gang of McGillivray's employees and had the lot of them arrested. Farmer accused them of acting "in so riotous, debauched, drunken manner of life that they were a nuisance to every family . . . and a pest to society."[77] A military court decided to punish the worst offender with 250 lashes and let the others go. By the time of Bartram's arrival, John McGillivray was recognized as one of the town's most prominent citizens and sat in the seldom-invoked general assembly.

Though we can only infer that Bartram called upon Charles Stuart and John McGillivray, we know that he took up quarters at Major Farmer's residence, Farm Hall on Tensaw Bluff. He traveled up the Tensaw River in a trading boat on August 5, having been invited by Major Farmer to "spend some days in his family."[78] Bartram declared Farmer a "worthy gentleman," and without doubt he was, but he was also one of the most controversial figures in British Mobile. As the commanding officer of the Thirty-fourth Regiment of Foot, he had an exaggerated opinion of his importance. He ruled Mobile with military discipline from October 20, 1763, until the arrival of Gov. George Johnstone on December 1, 1764, and even then maintained the independence of the military from the civil government. This led to continual and bitter disputes, many of them petty, between the irascible Johnstone and the stubborn Farmer. Johnstone had to remind Farmer that he was not in command of West Florida but merely the major of the Thirty-fourth Regiment stationed at Mobile.[79] Farmer did not recognize John Stuart's prerogative in Indian affairs and refused to shake Stuart's hand when the superintendent visited Mobile.[80] The long-suffering General Gage finally tired of the bombardment of accusations against Farmer and ordered a court-martial on charges of peculation brought by Johnstone.

Before he heard about the court-martial, Farmer embarked on an adventure that had elements of the heroic with undertones of farce. He took the 34th out of Mobile and up the Mississippi River to occupy the French Fort Chartres near Kaskaskia. He accomplished the mission by sheer willpower and iron discipline in spite of a chorus of complaints by his officers and desertions by his troops. He reached Chartres on December 2, 1765, and on May 17, 1766, received summons to appear in Pensacola for his court-martial.[81] By the time he arrived on December 11, 1766, his adversary, Governor Johnstone, had been recalled by an exasperated ministry.[82] The assembling of the requisite number of officers took more than a year, and the court finally convened on March 16, 1768, lasting thirty-eight days. Farmer benefitted from the fact that his military peers resented the attitude of the civil governor. The court acquitted him of the charges of illegally profiting by his office.[83] Farmer subsequently journeyed to London on business in 1769 and learned that his commission had been sold without his knowledge and that, like it or not, he was now a civilian.[84] He retired to his Tensaw property just below the Creek boundary set by Stuart's Indian congress in 1765. He remained a dominant figure in Mobile, and at the time of Bartram's visit he served in the assembly and acted as justice of the peace.

Bartram described Farm Hall with approval that he withheld from the town. Farmer had "a most delightful situation, commanding a spacious prospect up and down the river, and the low lands of his extensive plantations on the opposite shore."[85] The major owned sixty acres on the west bank of the Tensaw and thirty-four acres back of the bluff on the east side, and employed forty-five slaves and several white workers. He kept a herd of cattle as well as thirteen horses and sixteen jackasses. Farmer was fifty-eight in 1775, his wife, Mary Anderson of Yorkshire, much younger, and his children not out of their teens. Bartram met Anne, Catherine, Thomas, and Elizabeth; Robert, the eldest boy, studied in London with indifferent success. Although Farmer owned land above the Creek line, he did not attempt to occupy it. In fact, no white settlement lay above Farm Hall after the French abandoned their plantations in 1763 and the land declared Creek territory by treaty in 1765. The latter circumstance caused Farmer considerable anxiety, and he made a nuisance of himself by appealing for protection of his outpost.[86]

Bartram disliked contention but enjoyed discussion and probably agreed with Farmer's political views. The major deplored the worsening relationship between colonies and mother country. He understood that "the Americans only desire to participate with the Britains in the privileges and liberties of their happy constitution."[87] A full-scale war would redound to the benefit of Britain's rivals, France and Spain. When he learned of the British plan to involve the Indians in the war, he worried that the pro-American faction among the Creeks would fall upon the exposed frontiers of West Florida.[88]

In his continual search for curious shrubs, Bartram found one growing on Major Farmer's property. He called it *Myrica inodora*; the French called it "the wax tree."[89] The large berries of the tree are covered with a waxlike scale, and he learned that the locals preferred the tree wax to beeswax for candle making. On another day he decided to make a canoe excursion upriver to see what else he might find. Traveling alone in the maze of waterways would have been a risky business, but the interconnecting rivers had been carefully mapped by David Taitt in 1771, and river residents such as Major Farmer would have had copies. Bartram set out on the East Branch, the name given on Taitt's chart, and not the Tensaw, the later name. He had not gone far when he noticed a blooming plant. Expressing surprise at its beauty and its size, Bartram described it as "gilded with the richest golden yellow."[90] He went on about the plant at length in his report and for good measure drew its portrait. The plant, the primrose, is cherished today by the residents of Baldwin County, the more so because of Bartram's delight in discovering it.[91]

After camping on the riverbank, the explorer continued his excursion, passing abandoned French plantations and marveling at giant cypresses and bamboo canes. He was happiest alone like this, communing with nature. "What a sylvan scene is here," he exclaimed. "I recline on the verdant bank, and view the beauties of the groves."[92] His curiosity impelled him farther upriver to the confluence of the Tombigbee and the Alabama, where he again camped. The next day he passed a large lagoon covered with chinquapin plants and disembarked at a high bluff to see what the forest might contain. He found vestiges of what he thought was an old French fortification. Looking across to the east side of the river, he saw trees so large that "I shall forbear to describe them, because it would appear incredible." He would only say that the cypress, ash, poplar, and other hardwoods were "the tallest, straitest and every way the most enormous that I have seen or heard of."[93] Even the bamboo grew to a height of forty feet. Bartram's description of his river adventure inspires moderns to take to the canoe trail named in his honor just as his word pictures of the Cherokee mountains tempt his readers to explore those heights.

Back at Farm Hall, he came down with a fever. As Mobile historian Peter Hamilton commented about Bartram, "He was to learn that the beautiful swamp and sylvan scenes and piroguing the lower rivers in August is not very prudent."[94] In the unlikely event that further evidence is needed for William Bartram's energy of mind and body, it is the fact that, only partly recuperated, he traveled thirty miles upriver to find a plant with supposedly curative powers.

He located it (a species of stone root), drank its juice, and found its taste pleasant. "For the sake of variety" he took an even longer ride on horseback to find other plants (including the abundant blue sage and scarlet foxglove) and returned home "fully satisfied with the day's excursion" in spite of "feverish symptoms continuing to lurk about me."[95]

At Farm Hall another guest, Dr. Michael Grant, physician to the Pensacola garrison, told him that a trading boat was scheduled to leave Mobile for Manchac on the Mississippi River. The fever notwithstanding, Bartram resolved to be aboard that vessel. Major Farmer provided a bateau and crew for Bartram's return to Mobile. On the way Bartram and Dr. Grant chatted about the absence of honeybees in West Florida. If one needed confirmation of his powers of perception, it is that Bartram not only noticed what was there but also what was not there. He thought it "extraordinary and almost incredible that there were no bees around."[96]

IV

*Our captain kept on for Pensacola, where we arrived in
the evening.*

Harper, *Travels*

William Bartram intended simply to sail around Mobile Bay, but he found himself instead bound for Pensacola. He left his letters of introduction, "all my papers and testimonials," in Mobile.[97] The ship's captain told him that he wanted to investigate a wreck and possibly salvage the sails, and Bartram went along to see what he might see. They found the wreck on the east shore of the bay, but it had already been stripped so the captain decided on a quick visit to Pensacola, the capital of West Florida.

Without his papers and probably disheveled from camping out on the beach near the wreck the night before, the botanist thought he would not announce his arrival, just look around a bit to satisfy his curiosity and be ready to leave whenever the captain gave the order. After an inspection he concluded that Pensacola made a better appearance than Mobile. Robin Fabel, in a recent history of West Florida, described the town in fewer words than Bartram managed: "During the ten years of British rule the capital, Pensacola, had developed from the bleak collection of huts bequeathed by the Spanish into a pretty little town with perhaps 200 houses, wharves, warehouses and a gridiron of streets surrounding a central square, in which stood a fort."[98]

Bartram thought there were "several hundred habitations" in Pensacola though Bernard Romans counted only 180 in 1775.[99] Bartram was particularly impressed by the governor's house, built of stone by the Spanish and crowned by a tower. The wooden fort housed the council chambers, quarters for the officers, and barracks for the garrison. A defensive stockade surrounded the town.[100]

The fortifications Bartram described in passing happened to be a point of contention between the civil and military leaders of West Florida. When the Wrightsborough raids occurred during the winter of 1773–1774, West Florida's panic almost equaled that of the eastern colonies. On March 26, 1774, Gov. Peter Chester conveyed a council resolution to Lt. Thomas Hutchins, military engineer at Pensacola. The council expected a "sudden stroke from the merciless hands of the cruel savages," and Hutchins should improve the town's defenses forthwith.[101] On the same day, Governor Chester wrote to the officer commanding the Pensacola garrison to "be prepared for any sudden attack" and to the officer commanding the batteries at the entrance to the harbor "to secure the harbor and town."[102]

A party of friendly Creeks, unaware of the fright their appearance caused, came into town on a routine mission to secure powder and ball for their protracted war against the Choctaws. Governor Chester turned them away in conformity with Georgia's punitive ban on trade. The good people of Pensacola, their fears increased, threatened Hutchins the engineer for his lack of cooperation and collected four hundred pounds sterling to clear the thickets around the town to expose any Indians who might be lurking there.[103] The military men found one excuse after another to avoid taking orders from the civil authority until General Gage—with troubles of his own in Boston—ordered them to work on the fortifications. The improvements were ongoing when Bartram surveyed the situation.[104]

Bartram's intention of remaining incognito proved unrealistic. Dr. John Lorimer, physician to the garrison, learned that the son of John Bartram was in town and sent him an invitation, explaining that Governor Chester would like to interview the botanist. While Bartram pondered whether to accept and possibly miss the boat for Mobile, he received another note, this from Philip Livingston, Governor Chester's secretary, to call upon him at his residence. Bartram must have worked out an arrangement with the captain because he agreed to delay his departure and see both Livingston and Lorimer and the governor as well.

It is not surprising that Dr. Lorimer wanted to meet the Philadelphian, for he happened to be the resident naturalist in West Florida. Lorimer came to Pensacola as surgeon of the Thirty-first Regiment in 1765 and almost immediately found himself involved in a life-and-death struggle with disease. Pensacola deserved the name Graveyard for Britons when five hundred persons died in the first two years of occupation. The Thirty-first Regiment suffered terribly from typhoid fever. By 1767 Lorimer succeeded in getting healthier barracks, shaded by piazzas and drained properly. Drinking water was first boiled and a healthier diet imposed.[105] Meanwhile, Lorimer found himself involved in political disputes. With so few eligible for office in the colony and with unusually contentious governors such as George Johnstone and Montfort Browne, political disputes involved almost everyone. Lorimer charged fraud in the first election of the West Florida assembly in 1766, won his case, and was rewarded with the speakership.[106] Other advantages followed; in 1770 he obtained the dual position of deputy surveyor and auditor of revenues and secured large land grants on the Mississippi.[107]

A motive of Lorimer's in meeting with Bartram was their mutual interest in the flora and fauna of the country. Lorimer corresponded with the London naturalist and West Florida agent John Ellis, and he knew William G. DeBrahm and Bernard Romans, both of whom studied Florida's natural history. In 1769 the doctor was honored by election to the American Philosophical Society.[108] He would have been keenly interested in Bartram's research and one of the few who wanted to know more about Bartram's plants than events back east. Governor Chester thought so well of Lorimer's abilities that he nominated him to the unofficial position of provincial botanist at fifty pounds sterling per year. According to the governor, Lorimer "employed himself in making curious and useful observations on the Country, Climate and natural productions."[109]

Philip Livingston, the governor's secretary, belonged to the prominent Hudson River Livingstons of New York and came to West Florida with the governor in 1770. Chester showered Livingston with preferment. The secretary held nine offices and accumulated 150,000 acres in land grants, most of them on the Mississippi.[110] Livingston had a vested interest in welcoming newcomers such as Bartram because he collected fees on each grant of land. Livingston scored a major coup in 1773, when he entertained Col. Israel Putnam and Lt. Rufus Putnam, both of whom represented New England speculators of the Company of Military Adventurers. The history of the adventurers is complex, but Bartram would have been interested in the fact that members of the company were in fact establishing themselves on the Mississippi, where he intended to go.[111] Whereas Lorimer would have enjoyed discussing Bartram's plant specimens, Livingston would have been more interested in the intentions of the speculators who accompanied Bartram to Mobile. At the precise moment, however, events in the Indian country occupied their attention, and they, like most West Floridians, wondered how they might be affected.

News brought by sailing vessels arrived so belatedly that their information could hardly be called news. Land communication worked more efficiently. David Taitt kept Charles Stuart informed of events, and Stuart made frequent visits to Pensacola. The latest report Taitt sent down on August 27 related how the civil war had actually begun. The Augusta liberty boys had mistreated some of the king's friends, and one young gentleman had been tarred and feathered some three miles above Augusta. Taitt told Stuart that "our friend" Andrew McLean might be in trouble. He also related that Col. Thomas Fletchall rallied South Carolina loyalists and had them on the march to Augusta to attack the liberty men.[112]

Taitt's news was mostly accurate. The Augusta Sons of Liberty decided to make an example of the most vocal supporter of royal government, the young Yorkshireman Thomas Brown. On August 2 they crossed into Carolina and walked up to LeRoy Hammond's New Richmond plantation house where Thomas Brown resided when he was not at his Brownsborough plantation. After a dramatic debate about the meaning of liberty between the leaders of the crowd and the lone but defiant Brown, the crowd surged forward. Brown shot one man in the foot and held others off with swordplay until he was hit from behind with a rifle butt, fracturing his skull. Whether they applied tar and feathers is not clear, but they did enough, scalping in several places, burning his feet, and hauling him senseless around town as an object lesson. When he recovered, he retired into the Ninety-Six District of Carolina and found friends including Col. Thomas Fletchall.[113] In Charlestown and Savannah, as well as Pensacola, rumors circulated that Fletchall and a vengeful Brown were on the march upon Augusta. The Georgia Council of Safety sent a company of militia to Augusta in anticipation of a battle, and the Carolina council dispatched William Henry Drayton, Rev. William Tennent, and Rev. Oliver Hart to dissuade the country people from joining the loyalists.[114]

David Taitt would have trouble getting news henceforth except by word of mouth. The Augusta committee men, headed by George Wells, intercepted letters addressed to Taitt and made life miserable for merchants friendly to Taitt. The deputy expected more Augusta traders to move their stores to Pensacola or Mobile. During September disturbing reports continued to filter into West Florida. On the 7th Galphin's nephew David Holmes brought the Georgia powder taken from Maitland's ship to Eusitchees, a Lower Creek town. Holmes, who appeared uncomfortable in the role of revolutionary, delivered his speech, blaming Georgia's problems on the king, who wanted people to pay more money than they had. Taitt rebutted Holmes, assuring them that Governor Wright had sent for supplies and they would soon arrive.[115]

Indian runners brought news from John Stuart in St. Augustine. The Alabama King, a brother of the Cusseta King, talked to John Stuart in St. Augustine. Stuart gave him some powder and promised to send more. He warned his friends—the Cussetas and the other Creek people—to stay out of the quarrel between the white people and requested that the important men of the villages come see him in St. Augustine, where he would be glad to give them supplies and powder.[116] Unfortunately the Georgians intercepted the Alabama King's party, arrested the white trader with them, and took the precious powder so the Alabama King brought back only Stuart's talk.[117]

Stuart sent a similar talk to Attakullakulla, Ouconnostotah, and other Cherokee headmen, inviting the Cherokees to journey to St. Augustine. At the same time he chided them for harboring Houmachta and Sophia.[118] Of the several themes that run through Bartram's years on the southern frontier and link the Cession of 1773 to the Indian raids and to the resulting fear of British-instigated Indian warfare, surely the most curious is the saga of Houmachta and Sophia. Their deaths were proscribed by a formal treaty in Savannah in 1774 and by the Creek Nation. Yet, though the governors and superintendent continued to call for their capture, they remained at large.

We might wonder how anyone could willingly entertain the notion of leaving the Creek country to travel to St. Augustine, and more so, how could Stuart expect the Cherokee chiefs to leave their mountains for what might be no more than a five-hundred-mile social call? Yet the Lower Creeks responded. The Cusseta King (Blue Salt), the Pumpkin King of the Osechees, the Chiaha King, the Long Warrior of Chiaha, and even the unreliable Sempoyaffe of Coweta sent a reply to Stuart saying they would come see him.[119] A Cherokee delegation followed the Creeks to East Florida, but the Upper Creeks balked at going so far. Stuart's best friend, Emistisiguo, a man of eminently good sense, scolded Stuart for lingering in St. Augustine. Why did not Stuart come to Pensacola rather than send for the Indians to go to St. Augustine. "We did not expect you was at St. Augustine, but expected you at Pensacola," he said.[120]

By coincidence Governor Chester also issued an invitation to the Creek chiefs to come to Pensacola, and Charles Stuart relayed the message to Taitt. Taitt warned that the chiefs would bring retinues with them and Pensacola would be overwhelmed with the task of entertaining them. Taitt also knew that John Stuart disliked anyone other than himself calling an Indian conference. So Chester withdrew his invitation and instead sent seven hundred pounds of powder and three hundred balls, making it clear that this ammunition was merely loaned to Stuart's department. Chester urged Stuart to come to Pensacola, where he could more easily manage Indian affairs.[121]

These were some of the major preoccupations of Gov. Peter Chester when William Bartram met him. Among his minor frustrations was the fact that his Spanish-built stone house that William Bartram admired needed repair. Chester blamed the engineer for spending all the allotted funds, then discharging the workers and departing for England.[122]

When Peter Livingston introduced the botanist to the governor, Chester showed an enthusiasm for Bartram's pursuit of natural history. Indeed he had employed Bernard Romans to investigate the products of West Florida. He encouraged Bartram to remain through the seasonal changes to better document nature's offerings, enhancing the temptation by making it clear that his expenses would be covered and that his residence would be in the governor's own house. Bartram expressed gratitude for Chester's generosity but explained that he intended to complete his journey to the Mississippi, a goal he had long ago set for himself. Chester could not object. His enthusiasm for the rapid settlement of the Mississippi region matched his zeal for the study of natural history. He had recently toured the western parts of his province as far as Natchez. He and his council hoped to establish a town at the junction of the Amite and the Iberville, and he personally hoped that the dream of ministers and governors since 1763—the dream of diverting Mississippi commerce through the Iberville and thus avoiding New Orleans—could finally be realized.[123] Perhaps Bartram would advertise the advantages of West Florida and hasten settlement. In any case the governor was pleased to endorse Bartram's missions. He wrote a flowery testimonial, using all his titles, including captain general, governor in chief, and vice admiral, permitting Bartram to collect rare and useful plants and commanding all His Majesty's people not to interrupt him in his work. The deputy secretary wrote out the impressive statement and dated it September 5, 1775.[124]

After Bartram's departure from Pensacola, the town was thrown into another fit of consternation by an urgent message from David Taitt. Taitt had worried about the sulking Escochabey, fearful that the Coweta chief knew of some dark intentions of his friends in Havana. On September 24 Escochabey's son told Taitt that a Spanish fleet had attacked and taken St. Augustine and carried out a general massacre.[125]

When he heard the awful news, Chester called members of the council who lived nearby, including Charles Stuart and Philip Livingston, and issued a spate of orders to the military officers. The existing stockade had been erected in anticipation of no more than an Indian attack. Now with a new threat from the sea, the governor asked Maj. Alexander Dickson to erect a barrier on the sea side of the town; he wanted a party of soldiers to keep watch at the entrance to the harbor, and for good measure he had the drums beat for a militia muster.[126] Major Dickson informed Chester that his men would do the work provided the governor paid them a shilling a day for their labor. Chester considered this to be an unpatriotic as well as shortsighted position for Dickson to take. After all, the fortifications would be for his defense as well as the town's. Failing to get the cooperation of the military, Chester depended on his three companies of militia and the reconnoitering parties he sent out to get intelligence.[127]

In the midst of all this excitement, Taitt sent another message saying that his information was false, there had been no Spanish attack on St. Augustine.[128] Presumably Escochabey, through his son, played a trick upon the royal officials. Governor Chester argued with his superior that notwithstanding the false alarm, Pensacola needed better protection.[129]

Another message written on September 12 had graver implications for West Florida and for the entire southern frontier. Gen. Thomas Gage informed John Stuart that the Americans had used Indians against British troops in Boston. Therefore, Stuart must arrange to have the southern tribes "take arms against His Majesty's enemies and to distress them in all their power for no terms is now to be kept with them."[130] Thus, Gage ratified a policy already rumored throughout Georgia and Carolina and favored by Carolina's governor Lord William Campbell and his collaborators. In hindsight it is impossible to overemphasize the significance of Gage's instructions of September 12, 1775. If both sides sought friendly but neutral relations with neighboring Indians, the frontier people had little reason to choose one side or the other. The overreaching ambition of most pioneer farmers was for cheap land, land claimed by Indians as hunting grounds. When the frontier people thought royal policy favored Indians and when they believed that royal government would enlist Indians against them, they felt that they had sufficient reason to separate themselves from royal rule. Gage's instructions simply confirmed their determination. They would never ally themselves with those whose property they coveted. If the king loved the Indians more, they loved the king less.

Governor Chester and the West Floridians believed that because their side intended to bring the Indians into the war, the other side must be doing the same thing. Indeed, Chester sounded properly horrified when he wrote John Stuart that he had learned that the rebels solicited the help of Indians against His Majesty's government.[131] On the contrary, George Galphin continued his campaign to keep the Indians out of the conflict though he was increasingly handicapped by lack of powder and supplies. "We are just like a parcel of carpenters set to work to build a house without one single tool," he complained. In spite of that, he counted on his personal relationship with the Lower Creeks to keep them neutral. "They have every temptation to break with us and yet I think I could keep them peaceable, if it was not for the people on the ceded land," Galphin told one of the North Carolina Indian commissioners.[132]

On September 11, 1775, three backcountry brothers named Cloud made Galphin's work more difficult by firing upon a peaceful party of Cherokees from the village of Seneca who were then at Buffalo Lick in the ceded lands. One man died and two were badly wounded. When the survivors returned to Seneca, the Raven set up the war whoop. Alexander Cameron wrote Stuart that a Cherokee attack on Georgia might follow.[133] Galphin and his fellow commissioners managed to avoid retaliation by calling for a general meeting with the Cherokees at Salisbury, North Carolina.

Galphin's efforts to placate both Creeks and Cherokees did not please people such as George Wells, who preferred to exterminate them. Henry Laurens warned Galphin that the Rev. William Tennent, a colleague of William Henry Drayton, even suspected Galphin's attachment to the American cause.[134] Restless radicals in Augusta talked about confiscating Galphin's stores. They operated on the principal that if Galphin were a friend of Indians, he must also be a friend of the king.[135]

William Bartram admired George Galphin for the very reason radicals criticized him. Galphin treated the Indians with the respect that his fellow humans deserved.

V

My eyes having acquired sufficient strength to endure the
open daylight, and set off from Pearl Island for Manchac
on the Mississippi.

Harper, *Travels*

William Bartram almost did not make it to the Mississippi, and his *Travels* nearly went unwritten. He came close to death at a stranger's house on a lonely
island. The day after he returned to Mobile from Pensacola, the incipient malady he had felt before leaving Mobile flared again, accompanied by a high fever,
"an excessive pain" in the head, and severe watering of the eyes. His readers are
ready for him to be put to bed when he surprises them by setting off on another adventure in spite of his worsening condition.

He left Mobile in the company of a French gentleman who acted as the
"general interpreter for the Chactaw nation." This could have been John Stuart's employee Rene Roi, who had a plantation on the Pearl River.[136] The near
ninety-mile trip to the Frenchman's house must have been excruciating for
Bartram. He could not see where they were going because his eyes could not
stand daylight. Incessant tears chapped his face. They sailed past the mouth of
the Pascagoula River and later Biloxi, the first French settlement on the gulf,
now nearly deserted. Bartram seldom complained, but he admitted that by the
time they reached their destination he was "almost frantic and stupid" with
pain and the loss of sleep. None of the Frenchman's remedies worked. After
three days of torment Bartram almost gave up hope of recovery: "I expected to
sink under the malady, and I believe my friends here did."[137]

If Bartram was going to die, the Frenchman preferred he do it in an Eng-
lishman's house. Roi took the desperately ill botanist to an island twelve miles
distant, where James Rumsey lived. Rumsey worked as a commission merchant
in New Orleans when he was not at his plantation.[138] To his credit he took in
the suffering man, and Bartram testified that Rumsey treated him "with the
utmost humanity." The first night at Rumsey's, Bartram almost died, and he
admits that death would have seemed a relief. Surviving that crisis, he suggested his own cure, a concoction of "cantharides," or blister beetles, which Rumsey applied to his back. The strange remedy had an immediate effect. He slept
soundly and awoke free from pain for the first time in days. "I do not know how
to express myself on this occasion," he said, "all was peace and tranquility,
although I had my sight perfectly; yet my body seemed but as a light shadow;

and my existence as a pleasing delirium, for I sometimes doubted of its reality."[139] Even so, he could not expose his eyes to daylight for several weeks, and his sight never fully recovered.

Before leaving the island, which he called Pearl Island but which Frances Harper identified as Prevost Island, he examined its soil and plant life thoroughly. Despite its sandy composition, the island produced "almost every sort of esculent vegetable" as well as a variety of fruit trees. He especially liked Mrs. Rumsey's marmalade, made from local plums. His island retreat lay so far west of Pensacola he missed the excitement of the false report of a Spanish attack that so alarmed Governor Chester. However, Rumsey, his host, would have been keenly interested in Spanish intentions since his business centered in New Orleans, a town of some eight hundred houses inhabited by French people but since 1763 governed by Spanish officials. Occasional visitors to Rumsey's plantation brought news. While Bartram convalesced, Montfort Browne, former lieutenant governor of West Florida, stopped by on his way to his new assignment, that of governor of the Bahamas. The progress of the war in the North, the uncertain situation of John Stuart, and the confusion in the Indian country were of immediate interest. Browne, as acting governor of West Florida from Johnstone's departure in 1767 to Chester's arrival in 1770, gets low marks from historians for his administration of the colony. John Alden wrote that "he did nothing toward bringing order in the Indian trade" and provoked the Creeks by granting land in Creek territory along the Tensaw River above Major Farmer's place at Farm Hall.[140] Robin Fabel is harsher in his judgment, saying that Browne "had shown himself to be ignorant in administration and a petty tyrant."[141] The acquisition of property on the Mississippi concerned him most. He suggested to the British Board of Trade that a separate colony be created on the Mississippi, and he aspired to become its governor. He acquired extensive grants at a place called White Cliffs on the river twenty-three miles above Baton Rouge, in the vicinity of today's Port Hudson. Browne asked Bartram to explore his property and give him an evaluation of it, and Bartram had enough confidence in his recuperative powers to agree to it.[142]

When his eyes could stand daylight, Bartram took his leave of the Good Samaritans, the Rumsey family, and set off for the Mississippi. His "handsome, large boat," probably Rumsey's trading craft, had a crew of three black men. They coasted along the north shore of Lake Pontchartrain and camped on a sandy bank. Huge crocodiles shared their cove, but Bartram, accustomed to their habits, noted that "we rested quietly."[143] The next day the voyagers sailed past cypress swamps to the Tangiphoa River, where they saw scattered huts of fishermen. Continuing, they entered beautiful Lake Maurepas and came to the mouth of the Amite River. Bartram was disappointed at first sight of the sluggish stream. A sleepless night on a shore swarming with mosquitoes did not improve his opinion.

As they ascended the river the flow increased and the scenery improved. A Scottish gentleman invited Bartram to stay the night, but the explorer explained that he wanted to complete his journey as quickly as possible. So they went on to the junction of the Iberville, a river that figured prominently in British diplomacy and politics. The Iberville connected the Mississippi with the Amite-Maurepas-Pontchartrain waterway.

When the duke of Bedford negotiated the Treaty of Paris in 1763, he had in his possession a map that clearly showed that the Iberville offered a shorter alternative to West Florida than the Mississippi at New Orleans. The French gladly agreed to the Iberville as a boundary, allowing them to persuade their Spanish allies to accept the treaty by transferring the island of New Orleans to Spain.[144] Unfortunately the duke of Bedford's map did not reveal that the mouth of the Iberville was fifteen feet above the level of the Mississippi and dry most of the year. The Iberville flowed only when the Mississippi flooded. One might assume that the British would soon discover their mistake. However, an assumption once made by higher authority is not easily unmade. Capt. James Campbell and Maj. Robert Farmer inspected the river route and assured Governor Johnstone that an eight-foot channel could be cut in a month. Johnstone gratified the Board of Trade by reporting that the Iberville would soon be open to traffic: "There is nothing on which I would pawn my Reputation so soon."[145] General Gage added his endorsement: "It is judged that it may be cleared with much less labor than was at first imagined."[146] As a token of the importance of the new route, the military erected Fort Bute at the mouth of the Iberville, and the cluster of trading houses around the fort took the name of a nearby Indian tribe, the Manchacs. With enormous effort the Iberville channel was deepened by six feet. However, that served only infrequently when the Mississippi rose.[147] Nevertheless the dream lingered. As late as January 26, 1775, Gov. Peter Chester suggested to Lord Dartmouth that it would be a good idea to establish a customhouse at Manchac.[148]

William Bartram referred to the Iberville as a canal. It seemed so, but it was really a partially dredged riverbed, and it ended nine miles short of the junction with the Mississippi. A few trading stores occupied the banks at the head of navigation. Bartram thanked the crew and took to the road along the dried riverbed the rest of the way to Manchac. At last, on October 21, 1775, he reached his objective of the past two years of wandering—the mighty Mississippi. "I stood for a time as it were fascinated by the magnificence of the great sire of rivers," he wrote.[149] The sight wholly astonished him; he estimated its depth at forty fathoms, its width nearly a mile. The steep embankments, the towering grand forests, and the powerful current contributed to a "grand sublime" prospect. The banks at Manchac, though fifty feet above the river, showed the effects of erosion; some of the buildings seemed on the verge of collapsing into the river.[150] A few of the houses appeared substantial, particularly the store belonging to McGillivray and Swanson. A crude footbridge crossed the dry bed of the Iberville to the Spanish side, where a small Spanish garrison kept wary watch on their British rivals. Its counterpart north of the river, Fort Bute of such great expectations, stood in disrepair, abandoned by the military in 1768, three years after it was built. It might have reminded Bartram of Fort Prince George at Keowee. In both places trading houses replaced the garrisoned forts.

One of the remarkable features of Bartram's epic journey is the frequency of his encounters with hospitable people willing to do him favors. He met another such at Manchac in the person of William Dunbar. They came upon each other accidentally, and Dunbar invited Bartram to visit him at his plantation near Baton Rouge. Bartram welcomed the chance to explore the great river. He learned that the 26-year-old Scot came from a distinguished family. His father was Sir Archibald Dunbar of Dunbar Castle in Morayshire. He immigrated to America in 1771 as did so many other Scots during that time because of depressed conditions in Scotland and the greater opportunities in the New World. He joined John Ross of Philadelphia in a partnership, trading along the Ohio; the Ohio led him to the Mississippi. In 1773 he obtained a grant from Governor Chester, then traveled to Jamaica to purchase slaves, seven men and four women for fieldwork and three household domestics. With their labor he cleared his land and planted corn, rice, and indigo. By October 1775, when he met Bartram, he counted himself a success as a planter. He told Bartram that he intended to begin manufacturing barrel staves at his place.[151] Within the year the contagion of independence, spreading across the southern colonies, reached the shores of the Mississippi. Dunbar discovered a conspiracy among his slaves. Bewildered by it, he wrote in his diary: "Of what avail is kindness and good usage when rewarded by such ingratitude; tis true indeed they were kept under due subordination and obliged to do their duty in respect to plantation work, but two of the three had always behaved so well that they had never once received a stroke of the whip."[152] That was later; while Bartram was there, all seemed well.

As a crew of three blacks rowed them upriver, Bartram learned that most of the people living along the Mississippi, Indian, European or African by origin, had settled there recently. The Tensaws and Mobilians below Manchac left their lands because of pressure by the aggressive Creeks. The Alabamas, who gave their name to the river formed by the Coosa and Tallapoosa, moved when their allies, the French, lost eastern Louisiana. Their chief, Tamathlemingo, burned Fort Toulouse to prevent the British from having it.[153] Bartram and Dunbar interrupted their voyage to stop at the Alabama village, "delightfully situated on several swelling green hills," and the two acted the part of tourists, buying baskets and pottery before continuing upriver. Dunbar told Bartram about other displaced people, the Tonicas near his plantation and the Bioloxies and Pascagoulas on the other side. A few years earlier John Stuart's deputy to the small tribes, John Thomas, annoyed the Spanish authorities and incurred the displeasure of his own government by trying to entice the western Indians to move to the British side. Stuart fired Thomas and decided he did not need a deputy to the small tribes.

Rapidly filling in between the Indian settlements were colonists, who, like Dunbar, followed the Ohio River route. The most ambitious enterprise was that of the Company of Military Adventurers from New England, some of whom established themselves near Natchez in 1773. West Florida historian Robin Fabel listed other emigrant groups from Pennsylvania, New Jersey, and Virginia as well as two hundred families from North Carolina who followed the Tennessee River to the Mississippi.[154] Choctaws warned the newcomers not to settle above the Big Black River near the northern boundary of the province; they had John Stuart's pledge that their hunting grounds would be respected. Stuart's promise did not prevent settlers taking grants on the Big Black above Natchez.[155] Some Americans preferred to settle on the Spanish side. By 1773, 120 families from Virginia and North Carolina settled on a twenty-four mile straggle of plantations and farms on the right bank above Baton Rouge, called then and still called Pointe Coupee.[156]

Bartram witnessed the ongoing transformation of the lower Mississippi valley. A French-dominated frontier was rapidly being colonized by Anglo-Americans. On November 11, 1775, Gov. Peter Chester accelerated the process. In response to instructions from Lord Dartmouth, he announced that West Florida welcomed all persons loyal to His Majesty and promised one hundred acres for the head of family and fifty acres for each dependent. Most of the colonists who took advantage of the proclamation were people of some wealth. Historian J. Barton Starr noted that eighty-eight loyalists who applied for land brought an average of almost ten slaves per family. Unlike the earlier emigrants who originated in the northern colonies, most of the loyal refugees came from Carolina and Georgia.[157] West Floridians, anxious about Indians and hosts to loyalists, could not escape the American Revolution. Much less could William Bartram.

William Dunbar seemed to know many planters along the way. He and Bartram spent the night with one and visited several others before arriving at Dunbar's place, "a very delightful villa, with extensive plantations of Corn, Indigo, Cotton and some Rice."[158] Dunbar shared Bartram's interest in natural history and volunteered to accompany the botanist on an inspection of Gov. Montfort Browne's nearby property at the White Cliffs. They went by horseback and traveled a few miles to the north through forests of giant cane until they came to a stretch of open plains. Unfortunately for Montfort Browne the white chalky soil that gave the cliffs their designation happened to be sterile, "scarcely any vegetable growth to be seen," noted Bartram, "except short grass or crustaceous mosses."[159]

The day after the tour of the disappointing "White Plains," Dunbar took Bartram to see the French settlement at Pointe Coupee. On the two-mile crossing of the river, Dunbar's oarsmen raced after a swimming bear. The bear gained an island in the river and disappeared into the thickets to the chagrin of the crew and to Bartram's relief.

They arrived at Pointe Coupee in the evening and were guests of an elderly but hardy French gentleman. Bartram listened attentively to the man's history of the settlement. He and others originally lived farther upriver near the Natchez Indians, whom he described as "a very powerful and civilized nation of red men." The French commandant's arrogant and insulting attitude alienated the Indians, and they destroyed the garrison and killed many of the settlers. Some French people escaped in canoes and came down to this place. The narrator salvaged only one calf, but that calf was progenitor of the numerous herd Bartram saw.[160]

Either the Frenchman did not explain the consequences of the Natchez massacre, or Bartram decided not to record the rest of the story, but the 1729 incident profoundly affected colonial history. Louisiana governor Bienville resolved to destroy the Natchez with the assistance of the Choctaws. The Natchez fled for protection to their neighbors, the Chickasaws, who were traditional enemies of the Choctaws. The Chickasaws sought help from the English at Charlestown, and Carolina traders gladly furnished them with guns and ammunition. Despite repeated invasions, the French could never defeat the brave and defiant Chickasaws, and the Choctaws grew tired of fighting for the French. The effect of the Natchez affair, in short, was the polarization of the colonial frontier—the Chickasaws allied to the British, the Choctaws to the French with the Creeks cleverly playing one side against the other.

The old Frenchman's story about the Natchez piqued Bartram's interest in that once-powerful people. Before he wrote *Travels* he read du Pratz's *History of Louisiana*. The author, Antoine Simon Le Page du Pratz, resided at Natchez and survived the massacre.[161] Bartram learned that the Natchez originally lived near Mexico and incorporated the religious and governmental practices of the natives of that region into their culture. They migrated to the Mississippi sometime before the arrival of the Spanish and subjugated the people they found there. Others sharing linguistic patterns, notably the Choctaws, Chickasaws, and Creeks, came later, coincident with the Spanish invasions.[162]

Bartram learned much less about the Choctaws and Chickasaws. He admitted, "I was not in the interior of the Chactaw territories."[163] When he referred to those people he quoted others. For example, he wrote of the Choctaws: "They are supposed to be most ingenious and industrious husbandmen, having large plantations or country farms, where they employ much of their time in agricultural improvements . . . by which means their territories are more generally cultivated and better inhabited than any other Indian republic that we know of."[164] He had seen members of that nation in Manchac town and thought them "remarkably slovenly and negligent in every part of their dress," comparing unfavorably in that respect with the Creeks and Cherokees.[165] The curious shape of the men's heads intrigued him, and he learned that Choctaw mothers deliberately flattened the heads of male babies, both in back and in front, by placing sandbags on the foreheads and using slanted headrests in the cradle.

He said even less about the Chickasaws, a renowned warrior people. Although he saw some men of that tribe—enough to know what they looked like and how they spoke—he acknowledged that he had never seen a Chickasaw woman.[166] Bartram's authoritative comments were confined to the Creek and Cherokee people. If the botanist had extended his tour to the Chickasaw country, as he originally intended, he would have had the pleasure of meeting another of the Darien Scots he liked so much. John McIntosh, Stuart's deputy there, was brother to Rory McIntosh and son of one of the innumerable Johns;

this one had the distinction of being the natural son of Brig. William McIntosh of Borlum, hero of the failed rising of 1715. Unlike Rory, whose fierce temper almost started a war over the marking of the Creek boundary of 1763, John McIntosh got along well with the Indians. He took a Chickasaw wife and had mixed-blood children. Bartram would have enjoyed chatting with him about his relatives in Georgia.[167]

Bartram lingered in Pointe Coupee long enough to compare the French residents favorably with their American counterparts. They were "far more regular and commendable in the enjoyment of their earning than their neighbours the English," Bartram thought. He approved the way they wore clothing of their own manufacture, and he praised their good manners and morals.[168]

On the return to Dunbar's plantation, Bartram observed the White Cliffs closely; the stratified face of the hundred-foot-high embankment caused him to speculate about the geology of the land. Charles Lyell, the great English geologist who mused along the same lines and whose conclusions about the great age of the earth gave Darwin scope for proposing natural selection, visited the same cliffs in 1849 and commended Bartram's insights.[169]

Bartram hints that he would have liked to extend his exploration of the Mississippi in which case he might have learned more about the Choctaws and Chickasaws, but his eye trouble flared again, and he reluctantly decided to turn back. He remained friendly with William Dunbar, and Dunbar made his own mark on the history of West Florida. When the Spanish government later employed him to survey the thirty-first parallel, his report included a Bartram-like description of plants, animals, and soil.[170] Pres. Thomas Jefferson later enlisted him to explore and write about the Washita River country. By coincidence Jefferson first asked Bartram then Dunbar to go on the Red River expedition. Bartram declined; Dunbar went.[171]

They said their good-byes, and Dunbar's trading boat conveyed Bartram to Manchac. From there he went by land to the head of navigation of the Iberville and the next day sailed down the sluggish Amite River. On November 13 his vessel crossed Lake Maurepas and into Lake Pontchartrain, where he and the crew spent an uncomfortable night grounded on a sandbar. A brisk wind whipped up the lake next morning and helped dislodge the craft. As they coasted along the Mississippi gulf, Bartram saw the shoreline for the first time; earlier he had been blinded by his eye affliction on the way west. He took pleasure in ticking off the sights: the Bay of Pearls, Cat Island, the beautiful Bay St. Louis, Ship and Horn Islands, the bold coast of Biloxi, the narrow Aux Christian Pass, and Dauphin Island, where they stayed the night. The next day, November 16, 1775, they came "safe again" to the town of Mobile.[172]

When Bartram's adventures are viewed from the context of his times, interesting suppositions arise. Several students of Bartram's travels believe that reasons more weighty than botanizing drew Bartram to the Mississippi. British officials from Lord Dartmouth to Peter Chester encouraged immigration to West Florida. Chester and Montfort Browne hoped to profit by the escalation in value of their landholdings. An extant plan in the papers of Lord George Germain, Dartmouth's successor, shows that Browne's White Cliffs was considered as the new seat of government. It is logical to believe that Governor Chester would have wanted Bartram to survey the site, and there is Bartram's word that Browne asked him for a report. It is doubtful that his employer Fothergill had any knowledge of or interest in his agent's involvement in a real estate promotion, as the contributors to the 1979 Bartram Trail Conference report suggest. Fothergill, at the time of Bartram's western swing, wrote to Dr. Chalmers urging the botanist to stay in one place. Nor does it seem likely, as the authors of *Bartram Heritage* propose, that Bartram returned to the Southeast to boost the advantages of life on the Mississippi.[173]

VI

After having made up my collection of growing roots, seeds, and curious specimen, left them to the care of Messrs. Swanson and McGillivray, to be forwarded to Dr. Fothergill of London. I prepared to set off again to Augusta in Georgia, through the Creek Nation. . . .

Harper, *Travels*

Bartram spent ten days in Mobile completing his drawings and preparing his shipment to Fothergill in England. His journey through the Creek country occupied the entire month of December and rewarded him with some of his richest experiences among Indian people. While he visited among the Upper Creeks, the struggle between loyal and patriot factions represented by John Stuart and George Galphin reached new dimensions.

British Indian policy at the time of Bartram's departure from Mobile still consisted in the decade-long promotion of the Creek and Choctaw War. Bartram and other travelers between the Alabama and Escambia Rivers knew that they entered a battle zone. Bartram characterized the region from Mobile to the

Upper Creek villages as "the bloody field of Schambe, where those contending bands of American bravos, Creeks, and Choctaws, often meet in dire conflict."[174]

That policy changed when John Stuart received Gage's instructions of September 12, 1775, to be ready to employ Indians to assist the military. Stuart candidly revealed the new strategy in a letter to Cameron at Keowee: "I have received instructions to employ the Indians in my department to distress Her Majesty's rebellious subjects by all practicable means."[175] However, Stuart cautioned, he did not intend to launch an "indiscriminate" attack. The Indians must be guided. Exactly who should do the guiding Stuart did not say and probably did not know. His first duty was to persuade them to enter the struggle on behalf of the king. The means to gain their allegiance consisted of adequate supplies of powder and ball.

George Galphin and his friends in Georgia and South Carolina knew how the game should be played. William Henry Drayton, in a reckless moment, had promised powder to the Cherokees.[176] When Galphin and his fellow commissioners met the Cherokee delegates in Salisbury, North Carolina, on November 13, 1775, Galphin felt embarrassed at the small supply at his disposal. "I am afraid they will think but little of our presents," he said; "They will get so much from Mr. Stuart." He asked the Carolina Council of Safety for two thousand pounds of additional powder.[177] Henry Laurens replied for the council that they could not supply the powder: "We must of necessity trust to Rum and good words for soothing until we can satisfy the further demands of our Red friends."[178]

John Stuart's great advantage over Galphin lay in his having adequate supplies, including powder, and he had access to the Creek and Cherokee country by way of Pensacola and Mobile. Governor Chester relished the new strategic importance of his province, observing to Lord Dartmouth that the rebels would block every port except Quebec and West Florida, and Quebec was not good in wintertime.[179] Stuart's plan involved Pensacola. He intended to make that place his base of operations and would go there as soon as he had entertained the visiting delegations of Creeks and Cherokees in East Florida. Meanwhile he instructed his brother Henry Stuart to proceed with dispatch to Pensacola and confer with Governor Chester and Charles Stuart with the object of settling the Creek-Choctaw War. Next, Henry Stuart must send a message to John McIntosh to prepare the Chickasaws to cooperate when called upon. He should proceed to the Upper Creek country and talk to David Taitt and Emistisiguo. John Stuart cautioned his brother to tell Emistisiguo "in private" that he must help bring the king's rebellious subjects to a sense of their duty. Presumably, Emistisiguo was expected to be discreet with this information. Finally, Henry Stuart would procure a supply of ammunition from McGillivray and other storekeepers and convey it through the Creek country to the Cherokees.[180] Henry Stuart's mission caused consternation in Savannah and Charleston, and confirmed the earlier suspicions of a British-inspired Indian attack that led to John Stuart's exile from Carolina.

Thus the country through which Bartram traveled was far from static even though his prose portraits made the scenes timeless. While agents scurried about on their errands, delegations of Lower Creeks took the long road to see Stuart in Florida, and some Upper Creeks visited Governor Wright in Savannah. Handsome Fellow of Okfuskee led this last group, claiming to represent several villages. His purpose probably surprised Governor Wright. They requested a pardon for Houmachta, the outlaw. By now the beleaguered governor had larger problems than Houmachta, but he did not want to disappoint his visitors. Samuel Elbert and Robert Rae, both on the Council of Safety, made much of the visitors, hoping to lure them away from the royal service. Wright offered a deal. If the Creeks would put Sophia to death, he would pardon Houmachta. This correspondence is the last that mentions the Wrightsborough raiders; presumably they were never punished.[181] Nor is there any evidence that white outlaws Hezekiah Collins and Thomas Fee paid for the murders they committed.

Bartram intended to go to Georgia by way of the Florida coast and thus connect with the route he had explored in 1774, but he heard that Seminoles had killed a group of migrants at Appalachee Bay so he decided to accompany a trading caravan to the Creek country and there find someone to escort him to Augusta. His luck in choosing good companions failed in this instance. John Adam Tapley, the trader in charge of Bartram's company, had the reputation of a troublemaker. However, Tapley worked for George Galphin when he did not work for himself and took Bartram on as a favor to Galphin. The fact that Dep. Supt. David Taitt had arrested him for various felonies meant that they would avoid Taitt's town of Little Tallassee.[182]

On the trail Bartram kept his distance from Tapley and teamed up with a mustee, the son of a Choctaw mother and a father who had white and Creek Indian parents. They traveled by boat up the Tensaw River to Farm Hall, where Bartram had a pleasant reunion with Major Farmer and his family. Tapley's packhorsemen were there with more than twenty horses, sixteen of them

loaded with merchandise. Bartram said his thanks to the Farmers, and the caravan took to the familiar path.[183]

Bartram's description of the daily routine of the trading company is a classic.
The shouted commands in Indian language, the cracking of whips, the jangling
of bells, the loud cursing, and the killing pace—all this clatter and confusion Bartram found "unexpressably disagreeable."[184] His poor mount could not keep up
the pace despite the long rest it had enjoyed at Farm Hall. Tapley wanted an
extravagant price for a replacement and warned Bartram that if he could not keep
up he would surely perish at the hands of the Choctaws. Bartram took some comfort in the fact that some of the men sympathized with his plight. His luck held,
for a company of traders on their way to Mobile suddenly appeared up the road.
Bartram gave up his faithful steed who had served him well since Savannah and
included an additional ten pounds for a fresh, strong horse, and extracted the
promise that his old horse would not be used as a pack animal.[185]

Bartram recorded a particularly poignant incident soon after they entered
the Creek country. As his train of packhorses clattered along the road, the
traders encountered a party of emigrants from Georgia seeking safety and new
opportunities in West Florida. A family consisting of a man, his wife, and several young children together with a young woman and three young men made
up the group. Bartram exchanged pleasantries with them, and they went on
their way. He later learned that while the travelers camped that night a war
party of Choctaws attacked their camp and took them away as captives.[186] He
did not know their eventual fate. If he were not with the traders, the same thing
might have happened to him.

The long days on the trail gave Bartram a chance to appreciate the good
qualities of his Indian companion. The youth spoke English, having been
taught by his half-white father. Until recently he had lived in the Choctaw
country, the land of his mother's people. He showed a quick intelligence and
seemed anxious to learn all he could from Bartram about the natural world as
well as the white people's world.[187]

As they neared the Tallapoosa River, Tapley and the traders rode ahead to
their base towns to announce their arrival. To his amazement Bartram and the
young mustee inherited the job of bringing in the packhorses with their valuable
cargo. A relatively simple task became immensely more difficult because a heavy
rainfall had swollen a river they had planned to ford. The mustee explained that
they would have to ferry the cargo across and construct a raft to do it. Bartram
recorded in detail and with obvious amazement how his companion gathered

bundles of reeds, vines, and logs and fashioned the raft. Bartram helped all he could, admitting, "this was a novel scene to me and I could not, until finished and put into practice, well comprehend how it could possibly answer the effect desired."[188] When they finished the raft, the youth swam across the swift-flowing stream with the end of a vine in his teeth, the other end tied to the raft. Bartram held another vine tethered to the opposite side of the makeshift pontoon. They loaded the precious stores a little at a time and ferried them across, one pulling, the other slowly letting the line out. The last load contained Bartram's box of paints, papers, and specimens. He says he then stripped except for his "breeches." He kept them on because "they contained matters of more value and conse-quence than all the rest of my property put together" and he did not want alligators and snakes nipping; the double entendre seems deliberate. He then drove the horses into the river and plunged in after them. Alas the current carried the horses downriver, and when they clambered ashore they were separated from the two men and the pile of goods by a twenty-foot-wide stream flowing through steep banks into the river they had just crossed. Bartram's Indian friend amazed him again by cutting a sapling and placing it across the gap. Then he ran back and forth over the narrow bridge carrying a hundred pounds of cargo each time. Bar-tram sat astride the pole and gingerly eased himself across. They loaded the hors-es and without further incident reached the Shawnee town of Savannuca.[189]

They awoke next morning, alerted by a shout from Tapley across the river. The trader and several Indians clad only in breechclouts even though frost lay on the ground, crossed over in canoes, loaded the goods, and brought them to Muc-colossus, only a mile upriver.[190] The mustee followed with the horses.

Surprises continued to unfold on this adventure-filled journey. The mustee turned out to be something of a celebrity, and the villagers greeted him warm-ly. He had not told Bartram that his reason for going to the village was to marry the daughter of the chief and the sister of Tapley's Indian wife. Only now did Bartram learn that the young man had fled from the Choctaws to save his life. While in that country someone had discovered that he had Creek blood and accused him of being a spy. The Choctaw party that attacked the Georgia emi-grants had been chasing him. If Bartram had known that story while on the trail, he would not have slept as well as he did. The nuptial day for the young man and his bride was an occasion for general celebration. Bartram recorded a touching moment, when later in the evening several people called upon the bridegroom to give them some Choctaw songs. He sang beautifully to a hushed audience. One girl, a Choctaw captive adopted into the village, wept openly.

The villagers retired to their dwellings and bride and bridegroom to the bower prepared for them.[191]

The next day Tapley invited Bartram to go along to another celebration at the Tuskeegee village at the confluence of the Coosa and Tallapoosa Rivers, the site of historic Fort Toulouse. The fort was gone, burned in 1763 by the departing Alabama Indians whose new settlement on the Mississippi Bartram had visited. Several half-buried cannons marked the location of the fort, and an ancient mound testified to the long history of habitation of this desirable site. Beyond the mound a breathtaking view of the rivers merging to form the Alabama delighted the observer. Bartram declared the location "one of the most eligible situations for a city in the world." The present thriving city of Montgomery just below the junction of the rivers justifies his prediction.[192] The place where Bartram stood and gazed into the distance, fortunately for today's traveler, looks much the same as then except that the Coosa has eroded the steep embankment near the old mound. Fort Toulouse has been carefully reconstructed, and Bartram's visit is memorialized by the Bartram Arboretum. Only a few miles up the Coosa lay the town of Little Tallassee. Emistisiguo, perhaps the most important man in the Creek Nation, lived there, as did David Taitt. Lachlan McGillivray had his residence there before the war with the French, and Sehoy, his wife, and their daughters still lived in the village. Lachlan's son Alexander stayed with him in Savannah and worked at a countinghouse. Soon, when he had to make a choice, twenty-five-year-old Alexander would return to Little Tallassee and to the clan of his mother and in due time Alexander McGillivray would succeed Emistisiguo as the most important man in the Creek Nation.[193]

Bartram, if alone, might have called upon David Taitt and presented his letter from John Stuart. However, the growing antagonism between the friends of Stuart and friends of Galphin was obvious even to him. Besides, he came under Tapley's protection, and Tapley was Galphin's man. It is possible that Henry Stuart visited Taitt and Emistisiguo while Bartram lingered on the Tallapoosa. However discreet they might have been, the villagers could not keep secret the summons to enter the white man's war.

When they returned to Muccolossus, Bartram heard that a trading company for Augusta was preparing to leave Tuckabatchee village at the falls of the Tallapoosa. He arrived there too late but found that another caravan would depart from Atasi, a neighboring village, in a week or so. Back at Muccolossus another of the unusual adventures that marked this trip took place. John Adam

Tapley had gotten himself in serious trouble. Several Indians stood guard at Tapley's storehouse, and one of the chief men of the village and his friends threatened to kill Tapley if they could lay hands on him. While that warrior was away on a hunt Tapley had what Bartram called "an amorous intrigue" with the man's wife. The cuckolded husband and a posse of a dozen men lured Tapley into the square and beat him with clubs. As they prepared to cut off his ears, the usual punishment for adultery, Tapley leaped up and escaped into the woods.[194]

All this became of immediate interest to the botanist when Tapley managed to get a message to him next morning that he was hiding in, of all places, his father-in-law's house. A distraught Tapley confided to Bartram that the chief had agreed that Tapley must lose his ears and forfeit his stores, which amounted to one thousand pounds sterling. Only one thing could save his ears and fortune, and that was the intercession of George Galphin. Tapley begged Bartram to call upon Galphin at Silver Bluff and solicit his help. Bartram agreed to do so. In the meantime Tapley remained a virtual prisoner in Muccolossus.[195]

At some point during his stay at the town, and before Tapley's fall from grace, Bartram had the privilege of meeting one of the legendary figures among the Upper Creeks. Tapley and Bartram took their seats around a circle of the "beloved men" of the village, the counselors to the chief. A fire burned in the center of the circle. Then all stood to greet a quite elderly chief escorted by three young men. Despite his complete blindness, the chief was cheerful and alert as he took a place near Bartram. The aged man who struck Bartram "with awe and veneration" was the man the English called the Wolf King.[196] John Stuart had reported him dead the year before, along with another well-known leader, Enochtonachee of Okchoy, whom the traders knew as the Gun Merchant.[197] The Wolf's history spanned the Anglo-American southern colonial era. He told Bartram that he had walked to Charlestown before his village had horses. He had been one of the first to go see General Oglethorpe in Georgia. Even though his village was so close to French Fort Toulouse, he remained a staunch friend of the British. On several occasions he had saved the lives of British traders from angry Indians by taking them into his own house. Yet he could stand up to royal authorities when it mattered. Once in Charlestown he had shocked the pompous Gov. James Glen with his boldness. On this occasion the Wolf and other Upper Creek chiefs asked the governor why the traders charged the Creeks more than they did the Cherokees. When the governor gave an unsatisfactory answer, some of the headmen got up and left, but the Wolf said bluntly that it was no wonder that their traders charged high prices because they gave away so much to their women.[198] On another occasion the Wolf went down to Pensacola when the Spanish gave up that place to the British and warned the British officer that the land belonged to the Creeks. His influence contributed to setting the tidewater as the limit of British settlement. John Stuart honored the Wolf with a "great medal," a mark of distinction borrowed from the French.[199]

Bartram presented the chief with "a very fine handkerchief" and a twist of tobacco. The Wolf gave him his own stone pipe and spoke at length about his friendship with the English. Bartram did a careful drawing of a stone pipe, perhaps to show how he valued the old man's gift, and the drawing is in the Fothergill collection at the British Museum of Natural History in London.[200]

On his way from Muccolossus to Atasi, Bartram called upon his friend James Germany at Kolumi and enjoyed a brief reunion. Word spread through the Tallapoosa villages of his passing; as he said, everyone treated him with marks of friendship "even as though I had been their countrymen and relation."[201] He arrived early at Atasi and waited there a week for the traders to organize.

The week at Atasi would be the botanist's last in the Indian country. He lingered over the experience in his notes and in his book, as if reluctant to leave the subject, as he must have been reluctant to leave the country. He enjoyed meeting the beloved men of the village in the public square; he felt honored to sit with them in the great rotunda and to be privy to their rituals. He described in remarkable detail the ceremony of the black drink, even replicating the solemn notes sung by the gourd bearers as they presented the drink. He devoted respectful attention to the passing of the pipe, from chief to the great men of the village to the guests, and clearly felt honored in the sharing.[202]

Interestingly, after setting the scene for the important gathering, which included headmen from neighboring villages, Bartram neglected to record the subject under discussion. Given the date, close to the end of December, the topic could very well have been the dissemination of John Stuart's message, brought by Henry Stuart, that attacks on whites might be requested. If the theme concerned warfare, Bartram typically would have closed his notebook.

Before he left Atasi he drew its portrait in prose. He described the great square with its four buildings, the architecture of the counsel house, the decorations on the pillars and walls of the houses, and an ancient column of uncertain origin standing near the town.[203]

He departed Atasi on January 2, 1776, a cold day with frost blanketing the ground. He traveled with four men and about thirty horses, twenty loaded with skins. The return journey had none of the excitement and anticipation of sum-mer's westward expedition. They passed near the Chiaha town on the Chatta-hoochee without comment. The Long Warrior of Chiaha was one of the Lower Creek headmen who had recently returned from a meeting with John Stuart and Gov. Patrick Tonyn in Florida and had been honored by them with a commission.[204] Tonyn, more aggressive than Stuart, told the Long Warrior to seize traders from Georgia who came with presents and deliver them to St. Augustine.[205] Bartram's companions probably did not want to linger in the Chi-aha town.

They met with "nothing material" according to the botanist until they reached the Ocmulgee, now dangerously flooded. They encountered two com-panies of traders with seventy or eighty packhorses on the west bank who had lost six animals and their packs in the crossing. Bartram described how they rigged a portable leather boat by using saplings for the keel and ribs. Then they waited for the river to recede enough to try a crossing.[206]

Bartram confessed that at the time he felt dejected and wanted to be alone. Francis Harper guessed that the traders they spoke with brought news about the escalation of the Revolution. During early December an army of three thou-sand men under Col. Richard Richardson effectively stamped out loyalist opposition in the South Carolina upcountry in a campaign marked by a heavy snowfall.[207] Whether the news caused his low spirits or whether it was the real-ization that he had to leave the Indian country for civilization, one cannot say. Bartram could not talk to his companions; he found them "thoughtless to an extreme" so he sought solace where he usually found it, in nature. He turned to "the expansive fields, fragrant groves, and sublime forests."[208]

In his tour of the Cherokee mountains and more so in his travel through the Creek country, he had gained an understanding of and a respect for the manners and morals of the native people. Bartram realized that he differed from the many of those he met in polite society who despised the Indians as savages. He had met some who hated them blindly. He viewed the Indians as the human component of the natural world the botanist loved, a world func-tioning according to the ordinances of the divine ruler of the universe. Perhaps Bartram realized the responsibility he had assumed by his long journey. From now on he must become an advocate for these people. He had to raise his goals. Instead of taking notes for his report to Dr. Fothergill, he would use his notes to teach Americans about the Cherokees and the Muscogulges, those other Americans. It would be a life's work.

6

The Military Engagement

I

I took this opportunity of visiting my friend Doctor Wells
at his plantation near the city.

Harper, *Travels*

The traders ferried their cargo of skins across the still-swollen Ocmulgee in the makeshift leather boat, and the horses managed to swim across safely. They negotiated the Oconee in the same fashion. At the Ogeechee, Bartram tried crossing on horseback and regretted it. His horse lost his footing, and the current carried them downstream. "I got very wet, but I kept my seat and landed safe; however I suffered much, it being a cold freezing day," he wrote.[1] In two more days of hard traveling they reached Augusta. The traders went about their business, and Bartram called upon his friend Dr. Humphrey Wells. He needed a few days to outfit himself properly. He bought new clothes in Augusta; those he wore were more suited to the Indian country than town life.

In the judicious Dr. Wells, Bartram had the right person to give him an objective view of the situation in the backcountry. Humphrey Wells inclined toward moderation in contrast to his impetuous brother George, whose denunciation of the Tories helped elect him to the colonelcy of one of the local militia units and a seat in the Provincial Congress.

Bartram had heard rumors about the example the liberty boys made of Thomas Brown. Wells could explain the repercussions of that August 2, 1775, affair that had been bruited about in far-off Pensacola. The more radical committeemen went too far in their cruel treatment of Brown, nearly killing him.

With feet crippled from burning, head fractured from a blow by a rifle butt, and bandaged because of lacerations to his scalp, Brown left Augusta with the help of sympathizers. He found friends in the Ninety-Six District and threatened to march on Augusta. A general alarm swept through Georgia. The local committee appealed to Col. James Grierson to call out the militia, but Grierson refused to act unless ordered to do so by Governor Wright. The Augusta committee then called upon the Council of Safety in Savannah to send help. The council responded by ordering Capt. Samuel Elbert's Grenadier company to Augusta to be joined by militia from Ebenezer, the Ogeechee River settlements and the Kiokee district of St. Paul Parish.[2] The show of force intimidated the unorganized loyal faction. It might not have deterred Brown, but he had abandoned any intention of marching upon Augusta. He instead lent his considerable energy to rallying the king's friends and pledging them not to take up arms against the royal government. Brown claimed that he obtained four thousand pledges.[3]

Meanwhile the South Carolina Council of Safety dispatched William Henry Drayton, the Reverend William Tennent and the Reverend Oliver Hart to counteract the influence of such loyalists as Brown, Robert Cunningham, Joseph Robinson, and Moses Kirkland. The exasperated Drayton informed the Charlestown Council that Brown acted as spokesman, "and his bitterness and violence are intolerable."[4]

Both Drayton and Tennent visited Augusta, rousing support for their cause. Drayton, camped at LeRoy Hammond's house in what is now North Augusta, South Carolina, believed that Moses Kirkland intended to march on Augusta with an armed band. So Drayton issued a proclamation to the effect that anyone joining Kirkland would become a public enemy. Then Drayton raised an armed force of Carolinians and Georgians and, dragging four cannon, marched to Ninety-Six to arrest Moses Kirkland. Kirkland managed to elude capture and gained the safety of a British ship in Charlestown harbor.[5]

With his comrade Drayton on the march, the Reverend Tennent remained in Augusta, where every rumor caused consternation. "Every valuable house in Augusta is surrounded by a strong wooden fortification," Tennent reported. When he sought admittance to one, "They were greatly alarmed at our coming and received us with guns all prepared." He arranged for a system of signals so that barricaded people could recognize friend from foe. He called upon Rebecca, Edward Barnard's widow, and found that she and her family had thirteen loaded muskets ready to repel an attack.[6] As in the aftermath of the Wrightsborough raids two years earlier, the fear of Indians heightened tensions in town. William Tennent played upon these fears by holding meetings wherever he could and denouncing the "hellish and diabolical plot" of the British to launch an Indian attack.[7]

The result of all the sound and fury was the signing of an agreement between Drayton and loyalist militia colonel Thomas Fletchall on September 16, 1775, pledging not to aid British troops nor to dispute the authority of Congress.[8] Thomas Brown, disappointed at Fletchall's timid capitulation, went to Charlestown to confer with Lord William Campbell only to find that his lordship had taken refuge aboard the warship *Cherokee*. The governor sent word to Brown to join him in Savannah to confer on future operations.[9]

When Brown arrived in Savannah, the Georgia Council of Safety gave him ten days to leave. On December 2, before the ten days had elapsed, a second shipload of servants indentured to Brown and destined for Brownsborough arrived in Savannah aboard the *Marlborough*, a vessel belonging to Brown's father, Jonas Brown of Whitby.[10] Another group of emigrants attracted by Governor Wright's glowing but now outdated invitation to Georgia's ceded lands arrived during the same week in December. One of the newcomers wrote a sympathetic account of Brown's travails to a friend who knew the family in Whitby. He expressed dismay that Governor Wright, who had promised to welcome new settlers to Georgia, had been reduced to a "mere cypher" and that authority lay in the hands of a committee of "Barbers, Taylors, Cordwainers, etc. . . . whose insolence and pettiness would raise any Englishmen's indignation."[11] The sponsor of this second group, a Quaker sea captain from the Orkneys named William Manson, intended to establish a town near Wrightsborough and Brownsborough called Friendsborough. The new arrivals for both of the latter places straggled through Augusta in late December, their journey marked by rain, frost, and snow. One of their members expressed surprise that people around Augusta "are taught to believe that the Ministry have vowed Death and Destruction to the whole continent."[12] The Wrightsborough Quakers made their Friendsborough neighbors welcome, easing the transition to the strange new world. Within a few weeks William Manson could tell his parents in the Orkneys that they should not worry about the troublesome news out of America: "All the People are Settled much to their Satisfaction."[13] Unfortunately the Georgia frontier proved an unsuitable place for peaceable people, and the Friendsborough community did not outlast the Revolution.

The Brownsborough settlement might have dissipated except for the infusion of the *Marlborough* passengers. Some of the original people took advantage of their leader's misfortune to desert their indentures. One such was the teenaged Baika Harvey, who abandoned Brownsborough to join LeRoy Hammond's company in Drayton's march upon Ninety-Six. He remained with Hammond when the company joined Col. Richard Richardson to disperse the last of the upcountry loyalists under Robert Cunningham in the December Snow Campaign. Young Harvey estimated Richardson's army at more than twice its actual size in his letter to his godfather: "I am just returned from the Back parts where I seed eight thousand men in arms, all with riffeld Barrel guns which they can hit the bigness of a Dollar betwix two and three hundred yards distance the little boys no bigger than myself has all their guns and marches with their Fathers, and all ther Cry is Liberty or Death." LeRoy Hammond, an honest man, bought Harvey's time from James Gordon, Brownsborough's manager.[14] The young Orcadian bought liberty at a dear price; he died in the Battle of Savannah in 1779.[15] With the infusion of new people Brownsborough survived the Revolution, but soon after the war its people moved away to their own farms. None of the colonial backcountry "boroughs" endured into the new century.

Bartram might have wondered at the status of Fort James at the Broad River and the fate of his friends there. A group of backcountry patriots, emboldened by the Drayton-Tennent show of force, liberated Fort James in September and then gave it back to Thomas Water's rangers in October.[16]

Humphrey and Abigail Wells had been good hosts to the botanist. Ironically neither Humphrey nor his brother George outlived the Revolution. Irascible George died in a duel in 1780, Humphrey of natural causes soon afterward.[17]

At some time before he left Augusta, Bartram might have thought back to the summer of 1773, when few houses had stockades and when four hundred Indians came as guests. Then the royal officials Wright and Stuart sat in seats of honor, enjoying the gratitude of the people. Now the town huddled fearfully behind stockades lest those same Indians return at the behest of the same royal officials and do some fearful mischief. George Wells, sitting in the Georgia Provincial Congress as a delegate from St. Paul Parish, considered how he might launch a preemptive war upon the Indians with the Oconee strip as a prize.

William Bartram left the uneasy town with an uneasy feeling. He hated war, but he could justify the position of friends such as Humphrey Wells, Lachlan McIntosh, and Henry Laurens. He assumed that it was in the ordination of

Providence that Americans separate themselves from a corrupt old world and serve as an inspiration to mankind. He later said, "Let our actions in this memorable age of our establishment as a Nation of People be as a Mirror to succeeding Generations."[18] The time would soon come when this Quaker would overcome his scruples and take up arms in defense of Georgia's borderlands. But he could not abide the loose talk he heard about exterminating savages. "We unreasonably ask," he wrote, and one can imagine him saying the words to friends, "to what purpose do we observe any terms with cruel barbarous Savages who are continually seeking opportunities to massacre our Brethren and Relatives on the Frontier?" He answered the question, one he had heard so frequently, with several reasons. War against them would only bring retaliation; it would cause them to ally with America's European rivals. More important, he believed, religion teaches that all men are brethren under God: "We ought to consider them, as they are in reality, as our Brethren and fellow Citizens and treat them as such; notwithstanding their manners and modes of Government are somewhat different from ours."[19]

With troubling thoughts he undertook the short journey to Silver Bluff to see George Galphin, a man who understood Bartram's feelings about the treatment of Indians. Galphin's hopes of retiring to the genteel life of a planter had not materialized. The new demands imposed on him in his role as Indian commissioner did not allow him time to properly manage his small army of slave workers and the plantation's growing congregation of Separate Baptists. Galphin greeted Bartram warmly as suited their ten-year acquaintance. Bartram related his adventures since seeing Galphin last in April 1775; so much had happened since then. Galphin seemed to be better informed of conditions in the Creek country than Bartram, who had been there, but Galphin had not heard about the Tapley affair. Galphin listened to Bartram's account of the trader's plight and agreed that Tapley might well lose his ears. However, he promised to intercede for the man.[20] It is a gauge of Galphin's influence even among the Upper Creeks that Tapley was released to get into more mischief later.

Galphin felt honored when the Continental Congress ratified his appointment as one of the Indian commissioners for the Southern Department along with Robert Rae and Edward Wilkinson. James Adair, a veteran trader, dedicated his book on southern Indians, published in 1775, to George Galphin and Lachlan McGillivray, recommending both men for John Stuart's job.[21] Now, in a sense, Galphin had it even though he served Congress instead of the king.

He knew that Stuart resented his influence among the Indians; "Mr. Stewart has been my Enemy ever since I got the Indians to give up that body of Land in Georgia to pay their debts," he said.[22]

The chief impediments to his maintaining his influence were the Indian haters among the settlers and the lack of support from the Georgia and South Carolina Councils of Safety. "They have every reason to break with us," he said of the Indians, "and yet I think I could keep them peaceable if it was not for the people on the ceded lands." When Galphin used the term "those damned villains," he meant the whites, not the Indians.[23] He had to go up to Salisbury, North Carolina, in November to satisfy the Cherokees after the Cloud brothers killed two Senecas and wounded another on Georgia's ceded lands, but his long-term efforts were hampered by a lack of powder. He urged repeatedly that the councils permit traders to carry up at least a limited supply of powder so that the Indians could conduct their winter hunts.

Instead the councils gave him useless and even laughable advice. The Carolina council suggested that he explain to the Indians how Congress had established different Indian departments and appointed commissioners in each: "The novelty and dignity of this grand plan will excite their curiosity, Strike them with awe and tend to confirm their resolutions to remain neuter. . . ."[24] Galphin doubted whether the Indians would be more awed by Congress's commissioners than they were by the king's. What was the use of his being a commissioner if he could not compete with John Stuart in meeting the Indians' need for goods? He stood ready to bankrupt himself to supply his usual clients but knew that would not suffice.[25]

Galphin also knew that some people interpreted his consideration of the Indians as a lack of loyalty to the revolutionary movement. Prior to Bartram's visit to Silver Bluff, Galphin was accused by the influential Rev. William Tennent of disloyalty. Tennent reported to the Charlestown Council of Safety that Galphin had been heard to say, "Damn the Country, I have lost enough by it already." Because Tennent had previously made accusations about Galphin and because members of the council began to take him seriously, Henry Laurens conducted a special hearing, calling a Dr. David Gould before the council. Dr. Gould testified that Galphin had indeed made the subversive statement. Had he said anything else incriminating, Laurens asked. No, Gould answered. What provoked the remark? Gould asked Galphin to supply him with a horse because he was engaged in his country's service. Who authorized Gould to act in the country's service? No one. Was Gould a guest of Galphin at the time, enjoying his food and lodging? Yes. After the interrogation Laurens could see no subversion in Gould's being denied a horse. He wrote Galphin, "I have taken a Resolution, that whenever I learn or hear of a very Rascally attempt to traduce a Man's Character, I will call it Parson Tenents Goulden Evidence." Even so, Galphin had to send his own version of the affair to the council.[26]

Bartram could not help being swayed by Galphin's confidence in his ability to control Creek Indian conduct. Galphin explained that he had accepted the job of commissioner because of the rumor that Stuart meant to employ the Indians against Americans; "I knowing my interest in the Lower Creeks was so great, that it was not in the power of any Man to set them upon us if I opposed them—the Upper Creeks will take no steps without consulting the Lower Creeks and the Cherokees will do nothing that will disoblige them."[27] Galphin's assurance led Bartram to say, "Mr. Galphin was of the opinion that two thirds of the [Creek] confederacy were decidedly in favor of Congress."[28] The statement reflected Galphin's aspirations and proved to be an exaggeration. Bartram thought that Galphin succeeded in replacing Stuart's commissaries with his own deputies, and he questioned whether even one of the Creek towns, with the exception of the Seminoles, actually joined the British forces.[29] If he had remained longer on the southern frontier, Bartram would have learned differently.

Galphin worried about Stuart's meeting with the Creeks and Cherokees in Florida at that time. He learned from his friends among the Lower Creeks that Governor Tonyn joined Stuart in welcoming the Lower Creek delegation to Cowford on the St. Johns River. The Indians honored their hosts with the eagle dance, and Tonyn and Stuart returned the compliments by giving commissions to the Pumpkin King of Oseche and the Long Warrior of Chiaha. The two chiefs were treated to a tour of the British schooner *St. Lawrence.* They assured Stuart and Tonyn that they stood ready to join any of Her Majesty's troops.[30]

A problem that had plagued Indian management since Edmond Atkin assumed the newly created position of superintendent for the Southern Department in 1755 was the question of prerogative. Stuart liked to be considered the ultimate authority in Indian-related matters, but so did the governors. Tonyn, with a well-developed ego himself, felt a personality conflict with Stuart. He expressed his opinion candidly to Lord Dartmouth: "The real truth, my lord, Mr. Stuart cannot bear that anyone but himself should have any consequence with the Indians. He wants to make a wondrous mystery and difficulty in it where really and truly there is no mystery at all."[31]

Stuart had to put up with Tonyn's interference and vice versa when the Cowkeeper and the Seminoles visited St. Augustine, and on January 11, 1776, the Cherokee delegation finally arrived.[32]

Stuart had intended to leave for Pensacola three months earlier and probably regretted inviting the Indians into Tonyn's jurisdiction. As he prepared to depart after entertaining the Cherokees, he had to delay again. Thomas Brown, following him into exile, captivated Tonyn with a plan he and Gov. William Campbell had discussed. Brown based his proposal on the conviction that the thousands of loyalists he had recruited in the Carolina upcountry would rally to the king if British troops landed on the coast and the Indians threatened the frontiers. The success of the plan depended on raising a troop of rangers to ride with the Indians and regulate their behavior. Brown had never seen an Indian, but he volunteered to enter the Creek country and enlist white men who could speak the language of the Indians and could lead them into war. A second essential element in the plan involved getting a supply of powder and balls from Pensacola into Carolina for the purpose of arming the loyalists. Brown volunteered for that duty also. Tonyn listened, fascinated by the apparent feasibility of the plan and in admiration of the well-bred young Yorkshireman who talked so confidently about the ease of its execution. Fort Charlotte on the Carolina side could be easily taken. Despite its stockaded houses, Augusta would quickly surrender, and its fall would "distress the rebels beyond measure."[33] John Stuart, when he first listened to Brown, seemed to like the important role accorded to the Indians, but the more he considered it the more he worried about losing control of Indian management. Stuart delayed his departure for Pensacola and instead went to confer with Gen. Henry Clinton at Cape Fear, North Carolina.[34] The intrepid Thomas Brown plunged into the Indian country with Governor Tonyn's blessing and encouragement.[35] All these new developments Galphin learned by his network of traders and Indian friends. William Bartram certainly shared Galphin's interest in Indian affairs and welcomed the information. He would have occasion to observe firsthand the first fruits of Tonyn's efforts to enlist the help of Indians.

Bartram learned that one of the men who went to St. Augustine told Galphin that Stuart intended to go to Pensacola to make peace between the Creeks and Choctaws. Galphin also heard that Georgia, at Carolina's urging, intended to prohibit all exports, including deerskins. He had, or more technically his sons and nephew had skins worth four thousand pounds sterling aboard the *Inverness,* a ship belonging in part to Lachlan and John McGillivray. Apart from the fact that the loss of the shipment would be a drastic financial blow, it meant that the company would not be able to purchase supplies for the trade. If he could not supply the Creeks, they would certainly go to Pensacola and Mobile. Galphin pleaded with the Carolina council to ask Georgia to allow the shipment: "Georgia shoul'd be the last that would stop the Indian trade, as they are the first that woul'd feel an Indian War."[36]

Galphin would get no satisfaction from Carolina because that Council had stiffened Georgia's wavering resolution in the matter of enforcing the Continental Association against trade. Bartram seems to have heard Galphin's assurances rather than his misgivings. In any case the question of exportation became moot when British warships began appearing off Tybee Island on January 13, 1776.[37] By January 18 four men of war and their auxiliary vessels lay at the entrance of the Savannah River. The Council of Safety, represented by Joseph Habersham, placed Governor Wright on house arrest, accepting his parole not to join the warships. One-third of the militia of the western parishes was ordered to Savannah. All nonassociators were detained and made to give their parole not to communicate with the ships.[38] So as William Bartram headed for Savannah he fell in with militiamen going in the same direction. On the road Bartram happened to meet a new settler, perhaps one of the Friendsborough people on his way to Savannah. The man's interest in botany diverted Bartram's attention from what might lie ahead. Bartram showed his companion his favorite site along the Savannah Road, the Blue Springs. They amused themselves along the way by looking for arrowheads and other Indian artifacts.[39] And so they reached Savannah by the last day of January 1776. Whatever peace of mind he might have achieved by the botanical diversion at Blue Springs was dissipated by the panic and confusion he encountered in Savannah.

II

After five days pleasant travelling we arrived at Savanna in good health.

Harper, *Travels*

William Bartram's experience in the southern colonies was filled with greater and lesser ironies. One consisted of his friendships with the two opposing giants of Indian diplomacy, John Stuart and George Galphin. He had eaten at their tables, carried their letters, and continued to refer to both in cordial terms. He must have become aware of an even more surprising circumstance soon after his arrival in Savannah in February 1776. He could count two men as not only friends but also father figures. One, Henry Laurens, had rescued him from near death in 1766 at his failed Florida plantation. The other, Lachlan McIntosh, had taken him into his home and family, and Bartram called him "father friend." In the critical period of 1776, when Savannah frantically prepared to defend against a British invasion, Bartram's friends acted as authority figures for South Carolina and Georgia. Henry Laurens, president of Carolina's Council of Safety, watched over Georgia like a doting parent over an unreliable child. And the man Georgians turned to rescue them in the emergency was Lachlan McIntosh. The Georgia Provincial Congress in its January 20, 1776, sitting named McIntosh colonel of the first Georgia battalion, with Samuel Elbert as lieutenant colonel and Joseph Habersham as major. Both Laurens and McIntosh had to contend with radical factions—William Henry Drayton in Carolina and Button Gwinnett in Georgia. Hotspur Joseph Habersham informed Drayton that Congress first chose Gwinnett, who turned down the colonel's commission.[40] Gwinnett preferred a seat in the Continental Congress. However, the factions represented by McIntosh and Gwinnett threatened to tear poor Georgia apart. "I am afraid," wrote Joseph Habersham, "we shall find it too true that a house divided against itself can never stand."[41]

The perception that Georgia was not committed to the revolutionary movement infuriated Carolina radicals and vexed Henry Laurens. He wrote to the Georgia council on December 14, 1775, that he had heard "with astonishment and concern, that several vessels are loading at Savannah for Great Britain; some with rice, and others, one in particular, of Mr. Telfair's with indigo."[42] The rebuke stung even more because the offender in question, Edward Telfair, sat on the Council of Safety. Georgia sent Stephen Drayton and William Ewen to explain that the exportation would be prohibited as of the date recommended by the Continental Congress, March 1, 1776.[43] Laurens grumbled, "These gentlemen are now with us, but hitherto they have offered no Satisfactory reasons."[44] He added ominously that if Georgia persisted, "we shall be obliged to Speak in plain terms of resentment . . . if she will not be a friend, an honest faithful friend, She must be held to be an Enemy."[45] Laurens strongly advised the Georgia council to prohibit the export of the ships loaded with rice and deerskins then crowding the wharves at Savannah.[46] Even if Georgia wanted to permit those vessels to leave, the arrival of a British fleet on January 18, 1776, settled the matter.

Laurens chided Lachlan McIntosh also for violations of the Continental Association at Sunbury: "Tell me how Liberty thrives about the Swamps of Altamaha [and] why you suffer Vessels to transgress by loading at Sunbury and your Neighborhood."[47] Laurens might have had in mind the Frederica merchant William Panton. Though Laurens probably did not know that Governor Tonyn had commissioned Panton to supply Florida with needed provisions, he was aware that Panton loaded flour on Daufuskie Island on the South Carolina side of the Savannah River.[48]

William Bartram found a badly divided Savannah when he arrived. The Provincial Congress quarreled over the question of barring exports and adjourned, leaving the management of affairs to the Council of Safety headed by an insecure Archibald Bulloch. On February 15 Bulloch sent a confidential letter to Henry Laurens that a panic had gripped Savannah with the arrival of the British men of war. He could not rely upon the loyalty of the locals; he appealed to Carolina to send troops—otherwise they were "an undone people."[49] Laurens, on behalf of the Carolina council, ordered Col. Stephen Bull to muster the militia in the Beaufort district and march to Savannah. The movement had the appearance of a Carolina invasion of Georgia.

None of this confusion and uncertainty found its way into William Bartram's notebook. He did not discuss politics and other forms of unpleasantness. Yet he could not escape the turmoil. Instead of the anticipated tranquillity of Darien he found Lachlan McIntosh in Savannah and a colonel of an incipient Georgia battalion. McIntosh described Savannah that February as an "open, straggling, defenseless and deserted town." The Council of Safety had not met since January 19, 1776, because the council could not agree on a plan of action. McIntosh called it a time of "anarchy and confusion." "In this desperate state of affairs," he wrote to his new superior, general of the Continental army, George Washington, "I ventured to take command of the militia, lest the Colony should be tamely given up, though I must acknowledge with some reluctance."[50] McIntosh later added that "most of our fellow Citizens and by far the most weighty were either Neutral or joined our Enemy" and that the four hundred or so "disorderly and Raw Militia" added to the seriousness of the situation.[51]

If William Bartram might have intended to pay a courtesy call on Gov. Sir James Wright, a gesture routine to him, he soon learned that the governor could see no one. Since the arrival of the British ships Wright remained a prisoner in his own house with a militiaman on watch. The Council of Safety employed Wright's slaves to dig entrenchments around the town. On the night of February 11, 1776, the governor let himself out the backdoor of his house and escaped to John Mulryne's plantation at Bonaventure. Mulryne, who earlier had helped Stuart get away from his pursuers, rowed the governor down Tybee Creek. At 3:00 A.M. Capt. Andrew Barkley of HMS *Scarborough* was awakened by Governor Wright's hail to come aboard. The next day Wright wrote to the council that the British warships merely intended to purchase provisions, not bother the townspeople. The Georgians refused to believe him and accused him of dishonorably breaking his parole.

The near approach of the Carolina troops emboldened the Council of Safety to take a stand. On March 2, 1776, the council summoned all "friends of America" to come to the defense of the "metropolis." They would burn the ships in the river and the town itself rather than let the royal forces take possession. The council ordered Col. Lachlan McIntosh to unrig the ships in the river and to dismantle the rudders.[52]

As though they had heard about the order to immobilize the twenty merchant ships, and perhaps they had, the British made their move. On March 2, 1776, riding the flood tide after dark, a line of warships moved upriver, taking the seldom-used channel behind Hutchinson's island so that the island screened them from McIntosh's less-than-wary sentries. Capt. Andrew Barkley acted as commodore, and Maj. James Grant commanded the nearly two hundred troops. The fleet consisted of the *Hinchinbrook*, the *Cherokee*, the *St. John*, the *Symmetry*, and three schooners.[53] Once behind Hutchinson Island, the ships dislodged their troops, who waded across William McGillivray's rice field and boarded some of the merchant ships to the surprise of their crews. Only two seamen had the patriotic courage to cross the river and tell Colonel McIntosh the alarming news.

McIntosh, convinced that the British meant to attack the town, expected the warships to round the western end of Hutchinson Island and land on Yamacraw Bluff. He posted a battery there. Indeed, as he had supposed, on the morning of March 3, a Sunday, the schooner *Hinchinbrook* and the sloop *St. John* made their ominous appearance. McIntosh ordered his riflemen to fire at will upon the vessels. Marines in the warships returned the fire. The Battle of the Rice Boats had begun.[54]

The British captains hoped to take advantage of the ebb tide to escort the rice boats downriver, but the heavier *Hinchinbrook* went aground. Maj. Joseph Habersham's riflemen kept up a sporadic fire for several hours until a change in the tide freed the warship, and with its companion it retired around Hutchinson's Island.[55]

The militiamen in Savannah reported that Capt. Joseph Rice, who had gone aboard one of the merchant ships early that morning to dismantle the rudder, had been made prisoner. McIntosh wanted to find the truth of the matter. Raymond Demere II (first cousin of Bartram's "sylvan friend" of St. Simon's Raymond Demere Jr.) and Daniel Roberts volunteered to go among the merchant ships in a canoe and to make polite inquiries. They found Capt. Andrew Barkley himself aboard the *Charming Nancy*, and the captain promptly made prisoners of them. Barkley allowed the two to invite on board two emissaries authorized to negotiate. Capts. James Screven and John Baker, both of St. John, volunteered, and they took along a dozen armed men. Their rowboat came under the stern of Barkley's vessel, and with the British marines glaring down at them they demanded the immediate release of their comrades. Adding insult to effrontery, Captain Baker fired into the larger vessel. The marines returned fire, and the brash Americans beat a hasty retreat, their boat sinking beneath them.[56]

McIntosh now approved the measure proposed by the Council of Safety, the burning of the vessels. The first ship torched, the *Inverness*, held George Galphin's deerskins along with a cargo of rice. Lachlan McGillivray, who chaired a protest meeting at the Tondee Tavern in July but stopped short of taking up arms against the king, owned the ship, together with others including his cousin Capt. William McGillivray of Hutchinson Island.[57]

The burning ship adrift on the current must have presented a terrifying sight to the soldiers and sailors aboard the crowded rice ships. Without waiting for orders they abandoned the vessels and ran helter skelter across boggy Hutchinson Island to the jeers of the Georgians on the south bank. Unfortunately for the Georgians the *Inverness* ran aground before it collided with the other ships. The militiamen fired a schooner on their side of the river and set its sails toward the rice ships. It collided with the *Nelly*, which caught the flames as did three adjacent schooners. The four ships continued to burn during the night and made an eerie sight as they drifted back and forth on the tide. Surprisingly the five ships failed to make contact with any other vessels. But the militiamen had found a formula for destruction of the fleet.[58]

They did not have a chance to renew the battle by fire because that night most of the rice boats took advantage of the flood tide to get around Hutchinson Island and escape under the escort of the *Hinchinbrook*, the *St. John*, and the *Cherokee*. Governor Wright, aboard the *Scarborough*, considered the expedition a success because he counted fourteen or fifteen merchant vessels coming downriver and gaining the open sea.[59] By seizing the rice the royal navy had what it came for.[60]

Lachlan McIntosh considered it an American victory. He believed that he had saved the town of Savannah from impending destruction. There was more than a hint of boast in his informing George Washington that the British "have done us great Honor by being the Second Province on the Continent which they have attacked and were shamefully foiled."[61]

The more patriotic Georgians, buoyed by success, felt vindictive toward the less patriotic in their midst. In retaliation for the British capture of Rice, Demere, and Roberts, the Council of Safety ordered the arrest of the most prominent loyalists. Twelve men surrounded Chief Justice Anthony Stokes's country house at two o'clock in the morning on March 6, 1776. Two of them entered the dwelling and found him sick in bed. They told him that they meant to take him to Colonel McIntosh's quarters in town. Stokes replied that they might as well kill him where he lay because going out at night in his condition would surely kill him. The militiamen agreed to wait until daytime to bring him to Savannah.[62] On his arrival Stokes admitted to McIntosh that he opposed the Revolution, asked for no favors, but challenged his captors not to "disgrace human nature by cruelty and oppression."[63]

In addition to Stokes, James Edward Powell, John Mulryne, Josiah Tattnall, Lachlan McGillivray, and William McGillivray were made prisoners, together with two of the captains of the merchant vessels, Hugh Inglis and George Wardell. Rumors circulated that the hostages would be shot if the three Georgians were not released.[64]

Events took an uglier turn with the arrival of Col. Stephen Bull and his Carolina troops on March 10, 1776. His dispatches to Carolina reveal that he assumed authority in Savannah though publicly deferring to the Georgia council. He told how he dispersed his troops to monitor the remaining vessels in the harbor so that "I can in a few minutes turn out the Troops."[65] He decided to dismantle the ships and persuaded the Georgia council to give the order to make it appear "that Georgia was not so backward as was heretofore suspected."[66] Unfortunately for one of the most zealous Georgians, Major Joseph Habersham, one of the ships belonged to him. The Georgia council asked if Habersham's ship might be spared. Bull answered absolutely not. Aboard the *Scarborough*, Governor Wright said sadly that Carolina had taken possession of Georgia.[67]

Two observations caused a sinister plan to form in Bull's mind. At Jonathan Bryan's Brampton plantation, where Bartram would soon be a guest, Bull met a traveling party of about a hundred Cusseta and Yuchi Indians, seventy of them warriors. Ten of the men took part in the rice boat skirmish, and one was wounded. Stukychee, a headman of the Cussetas, declared that "as his Nephew joined us and got hurt in the first engagement he and his people would now join and assist us."[68]

If Bull's first thought was to use Indians in this battle, the second observation was that 150 slaves had sought freedom by joining the British on Tybee. They camped near the warships waiting to be taken aboard. Bull revealed his plan in a confidential dispatch to the Carolina council. "The matter is this," he wrote, "it is far better for the Public and the owners of the deserted Negroes on Tybee Island . . . to be shot if they cannot be taken . . . for if they are carried away, and converted into money . . . it will only enable our Enemy to fight us with our own money or property. . . ." Having decided upon the need to kill the slaves, Bull proposed a creative manner of accomplishing the deed: "Therefore all who cannot be taken had better be shot by the Creek Indians, as it perhaps may deter other Negroes from deserting and will establish a hatred or Aversion between the Indians and the Negroes."[69]

Here occurred another of those ironies we have noticed in William Bartram's southern sojourn. Col. George Wells, brother to Bartram's Augusta host, Humphrey Wells, was Bull's confidant in the scheme and carried Bull's dispatches to Charlestown. An unwilling participant on the Georgia council was Bartram's friend Benjamin Andrew. Bull said of him, "Some of the Council of Safety are timid, particularly one Mr. Andrews from St. John Parish Sunbury who has influence and through whose means Governor Wright has been enabled to carry on his Plans of late."[70] One wonders what William Bartram might have thought about the plan, what disappointment he must have felt. Lachlan McIntosh seems not to have played an active part in the ugly affair but must have given tacit approval. Archibald Bulloch would lead the Indians and the Georgians disguised as Indians.

Henry Laurens, writing for the Carolina council, expressed revulsion at the idea of executing the runaways; "the prospect is horrible," he said. However, in a tortured argument he decided that the end justified the means. He blamed the British for "every inglorious unavoidable act of necessity which we may be driven to commit."[71] Laurens added mysteriously that he hoped Colonel Wells "will succeed in everything he has in view." The Georgians waited for Wells before conducting their raid, or perhaps it was coincidental that the Tybee operations happened the day after Wells arrived back in Savannah.[72]

Fortunately for the slaves, as well as for the honor of the Georgians who carried out the raid, the slaves had already been taken aboard the transports. Governor Wright estimated that between two and three hundred refugees sought safety with the British fleet at Tybee. Disappointed at not finding the runaways, Archibald Bulloch's men, some disguised as Cussetas, killed and scalped a British soldier and fatally wounded three others. They burned houses of persons suspected of cooperation with the British and took several prisoners. Governor Wright believed they were looking for him.[73]

William Bartram never criticized his friends in print. But in private conversations with Lachlan McIntosh and Benjamin Andrew, he may have questioned this strategy of setting Indians upon black people. Did he ask why the same people who execrated and exiled John Stuart because of a rumor that he might use Indians themselves employed Indians in warfare?

The Tybee affair marked the end of the beginning of the military operations in Georgia. Captain Barkley released the three Americans whereupon the Georgia council allowed Anthony Stokes, the McGillivrays, and the others to leave Georgia. On March 31, 1776, the British fleet with the Georgia exiles and the captured rice left for Boston. The *Cherokee* and the *Raven* remained on guard at Tybee.[74]

On March 26 South Carolina adopted its first constitution and elected John Rutledge president and Henry Laurens vice president.[75]

III

When I was at Gen'l McIntoshes on the Alatamaha, the
English attempted to invade Georgia.
Bartram, "Some Hints and Observations . . ."

As a result of his three year travels, William Bartram had acquired an encyclopedic knowledge of plants and birds of the southern frontier and also a comprehension of the essential unity of the frontier. The Wrightsborough raids of the winter of 1773–1774 had ramifications from the Atlantic to the Mississippi; the resulting trade embargo affected all the colonies and the several Indian nations. The widening separation of colonies from mother country confused and divided the southeastern Indians as well as the colonists. During his last summer in the South, Bartram witnessed the dramatic climax of a chain of events in which he had been involved.

The Georgia Provincial Congress, concerned about the British ships at Tybee, took the precaution of meeting at Augusta. Still waffling between temerity and timidity and still goaded by Carolina, the congress drew up a short set of rules and regulations to serve as a framework of government. The rudimentary constitution created a presidency and four other offices and maintained the Council of Safety to act as council to the president. The congress adopted the rules and regulations on April 15 and elected Archibald Bulloch president and commander in chief.[76]

The uncertainty about the intentions of the great Indian nations worried the new governments of Georgia and Carolina. In his inaugural address on April 11, 1776, John Rutledge told the South Carolina congress that a principal grievance concerned the British effort "to engage barbrous nations to embue their hands in the innocent blood of helpless women and children." With characteristic lack of modesty, he concluded, "The eyes of every other Colony are on this— a Colony whose reputation for generosity and magnanimity is universally acknowledged."[77] At least Georgia watched.

Indian diplomacy occupied the attention of high strategists on both sides of the conflict. The Continental Congress approved the use of Indians in warfare and so notified General Washington.[78] Commissioners representing the Continental Congress, including George Galphin, Robert Rae, and Edward Wilkinson, met delegates from the Cherokee Nation at Fort Charlotte on April 15, 1776, the day Georgians adopted their new form of government.[79] A nervous headman spoke for his people: "The land now trembles, the Wind whistles from almost every quarter." The commissioners delivered John Hancock's message that the dispute was "a family quarrel between us and old England, you Indians are not concerned in it, we don't wish you to take up the hatchet against the king's troops" even though some of the Creek Indians, out of "their love for us . . . voluntarily turned to our assistance" in the recent skirmish with British troops in Savannah. Galphin explained that though he appreciated what the Creeks had done, he would tell them to stay home next time. As though Galphin and his friends knew about the British proposal to employ Indians in conjunction with troops, the commissioners warned the Cherokees not to be tempted to do so. The Indians could not fight their way through to join the redcoats, and the redcoats could not fight in the woods. Besides, he said, "the great Man above us is on our side." Galphin passed along John Rutledge's warning to the

Indians not to listen to the talk of Stuart and Cameron: "they want to make mischief between us."[80] Whatever advantage the commissioners might have gained was dissipated by the paucity of presents. The Good Warrior of Seneca showed his displeasure by refusing to accept any gifts.[81]

George Galphin sent out an invitation to the headmen of the Creek villages to meet with him and the other commissioners in Augusta on May 1, 1776. Meanwhile the Georgia congress enlisted the help of Governor Wright's antagonist Jonathan Bryan. Bryan liked to entertain visiting Indians at his Brampton plantation on the river just above Savannah. Bryan introduced Stephen Bull to the party of Cussetas and Yuchis there in March, with the raid on the blacks on Tybee as a result.[82] Bryan still had not given up hope of obtaining a huge tract of land in the northern part of East Florida. During April, Bryan organized an expedition to the Lower Creeks led by his son William and a well-known mixed-blood interpreter named Thomas Gray. The mission had as its primary purpose the securing of the allegiance of the Creek villages, secondly the arrest of David Taitt, and thirdly obtaining consent to Bryan's projected lease of land.[83] Bryan recruited seventy men to carry his presents and his talk.

It is likely that Bryan conferred with William Bartram about his plans. Bartram had just come from the Creek country and could speak with authority on the disposition of the Indians. Bryan certainly met with Bartram at some time during the rice boat fracas because Bryan invited the botanist to visit him at Brampton on the latter's return from a sojourn with the McIntoshes on the Georgia coast.

On the British side Gage's successor, Gen. Sir William Howe, considered the employment of Indians so essential to a southern military strategy that he dispatched a ship to St. Augustine for the purpose of transporting Stuart to Cape Fear, North Carolina, to confer with Gen. Henry Clinton, commander in the Southern Department. Stuart had just heard and apparently agreed with Thomas Brown's proposal to carry arms and ammunition to loyalists in Carolina and to raise a corps of rangers to ride with the Indians. He was about to set off on his already-delayed voyage to Pensacola when Howe's instructions diverted him to Cape Fear. He left St. Augustine on February 15, 1776, passed Governor Wright aboard the *Scarborough* at Tybee, and met Clinton and Lord William Campbell at Cape Fear by March 15, 1776.[84]

Clinton's hopes of a quick campaign were dashed by a premature rising of loyalists, mostly Highland Scots under Donald McDonald, who suffered defeat at the battle of Moore's Bridge, North Carolina. Royal governor John Martin complained that the rising was not premature; rather, Clinton was late.[85]

Patrick Tonyn expressed delight at Clinton's arrival in the South and described to him Thomas Brown's proposal to circle around Georgia to recruit two or more companies of rangers in Carolina who would regulate Indian warfare. Brown, he said, "is a very active, spirited, sensible young man . . . very deserving, confidential and of noble sentiments." Tonyn fancied himself operating under Clinton's command using Brown's rangers and Stuart's Indians: "If I do not restore Sir James Wright to his Government, I shall at least draw the Georgia troops from opposing your army."[86]

Clinton, already lobbied by Sir William Campbell on behalf of the plan to use Indians in conjunction with troops, readily endorsed the strategy. In fact, he adopted it as his own. On March 14 Clinton wrote out "My plan for fulfilling the object of the expedition." In part he proposed a landing in the Savannah River and a rapid march to Augusta, Fort Charlotte, and "all the backcountry which is in general friendly to government." Clinton might "show" the Indians as long as they were under British control so as not to push "their ravaging too far."[87] How to show the Indians and how to organize the right amount of ravaging remained a British problem.

On the way to Cape Fear, John Stuart's enthusiasm for the plan cooled. Outranked by Campbell and Tonyn, he could not oppose the employment of Indians, but he could and did set conditions. He first recited to Clinton the history of his administration, noting the problems caused by the interference of the governors in Indian affairs, deploring the way Governor Wright exalted George Galphin, and reviewed recent events such as the Fort Charlotte conference and Henry Stuart's mission to the Cherokees.[88] Even then, he explained, Henry Stuart was on his way with a caravan of munitions for loyalists in the Carolina upcountry. Stuart lingered at Cape Fear all during April while Tonyn chafed at St. Augustine, waiting for orders from Clinton. Stuart made his demands of Clinton in a letter dated May 8, 1776. He objected to military officers interfering in Indian affairs: "I wish to be in a situation not to be thwarted or counteracted in the management of my Indians." At least partly because Tonyn's rangers might outrank his deputies, he insisted on a colonelcy for himself and suitable ranks for his deputies: Taitt, Cameron, John McIntosh, and Henry Stuart. He needed two thousand pounds sterling for supplies for the Indians.[89]

Clinton acquiesced in the request for military rank and agreed to the subsidy but could not find a way to keep the governors, who claimed the title of commander in chief of their colonies, out of military operations. Clinton dispatched the *Hinchinbrook* of rice boat fame to carry Stuart to St. Augustine by June 8 and to Pensacola on July 24.[90]

Long before Stuart's return Tonyn lost confidence in the superintendent. Stuart was supposed to present Thomas Brown's plan to Clinton. What had happened? The superintendent instead had introduced new complications. Nothing could have been easier to execute: "There is no mistery in it, no difficulty," he wrote to Clinton. "It is cruel to continue doing nothing," he added, "it is always a losing game." In fact, events did not wait on Stuart. Tonyn expected an attack upon his borders by the Georgians; "The Rebels are assembling on the Banks, north of the River Saint Mary," he told Clinton in his letter of May 21, 1776.[91]

Tonyn revealed the extent of his exasperation in a letter to the American secretary, Lord George Germain, when he learned from Stuart that the Indians would not be involved as early as he had wished. He only found out about Gage's directive of September 12, 1775, on May 3, 1776. Stuart had not told him about the instruction to employ Indians. "I was my Lord in amazement," he wrote; "Nothing can be more explicit then the General's design." Stuart should have gone to Pensacola in October last in response to Governor Chester's invitation and Emistisiguo's urging to be in closer contact with the Creeks. If he, Tonyn, had known the contents of Gage's letter, he would not have invited the Creeks to visit East Florida in December: "I cannot help being exceedingly vexed that a whole year for Her Majesty's service is lost."[92]

Of course, Tonyn had not waited idly for word from Stuart. His protégé, Thomas Brown, had achieved some early success in the Creek country. With David Taitt's approval Brown recruited the Oconee King and sent him to Tonyn. The Cowkeeper had already offered his services. Therefore, Tonyn had Indians at his disposal to oppose the threat of Georgians on the Saint Marys. Brown intended to convey his train of ammunition to his friends in Carolina, but when he reached Chiaha, the Indians "expressed the greatest satisfaction at the sight of such quantity of Ammunition."[93] Only Brown's self-assurance enabled him to survive in a world new and strange to him. His journey through the Seminole villages to the Lower Creek towns obliged him to swim twenty-five rivers and creeks transporting the cargo on improvised rafts. When he reached Chiaha, he heard that Jonathan Bryan's party was on its way to the same place and that several of the towns meant to respond to George Galphin's invitation to attend a conference in Augusta on May 16. The fact that the Chiahas and Cowetas might decide to appropriate the powder he carried added to his problems. Brown did the prudent thing; he sent an urgent message to David Taitt at Little Tallassee to come quickly. Taitt obliged and on May 1, 1776, talked to the gathering of Lower Creeks at Chiaha. He told them not to go to Augusta to see George Galphin. Galphin had become poor, Taitt said, and had nothing to give them. Brown's impressive pack train lent credibility to his argument that the king could help them and Congress could not. He persuaded most of the towns to stay away from Augusta, but the Cowetas and some Cussetas and Hitchitas said they meant to go see their good friend George Galphin anyway. Taitt gained an important point by securing the consent of his listeners to have nothing to do with Jonathan Bryan's party. Should they venture here, he wrote Tonyn, "I am in hopes of being able to secure them."[94]

A few days after his meeting, Taitt expressed the hope that the Creeks would let Brown's caravan through on the promise that more powder would be sent to them. Taitt and a party of Upper Creeks would escort Brown and some Lower Creeks up the Coosa River Valley and into the Overhills Cherokee towns. Taitt proved far more cooperative than his superior, telling Tonyn that with the Oconee King's warriors and the Cowkeeper's Seminoles "your Excellency will have it in your power to employ them as you shall judge necessary."[95]

George Galphin could not compete with Taitt in supplying powder; he could, however, depend on the personal bonds created by forty years of association with the Lower Creeks. He could count on the loyalty of Coweta, where he maintained his trading house until the war with the French. Cowetans Sempoyaffe and Eschochabey were mistrusted by Stuart and Taitt partly because they were friends of Galphin. As the Cowetas rode to Augusta along their traditional trading path, a gang of backcountrymen led by the notorious Thomas Fee attacked them and killed a warrior. Rather than start a war then and there, the Cowetas rode on to Augusta to tell George Galphin about the incident. When the conference began on May 16, Galphin tried to make the best of a bad situation. The murdered Indian, he said, had stolen a horse from one of the white men. The Chavulky Warrior of Coweta told Galphin that it was not the custom to kill people for stealing a horse. His people must have satisfaction. Ten white people had fired on them and killed one, "and as we are all met here like brothers I hope that he may suffer."[96] Galphin had only soothing words and rum, and he applied both liberally. The Cowetas took his liquor but brooded over the death of their kinsman. Because of the wanton cruelty of Fee and his companions, the Americans lost their strongest ally; the Cowetas would soon wreak havoc on the backcountry.

George Galphin blamed George Wells for attempting to start an Indian war. "If he could get people enough to have joined him at the time of the Congress, I was told by a man that was in the plot to have seized all the ammunition, and to have fell upon the Indians and killed them and declared war with them," he wrote to the North Carolina Indian commissioner Willie Jones.[97] Whatever theoretical reasons William Bartram and his friends might have had in this developing war, people such as George Wells saw it as a practical opportunity to get rid of Indians and appropriate their land.

While Thomas Brown waited among the Lower Creeks until he could continue his expedition to his loyalist friends in Carolina, Henry Stuart finally reached Toquah in the Cherokee overhills on April 26 after a tedious journey through the Chickasaw country. He wrote John Stuart on May 7 that he delivered all his powder to the Cherokees, that several Carolina loyalists wondered where their supply was, and that the Cherokees seemed to be on the verge of war because of the continued encroachment upon their lands. Henry Stuart and Alexander Cameron urged them to wait for word from John Stuart.[98]

Georgians and Carolinians blamed the Stuarts and Cameron for inciting the Cherokees to war. None of these troubling events found their way into William Bartram's *Travels*. Of that period he simply writes, "I employed myself during the spring and fore part of the summer, in revisiting the several districts of Georgia and the East borders of Florida." The most exciting event, if we are to believe his chronicles, was his rediscovery of the Franklinia. Yet George Ord, a contemporary of Bartram whose biographical sketch of the botanist appeared in 1832, wrote that Bartram "volunteered and joined a detachment of men, raised by General Lachlan McIntosh, to repel a supposed invasion of that state from St. Augustine by the British."[99] Bartram must have given that tantalizing bit of information to Ord, and it prompted Francis Harper to speculate that McIntosh might have employed Bartram as a scout. Harper even suggests that Bartram's encounter with the lone angry Seminole who might have killed him occurred while Bartram scouted along the Saint Marys. However, Bartram's letter to Henry Knox in the John Pierpont Morgan Library in New York provides essential insight into his activity. "When I was at Gen'l McIntoshes on the Altamaha," he wrote, "the English attempted to invade Georgia."[100] Bartram was more involved in the war than Harper supposed, and his letter explained how.

After the rice boat affair Bartram had accompanied Lachlan McIntosh to Darien. The war fractured the once close-knit clan. Lachlan and his sons Lachlan Jr. and William served in the Continental army, as did Lachlan's brother, William, and his sons John and Lachlan. Their cousins John and William McIntosh remained in the Indian country in service of John Stuart. Eccentric Rory McIntosh would not betray the king and dared anyone to stop him from going to Florida. A family tradition has it that his relatives unsuccessfully tried to persuade him to join the Revolution by telling him that the Americans intended to put Prince Charles Stuart on the throne.[101] James Spalding of St. Simon suffered banishment, as did George Baillie for trading with Florida. George McIntosh, Lachlan's younger brother, served on the Council of Safety, but because he was connected with William Panton in a shipment of goods from Sunbury in June 1776 that found its way to Florida, he would become a target for the wrath of Georgia's radical faction.

By coincidence, while Bartram lodged with the McIntoshes, Henry Laurens spent the month of May at his Broughton Island and New Hope plantations.[102] Bartram would have made an effort to see him. Old friend Benjamin Andrew supervised the construction of Fort Morris at nearby Sunbury.[103] But it was not a time for convivial socializing. The incursions of Florida cattle raiders and rumors of invasion by Florida rangers and their Indian allies kept people on edge. There are no idylls in this chapter of *Travels*, no loitering with sylvan friends or jousting with alligators. Bartram's short chapter is almost entirely taken up with the rediscovery of the Franklinia plant.

His great military adventure began with a report by Capt. William McIntosh to the Council of Safety on May 14 about persons on the St. Marys who traded with the enemy.[104] Bartram knew some of them. Governor Wright's brothers, Charles and Jerym, had fortified one of their plantation houses and stored a supply of gunpowder there. Twenty loyalists and their slaves took refuge in Wright's fort. Martin Jollie, another planter on the border, supplied St. Augustine with cattle. Several boats belonging to loyalists anchored in the river. The council took umbrage at those activities, and President Bulloch ordered Captain McIntosh to put an immediate stop to all of it. With his troop of lighthorse he should take possession of Wright's fort, arrest its defenders, confiscate the powder, apprehend Martin Jollie, secure his gunpowder also, seize all boats belonging to unfriendly persons, and for good measure arrest any and sundry persons who might be dangerous to the liberties of America.[105]

Colonel Lachlan might have been concerned that President Bulloch neglected the chain of command in giving orders directly to his subordinate, who happened to be his brother. Clearly, Bulloch took his title of president and commander in chief seriously. The question of military supremacy led to disastrous consequences, not the least being a duel between Lachlan McIntosh and Bulloch's successor, Button Gwinnett—a duel fatal to Gwinnett. In this case Lachlan McIntosh accompanied the Continentals to the St. Marys with volunteers from the coastal Georgia counties, including William Bartram.

The best description of how the Georgians fared was supplied by Governor Tonyn of Florida, who heard about the Georgia raid almost immediately. He dispatched the *St. John* schooner with a captain's detachment of troops to the St. Marys. The schooner entered the river on May 29, 1776, but could not prevent the Georgians crossing over and making prisoners of Martin Jollie and two other planters. The Florida troops nearly intercepted the raiders on their return to Georgia. Both sides fired shots at each other across the river, and in the confusion two of the planters regained the Florida side of the river.[106] The Georgians failed to dislodge the loyalists from Wright's fort, and their raid prompted Tonyn to build up his defenses of the Florida border. The arrest of Martin Jollie represented the only successful outcome of this first Georgia incursion. The council ordered Jollie to be "detained in this Province, on his parole."[107]

The rumor swept through Georgia that Floridians planned an invasion. The council, again ignoring the military chain of command, ordered Lt. Col. Samuel Elbert to march with his Continentals to the defense of Savannah.[108] The council seemed to acknowledge Georgia's weakness by ordering Colonel McIntosh to hold the line not at the St. Marys but at the Satilla with the Altamaha as a fall-back position. On the same day, July 2, 1776, the council ordered the St. John militia under Col. John Screven "to support Lieutenant Colonel McIntosh with a sufficient number of men to make a stand against the troops of Indians from St. Augustine."[109]

More than anything else, the fear of Indians paralyzed the Georgians. Governor Tonyn knew as much, and that is why he dispatched the Cowkeeper to the Altamaha. "The Americans are a thousand times more in dread of the Savages than of any European Troops," he wrote to General Clinton.[110]

Martha Searcy, in her excellent study of the Georgia-Florida border warfare, suggests that "It was probably about this time that William Bartram, the naturalist, embarked on a reconnaissance mission between the Altamaha and the St. Marys for Captain Lachlan McIntosh."[111] Francis Harper tantalizes us with the thought that McIntosh sent Bartram on a scouting trip to the St. Marys and that at this time he encountered the angry Seminole and while on the Altamaha saw the eclipse of the moon.[112] We have seen evidence of Bartram's resourcefulness during his three years in the wilderness, and it is tempting to picture him as a James Fenimore Cooper prototype of Natty Bumpo. Unfortunately the descriptions of the 1773 exploration of the St. Marys does not accord with the 1776 situation. In 1773, after his meeting with the "intrepid Seminole," he crossed over to the Florida side of the river to a trading company store, where the traders welcomed him and told him that the Indian had been outlawed by his own countrymen.[113] Trade had ceased in 1776, and the trading houses on the St. Marys were abandoned. The blithe tone of his description of the 1773 excursion belies any notion of his being a spy on a dangerous mission.

His letter to Henry Knox may be the best insight we are allowed to have regarding his part in the war. He described how "the English attempted to invade Georgia." He explained that "They advanced to the Banks of St. Mary's, possess'd themselves of it, and took Shelter in the old Indian trading house. A few Indians were in company. A Small party of the Georgians marched from the Alatamaha to oppose them and they gain'd the banks before the Enemy had pass'd the Flood. Hostilities commenced by the parties firing at each other across the River. The British were under cover of the evacuated trading houses, and the Georgians shielded themselves behind the Trees, on the River Banks." Bartram's narrative achieved a crescendo as he continued: "The conflict had continued for some time when the Chief of the Indians threw down his Gun and boldly stepping out from the corner of a House he took off his Hat and whirling it up in the Air as he advanced to the River Side, amidst showers of Bullets, he spoke aloud to the Georgians, declaring that they were Brother's and friends and that he knew not any cause why they should spill each others Blood. Neither I (said he) nor my Companions the Red-Men, will fire another Gun. He turned about, shouted, and immediately le'd off the Indians. This put an end to the contest at that time."[114]

The chief in question was almost certainly Bartram's friend Ahaya, the Cowkeeper of Cuscowilla, who had given him the name Pug Puggy. Apparently, Bartram did not see the need to go into that detail with Secretary of War Knox. His story excites the imagination. Did the Cowkeeper recognize his friend across the river? Something of that sort caused the chief to stop fighting on this occasion. The Cowkeeper had no qualms about fighting in subsequent battles. In February 1777 the Cowkeeper and his band followed Thomas Brown to the fort on the Satilla River built by and named after Lachlan McIntosh. The Cowkeeper's war whoops, as much as the actual shooting, frightened the Georgia garrison into surrendering.[115] Throughout the war the Cowkeeper remained Governor Tonyn's best ally; however, on this occasion, perhaps, the chief decided not to shoot at Pug Puggy.

Governor Tonyn's dispatch to Lord George Germain adds a few details to the skirmish on the St. Marys. Earlier, the captain of the schooner *St. John* put his sick and wounded in Wright's fort on the Georgia side. On the opposite bank the old trading post had been occupied by a detachment of the Sixteenth Regiment. A Lieutenant Beecher set out from the *St. John* in a cutter to bring off some of the sick soldiers. A canoe carrying five men followed the cutter. As Bartram mentioned, before they passed the high-water mark the Georgians had hidden themselves on the riverbank near Wright's fort. Two guns were fired from the fort to warn the approaching boats, and then the Georgians opened fire, killing two and taking the cutter. The lieutenant and two officers were made prisoners and the cutter burned. The canoe escaped back to the *St. John*.

The soldiers and the Indians fired upon the Georgians from across the river and from the fort. Tonyn did not mention the part played by the Cowkeeper other than stating that Tonyn directed the chief to cut off the rebel raiders south of the St. Marys.[116] He also said that some of the Georgia troops had suffered because after the engagement the places where the soldiers hid showed blood.

Lachlan McIntosh reported on the skirmish to Gen. Charles Lee, newly arrived in Charlestown as commander of the troops in the Southern Department. Two hundred Indians, he wrote, had come to the river to cut off the retreat of the Georgians. William McIntosh's men "obliged them to desist." However, the Georgians thought it prudent to retire to the Satilla where they constructed Fort McIntosh.[117] There was no pursuit. The immediate danger of invasion from the South eased for the time being.

According to Bartram's first biographer George Ord, McIntosh offered the botanist a lieutenant's commission if he would stay in Georgia.[118] Bartram turned down the promotion. He could reconcile volunteering to oppose a threat to his friends, but his Quaker conscience would not let him become a professional in the business of war. Although it comes as no surprise that he declined the position, he certainly deserved the honor of the offer.

Thus ended Bartram's singular military adventure. His vast exotic garden from the Cherokee mountains to the Florida borderlands had become a battleground, and Pug Puggy had nearly become a warrior. It was time to go home.

7

Philadelphia

I

*I took leave of these Southern regions, preceding on my
return to Charleston.*

Harper, *Travels*

After his tour of service on the St. Marys and his retreat with Capt. William
McIntosh's militia to the Satilla, William Bartram returned to his Georgia
home and the McIntoshes. Sarah McIntosh made him welcome. Lachlan Jr.,
only seventeen but already a lieutenant in Capt. Arthur Carney's First Regiment, Georgia Continentals, had the duty of protecting Darien. William, or
Billy, served as an ensign in the Fifth Regiment, stationed in Savannah.[1] Sarah
kept the younger children, George, Henry, and Hetty, at their studies, and
William Bartram would have been glad to help out.[2]

As he lingered through September at the McIntoshes, Bartram's orderly
world collapsed. During the last days of June, Sir Peter Parker's fleet assaulted
Charlestown, with Henry Clinton's troops ready to land. Six men-of-war ranged
along the palmetto fort on Sullivan's Island commanded by Col. William
Moultrie and blasted twelve thousand pounds of cannon shot at the fort. Moultrie's gallant defenders returned almost five thousand pounds of shot, nearly
sinking the flagship *Bristol* with Lord William Campbell aboard. Sgt. William
Jasper earned lasting fame when in the heat of the June 28 battle he retrieved
the fallen flag and fixed it again in its place, to the cheers of the fort's defenders. The badly mauled fleet lingered off the bar during most of July, then sailed
for the northward.[3]

By coincidence the Cherokees, in the words of John Drayton, "poured down upon the frontiers of South Carolina, massacreing without distinction of age or sex, all persons who fell into their power."[4] The immediate provocation for the July 1 outbreak was Maj. Andrew Williamson's earlier dispatch of thirty men to Seneca to arrest loyalists being harbored there. John Rutledge solemnly announced to his legislature that the attacks from sea and mountain "convinces us of what, indeed, we had before little reason to doubt, of the indiscriminate atrocity and unrelenting tyranny of the hand that directs the British war."[5] Although British general Sir Henry Clinton approved such a simultaneous offensive, the Cherokee assault happened despite John Stuart and his deputies. Stuart frustrated Governor Tonyn by inviting the Indians to meet him in Pensacola, thus delaying any coordinated offensive. The facts mattered little; most Carolinians blamed Stuart for the Cherokee outbreak.

The Cherokees suffered terrible retribution. Gen. Charles Lee, who arrived in Charlestown just in time to take credit for the defense of the town, also took charge of the Cherokee campaign. He called upon the Virginians to attack the overhills and the Carolinians to march upon the lower settlements. William Henry Drayton's instructions to Francis Salvador, Andrew Williamson's fellow resident in the Ninety-Six District and a volunteer in the expedition, belied his earlier sugar-coated overtures to the Cherokees: "It is expected you make smooth work as you go that is, you cut up every Indian corn-field, and burn every Indian town, and that every Indian taken shall be the slave and property of the taker, that the nation be extirpated, and the lands become the property of the public."[6]

On August 1, 1776, Williamson's army invaded the apparently deserted village of Seneca. As they forded the river, the Senecas fired a volley from behind a palisade, fatally wounding Salvador, who rode at Williamson's side. Lt. Col. LeRoy Hammond led the charge across the river to the west bank, scattering the defenders. Williamson then proceeded to systematically destroy all the towns in the lower settlements. "I have now burnt down every town and destroyed all the corn, from the Cherokee line to the middle settlements," Williamson reported to Drayton.[7]

Williamson paused to furlough his men and erect Fort Rutledge on the eastern part of the town of Seneca. Seneca and the lower towns now belonged to Carolina as trophies of war. In September, with two thousand men, he resumed his mission of destruction. His army followed Bartram's route, crossing the Chattooga at Warwoman Creek, marching over Courthouse Gap, then

up the path to Watauga and Cowee, destroying everything in the middle settlements. Every town Bartram had visited the year before lay in ruins, but Bartram would write about them as he remembered them—peaceful villages,
proud people, and strawberry fields—and his readers for generations to come
would not know about the devastation.

William Bartram learned the awful lesson of the Cherokee War. As the
American people assumed responsibility for their own government, they had
to choose between Drayton's option of extermination of the Indians and the
alternative of accommodation. All Bartram's writings became a thinly disguised plea for accommodation. He may have been involved in the appeal that two of his friends made to Gen. Charles Lee after Lee's arrival in
Charlestown. Lachlan McIntosh and Jonathan Bryan, with John Houston as
a third, addressed a plea for help to General Lee. They stressed the large
number of Indian warriors on their borders and the immediate danger of a
rupture with them because of British tampering. Their solution, interestingly, was not a war of extermination but coexistence: "men, fortifications, and
a good understanding with the Indians." They acknowledged that Indians
should be well paid for their neutrality. Since gunpowder could not be supplied, the Georgians suggested cattle as the next best commodity. Their rea-
soning sounds like a line from Bartram: "We are of opinion this step would
answer many valuable purposes, and would have a tendency not only of
attaching them to our interest from gratitude but would also be a means
of civilizing them, and by fixing the idea of property, would keep them honest and peaceable with us."[8]

Backcountry Georgians preferred the Drayton method of dealing with
Indians. George Wells, brother of Humphrey and a partner in Stephen Bull's
proposed raid on Tybee refugees, got up a petition purporting to represent
the inhabitants of St. Paul, St. George, and the ceded lands, most of them
"people of no property," according to George Galphin.[9] The petition stressed
the danger of allowing Indians to come among the white settlements and the
desirability of appropriating the Oconee River as an outlet to the sea and concluded that the time had come "to exterminate and rout those savages out of
their nation." They asked the general to send an army to Georgia to accomplish
that result and said that they were ready to hazard their lives and fortunes in "so
desirable a purpose."[10] When Williamson requested Georgia's help in the campaign against the Cherokee because the town of Chote lay within Georgia's
boundaries, there were few volunteers. George Galphin noted sarcastically that

Georgia's captain, Leonard Marbury, "could not get one of these people to go with him that wants to declare war."[11]

Lee listened to the urgent messages of both the McIntosh and the Wells factions and agreed that Georgia deserved military attention but opted for neither accommodation nor extermination as his Indian policy. He would send an army to the Florida borderlands, not because he had any real expectation of reaching St. Augustine but because, as he confided to Pres. John Rutledge of South Carolina, a grand demonstration of this kind would awe the Indians. The expedition would "above all, make a salutary impression on the minds of the Creeks who now are thought to stand wavering."[12] Seldom if ever in American military annals has a parade for the purpose of awing Indians been disguised as an invasion. Lee intended the former; Tonyn of Florida interpreted it as the latter.

Except for the tragic aspects that Lee's expedition shared with all forms of warfare, Georgia's military efforts bordered on the burlesque. After reaching Savannah on August 19 and conferring with the authorities, Lee wrote to a subordinate in Charlestown that the Georgians were more "harum skarum" than the Carolinians. "They will propose anything," he said, "and after they have proposed it, discover that they are incapable of performing the least." After assuring him that they were ready to march, Georgia authorities found that they had no horses to go by land or boats to go by sea. "Upon the whole," he concluded , "I shou'd not be surprised if they were to propose mounting a body of mermaids on alligators."[13] Lee would have to employ several Carolina regiments now mustered into Continental service for the invasion.

The arrival of the regiments in Georgia coincided with the news of the Declaration of Independence, read aloud on August 8 by Pres. Archibald Bulloch at the liberty pole in Savannah. The presence of the troops greatly encouraged the Georgians in their celebration. On August 19 the Georgia battalion joined the Carolinians in impressive military maneuvers in Savannah. Then the trouble began. Dissension about precedence in command led to bickering between Carolinians and Georgians. With considerable difficulty the main body of Lee's army reached Sunbury and stopped there. Under the circumstances Lee felt rescued by an order to return to the northward. He took some of the troops with him in early September.

Before the Carolina troops left Georgia, they devastated Sunbury and Darien in their foraging. Ironically, friendly troops, not the enemy, destroyed Lachlan McIntosh's plantation and put an end to William Bartram's visit there.

Lachlan later appealed to Congress for compensation for the loss of his crop of rice, corn, peas, and potatoes, all "taken and destroyed by our own troops who burnt my fences and turned their horses into the fields." Eventually, McIntosh suffered worse losses. He did not make clear whether Americans, following a scorched earth policy, or British invaders caused the damage, but he lost his residence, barn and outbuildings, all his livestock, and twenty-four slaves. Presumably the slaves escaped to Florida. McIntosh did say that as a result of the damage to his property he had to remove his family to Savannah. Perhaps his promotion to the rank of brigadier general on September 16, 1776, provided some solace.[14]

With his last and favorite retreat closed to him, William Bartram had to follow his friends to Savannah. He might have pondered the irony that an expedition urged by Lachlan McIntosh should have displaced McIntosh's family. The greater irony was that the military operation meant to overawe the Indians not only made the American look inept but also led to a retaliation by the British and their Indian allies.

Before leaving Georgia, Bartram visited Jonathan Bryan's Brampton plantation. Bryan's spacious gardens with their rich variety of fruit trees and flowering shrubs revived Bartram's enthusiasm for botanizing. He expressed interest in two kinds of plants with large turniplike roots, relished by blacks because they tasted like sweet potatoes. He described how the passenger pigeons migrated to these regions in huge numbers and how the slaves captured them by torchlight as the pigeons roosted in trees.[15] Bryan, his host, sat on the Council of Safety as the Indian expert. He could brief Bartram on the spectrum of recent Indian activities, from the Cherokee war to Stuart's invitation to the Creeks and Choctaws to meet him in Pensacola and settle their war. Bryan's own efforts had not produced results. David Taitt proved too formidable a rival for Bryan's emissaries, his son William and the part-Indian Tom Gray. On September 1, 1776, Bryan sent Gray back to the Creek Nation with a new talk. On behalf of the council he stated that he only wished "to hold fast that love which has for many years subsisted between you and us." Bartram would have approved of that sentiment. Bryan went on, in an obvious reference to the ruined villages of the Cherokee country, to say that if the Creeks failed to be friendly, they would bring on themselves "Destruction and Ruin."[16] George Wells would have preferred that alternative. The Creeks responded with a mixed signal. The Cussetas would not allow Thomas Brown to arrest Tom Gray, but neither did they receive Bryan's talk.[17]

Bartram would have been interested to learn that Adam Tapley, the unpleasant trader he had traveled with, had a run-in with Brown, who had assumed the duties of policeman in the Creek country. Brown intercepted Tapley's trade caravan on its way from Mobile to Muccolossus and arrested the troublesome Tapley. Long-standing custom forbade such interference in trade, and a party of Creeks freed Tapley and scolded Brown.[18]

Thomas Brown considered the Tapley affair a minor problem compared to the premature Cherokee rising that effectively cut him off from his friends in Carolina. Stuart's Pensacola congress stymied him again. Nothing could be done until the Creeks returned to their villages. Rumors that Brown intended to bring the Indians down upon the frontier made backcountry Georgians as nervous as they were a year earlier, when Brown was said to be leading Carolina loyalists against Augusta.

Meanwhile, Brown's newly recruited rangers and their Seminole allies caused consternation in coastal Georgia. The Council of Safety ordered all cattle on the sea islands moved to the mainland by November 1, 1776, because of Georgia' s inability to defend those islands.[19] In early October the Florida raiders skirmished with Lt. Col. William McIntosh's lighthorse.[20] On October 7, 1776, the Council of Safety ordered Gen. Lachlan McIntosh to prepare defenses at Darien and Sunbury. Georgia seemed willing to sacrifice the land below the Altamaha, once again the "debatable" land as it had been in Oglethorpe's day.[21]

On October 30, 1776, James Bailey, Laurens's agent on Broughton Island, wrote a letter to Bartram that reveals the state of mind of those remaining on the coast. "I am in much perturbation of mind," he wrote, explaining that the recent alarm prevented his visiting Bartram in Savannah as he had promised. "The storm thickens fast in this quarter; I wish that I may get off safe with the remainder of the Negroes."[22] Bailey knew that Bartram intended to go to Charlestown on his way to Philadelphia and asked him to write from both places.

Georgia began drawing its permanent constitution while Bartram visited Brampton. Jonathan Bryan and the McIntoshes worried that the radical faction dominated the convention. Button Gwinnett, as president of the convention, chaired the committee charged with drafting the constitution. George Wells sat on the committee and spent much of his time denouncing the McIntoshes for Georgia's inability to protect its borders. Wells's criticisms caused Lt. Col. William McIntosh to resign his commission, and the factional gap widened.[23] Georgia might have served Bartram as a case study of the birth throes of the nation as a whole. Radical democrats were in control, leading the country in a social revolution as well as a political one. William Bartram clung to the conviction that Providence ordered all things for the better. For him the blemishes on the birth of Georgia and of America were faulty Indian policy and the perpetuation of the institution of slavery.

The muted wildflowers of autumn decorated the low country marshlands as William Bartram crossed the Savannah River at Zubly's Ferry and made his way to Charleston.[24] He commented on how the climbing asters flourished in the low, moist land.[25]

Charleston in November 1776 still celebrated its recent victory over the British fleet and its successful campaign against the Cherokees. Mary Lamboll Thomas welcomed Bartram as usual. Rev. John J. Zubly was now a frequent guest after his exile from Georgia. Although a staunch defender of American rights, he could not bring himself to break with the mother country. Zubly had been a friend of her father, and Mary risked the displeasure of some patriots by her kindness to him.[26] Mary's two girls, Mary, age six, and Elizabeth, one year younger, brightened the old house on King Street. William had no way of exporting his most recent collection of specimens with trade to England cut off so he left them with Mary.[27]

Bartram had to report on his adventures to Dr. Lionel Chalmers, Dr. Fothergill's intermediary. He observed that Chalmers, like several others who preferred continued union with Britain, had incurred the displeasure of the assertively patriotic element. The doctor attracted attention by taking as a patient John Stuart's wife, Sarah, now a virtual hostage in her Tradd Street house. Through Henry Laurens, Chalmers obtained permission to escort Mrs. Stuart out of her house for air and exercise.[28] Chalmers had received several letters from Fothergill inquiring after the whereabouts of the wandering botanist. Until Bartram returned to Charleston, however, Chalmers did not know where he was. Fothergill's instructions that Bartram should confine himself to a single place, "some small spot," and search that place thoroughly, must have seemed to Bartram advice coming too late.[29]

Henry Laurens's friendship with Dr. Alexander Garden protected Garden, another of Bartram's friends, in spite of his loyalist sympathies. Garden had been forced on his sickbed to sign the association by some rough liberty men but nevertheless remained loyal. He risked public displeasure by accepting Lord William Campbell as a patient after the governor had taken refuge aboard the *Cherokee* in September 1775.[30]

William Bartram's news of conditions on the Georgia coast were not calculated to cheer Laurens when the two met. Bartram could convey James Bailey's report and one from Lachlan McIntosh that the "Florida scout," as the rangers were called, together with the Indians had raided along the Altamaha causing in McIntosh's words "the utmost consternation" in the neighborhood. McIntosh tried and failed to raise militia in St. Andrew, Sunbury, and St. Catherine and Ossabaw Islands.[31] Laurens's New Hope plantation, across the Altamaha from Darien, had not escaped damage. Worse, George Aarons, the New Hope overseer, and five of Laurens's trusted slaves had joined the British.[32] Laurens considered the loss of his Georgia crops "no small sacrifice at the shrine of Liberty, and yet very small compared with that which I am willing to make."[33]

Laurens might have mentioned to Bartram that two acquaintances of the botanist were prisoners on parole. Capt. Peter Bachop, who ferried supplies to Bartram in Florida in 1766, and retired Lt. White Outerbridge, Bartram's companion on his 1773 sea voyage to Charlestown, a voyage that now seemed to belong to a different age, had been arrested for their loyalty to the king.

Charleston wore a brave front, but a tension born of insecurity pervaded the town. Everyone expected the redcoats to return, as they finally did in 1780. Bartram could contrast the Charleston of 1776 with the Charlestown of 1773. The bustle of business was missing; the extravagant rhetoric was muted at the coffee houses. He quickly said his last good-byes and left his friends, noting simply, "After a few days residence in Charleston, I set off on my return to my native land."[34]

His prose grew more prolix as his distance from the troubled region lengthened. November gave way to December, but plants blossomed in Bartram's notebook. By the time he crossed into North Carolina, a familiar country for him, nature had recovered some of the magic of his earlier adventures.

One incident caused him some anxiety. As he rode along a deserted stretch of the South Carolina coast, he saw a number of black men advancing toward him. When they were still at a distance, he dismounted to give his tired horse a brief rest, thinking he could leap into the saddle and dash off if need be. In these unsettled times bands of displaced and runaway slaves wandered about, living off the land. "When we drew near each other, I mounted and rode briskly up and though armed with clubs, axes, and hoes, they opened to right and left and let me pass peaceably."[35] It was a scene reminiscent of the "intrepid Seminole " encounter in 1773, and again the better side of human nature prevailed, which is why Bartram recorded the incident.

In North Carolina the Bartram family seat, Ashwood, was located on the right bank of the Cape Fear River about five miles northeast of today's Council in Bladen County. Today only a shallow cellar excavation marks the site.[36] A historical marker on Highway 87, the old colonial road, as it crosses the Cape Fear River, tells travelers that "Naturalists John and William Bartram in 1765, and later, used their kinsman's house Ashwood as operating base. Stood 2 mi. E."

Ashwood held pleasant memories for William. His uncle, Col. William Bartram, had invited him to stay with him and his family in 1761, promising that he would not be drafted to fight in the Cherokee War.[37] The colonel's son was also named William so Ashwood had a confusion of Williams. William Jr. of Ashwood, called Bill, traded places with this William, then called Billy, and went to live with John Bartram in Philadelphia. Colonel William and his two daughters, Mary and Sarah, treated Billy like one of the family during his four years at Ashwood from 1761 to 1765. During those years he worked for his living with a Brunswick merchant but much preferred botanizing in the Cape Fear region. A favorite place was Lake Waccamaw, southwest of the Cape Fear River. Thomas P. Slaughter in his study of John and William Bartram cites a family tradition that William and Mary Bartram became romantically involved.[38] We only know for certain that he grew to know and love the slaves and servants of the plantation. He later wrote Mary asking her to remember him to all the families of the black people: "They were kind and very seviceable to me." He added that "these acknowledgements at least are due from me to them, altho they are negroes and slaves."[39]

In 1765 William left Ashwood to embark on the famous journey with his father through Georgia and the Floridas. In 1770, burdened by debt in Philadelphia, he came back to Brunswick to collect old debts due him. Bartram's short second sojourn contrasted with the first happy visit because while he was a guest at Ashwood the much-loved and respected colonel died in 1770 followed by his son, William, in 1771. The latter had a promising future as a physician, and a tradition holds that he died from fever contracted while treating patients in Wilmington.[40] Eric Bolen, in a recent article about Ashwood, relates another bit of local lore. When the young doctor died, his fiancée, Polly White, drowned herself in the Cape Fear River. People whispered that her ghost haunted Ashwood.[41]

When our botanist visited Ashwood in December 1776, his two cousins were happily married to prominent Bladen County patriots. Mary's husband, Thomas Roberson, served as colonel of the county militia, and Sarah's husband, Thomas Brown, acted as his lieutenant colonel. Both men, like all Whigs in the Cape Fear district, still celebrated their victory over the royalist Highlanders at Moore's Bridge in May of the same year. The sisters and their servants made Bartram feel at home again.

Evidence of Bartram's thorough familiarity with the region is his exhaustive description of the geology and plant life in *Travels*. He must have used notes from his earlier searches through the woods in his listing of the "beautifully flowering and sweet scented shrubs." As Francis Harper observed, the plants listed, including the azalea and mountain laurel, do not bloom in December.[42] Bartram later wrote Mary about how much he enjoyed his days at Cape Fear: "I must confess that now I am grown old and consequently more sensible of the cold and frown of our winters, it is generally in the Autumn and Winter that these juvenile landskips of your fine temperate and flowery regions (where reigns Spring eternal) present to view and seem to beckon me to return."[43]

Reluctantly, Bartram left his North Carolina cousins and resumed his northward journey. He marveled at the growth of the town of Cross-Creek (in 1784 named Fayetteville). When he had been there on his first trip south, the town was newly laid out with twenty or so dwellings. In December 1776 the houses numbered over a thousand, and the town served as a busy market for a growing backcountry. For a while he forgot about war with its violence and destruction and contemplated a young and vigorous new country bustling with the kind of energy he witnessed at Cross-Creek.

But as the new year loomed and winter claimed the land, his adventures drew to a close. He decided that his readers knew enough about Virginia and Maryland and excused himself from narrating that last part of his journey. When he reached the frozen Susquehenna in his native state, "I began anxiously to look toward home." His anxiety prompted him to make a dangerous but successful crossing on the ice and at last "arrived at my father's house on the banks of the river Schuylkill, within four miles of the city."[44]

His father, whom he so admired and respected, and his loving mother, Ann, received him as one given up for dead. He had eight precious months to tell his father about his adventures before death claimed John Bartram on September 22, 1777, in his seventy-ninth year. Francis Harper imagines what it must have been like for those two rare spirits to talk about William's discoveries: "It is pleasant to believe that the elder Bartram's earlier doubts as to William's worth and ability were at last happily resolved. For surely, in listening to the tales of perserving endeavor and high adventure among primitive scenes and peoples, and in scanning the field journals brought back, he must have realized that his truly talented son had now attained full stature."[45]

Francis Harper, diligent Bartram devotee that he was, did not get his conclusion quite right. If William Bartram had done nothing more than survive his travels, he would not have mattered so much to the world. He attained his full stature only when he painstakingly reworked his notes, sometimes with eyes closed because they hurt so, and produced the book that raised the awareness of his readers and caused them to appreciate the natural wonders around them. He pricked the national conscience and urged the reform of official Indian policy.

II

"I forsee the Magnificent structure and would be instrumental in its development."
Bartram, "Some Hints and Observations . . ."

William had a few precious months with his father comparing each other's recent activities, talking about mutual friends, puttering about the garden, wondering about the war. The General Assembly of Pennsylvania required everyone to subscribe to an "Affirmation of Allegiance and Fidelity" by an act of June 13, 1777. William had made a similar affirmation in Georgia; he deferred doing so in his home state until August 26, 1778.[46] The delay did not imply a lack of patriotism because William believed that Providence directed events in America for the betterment of mankind, making patriotism an article of faith.

The Continental Congress convened in Philadelphia on March 5, 1777, and took up consideration of the Articles of Confederation and the conduct of the war. Henry Laurens came up from South Carolina on July 21, 1777, and took his seat in Congress. Did he make the short trip down the Schuylkill to visit his friends at Kingsessing? He must have. But Congress and the war kept Laurens busy. He intended to sit quietly, listen, and learn; however, on his first day he was startled to hear that the members were about to approve an invasion of West Florida by way of the Ohio and Mississippi Rivers in conjunction with a naval attack on Pensacola. Laurens could not refrain from telling his colleagues that it was a terrible idea. He listed several excellent reasons, not the least of which was that Congress had no available navy. The honorable members would do better to send help to Georgia. In a disillusioned mood he wrote to John Rutledge, "I can hardly forbear concluding that a great Assembly is in its dotage."[47]

Death spared John Bartram the inconvenience of the brief restoration of British rule in Philadelphia. He died peacefully on September 22, 1777, as members of Congress left the city for the comparative safety of York, Pennsylvania, while Gen. Sir William Howe's British forces occupied Philadelphia. Howe favored conciliation and put his troops on their best behavior so the Bartrams were bothered only by the curious. British captain E. S. Fraser wrote to John Jr. on December 15, 1777, saying that he considered himself a friend of John and William's brother Moses Bartram and would like to visit the garden.[48] Most likely he and other officers did so.

The British departed in June 1778, and Congress returned to Philadelphia in July 1778. When the secretary of the French legation saw the garden on October 16, 1779, he expressed disappointment. "It was in a state of neglect which caused us actual pain," he said.[49] However painful the appearance of the garden, the war might have extracted a greater toll if Philadelphia had been a battleground. As long as the war interfered with business, the Bartrams let the weeds grow.

William finished drawing pictures of birds and plants he had seen during the last of his travels for Dr. Fothergill. Bartram's patron played his own part in this war, a part unrecorded by Bartram if he knew about it. He acted as intermediary in 1775 between his friends Lord Dartmouth and Benjamin Franklin and worked out a compromise acceptable to them but ultimately rejected by Lord North. Disappointed, Fothergill wrote Dartmouth, "Was the whole of a[dministration] as cordially disposed to peace and as sensible of its advantages as Lord Dartmouth, I think that there would be very little difficulty in accomplishing it."[50] The good doctor died, greatly mourned by many, in 1780. Benjamin Franklin paid him a superb compliment: "I can hardly conceive that a better man existed."[51] Bartram's drawings and specimens subsequently did not get the attention they deserved from the British experts. Dr. Daniel Solander, deputed by Fothergill to classify the American plants, died in 1782. Dr. Joseph Banks acquired Fothergill's collection but did little with it. The original report Bartram sent to Fothergill, now in the library of the British Museum of Natural History, is stamped "Jos. Banks." By 1791, when *Travels* appeared in print, many of Bartram's discoveries had been listed by others.[52]

At home in his father's house, William treasured the memory of his southern adventures and the people he met along the way. Whig or Tory, they remained his cherished friends. It must have been a joyful day when Henry Laurens and Lachlan McIntosh, both his father figures, honored him by a visit to Kingsessing. He had already begun to write his book, and their presence encouraged him to get on with it.[53] Even before *Travels* made him better known to the public, he had to put up with the attention paid him as a minor celebrity. The University of Pennsylvania offered him the position of professor of botany in 1782, an honor he declined.[54] In 1783 the war ended, and the Bartrams tidied up their garden for inspection by customers and the curious.[55] A legacy of two hundred pounds sterling left by his father allowed him to pay off his old obligations, greatly easing his conscience. "What a pleasure it is to pay one's debts," he noted in his journal.[56] He suffered a severe setback in 1786, when he fell from a tree and broke his leg; the compound fracture left him bedridden for nearly a year.[57] His good friend Mary Lamboll Thomas sent him his trunk with its notebooks and specimens, and he used his convalescence to complete his book.[58]

The publication process proved to be a slow one. He contacted a Philadelphia publisher named Enoch Story Jr. with a proposal for printing the book by subscription, stressing the need to promote the study of American natural history: "It is not a little remarkable that the production of our own country (which are so numerous and various) should hitherto have been little attended to." Now that the United States had won its independence, he hoped that the richness of American flora and fauna would be better known and appreciated.[59]

The canvass for subscriptions for Bartram's book attracted some attention to him. During the 1787 Constitutional Convention in Philadelphia, the parade of notables who visited Bartram in his garden included George Washington, James Madison, Alexander Hamilton, George Mason, and John Rutledge. Many of them subscribed to his work.[60] Before the publication the French botanist André Michaux called on Bartram in preparation for his own excursion through the Cherokee country.[61]

In 1787 Benjamin Smith Barton, a young Philadelphian then in Scotland to study medicine, wrote to Bartram that Enoch Story had spread a false report that Barton intended to pirate Bartram's work and publish it in Europe. Barton denied the accusation and at the same time offered to publish the book at his own expense and divide the profits.[62] He pressed his case in a follow-up letter, saying that he acted from a desire "to rescue from obscurity (you will pardon the phrase) a work which could not fail to be of very essential benefit to the cause of science." He believed, correctly as it turned out, that a work on American natural history would sell well in Europe.[63] Evidently, Bartram accepted Barton's offer of collaboration. Nancy Hoffman, who has compared Bartram's draft chapters with the published book, believed that Barton or some other editor muted Bartram's fresh voice by interrupting the narrative with lists of plants in Latin terminology.[64] Even so, the lists must have come from Bartram's notebook.

In 1790 another Philadelphia firm, James and Johnson, issued an announcement of the publication of *Travels*. William expressed appreciation for Barton's help and for the younger man's interest in promoting "this our Native Country." William too yearned to contribute all he could to its promotion. He hoped that his book would serve that end. Providence planned a great destiny for America, no less than serving as a model for the nations of the world: "I forsee the Magnificent structure and would be instrumental in its advancement." That statement is the best insight into his motivation for writing his book.

He also intended his work to be a refutation of Buffon and other Europeans who denigrated American plants as inferior to those of Europe. But he hoped that the dozens of subtle hints and his not-so-subtle defense of Indian culture would have an ameliorating effect on the conduct of his countrymen. His book, the best tool he had for building the "magnificent structure," would depict a happy America, exorcized of wars and ugliness, filled with wonderful plants and animals for the betterment of mankind. He believed that if Americans would only respond to the innate moral laws endowed by their Creator, if they would live in communion with nature, then they could erect their magnificent structure for the world to see.

A more pointed directive is Bartram's essay titled "Some Hints and Observations Concerning the Civilization, of the Indians, or Aborigines of America." Kathryn Braund and Gregory Waselkov suggest that Bartram wrote the piece for a group of Philadelphia Quakers who then sent a transcription to Henry Knox, secretary of war in Washington's administration and charged with formulating Indian policy.[65] Although Bartram misconstrued the part Indians played in the recent war, assuming that few if any joined the British, his message conveyed a heartfelt plea for a benevolent American Indian policy. He denounced the "injustice and avarice" of those who wanted to make war on the Indians in order to take their land. He stated clearly that "no more elegeble or laudable step can be pursued, than the introduction of our Language, System of legislation, Religion, Manners, Arts and Sciences; and by the reestablishment of trade and Commerce, in a peaceable and friendly manner amongst them."[66] To what extent Bartram influenced Knox is impossible to tell, but Knox sounded like Bartram in his recommendation to President Washington that the federal government undertake a plan of civilization: "How different would be the sensation of a philosophic mind to reflect, that, instead of exterminating a part of the human race . . . we had . . . imparted our knowledge of cultivation and the arts to the aboriginals of the country, by which the source of future life and happiness had been preserved and extended."[67] Although ethnohistorians have criticized the effort to acculturate the native people, there can be little doubt that the efforts of Hawkins and others prepared the Muscogulges for an eventual accommodation that came in the twentieth century.[68]

Fairness for Indians as fellows and equals would be an essential part of the foundation of Bartram's "God-blessed" structure of America. But the structure would never attain the magnificence Bartram envisioned unless the builders addressed the problem of slavery. As if to compensate for ignoring the subject in his book, he summoned all the earnestness he could in penning an essay titled "Americans I Request Attention." The authors of *Bartram Heritage* assumed that Bartram intended to appear before Congress with his message because it included the salutation "Ye Chiefs in the National Council."[69] On the other hand, historians Braund and Waselkov dismiss the notion that Bartram intended to address Congress.[70] For one thing we cannot imagine the retiring Quaker attracting that kind of attention. For another, in addition to calling the chiefs of the nation to attention, he also summons "Christians," "Brethren," "Men," "People," and "Americans." His was an appeal to everyone though perhaps unheard and unread in his lifetime.

There is so much pent-up passion in the essay, tightly scrawled on the reverse of a catalog of plants for sale, that one feels compelled to do what he asks and pay attention. He calls the subject "the most interesting and important, the most indispensably deserving your serious consideration perhaps that ever hath or ever will come before you." He asks rhetorically if his readers believe in a just God and in an afterlife. He reminds them that Jesus said that what is done to others is done to him. Bartram cites "the first Articles of the constitution of the United States" but obviously means the Declaration of Independence with its affirmation of "an equal, unalienable right to Life, Liberty, and property."

After a lengthy but well-reasoned preliminary statement he makes his point by asking why Americans risk God's displeasure "by suffering the Black People who are fellow citizens of our Nation to be held in perpetual Bondage and slavery being drag'd in chains from Africa their Native Land, many and most of them for no crime whatever and none for any crime or harm they have caused us." Even if a person has been enslaved for a crime, he asks, what justification is there for enslaving that person's children? He knew from his experience in South Carolina that white children were suckled in infancy by black women and remarks how unjust it is to keep those women and their children in slavery.

He ends by warning that his generation of Americans by their unjust treatment of black people are endangering the happiness of future generations, "filling up the cup of their calamity and destruction." The day would come when those oppressed people would have full retribution unless "ye speedily take measures to do them justice."[1] He anticipated a slave rebellion, but the Civil War was calamity enough to justify his prediction. Two hundred years later the builders of the national structure accept Bartram's admonition that God is no respecter of persons and that "the Black, White, Red, and Yellow People are equally dear to Him" and must be dealt with equally under the law. The implementation of that understanding has proven elusive, and the hoped-for magnificence not yet achieved. Bartram's ardent plea may never have been voiced, but he had grasped the meaning of America and its promise to the world. His friend and correspondent Thomas Jefferson had written those principles into the Declaration of Independence. Abraham Lincoln reiterated them after a faulty national beginning. Woodrow Wilson and Franklin Roosevelt offered them to peoples everywhere as ideals to follow.

Bartram fulfilled his wish of influencing national development through his *Travels* in ways he could not have imagined. After its publication in 1791 a succession of students of natural history followed Bartram's trail. Georgia's John Eatton LeConte spoke for most of them when in 1854 he wrote, "I remember when it was much the custom to ridicule Mr. Bartram, and to doubt the truth of many of his relations. For my own part I must say that having travelled in his track I have tested his accuracy, and can bear testimony to the absolute correctness of all his statements. . . . Mr. Bartram was a man of unimpeached integrity and veracity, of primeval simplicity of manner and honesty unsuited to these times when such virtues are not appreciated."[2]

Protégés of Bartram specialized in branches of natural history: Benjamin Smith Barton in botany, Alexander Wilson in ornithology, and Thomas Say in conchology (the study of shells) and entomology (the study of insects).[73] Bartram aroused the curiosity of Charles Lyell, the English father of geology, who came to America to investigate the prehistoric shells on the Savannah River described by Bartram and the petrified logs at White Cliffs on the Mississippi. Lyell's computation of the amount of time required for the formation of rock strata provided Charles Darwin with the extent of time his theory of natural selection demanded. Bartram's description of the adaptation of plants to environment anticipated William Paley's argument that the perfection of design in nature could be explained only by a divine designer.[74] Charles Darwin read Paley and decided that Paley's conclusion was a reverent way of saying he did not know how adaptations occurred. Darwin himself assigned natural selection as the mechanism behind design. Bartram preceded Darwin in ascribing human attributes to animals. "Can any man of sense and candour . . . doubt that animals are rational creatures?" he asked Barton. He wondered why the great philosophers were so reluctant to admit that animals could reason. "What are they afraid of?" he asked.[75] Of course, he and Barton knew the answer. If animals could reason, then man would lose his place as the unique rational animal, and the boundaries between species would blur. A belief in an unchanging natural law governed the thinking of the era.

Bartram influenced American exploration by inspiring others to make discoveries. Thomas Nuttal went all the way to the Pacific in 1834 and wrote about his findings in a room reserved for him at Bartram Gardens.[76] The patron of explorers, Thomas Jefferson, invited Bartram to lead an expedition up the Red River in 1805. Bartram declined because of his age (sixty-four) and his poor eyesight but was flattered by the offer.[77]

Others were influenced by William's philosophy of a simple life in communion with nature. In one of his unpublished essays, William wrote that the more a man or woman attempts to live a life of "Honesty and Simplicity, the more he is accounted a Fool." He deplored the relentless pursuit of riches by so many.[78] He hated war. To Barton he addressed the question, "Can any action strike our understanding with more decisive and forcible ideas of Madness, Brutality, Wretchedness, and depravity of nature than National War."[79]

The "magnificent structure" Bartram helped build is in the realm of platonic ideals but nonetheless real. He tells Americans that their country has a divinely inspired destiny and that they must help advance it, that racism is wrong and should be replaced by respect for one's neighbor, that there is satisfaction in gardening, adventure in travel, excitement in discovery. "I see new beauty in every bird, plant or flower," Alexander Wilson wrote Bartram in 1804, and he thanked his mentor for opening his eyes.[80] Thousands of Americans hiking along Bartram trails thank him also. Charles Frazier, in his best-selling novel about a Confederate veteran coming home to the Cherokee mountains, puts into words the reason so many modern-day adventurers read Bartram. His hero carried a copy of *Travels* in his knapsack and read it now and then for inspiration and encouragement. He had been to the mountain Bartram climbed several times in different seasons. Bartram passed that way but once. Yet when the mountaineer thought about the scene from that lofty peak, he thought about it as Bartram described it rather than the way he experienced it.[81] Without Bartram's example, our frail imaginations would miss much of the magic.

William Bartram's last years passed quietly, almost serenely. He thought frequently about his southern adventures. He wrote his "father friend" Lachlan McIntosh in 1796 that he had been tempted to make further explorations in "your delightful southern regions," but at fifty-six he dared not try. He had to be content to retrace his journey in his mind. He expressed his delight at receiving a visit from Lachlan's nephew of the same name. The young man introduced himself as William McIntosh's son and gave Bartram an account of his friends in Darien. Bartram sent his fond regards to the older William McIntosh, to Lachlan's wife, Sarah, and to young Thomas Spalding, who was a toddler when Bartram last saw him. He asked to be remembered to James Spalding's widow, Thomas's mother, Margery McIntosh. Also he wished to be remembered "to good old Don'd McIntosh at the swamp between Sapelo and the great swamp where I had shelter during the tremendous thunder-storm and who treated a stranger with true hospitality."[82]

William Baldwin was another of those inspired by Bartram to go exploring. In 1817 he wrote William Darlington, "Could you only come and go up the beautiful St. Johns with me, with what delight would we pursue the steps of Bartram."[83] At St. Simon, Baldwin visited Margery McIntosh Spalding, who assured him that Bartram's account of alligator behavior was authentic.[84] Upon his return to Philadelphia, Baldwin hurried to tell Bartram about his adventures. He found the botanist "in the possession of good health, and all the faculties of his mind were as brilliant as in the morning of his life." Bartram's face brightened as Baldwin confirmed the veracity of his accounts. Messages from his Darien friends delighted him still more. He told Baldwin that such was his love "for that delightful country that he often fancied himself transported thither in his dreams by night."[85]

The best pen picture of Bartram is furnished by a visitor to Bartram's Garden. The playwright William Dunlap recorded his impressions in his diary: "We approached an old man who with a rake in his hand, was breaking the clods of earth in a tulip bed. His hat was old and flopped over his face, his coarse shirt was seen near his neck, as he wore no cravat or kerchief; his waistcoat and breeches were both of leather, and his shoes were tied with leather strings. We approached and accosted him. He eased his work, and entered into conversation with the ease and politeness of nature's nobleman. His countenance was expressive of benignity and happiness. This was the botanist, traveler, and philosopher we had come to see."[86]

On July 22, 1823, William Bartram finished an article about a plant, then stepped out of his house to take his morning stroll about the garden. An artery burst in his lung, and he died instantly. He was eighty-five.[87]

Some years earlier, in 1808, Charles Wilson Peale painted a portrait of Bartram that allows us a glimpse of the man in the evening of his life. His eyes are the striking feature. Set in a strong face, with a prominent nose and lips showing the barest hint of a smile, the eyes reveal an inner serenity, an acceptance of his lot in life, even a contentment. It is the face of a good man.

Epilogue

Remember me to my friends.
William Bartram to Mary Bartram Roberson,
September 7, 1788

During the last years William Bartram relived his southern adventures in imagination and cherished the memories of friends. Several of them died before his
book appeared in print. His chief mentors in Indian matters, those opposing
giants of influence among the southeastern tribes, John Stuart and George Galphin, did not outlive the war. Stuart died at Pensacola on March 21, 1779.
Crippled with gout and increasingly jealous of his prerogative in Indian affairs,
he spent prodigally on conferences and supplies designed to retain the allegiance of the several Indian nations. He never felt comfortable with the strategy of employing Indians in warfare. When ordered by Lord George Germain
to send Creek warriors against the Georgia and Carolina backcountry in cooperation with Lt. Col. Archibald Campbell's 1779 thrust inland to Augusta,
coordination proved impossible. A party of Creeks led by David Taitt and
Alexander McGillivray were a month late; Campbell had to abandon Augusta
before they arrived. Germain blamed Stuart; death spared the superintendent
the ignominy of removal from office.[1]

Alexander Cameron and Charles Stuart volunteered to run the agency,
and Cameron expected to succeed to the office for which he had been
groomed. However, Germain divided the Southern Department and assigned
the more prestigious eastern half, with jurisdiction over the Cherokees and
Creeks, to relative newcomer Thomas Brown, the favorite of Governor Tonyn.[2]
Charles Stuart died in 1780, as did John McIntosh, deputy to the Chickasaws.[3]
West Florida, once the remote refuge for loyalists, fell to the Spanish forces of
Gen. Bernardo de Galvez in 1781. Cameron thus lost his base and had to
remove to Savannah, where he died in 1781.[4] Bartram remembered him as

"the agreeable and liberal Mr. Cameron."[5] David Taitt became a Spanish prisoner of war in 1781. Considered especially dangerous because of his influence with the Creek Indians, he was sentenced to labor in the mines of Mexico. He escaped from a prison ship and made his way to Georgia, then to London, where he secured endorsements from Govs. Peter Chester and James Wright. By way of compensation he obtained an appointment as the first provost marshall of Nova Scotia. He lived to an honored old age of ninety-four in that province and is buried in St. Paul's Churchyard, Halifax.[6]

Bartram's West Florida acquaintances scattered after the war. Dr. John Lorimer, who shared Bartram's interest in plants, received a compensatory grant of 504 acres on Grand Caicos Island and died there in 1807.[7] Dr. Michael Grant joined Lorimer on Grand Caicos after finding Abaco Island unsuitable and died in 1797.[8] The Mississippi River planter William Dunbar moved to Natchez, above Spanish Florida. He achieved distinction as a scientist, surveyor, and explorer. For the Spanish government he accompanied Andrew Ellicott on a survey of the thirty-first parallel and wrote a report on the expedition. For Thomas Jefferson, with whom he maintained an active correspondence, he explored the Washita River and supervised the Red River expedition. He died October 1810.[9]

Bartram's friends at Fort James on Georgia's Broad River, Dr. Francis Begbie and Lt. Thomas Waters remained loyal to the king, and both settled in the Bahamas after the war.[10] Waters served Thomas Brown as deputy superintendent of Indian affairs and followed Brown to Abaco Island, as did many of Brown's rangers. Thomas Brown moved to Grand Caicos and St. Vincent island, where he finally became the planter he intended to be before the Liberty Boys interrupted his plans. He was one of the few of Bartram's southern contemporaries who outlived the botanist. He died at St. Vincent in 1825.[11]

Bartram's Florida associate Stephen Egan bravely defended Lord Egmont's property on Amelia Island during the border skirmishes but lost it all when England gave Florida to Spain in the peace treaty. He received a grant of 1,612 acres on Dominica Island.[12] Trader James Spalding's agent, Charles McLatchy, died in 1780. Job Wiggins, Bartram's traveling companion in Florida, married an African American woman and settled to a sedentary family life after the war; he died in 1810.[13]

Bartram's intermediary with Dr. Fothergill, Dr. Lionel Chalmers of Charleston, achieved his greatest professional success with his tract, *Account of the Weather and Diseases of South Carolina*, published in 1776, the year before

his death.[14] Dr. Alexander Garden remained loyal to Britain. Only his friendship with Henry Laurens and the general respect for his medical prowess
allowed him to remain at large in Charleston during the early years of the war.
He and other loyalists rejoiced when the British occupied Charleston in 1780,
only to be forced into exile when Nathanael Greene's Continentals recovered
the town in 1782. In London, Garden enjoyed his membership in the Royal
Society and his association with the intelligentsia. As a friend of the eminent
Sir Joseph Banks, president of the society, Garden could have been of help to
William Bartram. Banks had acquired Bartram's Fothergill specimens from
Dr. Daniel Solander and put them aside without crediting Bartram with his
discoveries. Garden would have been pleased to help John Bartram's son, but
William lacked the sort of self-promotion that might have enlisted Garden and
stirred Banks. Dr. Garden died on April 15, 1791, the year Bartram's *Travels*
appeared in print in London.[15]

Of all his friends and acquaintances, Henry Laurens achieved the largest
fame. Few Americans contributed so importantly to the cause of independence.
The "fugitive" Congress, meeting at York on November 11, 1777, must have
been impressed by Laurens's arguments regarding a naval operation against
West Florida (it will be remembered that he observed that Congress lacked a
navy) because the delegates elected him president. In the account of Bartram's
adventures, Henry Laurens has graduated from father figure to Bartram to that
of South Carolina and Georgia, and now he had to assume responsibility for the
new nation. During his watch Congress, crippled as it was, accomplished two of
its most important achievements: the adoption of the Articles of Confederation
(subject to ratification by the states) and the conclusion of the treaty of allegiance with France, an essential factor in the final victory.

Laurens resigned his post in December 1778, but in 1780 Congress
named him envoy to the Netherlands. En route his vessel fell in with a British
warship, and Laurens found himself shut up in the dreaded Tower of London,
charged with high treason. He endured fifteen months of bad treatment while
his gout worsened before being exchanged for Lord Cornwallis. His last service
to his country was as peace negotiator along with Benjamin Franklin, John Jay,
and John Adams. In 1784 he returned to Charleston and lived out the remaining six years of his life honored by his countrymen.[16]

The winners of the war suffered nearly as much as the losers, as evidenced
by Bartram's Georgia friends. When Lt. Col. Archibald Campbell passed Silver
Bluff on his march to Augusta, ninety of Galphin's slaves sought refuge behind

British lines. Campbell considered them hostages to Galphin's good behavior.[17] When Charleston surrendered in May 1780 to Gen. Sir Henry Clinton's British troops, Galphin surrendered to the man who has appeared so frequently in these pages, Lt. Col. Thomas Brown of the King's Rangers. As did most Georgians, Galphin thought the war was over when Benjamin Lincoln lost the entire southern army to Clinton at Charleston. In that belief, sadly, he died at Silver Bluff on December 1, 1780.[18] He had lost a fortune in the American effort.[19]

Dr. Humphrey Wells, Bartram's good host in Augusta, had to bury his fiery brother, George Wells. George helped Button Gwinnett craft Georgia's radically democratic constitution of 1777, then acted as Gwinnett's second in Gwinnett's fatal duel with Lachlan McIntosh. After Gwinnett's death George Wells kept up the vendetta against the McIntoshes. In 1780 he had worked himself into the position of acting governor, but his temper doomed him. He challenged Maj. James Jackson, an ally of the McIntoshes, to a duel, and Jackson's bullet found its mark. Humphrey Wells settled George's estate, but Humphrey outlived George by only a year.[20]

In this war in which the winners suffered as much as the losers, few families had to undergo the misfortunes that plagued Bartram's adopted family, the McIntoshes. The latent bad feeling between the patriots of St. John and the Scots of St. Andrew widened into factionalism that crippled Georgia during its struggle for independence. Button Gwinnett, as president of the convention that drafted the radical constitution of 1777, had George McIntosh arrested on suspicion of trading with the enemy. McIntosh's property, including slaves, was confiscated by Gwinnett's orders.[21] An indignant Gen. Lachlan McIntosh ordered his troops to remove George from an unhealthy jail and to escort him to Congress, where with Henry Laurens's help he was released for lack of evidence. But the animosity between Gwinnett and Lachlan McIntosh festered as a result. Gwinnett, who liked to think of himself as a military figure, ordered a second invasion of Florida. This 1777 adventure proved a worse fiasco than General Lee's military parade of 1776. Gwinnett's militia refused to cooperate with McIntosh's Continentals. Gwinnett blamed McIntosh, and McIntosh called Gwinnett a rascal and a scoundrel. Such words led to duels in those days when Georgians aspired to become gentlemen, and the two adversaries faced each other at a cruelly short distance. Both shots found their marks. McIntosh recovered from his wound, but gangrene infected Gwinnett's leg, and he died three days later. John Treutlen, Georgia's first governor under its new constitution, informed Congress that Gwinnett lost his life trying to maintain the independence of the civil power from the military. "While the command of the Continentals remains in the hands of the McIntoshes, our people will never think themselves safe," Treutlen complained.[22] The hue and cry raised against McIntosh by Gwinnett's faction caused Henry Laurens in Congress to arrange for McIntosh's transfer to Washington's command at Valley Forge. Sons Lackie and William went with him as aides. Washington gave McIntosh a brigade and stationed him at Fort Pitt. After Congress ordered McIntosh to launch a campaign against British-held Detroit, he constructed two forts west of the Ohio as bases and named them Forts McIntosh and Laurens.[23] Instead of overawing the British-allied Indians, the remote Fort Laurens became a target for hostile Shawnees. In February 1779 the Indians caught nineteen soldiers outside the fort, killed and scalped seventeen, and took two prisoners. McIntosh had to abandon his plan of attacking Detroit; it was all he could do to rescue the beleaguered garrison of Fort Laurens.[24]

Learning that a British army under Archibald Campbell had invaded Georgia, McIntosh requested a return to his native state in 1779. More trouble awaited him, compounded when he lodged with an old friend, Andrew McLean, widely (and correctly) suspected of harboring Tory sympathies. George Wells and his friends renewed their criticism of McIntosh, and the legislature asked Congress to transfer McIntosh a second time.[25] McIntosh participated in the failed siege of Savannah in October 1779 and in the greater disaster, the surrender of Charleston in May 1780.[26] After the war a less radical Georgia assembly acquitted McIntosh of any blame, and Congress promoted him to major general. Family deaths clouded any comfort he might have felt at his vindication. Son Lackie died in 1783. Oldest son, John, once Bartram's travel companion, lived out the war with an uncle in Jamaica, then came home to help his father manage his rice fields. John died in 1792. The next year Georgia did Lachlan the honor of giving the name McIntosh County to old St. Andrew Parish.[27] Though Lachlan struggled financially (as did most of the heroes of the war), he enjoyed the respect of his countrymen. William Bartram wrote him an affectionate letter in 1796 following a visit from Lachlan's nephew, also named Lachlan, but there are no extant letters McIntosh might have written in reply. The general died on February 20, 1806.[28]

Another good friend, James Spalding, spent the war as a reluctant loyalist in Florida, presumably at one of his stores on the St. Johns. Because he played a passive role and because of Margery McIntosh Spalding's connections, he was allowed to return home to St. Simon after the war. His exiled partner, Roger Kelsall, sent him seeds of long-staple cotton from the island of Exuma in the Bahamas in 1786. With his successful cultivation of sea island cotton, Spalding found that his reputation improved with prosperity. He died in 1794 at the age of sixty. Margery Spalding, who continued to manage their St. Simon plantation, sent her fond regards to William Bartram by William Baldwin in 1817, the year before her death.[29] The year 1817 marked the death of Bartram's Charleston friend and hostess Mary Lamboll Thomas, the "Charming Polly" of his adventures.[30]

There is no indication that William Bartram ever met Benjamin Hawkins, but Hawkins read *Travels* and agreed with Bartram's opinions regarding potential acculturation of southern tribes. As Indian agent, Hawkins achieved some success in converting hunters to farmers but in the process created a division among the Creeks between the "progressives" and the nativists.[31] Bartram must have applauded Hawkins's efforts but regretted the consequences. Tecumseh, the great nativist, found adherents among the Creeks, especially in the Upper Creek towns, and Red Eagle's warriors vented their frustration by the terrible massacre of the refugees at Fort Mims in the Tensaw region of Alabama in 1813. Andrew Jackson's decisive retaliation at Horseshoe Bend put an end to resistance and left accommodation as the only option.[32]

It was the Cherokees who seemed to justify William Bartram's predictions. In the message sent to Henry Knox, Bartram said that the Indians admired the Christian religion and would welcome missionaries, that they would set up schools "to instruct their children in reading, writing, and arithmetic," and that they could raise cattle and sheep, and produce cotton and wool for themselves and for trade. As for their language, "it would be an easy matter to translate the Bible and other useful books and have them printed and distributed among them in their own tongue."[33]

The Cherokees acted as if they followed Bartram's script, and he lived long enough to witness the beginnings of their remarkable transition. They invited Christian missionaries into their mountains, created a written language, opened schools, cultivated cotton, operated cotton gins, raised cattle, erected Virginia-style plantation houses and adopted a constitution modeled after that of the United States. Bartram did not live to see the formation of the Cherokee Republic, nor did he know the futility of the Indians' attempts to cling to their homeland. Accommodation would wait for Oklahoma. Bartram's admonition remained a challenge for subsequent generations: "We ought to consider them as they are in reality, as our Brethren and fellow citizens, and treat them as such. . . ."[34]

Notes

Prologue

1. John Bartram to Peter Collinson, n.d., John Bartram letter book; same to same, September 28, 1755, Bartram Papers, vol. 1, Simon Gratz Collection, Historical Society of Pennsylvania, Philadelphia, henceforth, HSP; Collinson to John Bartram, January 20, 1756, February 10, 1756, Bartram Papers, vol. 2, HSP.

2. Cited in Josephine Herbst, *New Green World* (New York: Hastings House, 1954), 150.

3. John Bartram, *Observations on the Inhabitants, Climate, Soil, Rivers, Productions, Animals and Other Matters Worthy of Notice* . . . (London: Printed for J. Whiston and B. White, 1751).

4. Address by Caroline Bartram Kelley, June 8, 1893, Bartram Papers, Miscellaneous Manuscripts, HSP.

5. William Bartram, "Some Account of the Late Mr. John Bartram, of Pennsylvania," *The Philadelphia Medical and Physical Journal* 1 (1804): part 1, 115–24.

6. Bartram Trail Conference, *Bartram Heritage, A Study of the Life of William Bartram* (Montgomery, Ala.: Bartram Trail Conference, 1979), 10.

7. John Bartram, "A Journey to Ye Catskill Mountains with Billy, 1753," Bartram Papers, vol. 1, HSP.

8. John Bartram to Peter Collinson, September 28, 1755, Bartram Papers, vol. 1, HSP.

9. Mr. John White acquired Collinson's collection of Bartram drawings and sold them to A. B. Lambert in 1798. They were purchased from Lambert's library in 1842 by the thirteenth earl of Derby. They are now at Knowsley Hall, Merseyside, in the present earl of Derby's estate. Thirteen sketches date from 1753 to 1757, Billy's fourteenth to seventeenth year.

10. William Bartram to John Bartram, May 18, 1761, Bartram Papers, vol. 1, HSP.

11. Peter Collinson to John Bartram, April 9, 1765, William Darlington, *Memorials of John Bartram and Humphry Marshall, with Notices of Their Botanical Contemporaries* (Philadelphia: Lindsay and Blakiston, 1849), 268. Henceforth, Darlington, *Memorials*.

12. William Stork, *An Account of East-Florida, with a Journal Kept by John Bartram of Philadelphia, Botanist to His Majesty for the Floridas* . . . (London: W. Nicoll, 1766).

13. John Bartram to Peter Collinson, June 1766, Darlington, *Memorials*, 281; John Bartram to William Bartram, July 15, 1772, Society Collection, HSP.

14. Henry Laurens to John Bartram, August 9, 1766, Darlington, *Memorials*, 438–42.

15. John Bartram to Peter Collinson, August 26, 1766, Darlington, *Memorials*, 283–85; John Bartram to William Bartram, April 28, 1767, Bartram Papers, vol. 4, HSP.

16. Peter Collinson to John Bartram, July 18, 1768, Darlington, *Memorials*, 300.

17. Peter Collinson to William Bartram, July 28, 1767, Darlington, *Memorials*, 288–91.

18. John Bartram to Dr. Fothergill, September 30, 1770, John Bartram Letters in the British Museum (photostats), 1769–1771, HSP; Fothergill to John Bartram, 1772, Darlington, *Memorials*, 343–45.

19. William Bartram, "Some Hints and Observations Concerning the Civilization of the Indians, or Aborigines of America," 1792, Henry Knox Papers, Gilder Lehrman Collection, John Pierpont Morgan Library, New York.

1. The Georgia Coast

1. Lionel Chalmers to John Bartram, April 7, 1773, Gratz Collection, Historical Society of Pennsylvania (hereafter HSP). William gave his drawing of the finch to Dr. Chalmers.

2. Francis Harper, ed., *The Travels of William Bartram, Naturalist's Edition* (New Haven: Yale University Press, 1958), 2. Henceforth Harper, *Travels*.

3. Harper, *Travels*, 2.

4. Ibid., xviii.

5. Edward J. Cashin, *Governor Henry Ellis and the Transformation of British North America* (Athens: University of Georgia Press, 1994), 138–40. Outerbridge is mentioned as a passenger in the *South Carolina Gazette*, April 5, 1773.

6. Edmund Berkeley and Dorothy Smith Berkeley, *The Life and Travels of John Bartram* (Tallahassee: University Presses of Florida, 1982), 158.

7. Francis Harper, ed., "Diary of a Journey through the Carolinas, Georgia, and Florida from July 1, 1765 to April 10, 1766 [by] John Bartram," *Transactions of the American Philosophical Society*, New Series 33 (December 1942): part 1, 13, 20. Henceforth John Bartram Diary.

8. A notation that Mrs. Lamboll created great excitement by planting a large and handsome garden about the year 1750 is in a loose paper in the Martha Logan folder, South Carolina Historical Society, Charleston (SCHS hereafter).

9. John Bartram to W. B., April 9, 1776, Bartram Papers, New-York Historical Society (NYHS hereafter).

10. Fothergill to John Bartram, July 18, 1768, Bartram Papers, HSP.

11. Arnold Nicholson, "The Bartrams' Curious Botanical Art," *Horticulture* 4 (April 1978): 38–45.

12. Fothergill to John Bartram, January 13, 1770, Fothergill Collection, 38/91, Society of Friends Library, London.

13. Fothergill to Chalmers, December 23, 1772, Fothergill Collection, 38/91, Society of Friends Library, London.

14. "Journal of Josiah Quincy, Junior, 1773," in Massachusetts Historical Society *Proceedings* 49 (June 1916): 441.

15. Walter J. Fraser Jr., *Charleston! Charleston! The History of a Southern City* (Columbia: University of South Carolina Press, 1989), 127.

16. Roy Merrens, *The Colonial South Carolina Scene, Contemporary Views, 1697–1774* (Columbia: University of South Carolina Press, 1977), 283.

17. "Charleston in 1774 as Described by an English Traveler," *South Carolina Historical and Genealogical Magazine* 47 (July 1946): 179–80.

18. George C. Rogers. Jr., *Charleston in the Age of the Pinckneys* (Norman: University of Oklahoma Press, 1969), 118. The Charleston building boom is described in the *South Carolina Gazette*, 7 March 1774.

19. Alice R. Huger Smith and D. E. Huger Smith, *The Dwelling Houses of Charleston, South Carolina* (New York: Diadem Books, 1917), 178. A document titled "Notes on Family History" puts the Lamboll House at 23 King Street, Lamboll Papers, SCHS. However, the house at 19 King Street is identified as the Lamboll House in Jonathan H. Poston, *The Buildings of Charleston: A Guide to the City's Architecture* (Columbia: University of South Carolina Press, 1997), 227.

20. Thomas Petigru Lesesne, *Landmarks of Charleston* (Richmond, Garrett and Massie Inc., 1932), 62.

21. Sermon by Rev. Josiah Smith on the death of Rev. John Thomas, Lamboll Papers, SCHS.

22. Samuel Beach Jones, "Genealogical Memo," Lamboll Papers, SCHS.

23. William Bartram to John Bartram, March 27, 1775, in Edmund Berkeley and Dorothy Smith Berkeley, eds., *The Correspondence of John Bartram, 1734–1777* (Gainesville: University Press of Florida, 1992), 768–70.

24. Mary Lamboll Thomas to William Bartram, May 11, 1785, Lamboll Papers, SCHS.

25. John Bartram to William Bartram, April 5, 1766, in Berkeley and Berkeley, eds., *Correspondence of John Bartram*, 661–62.

26. Peter H. Wood, "'Liberty Is Sweet' African-American Freedom Struggles in the Years before White Independence" in Alfred F. Young, ed., *Beyond the American Revolution, Explorations in the History of American Radicalism* (DeKalb: Northern Illinois University Press, 1993), 157.

27. There are several references to Galahan in William L. McDowell Jr., *Documents Relating to Indian Affairs, 1754–1765 Colonial Records of South Carolina* (Columbia: University of South Carolina Press, 1970), 525, 527, 528, 537, 574–75.

28. Robert M. Weir, *Colonial South Carolina, A History* (Millwood, N.Y.: KTO Press, 1983), 294–95, 301–2; Fraser, *Charleston! Charleston!*, 122.

29. Fothergill to Humphry Marshall, August 23, 1775, Marshall Collection, Clements Library, University of Michigan, Ann Arbor.

30. Fothergill, "Essays on the Weather and Diseases of London," *Gentleman's Magazine* (London, 1751–1754). Lionel Chalmers, M.D., *Essay on Fevers* (Charleston: Robert Wells, 1767). Chalmers, M.D., *An Account of the Weather and Diseases of South Carolina*, 2 vols. (London: Printed for E. and C. Dilly, 1776).

31. Fothergill to Chalmers, December 23, 1772, Fothergill Collection, 38/94, Society of Friends Library, London.

32. Harper, *Travels*, 469.

33. Edmund Berkeley and Dorothy Smith Berkeley, *Dr. Alexander Garden of Charles Town* (Chapel Hill: University of North Carolina Press, 1969), 209.

34. Ibid., 209–10.

35. Robert M. Weir, *Colonial South Carolina, A History*, 305.

36. Kinloch Bull Jr., *The Oligarchs in Colonial and Revolutionary Charleston: Lieutenant Governor William Bull II and His Family* (Columbia: University of South Carolina Press, 1991), 120.

37. Weir, *Colonial South Carolina*, 307–10.

38. Lionel Chalmers to John Bartram, April 7, 1773, Gratz Collection, HSP.

39. William Bartram to Fothergill, April 2, 1773, Friends Autographs 4/19, Society of Friends Library, London.

40. Alice R. Huger Smith and D. E. Huger Smith, *The Dwelling Houses of Charleston South Carolina* (New York: Diadem Books, 1917), 240–46. See also Poston, *The Buildings of Charleston*, 285–86.

41. John Richard Alden, *John Stuart and the Southern Colonial Frontier* (New York: Gordian Press, 1966), 156–69; see also J. Russell Snapp, *John Stuart and the Struggle for Empire on the Southern Frontier* (Baton Rouge: Louisiana State University Press, 1996). Snapp is critical of Stuart for his efforts to extend "imperial control" over the Indian trade and thus alienating colonial traders.

42. Alden, *John Stuart*, 61, n.19.

43. Ibid., 79–80.

44. Ibid., 85–86.

45. Ibid., 88.

46. Ibid., 101–4.

47. Montgomery's expedition is chronicled in the *South Carolina Gazette*, 31 May, 10, 14, 20 June, 19 July, 23 August, 1760, and in Public Records Office, Colonial Office 61/585–603 (hereafter PRO, CO).

48. I am indebted to Patrick Demere for the draft of his book "Demere of Georgia" (1995) which details the careers of Raymond and Paul Demere.

49. Amherst to Wright, December 28, 1760, PRO, CO 5/60.

50. "Journal of Lt. Col. James Grant Commanding an Expedition against the Cherokee Indians," *Florida Historical Quarterly* 12 (July 1933): 725–36 (hereafter *FHQ*).

51. Alden, *John Stuart*, 135–36.

52. Harper, *Travels*, 230.

53. Wright to Hillsborough, December 12, 1771, in Davies, ed., *Documents of the American Revolution, 1770–1783* (Dublin: Irish University Press, 1972), 3: 269–75; Hillsborough to Stuart, January 11, 1772, PRO, CO 5/73: Memorial of the principal traders to the Creek and Cherokee Nations to Governor Wright, n.d., *Colonial Records of Georgia* 28, part 2: 373–75 (hereafter CRG).

54. Stuart to Gage, February 15, 1773, Gage Papers, William Clements Library, Ann Arbor, Michigan (hereafter WLCL).

55. Harper, John Bartram Diary, 29.

56. Chalmers to John Bartram, April 7, 1773, Gratz Collection, HSP.

57. In *Travels* Bartram assigns twenty-four hours to the voyage to the Savannah: Harper corrects it to twelve hours, W. B. Report, 172.

58. "The New Light House is finished," James Habersham wrote to Governor James Wright, then in England, on December 4, 1772, Georgia Historical Society (hereafter GHS) *Collections* 6: 215–18.

59. *South Carolina Gazette*, 12 April, 1773.

60. Barratt Wilkin,"A View of Savannah on the Eve of the Revolution," *Georgia Historical Quarterly* (hereafter GHQ) 54 (1970): 577–84.

61. Joseph Frederick Waring, *Cerveau's Savannah* (Savannah: Georgia Historical Society, 1973), 1–2.

62. Ibid., 9–10. For Oglethorpe's plan, see Rodney M. Baine and Louis De Vorsey Jr., "The Provenance and Historical Accuracy of 'A View from Savannah as It Stood the 29th of March, 1734,'" GHQ 73 (Winter 1989): 784–813.

63. William G. De Brahm's 1770 map of Savannah is in Kings Ms. 210, p. 54, British Library. For other views of Savannah in the 1770s, see Fred Shelly, "The Journal of Ebenezer Hazard in Georgia, 1778," GHQ 41 (Fall 1936): 316–19, and John P. Corry, "The Houses of Colonial Georgia," GHQ 14 (Fall 1936): 181–201.

64. Henry Ellis, "An Account of the History of the Weather in Georgia," *London Magazine* (July 1759): 371–72; John W. Reps, "$C^2 + L^2 = S^2$? Another Look at the Origins of Savannah's Town Plan"; Harvey H. Jackson and Phinizy Spalding, *Forty Years of Diversity Essays on Colonial Georgia* (Athens: University of Georgia Press, 1984), 101–51.

65. Kenneth Coleman, *The American Revolution in Georgia* (Athens: University of Georgia Press, 1958), 35–36.

66. Kenneth Coleman, *Colonial Georgia: A History* (New York: Charles Scribner's Sons, 1976), 224.

67. House Minutes, February 11, 1773, CRG 15: 384.

68. House Minutes, March 12, 1773, CRG 15: 425–26.

69. Wright to Hillsborough, October 31, 1772, Dartmouth Papers, Staffordshire Record Office, Stafford, England.

70. Map enclosed in Wright to Dartmouth, August 10, 1773, CRG, 38, part 1A, following p. 29.

71. Council Minutes, September 1, 1772, CRG 12, 328–29.

72. Hillsborough to Stuart, January 11, 1772, PRO, CO 5/73; E. R. R. Green, "Queensborough Township," *William and Mary Quarterly*, 3rd series 17 (1960): 189–96.

73. A resolution was introduced in the House, thanking George Galphin and Lachlan McGillivray for their services in the matter of the treaty, House Minutes, June 28, 1773, *CRG* 15: 439.

74. Wright, "To All Persons . . . ," Bartram Papers, HSP.

75. W. B. Report, 134.

76. John Bartram Diary, 29–30.

77. Kenneth Coleman, *Colonial Georgia*, 239–40; for the countess of Huntingdon's efforts, see Edwin Welch, *Spiritual Pilgrim: A Reassessment of the Life of the Countess of Huntingdon* (Cardiff: University of Wales Press, 1995), 138–40. Piercy proved a poor president, and the Revolution completed the wreck of Bethesda. The institution was revived by Savannah's Union Society and exists today.

78. W. B. Report, 134.

79. Coleman, *Colonial Georgia*, 235.

80. W. B. Report, 134.

81. Harper, *Travels*, 3.

82. Ibid., 6.

83. W. B. Report, 135.

84. Harper, *Travels*, 5.

85. W. B. Report, 135.

86. Harper, *Travels*, 8.

87. W. B. Report, 135.

88. Charles E. Spalding, "Twice Twenty Years Ago, The Scotch in Georgia," Margaret Davis Cate Collection, Georgia Historical Society (hereafter GHS).

89. *Georgia Gazette*, 27 December 1769.

90. Nathan Bryllion Fagin, *William Bartram, Interpreter of the American Landscape* (Baltimore: Johns Hopkins University Press, 1933), 199.

91. Earnest Hartley Coleridge, "Coleridge, Wordsworth and the American Botanist William Bartram," Royal Society of Literature *Transactions*, 2nd series, 27, part 2 (London, 1906): 69–92.

92. J. P. Maclean, *An Historical Account of the Settlements of the Scotch Highlanders in America Prior to the Peace of 1783* (Cleveland: Hilman-Taylor, 1900), 152.

93. John Bartram Diary, 29.

94. Harper, *Travels*, 8.

95. For the background of the Darien Scots, see Anthony W. Parker, *Scottish Highlanders in Colonial Georgia, the Recruitment, Emigration, and Settlement at Darien, 1735–1748* (Athens: University of Georgia Press, 1997), and Edward J. Cashin, *Lachlan McGillivray, Indian Trader and the Shaping of the Southern Colonial Frontier* (Athens: University of Georgia Press, 1992).

96. Robert G. McPherson, ed., *The Journal of the Earl of Egmont: Abstract of the Trustees Proceedings for Establishing the Colony of Georgia, 1732–1738* (Athens: University of Georgia Press, 1962), 217–18.

97. Harvey H. Jackson, "The Darien Antislavery Petition of 1739 and the Georgia Plan." *W & MQ*, 3rd series, 34 (October 1977): 618–31.

98. John Mackintosh to Alexander Mackintosh, June 20, 1741, *CRG* 35: 340–43;

the best account of the siege is Larry Ivers, *British Drums on the Southern Frontier: The Military Colonization of Georgia, 1733–1749* (Chapel Hill: University of North Carolina Press, 1974).

99. Harvey H. Jackson, *Lachlan McIntosh and the Politics of Revolutionary Georgia* (Athens: University of Georgia Press, 1979), 4.

100. Anthony W. Parker, *Scottish Highlanders in Colonial Georgia*, 97–8.

101. "The Answer of Lachlan McIntosh to the Bill of the Complainant," Keith Read Collection, box 17, Hargrett Collection, University of Georgia Libraries; Jackson, *Lachlan McIntosh*, 6–19.

102. Chesnutt, David R. et al., eds., *The Papers of Henry Laurens* (hereafter *Laurens*) (Columbia: University of South Carolina Press, 1985), 10: 100.

103. Bessie Lewis, *They Called Their Town Darien* (Darien, Ga.: The Darien News, 1975), 27.

104. House Minutes, March 2, 1773, CRG 15: 395.

105. William Bartram to Lachlan McIntosh, May 31, 1796, Bartram Papers, NYHS.

106. Harper, *Travels*, 9.

107. Ibid., 9–10.

108. William Bartram to Lachlan McIntosh, May 31, 1796, Bartram Papers, NYHS.

109. Charles A. Spalding, "Twice Twenty Years Ago, the Scotch in Georgia," Margaret Davis Cate Collection, GHS.

110. "McIntosh Genealogy," Margaret Davis Cate Collection, folder 420, GHS. I am indebted to Robert Wylie, archivist at the Coastal Georgia Historical Society Museum of Coastal History, St. Simon's Island, Georgia, for information about McIntosh genealogy.

111. William Bartram to Lachlan McIntosh, May 31, 1796, Bartram Papers, NYHS.

112. Outerbridge's claim for compensation for his losses is in the Margaret Davis Cate Collection, folder 261, GHS.

113. Laurens to John Bartram, August 9, 1766, Darlington Collection, HSP.

114. Henry Laurens to Lachlan McIntosh, September 28, 1768, "McIntosh Genealogy," Margaret Davis Cate Collection, GHS.

115. Ibid.

116. Harper, *Travels*, 18.

2. The Ceded Lands

1. Harper, *Travels*, 337.

2. William Bartram to Robert Barkley, 1786, in the William Bartram Manuscripts, Fothergill Album, Library of the British Museum of Natural History. Bartram stated that he and his father first found the Franklinia "above 20 years ago."

3. Charles Jenkins, "The Historical Background of Franklin's Tree," *Pennsylvania Magazine of History and Biography* 57 (1933): 193–208.

4. Harper, *Travels*, 417.

5. The last time the Franklinia was seen in the wild was 1803. Harper, *Travels*, 417.

6. Margaret Davis Cate, *Our Todays and Yesterdays, A Story of Brunswick and the Coastal Islands* (1930; reprint, Spartanburg, S.C.: The Reprint Company, 1972), 171.

7. House Minutes, March 12, 1773, *CRG* 15: 425.

8. Edward J. Cashin, *The King's Ranger: Thomas Brown and the American Revolution on the Southern Frontier* (Athens: University of Georgia Press, 1989), 74.

9. Harper, *Travels*, 18.

10. W. B. Report, 135. Bartram omits his diversion to Brunswick in Harper, *Travels*.

11. W. B. Report, 135.

12. Coleman, *American Revolution*, 33.

13. Harper, *Travels*, 18.

14. Fothergill to William Bartram, September 4, 1773, Fothergill Collection, 38/94, Society of Friends Library, London.

15. Allan Gallay, *The Formation of a Planter Elite: Jonathan Bryan and the Southern Frontier* (Athens: University of Georgia Press, 1989), 89.

16. Harper wrote that John and William probably lodged at Dacre's Tavern in 1765, John Bartram Diary, 63. He assumed that William and John McIntosh stayed there in 1773; Harper, *Travels*, 341.

17. Coleman, *Colonial Georgia*, 235.

18. W. B. Report, 136.

19. Ibid., 137.

20. Harper, *Travels*, 414.

21. Ibid., 341.

22. Annie Blount Hamilton, "George Galphin of Silver Bluff," *Richmond County History* 13 (1981): 7–12.

23. For a discussion of the Augusta-based Indian trade, see Kathryn Braund, *Deerskins and Duffels, Creek Indian Trade with Anglo-America, 1685–1815* (Lincoln: University of Nebraska Press, 1993).

24. Cashin, *Lachlan McGillivray, Indian Trader*, 221; Stuart complained of Galphin's interference in Indian affairs in his to Dartmouth, October 25, 1775, PRO, CO 5/77.

25. E. R. R. Green, "Queensborough Township," *W&MQ*, 3rd series 17 (April 1960): 183–99.

26. For the dramatic story of David George and the founding of Springfield Baptist Church, the oldest African American Christian congregation, see Edward J. Cashin, *Old Springfield, Race and Religion in Augusta, Georgia* (Augusta: Springfield Village Park Foundation, Inc., 1995); David George's life is summarized in John Rippon, D.D., "Sketches of the State of Religion among Different Denominations of Good Men at Home and Abroad," *The Baptist Annual-Register* (London: 1790, 1791, 1792, and part of 1793).

27. Document titled "Some Hints and Observations Concerning the Civilization, of the Indians," Henry Knox Papers, John Pierpont Morgan Library, New York. I wish to thank Kathryn Braund for calling my attention to the document.

28. Samuel Cole Williams, ed., *Adair's History of the American Indians* (1930; reprint, New York: Promontory Press, 1974), 288–89.

29. Hawkins to Madison, July 11, 1803, C. L. Grant, ed., *Letters, Journals and Writings of Benjamin Hawkins*, 2 vols. (Savannah: Beehive Press, 1980), 2: 458–59.

30. William Bartram, Report, 137.

31. Edward J. Cashin, "Oglethorpe's Contest for the Backcountry, 1733–1749," in Phinizy Spalding and Harvey H. Jackson, eds., *Oglethorpe in Perspective Georgia's Founder after Two Hundred Years* (Tuscaloosa: University of Alabama Press, 1989), 99–111.

32. Harold S. Maness, *Forgotten Outpost: Fort Moore and Savannah Town, 1685–1765* (Pickens, S.C.: BPB Publications, 1986), 65–110.

33. Harold S. Maness, "Historic Beech Island," in *Beech Island Tricentennial Celebration* (Beech Island, S.C.: Beech Island Historical Society, 1986), 1–4.

34. Harper, *Travels*, 22.

35. Robert G. McPherson, ed., *The Journal of the Earl of Egmont* (Athens: University of Georgia Press, 1962), 193–95.

36. Heard Robertson and Thomas H. Robertson, "The Town and Fort of Augusta," in Edward J. Cashin, *Colonial Augusta "Key of the Indian Countrey"* (Macon: Mercer University Press, 1986), 66, n. 27.

37. Cashin, *Lachlan McGillivray, Indian Trader*, 208.

38. John Bartram Diary, 26. Harper's published version renders "Trevin's" as "Trains."

39. "Unfinished Memories of Robert Mackay," in Mackay–Stiles Papers, 42, Southern Historical Collection, University of North Carolina, Chapel Hill.

40. Edward J. Cashin, *The King's Ranger*, 115–18.

41. Humphrey and George Wells were sons of Dr. Richard Wells of Queen Anne County, Maryland. John Britton Wells III to author, February 28, 1997.

42. Helen Callahan, "Colonial Life in Augusta," in Edward J. Cashin, ed., *Colonial Augusta*, 96–119.

43. W. B. Report, 137.

44. Alden, *John Stuart*, 323–25.

45. For the roles of the principal Creek chiefs, see Cashin, *Lachlan McGillivray, Indian Trader*.

46. Habersham to Wright, August 20, 1772, *Collections*, GHS 6: 203–7; George Galphin to Willie Jones, October 26, 1776, in Force, ed., *American Archives*, 5th series, 3 vols. (Washington D.C.: M. St. Clair and Peter Force, 1848–53), 3: 648–50.

47. Talks from Emistisiguo and Gun Merchant, May 1, 1776, Davies, *Documents*, 3: 118–21.

48. Wright to Hillsborough, December 12, 1771, Davies, *Documents*, 3: 269–75.

49. W. B. Report, 138.

50. Robert S. Davis Jr., ed., *Quaker Records in Georgia: Wrightsboro, Friendsborough 1776–1777* (Augusta: Augusta Genealogical Society, 1986), 8–9.

51. W. B. Report, 138.

52. The church is located near the junction of Jackson and Wrightsboro Roads in West Augusta. Old Augustans remember the curious hill of white rocks.

53. William Skinner acquired the property owned by Humphrey Wells; the Skinner house (circa 1820) is still standing on the same site on Skinner Mill Road in West Augusta.

54. Stuart to Dartmouth, June 21, 1773, Davies, *Documents*, 6: 158–59.

55. Harper, *Travels*, 22.

56. Ibid., 307–8.

57. Ibid., 308.

58. Wright to Dartmouth, June 17, 1773, Davies, *Documents*, 6: 156–58.

59. Stuart to Dartmouth, June 21, 1773, Ibid., 6: 158–59.

60. W. B. Report, 138.

61. Harper, *Travels*, 22–23.

62. Ibid., 23.

63. Bartram's Young Warrior may also have been called Chavulky Warrior, head warrior of the Cowetas, who later told George Galphin that he "was the one who made the line and gave the land to the Virginia people." Congress at Augusta, May 16, 1776. Papers of the Continental Congress, 1774–1789, Library of Congress, Washington, D.C.

64. W. B. Report, 139.

65. David Nordan, "The Magic of Yellow Root," *Georgia Journal* (September–October, 1997): 11.

66. Harper, *Travels*, 27, 592.

67. Waldo Harris III, "Daniel Marshall: Lone Georgia Baptist Revolutionary Pastor," *Viewpoints Georgia Baptist History* 5 (1976): 51–64.

68. Robert S. Davis, *Quaker Records in Georgia*, 15–18; John, Robert, and Samuel Germany obtained grants in upper St. Paul Parish. Marion Hemperley, *English Crown Grants in the St. Paul Parish in Georgia 1755–1775* (Atlanta: State Printing Office, 1974), 66–67.

69. Plan of Wrightsborough is reproduced in Dorothy M. Jones, *Wrightsborough 1768, Wrightsborough 1799, McDuffie County, Georgia 1870* (Thomson, Ga.: Wrightsborough Quaker Community Foundation, 1982), 28.

70. W. B. Report, 139.

71. Pearl Baker, *The Story of Wrightsborough 1768–1964* (Thomson, Ga.: Wrightsborough Restoration Foundation, 1965), chapter 4 (pages not numbered).

72. Ibid.

73. Samuel Cole Williams, ed., *Adair's History of the American Indians* (1930; reprint, New York, Promotory Press, 1974), 295.

74. The original map of ceded lands by Philip Yonge is in the British Public Record Office. A copy is in the Hargrett Special Collections, University of Georgia Libraries.

75. W. B. Report, 179.

76. Marshall Forest, a 250-acre tract within the city limits of Rome, Georgia, claims to be the only virgin forest in the ridge and valley of the Appalachian range.

77. Harper, *Travels*, 344. The actual location of the "great" lick has been disputed, most recently by distinguished University of Georgia geographer Louis DeVorsey, who told an Oglethorpe County audience on November 25, 1997, that a study of the Yonge map led him to believe that the lick lay near Buffalo Creek.

78. The Treaty of 1773 is in *CRG* 39: 496–99.

79. Harper, *Travels*, 28.

80. Ibid., 27.

81. A marker just off Highway 78 in Oglethorpe County at the Clarke County line marks the site of the boundary tree. See also Marion R. Hemperley and Edwin L. Jackson, *Georgia's Boundaries: The Shapes of a State* (Athens: University of Georgia, 1993), 51–56.

82. W. B. Report, 140.

83. Ibid., 141, 180.

84. Harper, *Travels*, 28–29.

85. W. B. Report, 143.

86. Harper, *Travels*, 29; W. B. Report, 143.

87. Harper, *Travels*, 30; W. B. Report, 144.

88. David Hackett Fischer, *Albion's Seed: Four British Folkways in America* (New York: Oxford University Press, 1989); Grady McWhiney, *Cracker Culture: Celtic Ways in the South* (Tuscaloosa: University of Alabama Press, 1988).

89. Richard J. Hooker, ed., *The Carolina Backcountry on the Eve of the Revolution, The Journal and Other Writings of Charles Woodmason, Anglican Itinerant* (Chapel Hill: University of North Carolina Press, 1953), 27–64.

90. Stuart to Dartmouth, Augusta 5, 1773, Davies, *Documents*, 6: 200–201.

91. House Minutes, July 14, 1773, *CRG* 15: 455.

92. House Minutes, July 22, 1773, *CRG* 15: 465; Council Minutes, July 22, 1773, *CRG* 122: 379.

93. Stuart to Dartmouth, August 5, 1773, Davies, *Documents*, 6: 200–201.

94. Wright to Dartmouth, August 10, 1773, Ibid., 201–2.

95. Council Minutes, June 21, 1773, *CRG* 17: 706–7.

96. Proclamation of Sir James Wright, June 11, 1773, in claim of Thomas Brown, American Loyalist Claims, PRO, Audit Office 13/34.

97. Council Minutes, June 16, 1773, *CRG* 12: 363–64.

98. Wright to Dartmouth, June 17, 1773, Davies, *Documents*, 6: 156–58.

99. Council Minutes, July 15, 1773, *CRG* 12: 371–76.

100. Ibid., 375.

101. House Minutes, June 28, 1773, *CRG* 15: 439.

102. Allan Gallay, *The Foundation of a Planter Elite* , 122–23. Gallay wrongly identifies McGillivray as Alexander rather than Lachlan.

103. Traders' Petition, Taitt to Stuart, September 9, 1773, PRO, CO 5/75.

104. Traders' Petition, n.d., *CRG* 28, part 2: 373.

105. Wright to Dartmouth, August 10, 1773, PRO, CO 5/75.

106. Ibid.

107. Cameron to Stuart, October 11, 1773, PRO, CO 5/75.

108. Stuart to Dartmouth, December 21, 1773, PRO, CO 5/75.

109. Cameron to Stuart, October 11, 1773, *Documents*, 6: 231–33.

110. Stuart to Dartmouth, December 21, 1773, PRO, CO 5/75.

111. Wright to Dartmouth, December 27, 1773, Davies, *Documents*, 6: 266–67.

112. Wright to Dartmouth, January 31, 1771, Davies, *Documents*, 7: 30–32.

113. Taitt to Stuart, January 22, 1774, PRO, CO 5/75; Braund, *Deerskins and Duffels*, 159.

114. *Georgia Gazette*, February 2, 1774.

115. Ibid., February 2, 16, 1774.

116. Wright to Dartmouth, January 31, 1774, CRG 38, part 1A: 163–65.

117. Stuart to Dartmouth, February 13, 1774, Davies, *Documents*, 8: 48–59, *South Carolina Gazette*, February 14, 1774.

118. Stuart to Gage, May 12, 1774, Gage Papers, WLCL.

119. *Georgia Gazette*, March 16, 23, 1774.

120. Taitt to Stuart, January 3, 1774, PRO, CO 5/75.

121. House Minutes, March 6, 1774, CRG 17: 771.

122. Ibid., 769–70.

123. Wright to Dartmouth, January 31, 1774, Davies, *Documents*, 8: 30–32.

124. Taitt to Stuart, January 22, 24, February 25, 1774, PRO, CO 5/75.

125. Wright to Stuart, March 9, PRO, CO 5/75.

126. Stuart to Haldimand, February 3, 1774, Davies, *Documents*, 8: 353.

127. House Minutes, March 9, 1774, CRG 17: 774.

128. Charles Stuart to John Stuart, May 19, 1774, PRO, CO 5/75.

129. Wright to Stuart, January 27, 1774, PRO, CO 5/75; Stuart to Gage, May 12, 1774, Gage Papers, WLCL.

130. Stuart to Gage, May 12, 1774, Gage Papers, WLCL.

131. Galphin's talk in Taitt to Stuart, Feb 25, 1774, CO 5/75.

132. *Georgia Gazette*, March 30, 1774; Stuart to Gage, May 12, 1774, Gage Papers, WLCL.

133. Wright to Dartmouth, April 18, 1774, Davies, *Documents*, 8: 98–99.

134. Wright to Dartmouth, May 24, 1774, CRG 38, part 1A: 286.

135. Cameron to Stuart, March 1, 1774, PRO, CO 5/75.

3. East Florida

1. House Minutes, July 14, 1773, CRG, 15: 455.

2. House Minutes, July 30, 1773, CRG, 15: 474.

3. House Minutes, September 3, 7, 1773, CRG, 15: 512, 516.

4. House Minutes, September 7, 1773, CRG, 15: 515.

5. Harper, *Travels*, 31.

6. William Bartram to Lachlan McIntosh, May 31, 1796, Bartram Papers, NYHS.

7. Harper, *Travels*, 32.

8. Ibid., 346.

9. Ibid., 34.

10. Louis De Vorsey Jr. puts the site at Harris Neck; see his "Early Maps and the Land of Ayllon," in Jeannine Cook, ed., *Columbus and the Land of Ayllon: The Exploration and Settlement of the Southeast* (Darien, Ga.: Lower Altamaha Historical Society, 1992), 17–22.

11. Moultrie to Dartmouth, May 16, 1773, Davies, *Documents*, 6: 146.

12. Moultrie to Dartmouth, September 18, 1773, PRO, CO 5/553.

13. McIntosh Genealogy, Margaret Davis Cate Collection, 420, GHS.

14. "Memorial of Traders," in Wright to Hillsborough, December 12, 1771, in CRG 28, 2: 373–75.

15. Spalding to McLatchie, August 15, 1773, Bartram Papers, HSP.

16. Harper, *Travels*, 37.

17. William Bartram to John Bartram, March 27, 1775, Bartram Papers, HSP.

18. Lamboll to William Bartram, November 9, 1773, Bartram Papers, HSP.

19. Chalmers to William Bartram, December 15, 1773, Gratz Collection, HSP.

20. George W. Richards, ed., "Ministers of the German Reformed Congregation in Pennsylvania and Other Colonies in the Eighteenth Century," Margaret Davis Cate Collection, GHS.

21. Fothergill to Chalmers, January 7, 1774, Fothergill Collection, Society of Friends Library, London.

22. Moultrie to Dartmouth, February 21, 1774, PRO, CO 5/553.

23. William Bartram to John Bartram, March 27, 1774, Bartram Papers, HSP.

24. Harper, *Travels*, 13–14.

25. Marion Hemperley, *English Crown Grants in the Parishes St. David, St. Patrick, St. Thomas and St. Mary in Georgia, 1755–1775* (Atlanta: Georgia Surveyor General Department, 1913).

26. Harper, *Travels*, 339.

27. Ibid., 339.

28. Moultrie to Dartmouth, February 21, 1774, PRO, CO 5/554.

29. Tonyn to Dartmouth, May 19, 1774, PRO, CO 5/554.

30. Savery's Map, dated March 13, 1769, is in WLCL.

31. Harper, *Travels*, 17.

32. William Bartram to John Bartram, March 27, 1775, Bartram Papers, HSP.

33. Charles Loch Mowat, *East Florida as a British Province* (Gainesville: University of Florida Press, 1964), 83–85.

34. Tonyn to Dartmouth, March 27, 1774, PRO, CO 5/554.

35. Harper, *Travels*, 37.

36. W. B. Report, 144.

37. Bartram assumed mistakenly that Harrington Hall was Oglethorpe's former residence. Harper, *Travels*, 38.

38. Patrick M. Demere, "Demere of Georgia, The History of the Family of Raymond and Paul Demere," 1995, 12. I am indebted to Patrick Demere for a copy of his excellent manuscript on the Demeres, his ancestors.

39. Oglethorpe's report of the Battle of Bloody Marsh, dated July 30, 1742, is in *CRG* 36: 31–43; reprinted in Edward J. Cashin, ed., *Setting out to Begin a New World* (Savannah: The Beehive Press, 1995), 88–93.

40. Patrick Demere, "Demere of Georgia," 35–38.

41. Ibid., 53.

42. Harper, *Travels*, 38.

43. "Map Showing Colonial Land Grants in the Vicinity of the Town of Frederica, St. Simons Islands" is in Margaret Davis Cate, *Our Today and Yesterdays, A Story of Brunswick and the Coastal Islands* (Brunswick: Glover Brothers, 1930), 68.

44. Harper, *Travels*, 39.

45. Cate, *Our Todays and Yesterdays,* 133.

46. Harper, *Travels*, 41.

47. Governor Tonyn referred to these incidents in his letter to Dartmouth, May 19, 1774, PRO, CO 5/554.

48. Louis DeVorsey Jr., "Oglethorpe and the Earliest Maps of Georgia," in Phinizy Spalding and Harvey H. Jackson, eds., *Oglethorpe in Perspective* (Tuscaloosa: University of Alabama Press, 1989), 38–39.

49. Edward J. Cashin, *Governor Henry Ellis and the Transformation of British North America* (Athens: University of Georgia Press, 1994), 104.

50. William Ramsey, "The Final Contest for the 'Debatable Land': Fort William and the Frontier Defenses of Colonial Georgia," *GHQ* 77 (Fall 1993): 497–524.

51. Ibid; W. B. Report, 145.

52. Harper, *Travels*, 42.

53. Copy of DeBrahm map of Amelia Island in St. Augustine Historical Society.

54. W. B. Report, 145.

55. John Tate Lanning, *The Spanish Missions of Georgia* (Chapel Hill: University of North Carolina Press, 1935), 201–35; David Hurst Thomas, ed., *The Missions of Spanish Florida* (New York: Garland Publishing Company, 1991), xxi–xxii.

56. Rebecca Saunders, "Architecture of the Missions Santa Maria and Santa Catalina de Amelia," in Bonnie G. McEwan, *The Spanish Missions of La Florida* (Gainesville: University of Florida Press, 1993), 35–38.

57. Tonyn to Dartmouth, May 19, 1774, CO 5/554.

58. Harper, *Travels*, 46.

59. Arthur McKnight to Margaret Davis Cate, September 29, 1958, Margaret Davis Cate Collection, GHS. Fatio's descendants still live in St. Augustine. Mowat, *East Florida,* 46.

60. Harper, *Travels*, 48.

61. W. B. Report, 145.

62. Harper, *Travels*, 49–50.

63. Laurens to John Bartram, August 9, 1766, Bartram Collection, box 45, P. K. Yonge Library, University of Florida, Gainesville.

64. Chester to Haldimand, March 26, 1774, Gage Papers, WLCL.

65. Dunmore to Stuart, April 5, 1774, Gage Papers, WLCL.

66. Stuart to Dartmouth, May 6, 1774, Davies, *Documents*, 8:109–10. Wright to Dart, April 18, 1774, Davies, *Documents*, 8: 98–99; Stuart to Gage, May 12, 1774, Gage Papers, WLCL.

67. Tonyn to Dartmouth, May 19, 1774, PRO, CO 5/554.

68. Dartmouth to Wright, July 6, 1774, CRG 38, part 1A: 273.

69. Tonyn to Dartmouth, March 27, PRO, CO 5/554.

70. Frances C. Pyle, "William Bartram's Voyage," *Subtropical Gardening* (December 1939): 12–13.

71. John Bartram Diary, 35, 51.

72. Harper, *Travels*, 52–53.

73. William Henry Siebert, *Loyalists in East Florida 1774–1785*, 2 vols. (De Land: Florida State Historical Society, 1929), 2: 367–71; Mowat, *East Florida*, 71.

74. Bernard Romans, *A Concise Natural History of the East and West Florida* (1762; reprint, Gainesville: University of Florida Press, 1975), 270.

75. Bartram's barely legible essay on slavery is on the reverse of a catalog of plants, Broadside Collection, HSP.

76. Ibid., 39, 43.

77. Harper, *Travels*, 61.

78. Ibid., 61–62.

79. Stuart to Dartmouth, May 6, 1774, Davies, *Documents*, 6: 109–10.

80. Wright to Dartmouth, May 24, 1774, Davies, *Documents*, 6: 116–17; Chester to Haldimand, May 12, 1774, Gage Papers, WLCL.

81. Mowat, *East Florida*, 24–25; Tonyn to Wright, June 27, 1774, cited in Council Minutes, August 30, 1774, CRG 12: 406.

82. Tonyn to Dartmouth, August 5, 1774, PRO, CO 5/554.

83. Wright to Gage, June 29, 1774, Gage Papers, WLCL.

84. W. B. Reports, 146; Harper, *Travels*, 108.

85. Conversation with Bruce Chappell, June 11, 1993, P. K. Yonge Library, Gainesville.

86. Harper, *Travels*, 114.

87. Ibid., 118.

88. Ibid.

89. Ibid., 120.

90. Ibid., 122–23.

91. Ibid., 127.

92. Ibid., 131.

93. Fothergill to William Bartram, September, 4, 1773, Fothergill Collection, folder 38/94, Society of Friends Library, London; Chalmers to Bartram, May 17, 1774, Bartram Papers, HSP.

94. Fothergill to Chalmers, January 7, 1774, Betsy C. Corner and Christopher C. Barth, *Chain of Friendship, Selected Letters of Dr. John Fothergill of London 1735–1780* (Cambridge: Harvard University Press, 1971), 407–8.

95. Bartram, Report, 150; Chalmers to William Bartram, May 17, 1774, Bartram Papers, HSP.

96. Stuart to Gage, July 3, 1774, Gage Papers, WLCL.

97. Taitt to Stuart, July 7, August 18, 1774, Gage Papers, WLCL. David Corkran suggested that Oktulgi might have been Togulki, son of the Creek spokesman Malatchi. Such is unlikely; the two differed in temperament, and Taitt and Stuart knew Togulki well enough not to have misspelled his name. David Corkran, *The Creek Frontier*, 1540–1783 (Norman: University of Oklahoma Press, 1967), 282.

98. Wright to Stuart, June 13, 1774, Gage Papers, WLCL.

99. Talk of Pumpkin King, June 23, 1774, Gage Papers, WLCL.

100. Talks enclosed in Stuart to Gage August 8, 1774, Gage Papers, WLCL.

101. Cameron to Stuart, May 29, 1774, Gage Papers, WLCL.

102. Taitt to Stuart, December 18, 1774; Stuart to Gage, January 18, 1774, Gage Papers, WLCL.

103. Gage to Stuart, March 11, 1775, Gage Papers, WLCL.

104. Samuel Thomas to Taitt, December 10, 1774; Stuart to Gage, May 26, 1774, Gage Papers, WLCL.

105. Edward Wilkinson to Cameron, June 26, 1774, and Ogilvy to Haldimand, July 18, 1774, Gage Papers, WLCL.

106. J. Leitch Wright, *Florida in the American Revolution* (Gainesville: University of Florida Press, 1975), 7.

107. Harper, *Travels*, 64–65.

108. Ibid., 71.

109. Ibid., 71–72.

110. In his report to Fothergill, Bartram stated that he persuaded one of the traders to accompany him on this trip upriver. W. B. Report, 151.

111. Harper, *Travels*, 76.

112. Ibid., 77–78.

113. Ibid., 79.

114. Ibid., 80.

115. Ibid., 81.

116. Ibid., 90.

117. Bartram to Lachlan McIntosh, July 15, 1774, Dreer Collection, HSP.

118. Harper, *Travels*, 92. Bartram collapsed two different ascents up the St. Johns into one narrative in *Travels*.

119. Harper, *Travels*, 99.

120. Ibid., 100.

121. Ibid., 136.

122. Ibid., 140.

123. Bernard Romans, *A Concise Natural History of East and West Florida*, 185.

124. Harper, *Travels*, 143.

125. W. B. Report, 158.

126. I am indebted to John Meadows for information on the present condition of Manatee Spring.

127. Harper, *Travels*, 148–50.

128. Ibid., 154.

129. William Bartram to Lachlan McIntosh, July 15, 1774, Dreer Collection, HSP.

130. Although his account in *Travels* describes the hurricane as happening on his first journey to Lake Beresford, the report to Fothergill has it occur during the second trip.

131. Helen Hornbeck Tanner, "Pipesmoke and Muskets: Florida Indian Intrigues of the Revolutionary Era," in Samuel Proctor, *Eighteenth-Century Florida and the Revolutionary South* (Gainesville: University of Florida Press, 1978), 13–39.

132. Harper, *Travels*, 161.

133. Romans, *A Concise Natural History of East and West Florida*, 81.

134. Harper, *Travels*, 163.

135. Ibid., 164.

136. Ibid., 165. Bartram's chapter 10 interrupts his narrative with a discussion about snakes (167–73), frogs (173–75), various other animals (175–78), and birds (178–91).

137. Tonyn to Wright, June 27, 1774, cited in Council Minutes, August 30, 1774, CRG 12: 406.

138. Taitt to Stuart, July 7, 1774, Gage Papers, WLCL.

139. Council Minutes, August 30, 1774, CRG, 12: 408.

140. Wright to Gage, September 9, 1774, Gage Papers, WLCL.

141. Council Minutes, August 30, 1774, CRG 12: 408–9.

142. Stuart to Gage, September 14, Gage Papers, WLCL.

143. Taitt to Stuart, August 29, 1774, Gage Papers, WLCL.

144. Kenneth Coleman, *The American Revolution in Georgia, 1763–1789*, 41.

145. *Georgia Gazette*, 12 October 1774; other resolutions in the *Georgia Gazette*, 28 September 1774.

146. Ibid., 26 October 1774.

147. Ibid., 21 December 1774.

148. Taitt to Stuart, August 26, 1774, Gage Papers, WLCL. Cusseje Mico said they came from Oconee to the White House. Robert Mackay's house, originally Lachlan McGillivray's, was known as the White House and was a usual stopping place for Indian visitors to Augusta.

149. Stuart to Gage, October 6, 1774, Gage Papers, WLCL.

150. Original treaty enclosed in Stuart to Gage, November 29, 1774, Gage Papers, WLCL.

151. Wright to Dartmouth, September 23, 1774, CRG 38 part 1–B: 326–27.

152. Council Minutes, September 3, 1771, CRG 12: 35.

153. Helen Burr Smith and Elizabeth V. Moore, "John Mare: A Composite Portrait," *North Carolina Historical Review* 44 (Winter 1967): 38. I am grateful to John Britton Wells of Paintsville, Kentucky, for details of the history of his ancestors.

154. *Remarks on a Pamphlet Entitled Strictures on a Pamphlet Entitled the Case of George McIntosh, Esq. Published by Order of the Liberty Society* (1777), 20–21. Hazard Pamphlets, Library of Congress.

155. For Wells's short and volatile career, see Edward J. Cashin, "The Famous Colonel Wells: Factionalism in Revolutionary Georgia," *GHQ* 50 (supplement 1974): 137–56.

156. George White, *Historical Collections of Georgia* . . . (New York: Pudney and Russell, 1855), 283–84.

157. "To His Excellency General Lee . . . The Petition of the Inhabitants of the Parish of St. George, and St. Paul . . . July 31, 1776," *Collections* NYHS (1873), 181.

158. George Galphin identified Wells as the author of the petition to Lee, claiming "he got all the people in the ceded land of no property to sign it." Galphin to Willie Jones, October 26, 1776, in Peter Force, ed., *American Archives*, 5th series, 3: 648–50. In his letter to Jones, Galphin accused Wells and his followers of a plot to start a war with the Indians "at the time of the Congress." In a biographical sketch of George Wells, I suggest that Galphin referred to the great congress of 1773. However, I now believe the reference is to Galphin's meeting with the Creeks in July 1776. See "Wells, George," in Kenneth Coleman and Charles Stephen Gurr, eds., *Dictionary of Georgia Biography*, 2: 1044–45.

159. Extract of a letter from Savannah to a gentleman in Philadelphia, December 9, 1774, Peter Force, ed., *American Archives*, 5th series (1837–1846), 1: 1038–39.

160. *Remarks on a Pamphlet Entitled Strictures on a Pamphlet Entitled the Case of George McIntosh, Esq. Published by Order of Liberty Society* (1777), 21, Hazard Pamphlets, Library of Congress.

161. Jonathan Bryan to William Drayton, November 23, 1774, PRO, CO 5/26.

162. Waselkov and Braund, *William Bartram on the Southeastern Indians* (Lincoln: University of Nebraska Press, 1995), 202.

163. Allan Gallay, *The Formation of a Planter Elite*, 131–50.

164. Wright to Tonyn, October 21, 1774, PRO, CO 5/555.

165. Braund, *Deerskins and Duffels*, 162.

166. Taitt to Stuart, December 17, 1774, Gage Papers, WLCL.

167. Ibid.

168. Tonyn to Dartmouth, December 14, 1774, PRO, CO 5/555.

169. Mowat, *East Florida as a British Province*, 89–91.

170. Wright to Stuart, January 12, 1775, Gage Papers, WLCL.

171. Stuart to Gage, January 18, 1775, Gage Papers, WLCL.

172. Thomas to Taitt, December 10, 1774, Gage Papers, WLCL.

173. Gage to Stuart, March 11, 1775, Gage Papers, WLCL.

174. William Bartram to John Bartram, March 27, 1775, Gratz Collection, HSP. William mistakenly dated his letter 1774.

175. Charles Spalding, "Twice Twenty Years Ago, the Scotch in Georgia," in Margaret Davis Cate Collection, GHS.

176. *Strictures on a Pamphlet Entitled, The Case of George McIntosh, Esq.* (Savannah: Published by order of the Liberty Society, 1777), 14, in Hazard Pamphlets, Library of Congress.

177. Ibid.

178. The Committee of St. Johns to the Charleston Committee, February 9, 1775, in Allen A. Candler, ed., *The Revolutionary Record of Georgia*, 3 vols. (Atlanta: Franklin-Turner Company, 1908), 1: 59–61 (hereafter RRG).

179. Coleman, *American Revolution*, 43.

180. *Remarks on a Pamphlet Entitled Strictures on a Pamphlet Entitled, The Case of George McIntosh, Esq. Published by Order of the Liberty Society* (Savannah, 1777), 15, in Hazard Pamphlets, Library of Congress.

181. McIntosh to Walton, July 14, 1777, Papers of the Continental Congress, 1774–1789, Library of Congress.

182. William Bartram to Benjamin Smith Barton, December 23, 1792, Barton Papers, American Philosophical Society, Philadelphia (hereafter APS).

183. Slaughter, *Natures of John and William Bartram* (New York: Alfred A. Knopf, 1996), 203–4.

184. "Americans I Request Attention," loose paper in Broadside Collection, Bartram Papers, HSP.

185. Betty Wood, *Slavery in Colonial Georgia 1730–1775* (Athens: University of Georgia Press, 1984), 191–92.

186. CRG 29: 481–82; for a view casting doubts on the motives of the petitioners, see Harvey H. Jackson, "The Darien Anti-Slavery Petition of 1739 and the Georgia Plan," WMQ, 3rd series, 34 (1977): 618–31.

187. "In the Darien Committee, Thursday, January 12, 1775," *RRG* 1: 38–42.

188. Betty Wood, *Slavery in Colonial Georgia*, 202–3; Harvey H. Jackson, "American Slavery, American Freedom and the Revolution in the Lower South: The Case of Lachlan McIntosh," *Southern Studies* 19 (Spring 1980): 82–93.

189. Notice by Lachlan McIntosh, July 1775, Keith Read Collection, box 17, Hargrett Collection, University of Georgia Libraries.

190. John Houstoun to Lachlan McIntosh, June 10, 1775, Papers of the Continental Congress, 1774–1789, National Archives Microfilm Publications.

191. Extracts of Minutes of January 21, 1775, St. John Committee, *RRG* 1: 56.

192. Messrs. Jones, Bulloch, and Houstoun to President of the Continental Congress, April 6, 1775, *RRG* 1: 63–66.

193. Robert to Mary Mackay, January 24, 1775, Mackay–Stiles Papers, vol. 42, Southern Historical Collection, University of North Carolina, Chapel Hill (hereafter SHC).

194. In General Committee, Charlestown, S.C., February 8, 1775, *RRG* 1: 57.

195. The Committee from St. John's to the Charlestown Committee, February 9, 1775, *RRG* 1: 59–61.

196. Reply of the Committee of Correspondence in Charlestown, South Carolina, to the Committee from St. John's Parish, February 24, 1775, *RRG* 1: 61–62.

197. Coleman, *The American Revolution*, 50.

4. The Cherokee Country

1. Henry Laurens to John Laurens, December 12, 1774, *Laurens*, 10: 4.

2. Henry Laurens to John Laurens, January 4, 1775, *Laurens*, 10: 18.

3. Henry Laurens to John Laurens, January 18, 1775, *Laurens*, 10: 30.

4. Henry Laurens to John Laurens, January 22, 1775, *Laurens*, 10: 43–44.

5. Ibid.

6. Henry Laurens to William Manning, February 4, 1775, to Ralph Izard, March 27, 1775, *Laurens*, 10: 51, 87.

7. Laurens mentioned meeting McIntosh in his letter to James Habersham, March 29, 1775, *Laurens*, 10:91–92.

8. Ibid., 129. Fothergill to Franklin, December 3, 1774, William B. Wilcox, ed., *The Papers of Benjamin Franklin* (New Haven: Yale University Press, 1978), 21: 365.

9. James Laurens to Henry Laurens, August 1, 1775, *Laurens*, 10: 263.

10. Henry Laurens to James McKenzie, March 27, 1775, *Laurens*, 10: 90–91.

11. Harper, *Travels*, 194.

12. Laurens to James Habersham, March 29, 1775, *Laurens*, 10: 91–92.

13. Henry Laurens to John Laurens, January 22, 1775, *Laurens*, 10: 82.

14. Henry Laurens to John Laurens, April 22, 1775, *Laurens*, 10: 103–6; Bull to Dartmouth, May 1, 1775, Davies, *Documents*, 9: 11–13.

15. Innes to Dartmouth, May 1, 1775, Davies, *Documents*, 9: 113–16.

16. William Bartram to John Bartram, March 27, 1775, Bartram Papers, HSP.

17. Cameron to Stuart, March 2, 1775, PRO, CO 5/76.

18. Stuart to Dartmouth, March 28, 1775, PRO, CO 5/76.

19. Harper, *Travels*, 207. Bartram indicates that his were letters of recommendation from Stuart to Cameron, but in the poisoned climate of the time, those would have been cause for suspicion.

20. Harper, *Travels*, 201.

21. Ibid., 380.

22. Gervais indicates that Bartram would have a letter from "our friend Mr. Laurens," Gervais to Williamson, April 18, 1775, Bartram Papers, HSP.

23. William Bartram to Fothergill, April 20, 1775, Gratz Collection, HSP.

24. General Committee to Delegates for South Carolina at Philadelphia, May 8, 1775, *Laurens*, 10: 114.

25. Henry Laurens to John Laurens, May 15, 1775, *Laurens*, 10: 118–20.

26. John Stuart to Dartmouth, July 21, 1775, Randolph Boehm, ed., Records of the British Colonial Office, class 5, part 1, microfilm, Hatcher Library, University of Michigan.

27. Cited in Peter H. Wood, "'Liberty Is Sweet' African-American Freedom Struggles in the Years before White Independence," in Alfred F. Young, *Beyond the American Revolution Explorations in the History of American Radicalism* (DeKalb: Northern Illinois University Press, 1993), 167–68.

28. Henry Laurens to John Laurens, August 20, 1775, *Laurens*, 10: 319–28; Lord William Campbell to Dartmouth, August 31, 1775, Davies, *Documents*, 11: 93–98.

29. *Laurens*, 10: 160n.

30. Stuart to Gage, May 26, 1775, Gage Papers, WLCL.

31. Stuart to Gage, July 9, 1775, Gage Papers, WLCL.

32. John Drayton, *Memoirs of the American Revolution*, 2 vols. (1821; reprint, New York: New York Times and Arno Press, 1969), 1: 308–9 (hereafter *Memoirs*).

33. William Bartram to Mary Lamboll Thomas, July 15, 1786, Bartram Papers, NYHS. For information on the Lambolls, see Elise Pinckney, *Thomas and Elizabeth*

Lamboll: Early Charleston Gardeners (Charleston, S.C.: The Charleston Museum, 1969).

34. Drayton, *Memoirs*, 1: 222.

35. Wright to Gage, April 24, 1775, CRG 38: 1B

36. Harper, *Travels*, 195–96.

37. Ibid., 196–97.

38. Ibid., 198.

39. David Colin Crass et al., "Archaeological Testing at Silver Bluff," Paper presented at the Conference of the Society for Georgia Archaeology, Augusta, Ga., May 3, 1997.

40. Braund, *Duffels and Deerskins*, 55.

41. Galphin to Messrs. Graham et al., April 30, 1775, Bartram Papers, NYHS.

42. Harper, *Travels*, 200.

43. James Habersham to Samuel Floyd, November 21, 1771, GHS *Collections* 6: 149–50.

44. Alden, *John Stuart*, 353–55; Bartram should have been alerted to the probability of a meeting with Hammerer. On May 28, 1766, Peter Collinson wrote to John Bartram mentioning "a good, sensible man named Hammerer, a foreigner long in London who went to the Cherokees in order to try to bring them to a sense of moral duties," cited in William Darlington, *Memorials of John Bartram and Humphry Marshall with Notices of Their Botanical Contemporaries* (Philadelphia: Lindsay and Blakiston, 1849), 278–80.

45. Ted Ruddock, ed., *Travels in the Colonies in 1773–1775 Described in the Letters of William Mylne* (Athens: University of Georgia Press, 1993), 60.

46. Ibid., 59.

47. Ibid., 60.

48. Cashin, *The King's Ranger*, 26–29.

49. Harper, *Travels*, 204.

50. Ibid., 382–83.

51. Ibid., 204–5.

52. Thomas Brown to Governor Tonyn, February 24, 1776, Clinton Papers, WLCL.

53. A list of Rangers stationed at Fort James is in the Loyalist claim of Thomas Waters, Public Record Office, PRO, AO 13/36-A.

54. White, *Historical Collections of Georgia*, 230.

55. Georgia State Park Bobby Brown occupies the site of the proposed town of Dartmouth. When the waters of Clarks Hill Resevoir are low, the foundations of some of the buildings of old Petersburg can be seen.

56. "A Map of North and South Carolina, Accurately Copied from the Old maps of James Cook. Published in 1771 and of Henry Mouzon in 1775," provided by Frederick Holder.

57. Harper, *Travels*, 207.

58. John L. Nichols, "Alexander Cameron, British Agent among the Cherokee, 1764–1781," *South Carolina Historical Magazine* 97 (April 1996): 94–114. John

Alden suggested that Cameron's real name was MacLeod and that he migrated to Darien with the clan Chattan Highlanders, Alden, *John Stuart*, 187.

59. John H. Logan, *A History of South Carolina from the Earliest Periods to the Close of the War of Independence* (Columbia, S.C., 1859; reprint, Spartanburg, S.C., 1960), 315–16.

60. Alden, *John Stuart*, 199.

61. Extract, Colonel William Preston to Governor Earl of Dunmore, January 23, 1775, Davies, *Documents*, 9: 33–34.

62. Stuart to Gage, January 18, 1775, Gage Papers, WLCL.

63. Drayton, *Memoirs*, 1: 231.

64. Harper, *Travels*, 208.

65. Richard Maxwell Brown, *The South Carolina Regulators* (Cambridge, Mass.: Belknap Press, 1963), discusses the main vigilante movement of late colonial South Carolina.

66. Wright to Dartmouth, May 24, 1775, Davies, *Documents*, 8: 116–17.

67. William Henry Drayton to Francis Salvador, July 24, 1776, Robert W. Gibbes, *Documentary History of the American Revolution* (1853; reprint, 3 vols. in 1, New York: New York Times and Arno Press, 1971), 2: 28–30 (hereafter, *Documentary History*).

68. Harper, *Travels*, 209.

69. For Williamson's campaign, see E. F. Rockwell, ed., "Parallel and Combined Expeditions against the Cherokee Indians in South and North Carolina in 1776," *Historical Magazine and Notes and Questions*, New Series 2 (October 1867): 212–20.

70. Bartram treats of agriculture in part 4, Harper, *Travels*, 325–26; Gary C. Goodwin, *Cherokees in Transition: A Study of Changing Culture and Environment Prior to 1775* (Chicago: Research Paper 181, Department of Geography, University of Chicago; no. 18, 1977), 55.

71. George C. Rogers Jr., "The Papers of James Grant of Ballindalloch," *South Carolina Historical Magazine* 77 (July 1976): 145–60.

72. Harper, *Travels*, 209–10.

73. Glen to Board of Trade, August 26, 1754, Records in the Public Record Office relating to South Carolina, S.C. Archives, microcopy, vol. 26.

74. Alden, *John Stuart*, 87–88.

75. Ibid., 103–4.

76. *South Carolina Gazette*, 10 June, 1760.

77. Alden, *John Stuart*, 111, 130; Harper, *Travels*, 210; of the many war women among the Cherokee, see Theda Perdue, *Cherokee Women, Gender and Culture Change, 1700–1835* (Lincoln: University of Nebraska Press, 1998), 54.

78. Harper, *Travels*, 210.

79. Ibid., 211.

80. Ibid., 211–12. Margaret Mills Seaborn drew a remarkably detailed map showing the placement of Cherokee towns based on historic maps in what is now Oconee County, South Carolina, including some correctly marked segments of William Bartram's route

through the region. Seaborn, *From 1730 through 1776: Cherokee Indian Towns of Oconee*, map (Walhalla, S.C.: Oconee County Library, 1974).

81. Rockwell, "Expeditions against the Cherokee Indians," 212–20. Alexander Garden, *Anecdotes of the American Revolution* (Charleston: A. E. Miller, 1828) 83–86, extract in Anne Sheriff, ed., *Cherokee Villages in South Carolina* (Easley, S.C.: Forest Acres/ McKissick Quest Program, 1990), 88. I am grateful to Frederick C. Holder, secretary of Oconee County Historical Society, for making this extraordinary valuable compilation of original source material available.

82. Historian Frederick Holder of Seneca, S.C., believes that Bartram crossed the Oconee range at Station Mountain. The South Carolina Department of Parks, Recreation and Tourism maintains the Oconee Station Historic Site, with its 1792 blockhouse.

83. Harper, *Travels*, 212.

84. Earl's Ford Road, a seldom-traveled, narrow dirt lane is only slightly improved since Bartram went that way.

85. Rockwell, "Expedition against the Cherokee Indians," 212–20.

86. Hawkins Journal, November 26, 1796, GHS *Collections* 9: 16. For a detailed description of Hawkins's route from Seneca to Earl's Ford, see Margaret Mills Seaborn, *Benjamin Hawkins' Journey through Oconee County, South Carolina in 1796 and 1797* (Columbia, S.C.: R. L. Bryan Company, 1973).

87. Waselkov and Braund, *Southeastern Indians*, 153.

88. Harper, *Travels*, 216.

89. Ibid., 386. Today's Bartram Trail is honorary rather than historic, in that it follows the ridge rather than the road.

90. Hawkins Journal, November 26, 1796, GHS *Collections* 9: 16.

91. Harper, *Travels*, 217–18.

92. Francis Lee Utley and Marion R. Hemperley, eds., *Placenames of Georgia: Essays of John W. Goff* (Athens: University of Georgia Press, 1975), 73.

93. Harper, *Travels*, 219–20.

94. I am indebted to Michael Hill of the Research Branch of the North Carolina Department of Cultural Resources for an account of the historical basis for the recent relocation of the marker "Cherokee Defeat" below the town of Otto, commemorating Grant's 1761 encounter and that of the marker "Cherokee Victory" north of Otto, marking Montgomery's battle of 1760. The markers were incorrectly located on Highway 28 north of Franklin in 1939.

95. There is still an Indian mound on the right bank of the Little Tennessee at Dillard, Georgia, which may have marked the site of Estatoe Old Fields.

96. Laurens to John Ettwein, July 11, 1761, *Laurens*, 3: 73–76.

97. Ibid.

98. James C. Kelley, "Notable Persons in Cherokee History: Attkullakulla," *Journal of Cherokee Studies* 3 (Winter 1978): 3–4.

99. Barbara McRae, *Franklin's Ancient Mound* (Franklin, N.C.: Fererita Press, 1993), 46. For Thomas Griffiths's journal, see William L. Anderson, ed., "Cherokee Clay, from Duché to Wedgwood: The Journal of Thomas Griffiths, 1767–1768,"

North Carolina Historical Review 63 (October 1986): 477–510. See also Hensleigh C. Wedgewood, *A Mission for Mr. Wedgewood* (New York: American Heritage Publishing Company, 1970).

100. Harper, *Travels*, 222–23.

101. Ibid., 222.

102. Ibid., 223.

103. Waselkov and Braund, *William Bartram on the Southeastern Indians*, 184.

104. Ibid., 150.

105. Captain Christopher French, "Journal of an Expedition to South Carolina," *Journal of Cherokee Studies* 2 (Summer 1997): 286.

106. James Grant, Journal, *FHQ* 12 (July 1933): 33.

107. Harper, *Travels*, 224.

108. Ibid., 225.

109. Ibid.

110. Ibid., 226. Bartram might have credited the maidens with a greater degree of innocence than they deserved. Theda Perdue, authority on the behavior of Cherokee women, writes, "Unmarried women engaged in sex with whomever they wished as long as they did not violate incest taboos against intercourse with members of their own clans or the clans of their fathers," *Cherokee Women*, 56.

111. Kelly, "Notable Persons in Cherokee History: Attakullakulla," 26; Hatley, *The Dividing Paths*, 217–18.

112. Stuart to Dartmouth, 21 July, 1775, Davies, *Documents*, 9: 53–54.

113. Harper, *Travels*, 227, 390–91. I have followed Harper's route through Wayah Gap rather than the route through Kyle proposed in *Bartram Heritage* (Montgomery, Ala.: The Bartram Trail Conference, 1979), 97.

114. Ibid., 228–29.

115. Ibid., 229.

116. Ibid., 230.

117. Ibid., 230–31.

118. Tom Hatley wrote that Attakullakulla was on his way to a conference in Augusta, but there was no such conference until Galphin scheduled one in July 1776, Hatley, *The Dividing Paths*, 216.

119. Stuart's talk to the Great Warrior, Attakullakulla, et al., August 30, 1775, PRO, CO 5/76.

120. Stuart to Dartmouth, July 21, 1775, Davies, *Documents*, 9: 53–54.

121. Harper, *Travels*, 235.

122. For Bartram's list of Cherokee towns, see ibid., 235–36.

123. Waselkov and Braund, *Southeastern Indians*, 125.

124. Harper, *Travels*, 232–33; the ballplay dance is described in Frank Gouldsmith Speck and Leonard Broom, *Cherokee Dance and Drama* (Berkeley: University of California Press, 1951), 55–62.

125. Ibid., 233–34.

126. Ibid., 235.

127. Drayton, *Memoirs*, 1: 253.

128. Ibid., 255.

129. Henry Laurens to John Laurens, June 13, 1775, *Laurens*, 10: 186–96.

130. Deposition of Robert Goudey, sworn before James Mayson, July 9, 1775, Miscellaneous Collections, South Caroliniana Library, Columbia.

5. The Creek Country

1. Harper, *Travels*, 237. The pay bill lists the names of Barnard's troops of Rangers, in loyalist claim of Thomas Waters, PRO, AO 13/36-A.

2. Coleman, *American Revolution*, 52.

3. Houstoun to Lachlan McIntosh, June 10, 1775, Papers of the Continental Congress 1774–1789, National Archives Microfilm Publications, U.S. Continental Congress.

4. Laurens to Gervais, December 28, 1771, *Laurens*, 8:137–40.

5. On November 15, 1771, St. Pierre petitioned the Board of Trade for 20,000 acres in Georgia, compensating him for the 40,000 he had been granted in Nova Scotia. CRG, 28, part 2: 376–78.

6. Laurens to Thomson, July 16, 1775, *Laurens*, 10: 225–27.

7. Ibid.

8. Williamson to Council, July 14, 1775, *Laurens*, 10: 222–24.

9. Abstract of Gervais to Cameron, June 27, 1775, in Stuart to Dartmouth, January 19, 1776, PRO, CO 5/77.

10. Cameron to Stuart, July 21, 1775, PRO, CO 5/77.

11. Ibid.

12. Campbell to Dartmouth, July 19, 1775, Clinton Papers, WLCL.

13. Campbell to Gage, July 18, 1775, Gage Papers, WLCL.

14. For the formulation and execution of the southern strategy, see Cashin, *The Kings Ranger*.

15. William Henry Drayton to William Drayton (of Florida), July 4,1775, Davies, *Documents*, 9: 36–37.

16. Wright to Dartmouth, July 8, 1775, Davies, *Documents*, 11: 37–43.

17. *Georgia Gazette*, 28 June 1775.

18. Coleman, *American Revolution*, 57.

19. Harvey H. Jackson, "Georgia Whiggery, The Origins and Effects of a Many-Faceted Movement," in Harvey H. Jackson and Phinizy Spalding, eds., *Forty Years of Diversity, Essays on Colonial Georgia* (Athens: University of Georgia Press, 1984), 251–73.

20. Drayton, *Memoirs*, 1: 268–69; *Laurens*, 10: 220.

21. Deposition of Richard Maitland, September 22, 1775, CRG, 38, part 1B: 606–16.

22. *Laurens*, 10: 220, 230. Ebenezer Platt, one of the Savannah liberty men involved in the seizure of powder, was later identified by Captain Maitland and arrested in Jamaica for treason. Incarcerated in London, his case drew the attention of Benjamin Franklin in Paris and of the American Congress. His defenders argued that he should be treated as a prisoner of war, not a traitor. The Privy Council decided that

Platt had become a nuisance and ordered his release on bail. After several misadventures, he found his way back to America. See Charles Coleman Sellers, *Patience Wright: American Artist and Spy in George III's London* (Middletown, Conn.: 1976). (Patience Wright lobbied for Platt's release.)

23. Council to Galphin, July 24, 1775, *Laurens*, 10: 243–44.

24. Wright to Dartmouth, July 18, 1775, *CRG*, 38, part 1B: 511–15.

25. A huge excavation pit marks the site of Flat Rock today, on Route 80 just north of Interstate 20.

26. Robert S. Davis, *Quaker Records in Georgia*, 158.

27. Abraham Marshall, "Daniel Marshall," in David Benedict, *A General History of the Baptist Denomination in America and Other Parts of the World*. 2 vols. (1813; reprint, Freeport, N.Y.: Books for Library Press), 1: 2.353,

28. Baikia Harvey to Thomas Baikia, December 30, 1775, Balfour Papers, Orkney Islands Archives, Kirkwall, Scotland.

29. Robert S. Davis Jr., "The Last Colonial Enthusiast: Captain William Manson in Revolutionary Georgia," *Atlanta Historical Quarterly* 28 (Spring 1984): 23–28; Utley and Hemperley, *Placenames of Georgia*, 197, 210.

30. Robert G. Mitchell and Warner O. Moore, "Land and Growth in St. Paul Parish." *RCH* 10 (Winter 1978): 36–45.

31. The trader, Hugh Simpson, worked for Martin Campbell. Newton D. Mereness, "Journal of David Taitt," in *Travels in the American Colonies* (1916; reprint, New York, Antiquarian Press, 1961), 504–5.

32. Stuart to Dartmouth, January 19, 1776, PRO, CO 5/77; see also original manuscript "Journal of Andrew McLean," Georgia Historical Society, Savannah.

33. For John McGillivray's Revolutionary War activity, see Cashin, *Lachlan McGillivray*, 293–96.

34. Taitt to Stuart, August 1, 1775, PRO, CO 5/76.

35. Extract of Wright to Taitt, July 6, 1775, in Chester to Dartmouth, PRO, CO 5/592.

36. Stuart to Dartmouth, May 30, July 31, 1775, PRO, CO 5/76.

37. Wright to Stuart, July 6, 1775 (citing Taitt's of May 24, 1775), Gage Papers, WLCL.

38. Taitt to Stuart, July 6, August 1, 1775, PRO, CO 5/76.

39. Taitt to Charles Stuart, August 27, 1775, PRO, CO 5/591.

40. Harper, *Travels*, 243.

41. My son and I followed Bartram's route to Mobile during July 1997, the same month he traveled across Georgia and Alabama.

42. Harper, *Travels*, 240.

43. Ibid., 241.

44. Wright to Dartmouth, November 1, 1775, Davies, *Documents*, 9: 176.

45. Harper, *Travels*, 241.

46. Ibid.

47. John R. Swanton, *Early History of the Creek Indians and Their Neighbors* (Washington, D.C.: Government Printing Office, 1922), 288–312.

48. Harper, *Travels*, 246.

49. Ibid., 248.

50. Benjamin Smith Barton's Queries to William Bartram as copied by John Howard Payne, Query 14th, Bartram Papers, HSP. Payne transcribed the name "Boston," but "Bo'sun" is short for Boatswain.

51. Ibid.

52. Harper, *Travels*, 251.

53. I am indebted to Ned Jenkins, director of Fort Toulouse–Jackson Park, for showing us the site of Old Kolumi. The principal mound rises steeply to a height of about fifteen feet. An artificial elevation marks the village square. A heavy growth of trees and brush conceals the second mound on the riverbank and obscures the view of the river.

54. Cashin, *Lachlan McGillivray*, 74–75.

55. Harper, *Travels*, 284.

56. Taitt to Stuart, August 1, 1775, PRO, CO 5/76.

57. Surprisingly, the old route is marked by an almost invisible line on a 1997 AAA map of Alabama, beginning above Snowdoun and running just west of Highway 65 to the Escambia County line.

58. Harper, *Travels*, 252.

59. Ibid., 253.

60. Ibid., 255.

61. Davida Hastie, local historian and gracious hostess, took us to the rather desolate "Gopher Hill."

62. Harper, *Travels*, 404.

63. Research by Davida Hastie reveals that Joshua Kennedy owned the site, and his deed referred to it as Farmer's Bluff. The property was acquired by William Kitchin, who laid out the present town of Stockton at a crossroads a short distance away.

64. *Mobile Press Register*, 7 March, 1976, Bartram Trail File, Mobile Public Library. The Tensaw region is rich in history, and its people are justly proud of it. Laura Hastie Thompson, a native of Stockton, has written a monumental history of William Weatherford (Red Eagle) and the early years of settlement, *William Weatherford, His Country and His People* (Bay Minette, Ala.: Lavender Publishing, 1991). John F. Shaw of Mobile has drawn an excellent map of the region, "Big Delta Guide," 1995; I am grateful to Jim Bryars of Holley Creek Fishing Camp for a copy.

65. Harper, *Travels*, 255.

66. Ibid., 256.

67. Robert R. Rea, *Major Robert Farmer of Mobile* (Tuscaloosa: University of Alabama Press, 1990), 53.

68. Ibid., 121.

69. Lawrence Henry Gipson, *The Triumphant Empire*, vol. 9 in *The British Empire before the American Revolution* (New York: Knopf, 1956), 213.

70. Robin F. A. Fabel, *The Economy of British West Florida, 1763–1783* (Tuscaloosa: University of Alabama Press, 1994), 18.

71. Ibid.

72. Alden, *John Stuart*, 315.

73. John Stuart to Gage, May 12, 1774, Gage Papers, WLCL.

74. Charles Stuart to John Stuart, May 19, 1774, Gage Papers, WLCL.

75. Taitt to John Stuart, August 1, 1775; John Stuart to Dartmouth, October 25, 1775, PRO, CO 5/76.

76. I am indebted to Lynn Hastie Thompson of Stockton, Alabama, for a copy of John McGillivray's will dated December 1767.

77. Rea, *Major Robert Farmer*, 42–43.

78. Harper, *Travels*, 256.

79. Rea, *Major Robert Farmer*, 49.

80. Farmer and Stuart had a "heated altercation" in the street, Alden, *John Stuart*, 199.

81. Rea, *Major Robert Farmer*, 71, 82.

82. Robin F. A. Fabel, *Bombast and Broadsides, The Lives of George Johnstone* (Tuscaloosa: University of Alabama Press, 1987), 54.

83. Rea, *Major Robert Farmer*, 106–7.

84. Ibid., 109.

85. Harper, *Travels*, 257.

86. Rea, *Major Robert Farmer*, 132.

87. Ibid., 140.

88. Ibid.

89. Harper, *Travels*, 257.

90. Ibid; Taitt's map is in PRO, CO 5/75; I am indebted to Davida Hastie for a copy.

91. Bernice McMillan, "The Evening Primrose," in Dess and Tom Sangster, eds., *Fort Mims and the Tensaw Settlement* (Bay Minette, Ala.: Lavender Publishing, 1993). The principal restaurant in Stockton displays a print of Bartram's primrose.

92. Harper, *Travels*, 258.

93. Ibid., 260.

94. Peter J. Hamilton, *Colonial Mobile* (1910; reprint, Tuscaloosa: University of Alabama Press, 1976), 301.

95. Harper, *Travels*, 261.

96. Ibid., 261–62.

97. Ibid.

98. Fabel, *Economy of British West Florida*, 167–68.

99. Bernard Romans, *A Concise Natural History of East and West Florida* (1775; reprint, Gainesville: University of Florida Press, 1962), 303.

100. Harper, *Travels*, 263.

101. Council Resolution, March 26, 1774, in Chester to Gage, June 20, 1774, Gage Papers, WLCL.

102. Chester to Dickson, March 26, 1774, Gage Papers, WLCL.

103. Dickson to Gage, May 9, 1774, Gage Papers, WLCL.

104. Gage to Dickson, September 12, 1774, Gage Papers, WLCL.

105. Robert Rea, "Graveyard for Britons: West Florida, 1763–1781," *FHQ* 47 (1969): 254.

106. Cecil Johnson, *British West Florida, 1763–1783* (New Haven: Yale University Press, 1942), 86–87.

107. Rea, "Graveyard for Britons," 350.

108. Ibid., 363.

109. Chester to Dartmouth, April 10, 1776, PRO, CO 5/592.

110. Johnson, *British West Florida*, 130.

111. Fabel, *Economy of British West Florida*, 168.

112. Taitt to Charles Stuart, August 27, 1775, PRO, CO 5/592.

113. Cashin, *The King's Ranger*, 27–29.

114. Minutes of Council, August 15, 1775, CRG 12: 437, Wright to Dartmouth, August 17, 1775, September 16, 1775, GHS *Collections* 3: 206–11.

115. Taitt to Stuart, Sept. 20, 1775, PRO, CO 5/77.

116. Stuart's talk, August 15, 1775, PRO, CO 5/76.

117. Tonyn to Dartmouth, September 15, 1775 PRO, CO 5/555.

118. Stuart's talk, Cherokees, August 30, 1775, PRO, CO 5/77.

119. Creek chiefs to Stuart Sept. 29, 1775, PRO, CO 5/77.

120. Emistisiguo's talk, September 2, 1775, Clinton Papers, WLCL.

121. Chester to Stuart, November 17, 1775, PRO, CO 5/592.

122. Chester to Dartmouth, April 22, 1775, PRO, CO 5/592.

123. Chester to Dartmouth, January 26, 1775, PRO, CO 5/592.

124. Chester's endorsement of September 5, 1775, is in Bartram Papers, HSP.

125. Taitt to Chester, September 24, 26, 1775, PRO, CO 5/592.

126. Council Minutes, October 5, 1775, PRO, CO 5/592.

127. Chester to Dartmouth, November 10, 1775, PRO, CO 5/592.

128. Chester to Dartmouth, November 18, 1775 Davies, *Documents*, 9: 183–85.

129. Chester to Dartmouth, November 10, 1775, PRO, CO 5/592.

130. Gage to Stuart, September 12, 1775, Gage Papers, WLCL.

131. Chester to Stuart, November 17, 1775, PRO, CO 5/592.

132. George Galphin to Willie Jones, October 26, 1776, in Peter Force, ed., *American Archives*, 5th series, 3: 648–50.

133. Cameron to Stuart, November 9, 1775, PRO, CO 5/77.

134. Laurens to Galphin, October 4, 1775, *Laurens*, 10: 447.

135. Enclosure in Thomas Brown to Tonyn, November 8, 1776, East Florida Papers, WLCL.

136. Alden, *John Stuart*, 212. David Taitt's map shows that Rene Roi had a plantation on the Alabama River just above the fork of the Mobile and East Branch where Bartram camped on his upriver excursion. He might have met Roi then. Taitt's map is in PRO, CO 5/75; James M. Stevens suggests that Bartram's companion was Jean Favre. A man of this name had a home one mile north of Pearlington on the Pearl River. *Bartram Heritage*, 102.

137. Harper, *Travels*, 266.

138. Fabel, *Economy of British West Florida*, 105, 228.

139. Harper, *Travels*, 266–67.

140. Alden, *John Stuart*, 317.

141. Fabel, *Economy of British West Florida*, 160.

142. Harper, *Travels*, 273.

143. Ibid., 268.

144. Zenab Esmat Rashed, *The Peace of Paris, 1763* (Liverpool: Liverpool University Press, 1951).

145. Fabel, *Bombast and Broadsides*, 43.

146. Gage to Halifax, May 21, 1764 PRO, CO 5/83/34.

147. Gibson, *Triumphant Empire*, 216.

148. Chester to Dartmouth, January 26, 1775, PRO, CO 5/592.

149. Harper, *Travels*, 271.

150. Harper estimated the embankment to be fifteen feet. *Travels*, 409.

151. Eron Rowland, ed., *Life, Letters and Papers of William Dunbar of Elgin, Morayshire, Scotland and Natchez, Mississippi* (Jackson: Press of the Mississippi Historical Society, 1930).

152. Ibid., Diary, July 12, 1776, 26–27.

153. Jean-Bernard Bossu, *New Travels in North America*, ed. Samuel David Dickinson (Natchez: Northwestern State University Press, 1982), 54–55, 74–75.

154. Fabel, *Economy of West Florida*, 174–75.

155. Ibid., 176.

156. Ibid., 175.

157. J. Barton Starr, *Tories, Dons, and Rebels: The American Revolution in British West Florida* (Gainesville: University Presses of Florida, 1976), 48–49.

158. Harper, *Travels*, 272.

159. Ibid., 273.

160. Ibid., 274–75.

161. Le Page DuPratz, *The History of Louisiana* (1774; reprint, Baton Rouge, La.: La Claitor Publishing, 1972).

162. William Bartram, "Observations on the Creek and Cherokee Indians," in Waselkov and Braund, *Southeastern Indians*, 140–41.

163. Harper, *Travels*, 332.

164. Ibid., 329.

165. Ibid.

166. Ibid., 307.

167. Alden, *John Stuart*, 212.

168. Harper, *Travels*, 275.

169. "William Bartram's influence on Charles Lyell and thus individually on Charles Darwin, is a subject of further research," *Bartram Heritage*, 24.

170. Rowland, *William Dunbar of Elgin*, 78–79.

171. Ibid., 12.

172. Harper, *Travels*, 277.

173. "A Safe Haven in the Loyal Colony of West Florida," in *Bartram Heritage*, 180–95.

174. Harper, *Travels*, 277.

175. Stuart to Cameron, December 16, 1775, Davies *Documents*, 21: 210–11.

176. Drayton, *Memoirs*, 2: 64.

177. Galphin to Council, December 9, 1775, *Laurens*, 10: 557–59.

178. Council to Galphin, December 18, 1775, *Laurens*, 10: 572–73.

179. Chester to Dartmouth, November 20, 1775, PRO, CO 5/592.

180. John Stuart to Henry Stuart, October 24, 1775, PRO, CO 5/76.

181. Wright to Stuart, November 16, 1775, PRO, CO 5/77.

182. Walker and Braund, *Southeastern Indians*, 258.

183. Harper, *Travels*, 278.

184. Ibid.

185. Ibid., 279–80.

186. Ibid., 281, 322.

187. Ibid., 321.

188. Ibid., 280–81.

189. Ibid., 281.

190. Ibid., 281–82.

191. Ibid., 282, 322.

192. I am indebted to Ned Jenkins, director of Fort Toulouse–Jackson Park, for hosting our visit to the park, August 11, 1997.

193. James H. O'Donnell, "Alexander McGillivray: Training for Leadership, 1777–1783," *GHQ* 49 (June 1965): 182.

194. Harper, *Travels*, 283.

195. Ibid., 283–84.

196. Ibid., 316. Harper reviews several references that mention the Wolf King, 473.

197. Taitt to Stuart, June 3, 1774, Gage Papers, WLCL.

198. Glen to Board of Trade, June 25, 1753, PRO, S.C., 25.

199. Stuart to Egremont, June 1, 1763, PRO, CO 5/65; Stuart to John Pownall, August 24, 1765, PRO, CO 5/66.

200. Though I had access to Bartram's notes on my visit to the British Museum, December 10, 1996, Bartram's drawings were out on exhibition.

201. Harper, *Travels*, 284.

202. Ibid., 286, for a discussion of the black drink ceremony. See Charles H. Fairbanks, "The Function of Black Drink among the Creeks," *FHQ* 9 (October 1980): 73.

203. Harper, *Travels*, 286–87.

204. Tonyn to Dartmouth, December 18, 1775, PRO, CO 5/556.

205. Tonyn to Stuart, April 20, 1776, Davies, *Documents*, 12: 108–10.

206. Harper, *Travels*, 289–90.

207. Drayton, *Memoirs*, 2: 127–35.

208. Harper, *Travels*, 290.

6. The Military Engagement

1. Harper, *Travels*, 290–91.

2. James M. Johnson, *Militiamen, Rangers and Redcoats, The Military in Georgia, 1754–1776* (Macon, Ga.: Mercer University Press, 1992), 120–21.

3. Thomas Brown to Jonas Brown, November 10, 1775, in possession of Joan Leggett, descendant of Thomas Brown. I am grateful to her for a copy of the letter.

4. Drayton to Council of Safety, August 21, 1775, in Gibbes, *Documentary History*, 1: 149–54.

5. Charles Drayton to William Henry Drayton, September 16, 1775, in ibid., 1: 183–84.

6. A fragment of a journal kept by Rev. William Tennent, in ibid., 1: 236.

7. Tennent to Laurens, August 20, 1775, to Council of Safety, September 1, 1775, in ibid., 1: 145–46, 149–54.

8. Treaty of Ninety-Six in Drayton to Council of Safety, September 16, 1775, September 17, 1775, in ibid., 1; 184–85.

9. Thomas Brown to Jonas, November 10, 1775, private possession, Joan Leggett.

10. *Georgia Gazette,* 20 December 1775.

11. Dr. Thomas Taylor to Mr. Morrison, December 26, 1775, in Margaret Wheeler Willard, ed., *Letters on the American Revolution, 1774–1776* (Boston: Houghton Mifflin, 1925), 245–46. For Taylor's career, see Robert S. Davis, "A Georgia Loyalist's Perspective on the American Revolution: The Letters of Dr. Thomas Taylor, 1776–1782," *GHQ* 81 (Spring 1997): 118–78.

12. Thomas Taylor to Rev. Thomas Percy, January 13, 1776, Miscellaneous Collections, WLCL.

13. Manson to his mother, April 8, 1776, Balfour Collection, Orkney Island Archives, Kirkwall Public Library, Scotland.

14. Baikia Harvey to Thomas Baika, December 30, 1775, Balfour Collection, Orkney Island Archives, Kirkwall Public Library, Scotland.

15. Bobby Gilmore Moss, *Roster of South Carolina Patriots in the American Revolution* (Baltimore: Genealogical Publishing Company, 1983), 423.

16. William Thomson to the Council of Safety, September 29, 1775, *Laurens*, 10: 438–40; Wright to Dartmouth, October 14, 1775, GHS *Collections* 3: 215; Coleman, *American Revolution*, 63.

17. Edward J. Cashin, "The Famous Colonel Wells: Factionalism in Revolutionary Georgia," *GHQ* 58 (supplement, 1974): 137–56.

18. "Some Hints and Observations," Henry Knox Papers, J. P. Morgan Library, New York. I am indebted to Kathryn Braund for telling me about this important document.

19. Ibid.

20. Harper, *Travels*, 292.

21. Samuel Cole Williams, ed., *Adair's History of the American Indians* (1930; reprint, New York: Promontory Press, 1974), xxxiii.

22. Galphin to Gentlemen, February 7, 1776, in *Laurens*, 11: 93–97.

23. Galphin to Willie Jones, October 26, 1776, in Peter Force, ed., *American Archives*, 3: 648–50.

24. Council to Galphin, October 22, 1775, *Laurens*, 10: 491–92.

25. Galphin to Council, October 15, 1775, ibid., 10: 467–69.

26. Council to Galphin, October 4, 1775, ibid., 10: 447–49.

27. Galphin to Council, February 7, 1776, Ibid., 11: 93–97.

28. "Some Hints and Observations," Knox Papers, J. P. Morgan Library, New York.

29. Ibid.

30. Tonyn to Dartmouth, December 18, 1775, PRO, CO 5/556.

31. Ibid.

32. Tonyn to Dartmouth, January 11, 1776, PRO, CO 5/556.

33. Brown to Tonyn, February 24, 1776, Clinton Papers, WLCL.

34. John Stuart to Clinton, March 15, 1776, Clinton Papers, WLCL.

35. Tonyn to Clinton, February 15, 1776, Clinton Papers, WLCL.

36. Galphin to Council, February 7, 1776, *Laurens*, 11: 93–97.

37. Council of Safety Minutes, January 13, 1776, *RRG*, 1: 97–98.

38. Council of Safety Minutes, January 18, 1776, *RRG*, 1: 101–2.

39. 292.

40. Gibbes, *Documentary History*, 1: 259.

41. Ibid.

42. *Laurens*, 10: 563–65.

43. Council of Safety Minutes, January 8, 1776, *RRG*, 1: 89.

44. Laurens to Stephen Bull, December 29, 1775, *Laurens*, 10: 597–98.

45. Ibid.

46. Laurens to Stephen Drayton and W. Ewen, January 1, 1776, *Laurens*, 10: 603–6.

47. Laurens to McIntosh, January 27, 1776, *Laurens*, 11: 74.

48. Tonyn to Dartmouth, December 18, 1775, PRO, CO 5/556; Laurens to Georgia Provincial Congress, January 24, 1776, *Laurens*, 11: 60–62.

49. Drayton, *Memoirs*, 1: 204.

50. McIntosh to Washington, March 8, 1776, Lilla M. Hawes, ed., GHS *Collections*, 12: 1–4.

51. McIntosh to Lee, August 26, 1776, Lilla M. Hawes, ed., *Lachlan McIntosh Papers in the University of Georgia Library*, University of Georgia Libraries Miscellanea Publications (Athens: University of Georgia Press, 1968), 16–17.

52. RRG, 1: 110–12; Captain Andrew Barkley to Clinton, February 23, 1776, Clinton Papers, WLCL.

53. Master's log of the H. M. S. Armed Vessel *Cherokee*, March 1–4, 1776, William Bell Clark, ed., *Naval Documents of the American Revolution* (Washington: U.S. Government Printing Office, 1969), 4:166–67.

54. Coleman, *American Revolution*, 69–70; Harvey H. Jackson, "The Battle of the Riceboats: Georgia Joins the Revolution," *GHQ* 68 (Summer 1974): 229–43.

55. James M. Johnson, *Militiamen, Rangers, and Redcoats: The Military in Georgia, 1754–1776* (Macon, Ga.: Mercer University Press, 1992), 148.

56. Ibid.

57. Governor Wright testified that Lt. Gov. John Graham suffered a great loss in the destruction of his rice aboard the *Inverness*. Wright to Germain, March 26, 1776, GHS *Collections* 3: 232.

58. Johnson, *Militiamen, Rangers, and Redcoats*, 150–51.

59. Wright to Dartmouth, March 10, 1776, GHS *Collections* 3: 233–34.

60. Among the merchant ships were the *Marlborough*, owned by the father of Thomas Brown, and the *Whitby*, in which Brown himself had an interest: "A list of the ships and vessels liberated from the Rebels of Savannah . . . " Clark, ed., *Naval Documents*, 4: 172. The *Whitby* was used as a transport.

61. McIntosh to Washington, March 8, 1776, GHS *Collections* 12: 14.

62. Anthony Stokes, *A Narrative of the Inner Temple, London* (London, 1784), 27.

63. Ibid., 29.

64. Johnson, *Militiamen, Rangers, and Redcoats*, 154.

65. Bull to Council, March 12, 1776, *Laurens*, 11: 152–54.

66. Bull to Council, March 15, 1776, *Laurens*, 11: 168–70.

67. Wright to Germain, March 20, 1776, GHS *Collections* 3: 239–41.

68. Bull to Council, March 13, 1776; Council to Georgetown Committee, March 15, 1776, *Laurens*, 11: 155–56, 164–65.

69. Bull to Council, March 14, 1776, *Laurens*, 11: 162–64.

70. Ibid.

71. Council to Bull, March 16, 1776, *Laurens*, 11: 171–73.

72. Henry Laurens's letter of March 24, 1776, to Lachlan McIntosh was carried by Colonel Wells. The Tybee raid occurred the night of March 25, 1776. William Ewen, writing for the Georgia Council of Safety, used the same cryptic language, stating they had heard through Wells about "a particular business which by your assistance we hope he will soon have effected." Clark, ed., *Naval Documents*, 4: 371–73.

73. Wright to Germain, March 20, 1776, postscript dated March 26, GHS *Collections* 3: 239–41; Wright to Clinton, March 29, 1776, Clinton Papers, WLCL.

74. Wright to Germain, April 26, 1776, GHS *Collections* 3: 243–44; McIntosh to George Washington, April 28, 1776, GHS *Collections* 12: 4–5.

75. Henry Laurens to John Laurens, March 28, 1776, *Laurens*, 11: 95–96.

76. "Rules and Regulations," April 15, 1776, *RRG*, 1: 274–77.

77. Gibbes, *Documentary History*, 1: 274–75.

78. Martha Condray Searcy. *The Georgia-Florida Contest in the American Revolution* (Tuscaloosa: University of Alabama Press, 1985), 28.

79. Bartram's acquaintance George Whitfield had been allowed to remain on his property as caretaker. Tennent's journal, in Gibbes, *Documentary History*, 1: 234.

80. Journal of Congress at Fort Charlotte, April 15–25, Papers of the Continental Congress, microfilm.

81. Chief Double-Head said bitterly that the people who saw Stuart in Pensa-

cola warned that he would get nothing from the Americans. He said he was ashamed to go home. He thought he would now have to get supplies from Stuart.

82. Bull to Council, March 13, 1776, *Laurens,* 11:155–56.

83. Tonyn to Taitt, April 20, 1776, Davies, *Documents,* 12: 108–10.

84. Stuart to Germain, March 20, 1776, PRO, CO 5/77; Tonyn to Clinton, February 15, 1776, Clinton Papers.

85. Governor Josiah Martin to Clinton, March 20, 1776, Clark, ed., *Naval Documents,* 4: 429–30.

86. Tonyn to Clinton, February 15, 1776, Clinton Papers, WLCL.

87. "My plan for fulfilling the object of the expedition," March 14, 1776, in Clinton Letterbook, Clinton Papers, WLCL.

88. Stuart to Clinton, March 15, 1776, Clinton Papers, WLCL.

89. Stuart to Clinton, May 9, 1776, Clinton Papers, WLCL.

90. Searcy, *Georgia-Florida Contest,* 29–30.

91. Tonyn to Clinton, May 21, 1776, Clinton Papers, WCLC.

92. Tonyn to Germain, June 10, PRO, CO 5/556.

93. Brown to Tonyn, May 8, 1776, Clinton Papers, WLCL.

94. Taitt to Tonyn, May 8, 1776, PRO, CO 5/556.

95. Ibid.

96. The culprit's name is given as Thomas Few in the *Journal of the Council of Safety,* May 14–16, 1776, *RRG,* 1: 122–23; David H. Corkran, *The Creek Frontier, 1540–1783* (Norman: University of Oklahoma Press, 1967), 297.

97. Galphin to Willie Jones, October 26, 1776, *American Archives,* 5th series, vol. 3: 648.

98. Henry Stuart to John Stuart, May 7, 1776, Davies, *Documents,* 12: 191.

99. Harper, *Travels,* 416.

100. William Bartram, "Some Hints and Observations . . .," Knox Papers, J. P. Morgan Library, New York.

101. George White, *Historical Collections of Georgia* (New York: Pudney and Russel, 1855), 470.

102. Henry Laurens to John Laurens, August 14, 1776, *Laurens,* 11: 222–26.

103. Council of Safety, July 30, 1776, *RRG,* 1: 169.

104. Council Minutes, May 14, 1776, *RRG,* 1: 123.

105. Bulloch to Captain William McIntosh, May 14, 1776, *RRG,* 1:124.

106. Tonyn to Clinton, June 8, 1776, PRO, CO 5/556.

107. Council Minutes, June 21, 1776, *RRG,* 1: 144.

108. Council Minutes, June 25, 1776, *RRG,* 1: 145.

109. Council Minutes, July 2, 1776, *RRG,* 1: 148.

110. Tonyn to Clinton, June 8, 1776, PRO, CO 5/556.

111. Searcy, *Georgia-Florida Contest,* 211, n. 96.

112. Harper, *Travels,* 416, 417.

113. Ibid., 15, 16.

114. William Bartram, "Some Hints and Observations . . .," Knox Papers, J. P. Morgan Library, New York.

115. Cashin, *The King's Ranger*, 59–61.

116. Tonyn to Germain, July 18, 1776, PRO, CO 5/556.

117. Lachlan McIntosh to Lee, July 29, 1776, GHS *Collections* 12: 10–11.

118. Harper, *Travels*, 416.

7. Philadelphia

1. White, *Historical Collections*, 94.

2. Lachlan McIntosh Jr. to Lachlan McIntosh, GHS *Collections* 12: 54–55.

3. John Drayton, *Memoirs*, 2: 290–309. A particularly useful study of the battle is found in Terry W. Lipscomb, *The Carolina Lowcountry: April 1775–June 1776* (Columbia: South Carolina Department of Archives and History, 1991).

4. Drayton, *Memoirs*, 2: 339.

5. John Rutledge to Constitutional Assembly, September 19, 1776, Force, ed., *American Archives*, 5th series, 2: 19.

6. Drayton to Salvador, July 24, 1776, Gibbes, *Documentary History*, 2: 28–30.

7. August 22, 1776, Gibbes, *Documentary History*, 2: 32.

8. Report on Conditions of Georgia, July 5, 1776, RRG, 1: 302–3.

9. Galphin to Willie Jones, October 26, 1776, in Force, ed., *American Archives*, 5th series, 3: 648–50.

10. Petition of the inhabitants of the Parish of St. George and St. Paul including the ceded lands . . ., July 31, 1776, NYHS *Collections* 2: 181–82.

11. Ibid.

12. Lee to Rutledge, August 1, 1776, NYHS *Collections* 2: 186–87.

13. Lee to John Armstrong, August 27, 1776, Ibid., 246–47.

14. Lachlan McIntosh deposition, Keith Read Papers, Hargrett Collection, University of Georgia Libraries.

15. Harper, *Travels*, 418.

16. Gallay, *The Formation of a Planter Elite*, 51–52.

17. Cashin, *The King's Ranger*, 55–56.

18. Williamson to Drayton, June 27, 1776, Gibbes, *Documentary History*, 2: 22–23.

19. Council Minutes, August 29, 1776, RRG, 1: 193.

20. McIntosh was promoted to a lieutenant colonelcy in September. Searcy, *Georgia-Florida Contest*, 67–68.

21. Council Minutes, October 7, 1776, RRG, 1: 206.

22. James Bailey to Bartram, October 30, 1776, Bartram Papers, HSP.

23. Lachlan McIntosh to Lt. Col. William McIntosh, December 19, 1776; John Wereat to George Walton, August 30, 1777, GHS *Collections* 12: 25–26, 66–74.

24. Carolina's constitution changed the spelling of Charlestown to its modern form.

25. Harper, *Travels*, 298.

26. Samuel Beach Jones, Lamboll family history, Lamboll Papers, SCHS.

27. William Bartram to Mary Lamboll Thomas, July 15, 1786, Bartram Papers, NYHS.

28. Laurens to Lionel Chalmers, Feb 15, 1776, *Laurens*, 11: 105.

29. Fothergill to John Bartram, May 6, 1776, Miscellaneous Collections, WLCL. Fothergill mentioned that he had written Chalmers "by every opportunity."

30. Berkeley, *Alexander Garden*, 267; *Laurens*, 11: 232.

31. McIntosh's letter of October 29, 1776, GHS *Collections* 12: 11–12.

32. Lachlan McIntosh Jr. to Lachlan McIntosh, GHS *Collections* 12: 54–55; *Laurens*, 11: 224.

33. Laurens to John Laurens, August 14, 1776, *Laurens*, 11: 223.

34. Harper, *Travels*, 298.

35. Ibid., 298–99.

36. Eric G. Bolen, "The Bartrams in North Carolina," *Wildlife in North Carolina* (May 1996): 18.

37. Berkeley and Berkeley, *The Life and Travels of John Bartram* (Tallahassee: University of Florida Press, 1982), 195.

38. Thomas P. Slaughter, *The Natures of John and William Bartram* (New York: Knopf, 1996), 164.

39. William Bartram to Mary Bartram Roberson, September 7, 1788, Gratz Collection, HSP.

40. For this and other information on Ashwood, I am indebted to Dr. Henry A. McKinnon Jr. of Lumberton, North Carolina.

41. Bolen, *The Bartrams of North Carolina*, 21.

42. Dr. Nancy Hoffman has studied Bartram's manuscript and believes that the list of plants and birds were added to the original, possibly by the editor. Nancy Hoffman, "The Construction of William Bartram's Narrative Natural History: A Genetic Text of the Draft Manuscript for *Travels through North and South Carolina, Georgia East and West Florida*." (Ph.D. diss., University of Pennsylvania, 1996).

43. William Bartram to Mary Bartram Roberson, September 7, 1788, Gratz Collection, HSP.

44. Harper, *Travels*, 304.

45. Ibid., 422.

46. Waselkov and Braund, *Southeastern Indians*, 21.

47. Laurens to Rutledge, August 12, 1777, *Laurens*, 11: 443–52.

48. Captain E. S. Fraser to John Bartram Jr., December 15, 1777, Bartram Papers, HSP.

49. Berkeley and Berkeley, *John Bartram*, 301.

50. Fothergill to Franklin, December 3, 1774, Willcox, ed., *The Papers of Benjamin Franklin*, 21: 365.

51. *Dictionary of National Biography*, vol. 7, 508.

52. Harper, *Travels*, xxi, xxii; Waselkov and Braund, *Southeastern Indians*, 19, 226. Bartram's drawings are housed in the Library of the British Museum of Natural History. Some were out on exhibition the day of my visit to the inner sanctum of the grand museum. Dr. Solander's delay in cataloging Bartram's discoveries might be attributed to Banks's prior claim on him to examine the collection Sir Joseph brought

back from his expedition with Capt. James Cook. However, Peter Collinson had a dim view of Dr. Solander's work habits; he once confided to John Bartram that "Dr. Solander is a strange, idle man; [I] can't get thy specimens from him." Darlington, *Memorials of John Bartram*, 270.

53. Harper, *Travels*, xxi. Exactly when Laurens and McIntosh called on Bartram is uncertain. Waselkov and Braund suggest 1782, but Laurens was a prisoner in the Tower of London then. Waselkov and Braund, *Southeastern Indians*, 226.

54. William Darlington, *Memorials of John Bartram*, 288.

55. John David Schoeff made "an appreciative account of the Garden" in 1783. Harper, *Travels*, xxix.

56. Slaughter, *Natures of John and William Bartram*, 226.

57. William Bartram to Lachlan McIntosh, May 31, 1796, Bartram Papers, NYHS.

58. William Bartram to Mary Lamboll Thomas, July 15, 1786, Bartram Papers, NYHS.

59. William Bartram Jr., "Printed Proposal for Printing by Subscription," n.d.; Enoch Story Jr. to Benjamin Franklin, 1789?, Franklin Papers, American Philosophical Society, Philadelphia.

60. Harper, *Travels*, xxix.

61. Ibid.

62. Benjamin Smith Barton to William Bartram, August 26, 1787, Bartram Papers, HSP.

63. Benjamin Smith Barton to William Bartram, February, 19, 1788, Bartram Papers, HSP.

64. Nancy Hoffman, "The Construction of William Bartram's Narrative Natural History . . ." pp. xi–xiv.

65. Waselkov and Braund, *Southeastern Indians*, 189.

66. "Some Hints and Observations Concerning the Civilization of the Indians, or Aborigines of America," John Pierpont Morgan Library, New York.

67. Cited in Perdue, *Cherokee Women*, 110; for a complete review of American policy, see Francis P. Prucha, *American Indian Policy in the Formative Years* (Cambridge: Harvard University Press, 1962).

68. Hawkins reported to President James Madison that the "plan of civilization" was working in the Creek country. Hawkins to Madison, July 11, 1803, in C. L. Grant, ed., *Letters, Journals, and Writings of Benjamin Hawkins* (Savannah: Beehive Press, 1980), 2: 458–59.

69. *Bartram Heritage*, 17, 54, 144. Excerpts of the essay are in N. Bryllion Fagin, *William Bartram: Interpreter of the American Landscape* (Baltimore: Johns Hopkins University Press, 1933), 16–17, reprinted in *Bartram Heritage*, 144.

70. Waselkov and Braund, *Southeastern Indians*, 280.

71. The document is in Broadside Collection, Bartram Papers, HSP.

72. Harper, *Travels*, xxxv.

73. *Bartram Heritage*, 21.

74. William Paley, *Natural Theology; or Evidence of the Existence and Attributes of the Deity, Collected from the Appearances of Nature* (London: R. Faulder, 1803).

75. William Bartram to Benjamin Smith Barton, December 23, 1792, Barton Papers, APS.

76. Harper, *Travels*, xxxiv.

77. William Bartram to Benjamin Smith Barton, November 30, 1805, Barton Papers, APS.

78. Loose essay in Bartram Papers, HSP.

79. William Bartram to Benjamin Smith Barton, December 23, 1792, Barton Papers, APS. Henry David Thoreau expressed the same ideas, and several utopian communities experimented with them.

80. Slaughter, *Natures of John and William Bartram*, 252.

81. Charles Frazier, *Cold Mountain* (New York: Atlantic Monthly Press, 1997), 276.

82. William Bartram to Lachlan McIntosh, May 31, 1796, Bartram Papers, NYHS.

83. William Darlington, *Reliquiae Baldwiniance, Selections from Correspondence of the Late William Baldwin, M.D.* (Philadelphia: Kimber and Sharpless, 1843), 197.

84. William Baldwin to William Darlington, May 30, 1817, Darlington, *Reliquiae Baldwiniance*, 197.

85. William Baldwin to William Darlington, August 20, 1817, Darlington, *Reliquiae Baldwiniance*, 238.

86. Harper, *Travels*, xxxi.

87. Slaughter, *Natures of John and William Bartram*, 11.

Epilogue

1. Cashin, *The King's Ranger*, 94.

2. Lord George Germain to Brown and Cameron, June 25, 1779, PRO, CO 5/242, also in Clinton Papers, WLCL.

3. Alden, *John Stuart*, 212.

4. Cashin, *The King's Ranger*, 147.

5. Harper, *Travels*, 208.

6. Alden, *John Stuart*, 297; David Taitt's claim for compensation is in CO, AO 13/37; I am indebted to Dr. Robert J. Morgan, University College of Cape Breton, for information about David Taitt's Nova Scotia career.

7. Lydia Austin Parrish, "Records of Some Southern Loyalists . . .," typescript on microfilm, P. K. Yonge Library, University of Florida, 386.

8. Sandra Riley, *Homeward Bound: A History of the Bahama Islands to 1850*, Appendix E, 270–74.

9. Eron Rowland, ed., *Life, Letters, and Papers of William Dunbar of Elgin, Morayshire, Scotland, and Natchez, Mississippi* (Jackson: Press of the Mississippi Historical Society, 1930), 12, 78–99.

10. For Begbie, see Parrish, "Records of Some Southern Loyalists," 131; for Waters, see Riley, *Homeward Bound*, 274.

11. Cashin, *The King's Ranger*, 218.

12. Wilbur Henry Siebert, *Loyalists in East Florida, 1774 to 1785*, 2 vols. (De Land, Florida, Florida State Historical Society, 1929), 2: 362.

13. I thank Bruce Chappel of the P. K. Yonge Library in Gainesville for information about McLatchy and Wiggins.

14. Harper, *Travels*, 469.

15. Berkeley and Berkeley, *Alexander Garden of Charles Town*, 324.

16. Introduction in Philip M. Hamer, et al., *Laurens*, 1: xviii–xx.

17. Colin Campbell, ed., *Journal of an Expedition against the Rebels of Georgia in North Carolina under the Orders of Archibald Campbell, Esquire, Lieut. Colol. of His Majesty's 71st Regiment, 1778* (Darien, Ga.: Ashantilly Press, 1981), 52, 56.

18. Cashin, *The King's Ranger*, 106.

19. Galphin's heirs waged a protracted legal battle for compensation for Galphin's wartime losses. In 1850 the federal government paid $43,518.97, the equivalent in 1850 currency of £9,791,15s., 5d., due Galphin as part of the proceeds of the 1773 cession. The payment of $191,352.89 interest caused heated controversy. See William P. Brandon, "The Galphin Claim," *GHQ* 15 (June 1931): 113–41, and Gerald S. Greenberg, "Ohioans vs. Georgians: The Galphin Claim, Zachary Taylor's Death, and the Congressional Adjournment Vote of 1850," *GHQ* 76 (Winter 1990): 575–98.

20. Cashin, "The Famous Colonel Wells: Factionalism in Revolutionary Georgia," *GHQ* 58 (supplement, 1974).

21. For George McIntosh's version of his arrest and treatment, see "Petition of George McIntosh, October 8, 1777," Papers of the Continental Congress, Georgia State Papers, 1778–1788. See also Jackson, *Lachlan McIntosh*, 56–57, 64–66.

22. Treutlen to John Hancock, June 19, 1777, Papers of the Continental Congress, Georgia State Papers, 1778–1788.

23. Jackson, *Lachlan McIntosh*, 81–86.

24. Thomas I. Pieper and James B. Gideny, *Fort Laurens 1778–1779, The Revolutionary War in Ohio* (Kent, Ohio: Kent State University Press, 1976), 59.

25. Cashin, "George Walton and the Forged Letter," *GHQ* 62 (Summer 1978): 133–45.

26. Jackson, *Lachlan McIntosh*, 105–10.

27. Ibid., 128, 149, 150.

28. Ibid., 157.

29. Charles W. Spalding, "Twice Twenty Years Ago. The Scotch in Georgia," Margaret Davis Cate Collection, GHS; Parrish, "Records of Some Southern Loyalists," P. K. Yonge Library, Gainesville, Fla., 377.

30. Samuel Beach Jones, "Family History," Lamboll Papers, SCHS.

31. Kathryn Braund notes that Hawkins's reforms contributed to Creek involvement in the War of 1812. *Deerskins and Duffels*, 186–88.

32. See Lynn Hastie Thompson's detailed account of William Weatherford (Red Eagle) and the Creek War, *William Weatherford, His Country and His People*.

33. William Bartram, "Some Hints and Observations . . .," Henry Knox Papers, J. P. Morgan Library. The definitive work on the subject of missionaries to the Cherokee is William Gerald McLoughlin, *Cherokees and Missionaries 1739–1839* (New Haven: Yale University Press, 1984).

34. William Bartram, "Some Hints and Observations . . .," Henry Knox Papers, John Pierpont Morgan Library, New York.

Bibliography

Published Collections and Contemporary Sources

Armstrong, Alan W. *"Forget Not Mee and My Garden" The Selected Letters of Peter Collinson, F. R. S. 1721–1768.* Haverford, Eng.: Alan W. Armstrong, 1992.

Benedict, David. *A General History of the Baptist Denomination in America and Other Parts of the World.* 1813. Reprint, Freeport, N.Y.: Books for Library Press, 1971.

Britt, Albert Sidney Jr., and Anthony Roane Dees, eds. *Selected Eighteenth Century Manuscripts.* Savannah: Georgia Historical Society, 1980.

Campbell, Colin, ed. *Journal of an Expedition against the Rebels of Georgia in North America under the Orders of Archibald Campbell Esquire, Lieu. Colol. of His Majesty's 71st Regimt. 1778.* Darien, Ga.: Ashantilly Press, 1981.

Candler, Allen D., ed., *The Revolutionary Records of the State of Georgia.* 3 vols. Atlanta: Franklin-Turner Co., 1903.

Candler, Allen D. et al., eds. *The Colonial Records of the State of Georgia.* 30 vols. Atlanta: Various printers 1904–1916, 1979–1982; vols. 29–39 in typescript and microfilm at the Georgia Department of Archives and History, Atlanta.

Clark, William Bell et al., eds. *Naval Documents of the American Revolution.* 10 vols. Washington, D.C.: U.S. Printing Office, 1964–1996.

Collections. 20 vols. Savannah: Georgia Historical Society, 1840–1980. Vol. 3 contains the letters of Governor Wright; vol. 12 contains the letters of Lachlan McIntosh.

Corner, Betsy C., and Christopher C. Barth. *Chain of Friendship, Selected Letters of Dr. John Fothergill of London 1735–1780.* Cambridge: Harvard University Press, 1971.

Darlington, William. *Memorials of John Bartram and Humphry Marshall, with Notices of Their Botanical Contemporaries.* Philadelphia: Lindsay and Blakiston, 1849.

———. *Reliquiae Baldwiniance, Selections from the Correspondence of the Late William Baldwin, M.D.* Philadelphia: Kimber and Sharpless, 1843.

Davies, K. G., ed. *Documents of the American Revolution 1770–1783.* 21 vols. Shannon: Irish University Press, 1972–1981.

Davis, Robert Scott Jr. *Quaker Records in Georgia: Wrightsborough, 1772–1793, Friendsborough, 1776–1777.* Roswell, Ga.: W. H. Wolfe Associates, 1986.

DuPratz, Le Page. *The History of Louisiana.* 1774. Reprint, Baton Rouge: La Claitor Publishing, 1972.

Force, Peter, ed. *American Archives.* 5th ser. 3 vols. Washington, D.C.: M. St. Clair and Peter Force, 1848–1853.

Gibbes, Robert W. *Documentary History of the American Revolution.* 1853. Reprint. 3 vols. in 1. New York: New York Times and Arno Press, 1971.

Grant, C. L., ed. *Letters, Journals, and Writings of Benjamin Hawkins.* 2 vols. Savannah: Beehive Press, 1980.

Hamer, Philip M., George Rogers Jr., and David R. Chesnutt, eds. *The Papers of Henry Laurens.* 14 vols. Columbia: University of South Carolina Press, 1968–1994.

Harper, Francis. "Travels in Georgia and Florida, 1773–1774, A Report to Dr. John Fothergill, William Bartram." *Transactions of the American Philosophical Society.* New Series 33, part 2 (November 1943).

———. *The Travels of William Bartram, Naturalist's Edition.* New Haven: Yale University Press, 1958.

Hawes, Lilla. *Lachlan McIntosh Papers.* Athens: University of Georgia Miscellanea Publications, no. 7, 1968.

Hemperley, Marion, ed. *English Crown Grants for Parishes of St. David, St. Patrick, St. Thomas, St. Mary in Georgia 1755–1775.* Atlanta: State Printing Office, 1973.

Hooker, Richard J., ed. *The Carolina Backcountry on the Eve of the Revolution, The Journal and Other Writings of Charles Woodmason, Anglican Itinerant.* Chapel Hill: University of North Carolina Press, 1953.

Juricek, John T., ed. *Georgia Treaties, 1733–1763.* Frederick, Md.: University Publications of America, 1989. Vol. 11 in Alden T. Vaughan, ed. *Early American Indian Documents: Treaties and Laws, 1607–1789.*

McDowell, William L. Jr., ed. *Colonial Records of South Carolina: Documents Relating to Indian Affairs.* Columbia: South Carolina Archives Department, 1958.

McPherson, Robert G., ed. *The Journal of the Earl of Egmont: Abstract of the Trustees Proceedings for Establishing the Colony of Georgia, 1732–1738.* Athens: University of Georgia Press, 1962.

Merrens, H. Roy. *The Colonial South Carolina Scene, Contemporary Views, 1697–1774.* Columbia: University of South Carolina Press, 1977.

New York Historical Society Collections for the Year 1872. New York: New York Historical Society, 1873.

Romans, Bernard. *A Concise Natural History of the East and West Florida.* 1775. Reprint, Gainesville: University of Florida Press, 1962.

Rowland, Eron., ed. *Life, Letters, and Papers of William Dunbar of Elgin, Morayshire, Scotland, and Natchez, Mississippi.* Jackson: Press of the Mississippi Historical Society, 1930.

Ruddock, Ted, ed. *Travels in the Colonies in 1773–1775 Described in the Letters of William Mylne.* Athens: University of Georgia Press, 1993.

Salley, A. S. Jr. "George Hunter's Map of the Cherokee County and the Path Thereto in 1730." *Bulletin of the Historical Commission of South Carolina,* no. 4. Columbia: The State Company, 1937.

Saunders, William L., ed. *The Colonial Records of North Carolina,* vol. 10. Raleigh: Josephus Daniels, Printer to the State, 1890.

Slaughter, Thomas P., ed. *William Bartram: Travels and Other Writings.* New York: The Library of America, 1996.

Stokes, Anthony. *A Narrative of the Inner Table, London.* London: 1784.

Stork, William. *An Account of Earl Florida with a Journal Kept by John Bartram. . . . Upon a Journey from St. Augustine up the River St. John's.* London: Sold by W. McColl and G. Woodfall, 1766.

Willard, Margaret Wheeler, ed. *Letters on the American Revolution, 1774–1776.* Boston: Houghton Mifflin, 1925.

Willcox, William B., ed. *The Papers of Benjamin Franklin,* vol 21. New Haven: Yale University Press, 1978.

Williams, Samuel Cole. *Adair's History of the American Indians.* 1930. Reprint. New York: Promontory Press, 1974.

Secondary Works

Books

Alden, John R. *John Stuart and the Southern Colonial Frontier.* New York: Gordian Press Inc., 1968.

Baker, Pearl. *The Story of Wrightsboro 1768–1964.* Thompson, Ga.: Wrightborough Restoration Foundation, 1965.

Berkeley, Edmund, and Dorothy Smith Berkeley. *The Correspondence of John Bartram, 1734–1777.* Gainesville: University Press of Florida, 1992.

———. *Dr. Alexander Garden of Charles Town.* Chapel Hill: University of North Carolina Press, 1969.

———. *The Life and Travels of John Bartram.* Tallahassee: University Press of Florida, 1982.

Bossu, Jean Bernard. *New Travels in North America.* Edited by Samuel David Dickinson. Natchez: Northwestern State University Press, 1982.

Braund, Kathryn. *Deerskins and Duffels, Creek Indian Trade with Anglo-America, 1685–1815.* Lincoln: University of Nebraska Press, 1993.

Brown, Richard Maxwell. *The South Carolina Regulators.* Cambridge: Belknap Press, 1963.

Bull, Kinloch Jr. *The Oligarchs in Colonial and Revolutionary Charleston: Lieutenant Governor William Bull II and His Family.* Columbia: University of South Carolina Press, 1991.

Calloway, Colin G. *The American Revolution in Indian Country: Crisis and Diversity in Native American Communities.* New York: Cambridge University Press, 1995.

Cashin, Edward J. *Colonial Augusta "Key of the Indian Countrey."* Macon, Ga.: Mercer University Press, 1986.

———. *The King's Ranger: Thomas Brown and the American Revolution on the Southern Frontier.* Athens: University of Georgia Press, 1989.

———. *Lachlan McGillivray, Indian Trader and the Shaping of the Southern Colonial Frontier.* Athens: University of Georgia Press, 1992.

———. *Old Springfield: Race and Religion in Augusta, Georgia.* Augusta: The Springfield Village Park Foundation, Inc., 1995.

Cate, Margaret Davis. *Our Todays and Yesterdays: A Story of Brunswick and the Coastal Islands.* Brunswick, Ga.: Glover Brothers, 1930.

Coleman, Kenneth. *The American Revolution in Georgia.* Athens: University of Georgia Press, 1958.

———. *Colonial Georgia: A History.* New York: Charles Scribner's Sons, 1976.

———, and Charles Stephen Gurr, eds., *Dictionary of Georgia Biography.* 2 vols. Athens: University of Georgia Press, 1983.

Cook, Jeannine. *Columbus and the Land of Ayllon: The Exploration and Settlement of the Southeast.* Darien, Ga.: Lower Altamaha Historical Society, 1992.

Corkran, David. *The Cherokee Frontier: Conflict and Survival, 1740–1762.* Norman: University of Oklahoma Press, 1962.

———. *The Creek Frontier, 1540–1783.* Norman: University of Oklahoma Press, 1967.

Cruickshank, Helen Gere, ed. *John and William Bartram in America.* New York: Devon-Adair Company, 1957.

Ernest, Earnest. *John and William Bartram: Botanists and Explorers 1699–1777, 1739–1823.* Philadelphia: University of Pennsylvania Press, 1940.

Ewan, Joseph. *William Bartram Botanical and Zoological Drawings 1756–1788.* Philadelphia: American Philosophical Society, 1968.

Fabel, Robin F. A. *Bombast and Broadsides: The Lives of George Johnstone.* Tuscaloosa: University of Alabama Press, 1987.

———. *The Economy of British West Florida, 1763–1783.* Tuscaloosa: University of Alabama Press, 1988.

Fagin, Nathan B. *William Bartram, Interpreter of the American Landscape.* Baltimore: Johns Hopkins University Press, 1933.

Fraser, Charles. *Reminiscences of Charleston.* Charleston, S.C.: 1854. Reprint, Charleston, S.C.: Garnier, 1969.

Fraser, Walter J. *Charleston! Charleston! The History of a Southern City.* Columbia: University of South Carolina Press, 1989.

Frazer-Mackintosh, Charles. *An Account of the Confederation of the Clan Chattan: Its Kith and Kin.* Glasgow: John Mackay, 1898.

Frazier, Charles. *Cold Mountain.* New York: Atlantic Monthly Press, 1997.

Gallay, Allan. *The Formation of a Planter Elite: Jonathan Bryan and the Southern Frontier.* Athens: University of Georgia Press, 1989.

Garden, Alexander. *Anecdotes of the American Revolution.* Charleston: A. E. Miller, 1828.

Gipson, Lawrence Henry. *The Triumphant Empire.* Vol. 9 in *The British Empire before the American Revolution.* New York: Knopf, 1956.

Goodwin, Gary C. *Cherokee in Transition: A Study of Changing Culture and Environment Prior to 1775.* Chicago: University of Chicago Department of Geography. Research paper no. 181, 1977.

Hamilton, Peter J. *Colonial Mobile.* 1910. Reprint, University of Alabama: University of Alabama Press, 1976.

Hatley, M. Thomas. *The Dividing Paths: The Encounters of the Cherokees and the South Carolinians in the Southern Mountains, 1670–1785*. Oxford: Oxford University Press, 1993.

———. "The Three Lives of Keowee: Loss and Recovery in Eighteenth-Century Cherokee Villages." In *Powhatan's Mantle: Indians of the Colonial Southeast*. Edited by P. H. Wood, G. A. Waselkov, and M. T. Hatley. Lincoln: University of Nebraska Press, 1989.

Herbst, Josephine. *New Green World*. New York: Hastings House, 1954.

Ivers, Larry. *British Drums on the Southern Frontier: The Military Colonization of Georgia, 1733–1749*. Chapel Hill: University of North Carolina Press, 1974.

Jackson, Harvey H. *Lachlan McIntosh and the Politics of Revolutionary Georgia*. Athens: University of Georgia Press, 1979.

Jackson, Harvey H., and Phinizy Spalding. *Forty Years of Diversity Essays on Colonial Georgia*. Athens: University of Georgia Press, 1958.

Johnson, Cecil. *British West Florida 1763–1783*. New Haven: Yale University Press, 1943.

Johnson, James M. *Militiamen, Rangers, and Redcoats: The Military in Georgia, 1754–1776*. Macon, Ga.: Mercer University Press, 1992.

Jones, Dorothy M. *Wrightsborough 1768, Wrightsboro 1799, McDuffie County Georgia 1870*. Thomson, Ga.: Wrightsboro Quaker Community Foundation, 1982.

King, Duane H. *The Cherokee Indian Nation: A Troubled History*. Knoxville: University of Tennessee Press, 1979.

Lanning, John Tate. *The Spanish Missions of Georgia*. Chapel Hill: University of North Carolina Press, 1935.

Lesesne, Thomas Petigru. *Landmarks of Charleston*. Richmond: Garrett and Massie, Inc., 1939.

Lewis, Bessie. *They Called Their Town Darien*. Darien, Ga.: The Darien News, 1975.

Logan, John H. *A History of the Upper Country of South Carolina from the Earliest Periods to the Close of the War for Independence*. Columbia, S.C.: S. G. Courtenay and Company. 1859. Reprint, Spartanburg, S.C.: The Reprint Company, 1960.

Mackintosh, A. M. *The Mackintoshes and Clan Chattan*. Edinburgh: Printed for the author, 1903.

Maclean, J. P. *An Historical Account of the Settlements of the Scotch Highlanders in America Prior to the Peace of 1783*. Cleveland: Hilman-Taylor, 1900.

Maness, Harold S. *Forgotten Outpost: Fort Moore and Savannah Town, 1685–1765*. Pickens, S.C.: BPB Publications, 1986.

May, Henry F. *The Enlightenment in America*. New York: Oxford University Press, 1976.

McRae, Barbara. *Franklin's Ancient Mound*. Franklin, N.C.: Fererita Press, 1993.

McWhiney, Grady. *Cracker Culture: Celtic Ways in the South*. Tuscaloosa: University of Alabama Press, 1988.

Medeiros, Patricia M. "Three Travelers: Carver, Bartram, and Woolman." In *American Literature, 1764–1789: The Revolutionary Years*. Edited by Everett Emerson. Madison: University of Wisconsin Press, 1977.

Merrens, H. Roy, ed. *The Colonial South Carolina Scene Contemporary Views, 1697–1774.* Columbia: University of South Carolina Press, 1977.

Mowat, Charles Loch. *East Florida as a British Province.* Gainesville: University of Florida Press, 1964.

Perdue, Theda. *Cherokee Women: Gender and Culture Change, 1700–1835.* Lincoln: University of Nebraska Press, 1998.

Pieper, Thomas I., and James B. Gideny. *Fort Laurens 1778–1779, The Revolutionary War in Ohio.* Kent, Ohio: Kent State University Press, 1978.

Pinckney, Elise. *Thomas and Elizabeth Lamboll: Early Charleston Gardeners.* Charleston, S.C.: The Charleston Museum, 1969.

Proctor, Samuel. *Eighteenth Century Florida and the Revolutionary South.* Gainesville: University Presses of Florida, 1976.

Rashed, Zenab Esmat. *The Peace of Paris, 1763.* Liverpool: Liverpool University Press, 1951.

Rea, Robert R. *Major Robert Farmer of Mobile.* Tuscaloosa: University of Alabama Press, 1990.

Riley, Sandra. *Homeward Bound: A History of the Bahama Islands to 1850 with a Definitive Study of Abaco in the American Loyalist Plantation Period.* Miami: Island Research, 1983.

Rogers, George C. Jr. *Charleston in the Age of Pinckneys.* Norman: University of Oklahoma Press, 1969.

Sanger, Marjory Bartlett. *Billy Bartram and His Green World.* New York: Farrar, Straus, and Geroux, 1972.

Sangster, Dess, and Tom Sangster, eds. *Fort Mims and the Tensaw Settlement.* Bay Minette, Ala.: Lavender Publishing, 1993.

Saunders, Rebecca. "Architecture of the Mission Santa Maria and Santa Catalina de Amelia." In *The Spanish Missions of La Florida.* Edited by Bonnie G. McEwan. Gainesville: University Press of Florida, 1993.

Searcy, Martha Condray. *The Georgia-Florida Contest in the American Revolution, 1776–1778.* Tuscaloosa: University of Alabama Press, 1985.

Sellers, Charles Coleman. *Patience Wright: American Artist and Spy in George III's London.* Middletown, Conn: 1976.

Sheriff, Anne, ed. *Cherokee Villages in South Carolina.* Easley, S.C.: Forest Acres/McKissick Quest Program, 1990.

Siebert, William Henry. *Loyalists in East Florida 1774 to 1785.* 2 vols. De Land: Florida State Historical Society, 1929.

Sheftall, John McKay. *Sunbury on the Medway.* Atlanta: The Georgia Department of Natural Resources, 1977.

Slaughter, Thomas P. *The Natures of John and William Bartram.* New York: Alfred A. Knopf, 1996.

Smith, Alice R. H., and D. E. Huger Smith. *The Dwelling Houses of Charleston, South Carolina.* 1917. Reprint, New York: Diadem Books, 1974.

Snapp, J. Russell. *John Stuart and the Struggle for Empire on the Southern Frontier.* Baton Rouge: Louisiana State University Press, 1996.

Bibliography

Spalding, Phinizy, and Harvey H. Jackson, eds. *Oglethorpe in Perspective: Georgia's Founder after 200 Years*. Tuscaloosa: University of Alabama Press, 1989.

Starr, J. Barton. *Tories, Dons, and Rebels: The American Revolution in British West Florida*. Gainesville: University Press of Florida, 1976.

Swanton, John R. *Early History of the Creek Indians and Their Neighbors*. Washington, D.C.: U.S. Government Printing Office, 1922.

Thomas, Daniel H. *Fort Toulouse: The French Outpost at the Alabamas on the Coosa*. Tuscaloosa: University of Alabama Press, 1989.

Thomas, David Hurst. *The Missions of Spanish Florida*. New York: Garland Publishing Company, 1991.

Thompson, Lynn Hastie. *William Weatherford, His Country and His People*. Bay Minette, Ala.: Lavender Publishing Company, 1991.

Utley, Frances Lee, and Marion R. Hemperley. *Placenames of Georgia: Essays of John H. Goff*. Athens: University of Georgia Press, 1975.

Waring, Joseph F. *Cerveau's Savannah*. Savannah: The Georgia Historical Society, 1973.

———. *A History of Medicine in South Carolina*. Columbia, S.C.: South Carolina Medical Association, 1964.

Waselkov, Gregory, and Kathryn Braund. *William Bartram on the Southeastern Indians*. Lincoln: University of Nebraska Press, 1995.

Weir, Robert M. *Colonial South Carolina, A History*. Millwood N.Y.: KTO Press, 1983.

White, George. *Historical Collections of Georgia*. New York: Pudney and Russell, 1855.

Wood, Betty. *Slavery in Colonial Georgia 1730–1775*. Athens: University of Georgia Press, 1984.

Wood, Peter. "The Dream Deferred': Black Freedom Struggles on the Eve of White Independence." In *In Resistance: Studies in African, Caribbean, and Afro-American History*. Gary Y. Okihiro. Amherst: University of Massachusetts Press, 1986, 166–87.

———. "'Liberty Is Sweet' African-American Freedom Struggles in the Years before White Independence." In *Beyond the American Revolution: Explorations in the History of American Radicalism*. Alfred F. Young. DeKalb: Northern Illinois University Press, 1993, 149–84.

Wright, J. Leitch Jr. *Florida in the American Revolution*. Gainesville: University Presses of Florida, 1975.

Articles

Anderson, William R. "Cherokee Clay: From Duché to Wedgwood." *North Carolina Historical Review* 63 (October 1986): 477–510.

Bartram, William. "Some Account of the Late Mr. John Bartram, of Pennsylvania." *The Philadelphia Medical and Physical Journal* 1 (1804): part 1, 115–24.

Billings, John Shaw. "Analysis of the Will of George Galphin." *Richmond County History* 13 (1981): 29–37.

Bolen, Eric G. "The Bartrams of North Carolina." *Wildlife in North Carolina* 60 (May 1996): 16–21.

Brown, Ian. "William Bartram and the Direct Historic Approach." In *Archaeology of Eastern North America, Papers in Honor of Stephen Williams.* Edited by James B. Stoltman. Archaeological Report no. 25. Jackson: Mississippi Department of Archives and History, 1993.

Cappon, Lester J. "Retracing and Mapping the Bartrams' Southern Travels." *Proceedings of the American Philosophical Society* 118, no. 6 (December 1974): 507–13.

Claussen, Henry H. "George Galphin in Ireland." *Richmond County History* 13 (1981): 113–18.

Coleridge, Earnest Hartley. "Coleridge, Wordsworth and the American Botanist William Bartram." *Royal Society of Literature Translations,* series 2, vol. 27, part 2 (London, 1906): 69–92.

Cone, Susan French. "Bartram Trail a Haven for Nature Lovers." *Mobile Register,* 22 June 1997.

Edwards, Elliott O. "A Sketch of the William Bartram Trail in Georgia." *Tipularia : A Botanical Magazine* 11 (1996): 16–25.

Goff, John H. "Some Major Indian Trading Paths across the Georgia Piedmont." *Georgia Minerals Newsletter* 6 (Winter 1953): 122–31.

Gordon, G. Arthur. "The Arrival of the Scotch Highlanders at Darien." *Georgia Historical Quarterly* 20 (September 1936): 199–209.

Hamilton, Annie Blount. "George Galphin of Silver Bluff." *Richmond County History* 13 (1981): 7–12.

Hamilton, Peter J. "Indian Trails and Early Roads." *Publications of the Alabama Historical Society* 7 (1901): 422–29.

Harper, Francis."The Name of the Florida Wolf." *Journal of Mammalogy* 23 (14 August 1942): 339.

———. "Two More Available Plant Names of William Bartram." *Bartonia* 21 (May 1942): 6–8.

———. "William Bartram's Names of Birds." *Proceedings of the Rochester Academy of Science* 8 (10 September 1942): 208–21.

Harris, Waldo III. "Daniel Marshall: Lone Georgia Baptist Revolutionary Pastor." *Viewpoints Georgia Baptist History* 5 (1976): 51–64.

Jenkins, Charles F. "The Historical Background of Franklin's Tree." *Pennsylvania Magazine of History and Biography* 57 (1933): 193–208.

Kelly, James C. "Notable Persons in Cherokee History: Attakullakulla." *Journal of Cherokee Studies* (Winter 1978): 2–34.

Knefler, Abraham E. "Eighteenth Century Cherokee Educational Efforts." *Chronicles of Alabama* 20 (1942): 55–61.

Lawrence, Alexander A. "General Lachlan McIntosh and His Suspension from Continental Command during the Revolution." *Georgia Historical Quarterly* (June 1954): 101–41.

Lewis, Bessie Mary. "Darien: A Symbol of Defiance and Achievement." *Georgia Historical Quarterly* 20 (September 1936): 185–98.

MacDonnell, Alexander R. "The Settlement of the Scotch Highlanders at Darien." *Georgia Historical Quarterly* 20 (September 1936): 250–62.

Bibliography

Mohr, Charles T. "History of the Earlier Botanical Explorations of Alabama, William Bartram." *Contributions from the United States National Herbarium* 8 (July 1901): 13–151.

Nordan, David. "The Magic of Yellow Root." *Georgia Journal* 17 (September–October 1997): 11.

Rea, Robert R., and Holmes, Jack D. L. "Dr. John Lorimer and the Natural Sciences in British West Florida." *Southern Humanities Review* 4 (1970): 363–72.

"Graveyard for Britons: West Florida 1763–1781." *Florida Historical Quarterly* 47 (1969): 345–46, 359–62.

Shelley, Fred. "The Journal of Ebenezer Hazard in Georgia, 1778." *Georgia Historical Quarterly* 41 (1957): 316–19.

Smith, Helen Burr, and Elizabeth V. Moore. "John Mare: A Composite Portrait." *The North Carolina Historical Review* 44 (Winter 1967): 18–52.

Strong, Mrs. Paschal N., Sr. "Glimpses of Savannah, 1780–1825." *Georgia Historical Quarterly* 33 (1949): 26–35.

Wilkins, Barrett. "A View of Savannah on the Eve of the Revolution." *Georgia Historical Quarterly* 54 (1970): 577–84.

Manuscript Collections

American Philosophical Society, Philadelphia
  Benjamin Smith Barton Papers
  Diary of William Bartram 1802–1803
  William Bartram Prints
  Benjamin Franklin Papers
  Miscellaneous Manuscript Collections
British Public Record Office, London
  Audit Office
  Colonial Office
Georgia Historical Society, Savannah
  Margaret Davis Cate Collection
  Andrew McLean Ledger
Historical Society of Pennsylvania, Philadelphia
  American Scientific Collection
  American Physicians Collection
  Bartram Papers
  William Bartram's Commonplace Book 1773 to 1777
  William Bartram's Pharmacopaedia
  Ferdinand J. Dreer Collection
  Etting Collection
  Simon Gratz Collection
  Society Miscellaneous Collection

Hargrett Special Collections, University of Georgia Libraries
	Keith Read Collection
	Telamon Cuyler Collection
John Pierpont Morgan Library, New York
	Henry Knox Papers, Gilder Lehman Collection
Kirkwall Public Library, Orkney Islands Archives, Kirkwall, Scotland
Knowsley Hall, Merseyside, England
	Bartram Prints 1755–1765. Originally collection of Peter Collinson.
Library Company of Philadelphia
Library of Congress
	Papers of the Continental Congress 1774–1789. Indian Affairs.
	Hazard Pamphlets
Linnean Society Library, Burlington House, London
	Peter Collinson Manuscripts
Mobile Public Library, Local History Division
	Bartram Trail File
New-York Historical Society
	Papers of John and William Bartram
	Lachlan McIntosh Papers
New York Public Library
	McIntosh Papers, Thomas Addis Emmet Collection
P. K. Yonge Library, University of Florida, Gainesville
	Lydia Austin Parrish Records of Some Southern Loyalists . . . (typescript)
Scottish Record Office, Edinburgh
	Frazer Mackintosh Collection
South Carolina Historical Society, Charleston
	Lamboll Papers
	Martha Logan Papers
South Caroliniana Library, Columbia
	Deposition of Robert Goudy, 10 July 1775
Southern Historical Collection, University of North Carolina, Chapel Hill
	Mackay-Stiles Papers
Society of Friends Library, London
	Fothergill Collection
	Friends Autographs
St. Augustine Historical Society
	Bartram Folder
The Library of the British Museum of Natural History
	Fothergill Album
	William Bartram Manuscripts
West Florida University Library, Pensacola
	West Florida Papers
Western Carolina College, Special Collections
	Cherokee material

William L. Clements Library
    Sir Henry Clinton Papers
    General Thomas Gage Papers
    Humphry Marshall Papers
    Miscellaneous Collections

Dissertations

Anderson, Kenneth Marshall Jr. "The Travels of William Bartram." Ph.D. dissertation, Columbia University, 1971.

Deaton, Stanley Kenneth. "Revolutionary Charleston, 1765–1800." Ph.D. dissertation, University of Florida, 1997.

Hoffman, Nancy. "Travels through North and South Carolina, Georgia, East and West Florida." Ph.D. dissertation, University of Pennsylvania, 1996.

Mitchell, Robert Gary. "Royalist Georgia." Ph.D. dissertation, Tulane University, 1964.

Peters, Thelma. "The American Loyalists and the Plantation Period in the Bahama Islands." Ph.D. dissertation, University of Florida, 1960.

Index